T5-DGS-543

ST. MARY'S COLLEGE OF MARYLAND
ST. MARY'S CITY, MARYLAND   20686

Hooliganism

Studies on the History of Society and Culture
Victoria E. Bonnell and Lynn Hunt, Editors

Hooliganism

Crime, Culture, and Power in
St. Petersburg, 1900–1914

Joan Neuberger

University of California Press

BERKELEY   LOS ANGELES   LONDON

University of California Press
Berkeley and Los Angeles, California

University of California Press, Ltd.
London, England

© 1993 by
The Regents of the University of California

Library of Congress Cataloging-in-Publication Data

Neuberger, Joan.
    Hooliganism : crime, culture, and power in St. Petersburg,
1900–1914 / Joan Neuberger.
        p.   cm.—(Studies on the history of society and culture ;
19)
    Includes bibliographical references and index.
    ISBN 0-520-08011-4 (alk. paper)
    1. Crime—Russia (Federation)—Saint Petersburg.
2. Hoodlums—Russia (Federation)—Saint Petersburg.   3. Saint
Petersburg (Russia)—Social conditions.   I. Title.   II. Series.
HV7015.S24N48   1993
364.947′453′09041—dc20   92–34003
                                                                      CIP

Printed in the United States of America
9 8 7 6 5 4 3 2 1

The paper used in this publication meets the minimum requirements of
American National Standard for Information Sciences—Permanence of
Paper for Printed Library Materials, ANSI Z39.48-1984. ⊗

I am proud to have portrayed for the first time the real man of the Russian majority, and for the first time to have exposed his tragic and misshapen side. . . . Underground, underground, "Poet of the Underground"—our feuilletonists have been repeating this as if it were something derogatory to me. Fools—this is my glory, for that is where the truth lies.

—Fedor Dostoevsky
Notebooks for *A Raw Youth*

For Charters and Max

Contents

Illustrations

All illustrations were originally published in *Peterburgskii listok*.

Tables

Acknowledgments

Charters Wynn has read every word I have written and has done so with enthusiasm, patience, and countless valuable comments. I thank him for this and for everything else we have shared.

This book began life as a dissertation, and I want to thank those who helped make it a better one, beginning with my graduate advisor, Terence Emmons, whose style of pedagogy and superior standards of scholarship allowed me to pursue an unconventional subject while striving to meet those standards. Reginald Zelnik provided essential guidance in my early struggles with Russian history, and continuing support ever since, for which I am deeply grateful. I would also like to thank all my teachers and friends at Grinnell College, who helped turn a student's infatuation with Dostoevsky into a scholarly curiosity about all things Russian and who made the process so much fun.

In search of not one but two jobs in this field, I have been welcomed by a number of institutions, all of which have provided a stimulating environment for talking and thinking about hooliganism; many thanks to my colleagues at the University of Iowa, the University of Houston, Lafayette College, and the University of Texas at Austin, particularly my friends on the fourth floor, where in the absence of windows, many doors remain open. Louise McReynolds and Jerry Surh commented on substantial portions of this study and shared with me their love for the city it explores. I want to thank everyone else who read the manuscript in various stages and incarnations: Laurie Bernstein, David Crew, Alexander Dallin, Sheila Fitzpatrick, Stephen Frank, Chris Gilmartin, Peter Jelavich, Sidney Monas, Martha Newman, Richard Stites, Bob Weinberg, and in particular Laura Engelstein, all of whom provided an abundance of good advice, friendly support, and critical commentary. William Todd introduced me to narrative theory and has always generously offered his critical perspective on my forays into literary territory. Michael Katz helped translate the songs. Sheila Levine at the University of California Press offered persistent encouragement and support, which I sincerely appreciate.

Funding for research and writing was supplied by Stanford University, the International Research and Exchanges Board, the Mabelle McLeod Lewis Fund, the Mellon Foundation, the Hoover Institution, the University of Houston, and the University of Texas at Austin. Bibliographers and librarians at what were then the Saltykov-Shchedrin Library and the

Library of the Academy of Sciences in Leningrad provided generous and knowledgeable assistance and a ready supply of their own crime stories and opinions about hooliganism. I am indebted to the staffs at the Stanford and Hoover libraries and at the Columbia University Law Library, and especially to Mary Person and Dave Warringer at the Harvard University International Law Library.

In the end the "work" cannot be disentangled from the "life." My greatest debts are to my family and friends: to my parents for encouragement of all kinds, but most of all for making me believe I could do anything I wanted; to Tania, Nina, and Galia for their friendship on the other shore; to Jan Burstein for everything under the sun (and the moon), and to Max, my wild thing, you make my heart sing.

o   o   o   o

The transliteration used in this study aims for readability in the text and accuracy in the notes. I follow the Library of Congress system for the social sciences, but in the text I give common names in common forms and I drop soft and hard signs, while preserving the original in the reference matter (e.g., Gorky in the text, Gor'kii in the notes). Dates are given according to the Julian calendar in use at the time. Translations are mine unless otherwise noted. Parts of chapters 1 and 2 originally appeared in "Stories of the Street: Hooliganism in the St. Petersburg Popular Press," *Slavic Review*, vol. 48, no. 2 (1989), reprinted here with permission.

Introduction
Crime and Culture

A terrible situation has seized our city and, under the name
of hooliganism, takes forms that threaten the security of our
society. Malicious assaults, fistfights, knifings, disgusting
forms of depravity, and inexcusable drunkenness occur on
our streets—and are committed not only by grown men but
by women and children as well. The situation has become so
grave that it is necessary to take serious measures to
eradicate an evil that no civilized country would tolerate.
—*Urban Affairs*
St. Petersburg, 1913

At the beginning of the twentieth century St. Petersburg was gripped by
fears of crime. This book is about those fears, the crimes that provoked
them, and their role in shaping urban Russian culture in the last years
before World War I. Crime of all kinds was on the increase, but it was
a peculiar concoction known as *hooliganism* that made headlines in St.
Petersburg and within a few years grew to acquire symbolic stature.
Around 1900 the Petersburg boulevard press began reporting an increasing
number of cases of annoying public disturbances, rowdiness, drunkenness,
rock throwing, shouting of obscenities, and the like. Soon, more serious
crimes were added to this list: armed assault, mugging, and brawling.
None of these crimes were new, and they seem to have little in common
with one another, yet they were all lumped together and collectively portrayed as a new urban blight. When this diverse assortment of offenses
was dubbed "hooliganism," the word—imported from England, where it
recently had been coined—was quickly absorbed into Russian usage.

Crime itself and the fear of crime were hardly new in the year 1900,
nor were they unique to urban Russia, but crime and the outrage it pro-
vokes always acquire meanings specific to their place and time.[1] Because

1. Although some of the best European historians have studied crime as an aspect
of social and cultural history, it is only now beginning to receive attention from
Russian scholars. See Stephen Frank, "Cultural Conflict and Criminality in Rural
Russia, 1861–1900" (Ph.D. diss., Brown University, 1987); id., "Popular Justice,

crime engages words and actions about every aspect of social interaction—political, economic, cultural—it can illuminate processes of change in ways other subjects cannot. Hooliganism involved offensive pranks and horrendous crimes, but what makes it important historically is that the hooligans' reckless behavior hinted at deeper discontents while at the same time the published discussion about hooliganism transcended the specific crimes to focus on the larger social, political, and cultural issues that hooliganism seemed to explain.

In published discussions disparate crimes were lumped together because they seemed to reveal a new mentality of defiance among petty criminals and later among the lower classes generally. On the streets the hooligans themselves were forging a new kind of power—new for turn-of-the-century Petersburgers, though familiar to every city dweller today—by exploiting their ability to mock and intimidate the respectable pedestrians who stood above them on the social and economic ladder. Hooligans did not defy institutions of power directly but used public and symbolic behavior to challenge existing hierarchies of everyday life. They threatened established forms of social authority openly, but they also reached below the surface to tap some of the as-yet unarticulated hostilities, fears, and insecurities emerging in the new Russian metropolis. This whole discourse—word and deed—is what elevated hooliganism from a crime wave to a full-fledged symbol: hooligan acts and charges of hooliganism articulated important messages that could not be expressed more directly.[2] The

---

Community, and Culture among the Russian Peasantry, 1870–1900," *Russian Review*, vol. 46, no. 3 (1987); Laurie Bernstein, "Sonia's Daughters: Prostitution and Society in Russia" (Ph.D. diss., University of California, Berkeley, 1987); Richard Sutton, "Crime and Social Change in Russia after the Great Reforms: Laws, Courts, and Criminals, 1874–1894" (Ph.D. diss., Indiana University, 1984); Bruce Adams, "Criminology, Penology, and Prison Administration in Russia, 1863–1917" (Ph.D. diss., University of Maryland, 1981); Cathy Frierson, "Crime and Punishment in the Russian Village: Concepts of Criminality at the End of the Nineteenth Century," *Slavic Review*, vol. 46, no. 1 (1987); Eric Naiman, "The Case of Chubarov Alley: Collective Rape, Utopian Desire, and the Mentality of NEP," *Russian History*, vol. 17, no. 1 (1990).

2. I use the word *discourse* to signify the whole gamut of hooligan behaviors and the diverse messages they sent, the construction of public images of hooliganism in the media, the preconceptions those images tapped and articulated, and the uses to which those images were put, as well as the hooligans' continuing ability to destabilize and influence the published discourse even as the printed images classified and ostracized hooligans. This usage obviously derives from Michel Foucault's work, but I give more weight than he would to the social facts of hooligan offenses and to the hooligans' ability to shape and reshape the discourse even while being subjected to its power. See Michel Foucault, *Power/Knowledge: Selected Inter-*

extraordinary potency and usefulness hooliganism acquired as a symbol lay in its ability to speak about critical issues to multiple audiences at numerous levels. Because hooliganism was so rich in symbolic resonance, so obviously constructed, and within a few years so widely adopted, an understanding of its uses and meanings provides an entrance into the social and cultural world of the Russian city.

Hooliganism in St. Petersburg was an example of what sociologist Stanley Cohen identified as a "moral panic": an episode in which part of the population responds briefly, suddenly, and intensively to some new feature of lower-class behavior.[3] At the turn of the century, crime waves similar to hooliganism took place in a number of Western capitals, when seemingly marginal conflicts managed to capture and symbolize some of society's central issues and basic preoccupations. In Russia, however, in contrast to London, New York, Paris, and Berlin, the power of hooliganism to provoke and explain has endured. Hooliganism became an important issue in the social campaigns and cultural discourses of the 1920s, and it has retained its usefulness in a variety of changing contexts since.[4] This study of the emergence of hooliganism in the period 1900–1914 helps explain the conflicts and concerns of that era of unprecedented change in urban Russia, but it also addresses some persistent strains in Russian culture—an abiding preoccupation with the friction between defiance and obedience, authority and change, and barbarism and civilization—and it examines the birth of a new trope for representing that friction. Hooliganism started out as a marginal phenomenon of the boulevard press, a

---

views and Other Writings, 1972–1977, ed. and trans. Colin Gordon (New York, 1980); and Michel Foucault, *The Order of Things: An Archeology of Human Sciences* (New York, 1973); Michel de Certeau, *The Practice of Everyday Life,* trans. Steven Rendall (Berkeley, 1988).

3. Stanley Cohen, *Folk Devils and Moral Panics: The Creation of the Mods and Rockers* (London, 1972), 9.

4. In Great Britain and the United States, hooliganism has *come back* as a label for the violent acts of sports fans; but in Russia the term has been used without interruption since the beginning of the century. For contemporaneous hooligans, see Stephen Humphries, *Hooligans or Rebels? An Oral History of Working-Class Childhood and Youth, 1889–1939* (Oxford, 1981); Geoffrey Pearson, *Hooligan: A History of Respectable Fears* (London, 1983); Christopher Stone, "Vandalism: Property, Gentility, and the Rhetoric of Crime in New York City, 1890–1920," *Radical History Review* 26 (1982); Eve Rosenhaft, "Organizing the 'Lumpenproletariat': Cliques and Communists in Berlin during the Weimar Republic," in *The German Working Class, 1888–1933,* ed. Richard J. Evans (London, 1982); Robert A. Nye, *Crime, Madness, and Politics in Modern France: The Medical Concept of National Decline* (Princeton, 1984).

conflict between relatively small, neglected, and largely powerless sectors of the middle and lower classes, but it quickly evolved into a useful symbol and an enduring cultural category. One of the goals of this book is to explain how hooliganism emerged from the ranks of a simple moral panic to enter and remain in Russian national discourse as an evocative symbol of social disintegration and cultural difference and decay.

In its early stages hooliganism arose and flourished at the intersection of social and cultural changes taking place at the turn of the century in connection with rapid urbanization, industrialization, demographic shift, the spread of education, the inception of a more public, open society, and the first tremors of the revolutionary era. New economic classifications were beginning to overlay old social and legal categories. New occupations, as well as recently acquired wealth and education, cut across old demarcations of social status and privilege, and new groups were emerging within traditional social categories. Above all, peasant migration flooded the city with new people, new cultures, and new problems. Such changes in the social structure produced both confusion about social identity and, confusion's companion, acute self-consciousness.[5] In the attempt to define and assert new social identities, people drew sharp distinctions between themselves and groups they saw above and below. Those distinctions were often based on judgments about public behavior, customs, and underlying values: on *culture*, broadly defined.[6] Hooliganism, and the discussion it provoked about the culture of the lower and middle classes and about

5. On the transformation of the social structure, see Gregory Freeze, "The Estate (*Soslovie*) Paradigm and Russian Social History," *American Historical Review*, vol. 91, no. 1 (1986); James H. Bater, "Between Old and New: St. Petersburg in the Late Imperial Era, " in *The City in Late Imperial Russia*, ed. Michael F. Hamm (Bloomington, Ind., 1986); Daniel Brower, *The Russian City between Tradition and Modernity, 1850–1900* (Berkeley, 1990); id., "Urban Russia on the Eve of World War I: A Social Profile," *Journal of Social History*, vol. 13, no. 3 (1980); Daniel Orlovsky, "The Lower Middle Strata in Revolutionary Russia," in *Between Tsar and People: Educated Society and the Quest for Public Identity in Late Imperial Russia*, ed. E. W. Clowes, S. D. Kassow, and J. L. West (Princeton, 1991), 248–68. On confusion about social status and social roles see Jeffrey Brooks, *When Russia Learned to Read: Literacy and Popular Literature, 1861–1917* (Princeton, 1985), 355; Alfred J. Rieber, *Merchants and Entrepreneurs in Imperial Russia* (Chapel Hill, N.C., 1982), 415–17; Terence Emmons, *The Formation of Political Parties and the First National Elections in Russia* (Cambridge, Mass., 1983), 1–4, 173–74.
6. For a discussion of the ways the concept of culture is used in this study, see below.

Russian society as a whole, helped determine the content of those identities.

Recent social history of the late imperial period has furnished us with portraits of some of the new social groups as well as more nuanced views of the traditional *sosloviia* (legal estates). But even these recent studies have generally focused on one particular group rather than on interaction between groups.[7] Yet it is interaction, after all, that is the critical ingredient in the social soup that boils over into revolution. I am not speaking here of the open political battles historians have studied, such as those between the intelligentsia and the state or between labor and management, but of the divergent ways in which people attributed meaning to the events unfolding around them and how those meanings coalesced in language or public behavior to represent conflicting interests. The search for meaning and self-definition is what allows people to make sense of their economic or political position in society, particularly in a society undergoing rapid change. What Frank Kermode once wrote about fiction is equally true of the ways people understand everyday life: "It is not that we are connoisseurs of chaos, but that we are surrounded by it, and equipped for co-existence with it only by our fictive powers."[8] It is not that we are connoisseurs of fiction either, but the history of urbanization cannot be understood apart from the symbols and rituals people devised to represent themselves and stake out their place within society. Crime is an ideal subject for studying the sort of social interaction through which people define themselves, because it provides one of the few instances in which classes actually interact, right on the street. Or for the more fortunate, crime encounters provided riveting, if anxiety-provoking, reading material about interaction. Hooliganism, in particular, was at heart a dialogue. The public behavior and published commentary took on meaning in response to one another, and the two continually interacted to generate new behaviors and new interpretations.

This study follows hooliganism as it proliferated and evolved both on the page and on the streets. Chapter 1 treats the original discussion of

7. Exceptions include Mark Steinberg, "Culture and Class in a Russian Industry: The Printers of St. Petersburg, 1860–1905," *Journal of Social History*, vol. 23, no. 3 (1990); Laura Engelstein, *Moscow, 1905: Working-Class Organization and Political Conflict* (Stanford, 1982); and Joseph Bradley, *Muzhik and Muscovite: Urbanization in Late Imperial Russia* (Berkeley, 1985). Bradley also discusses attempts to reform the unruly lower classes by imposing on them notions of "respectability."
8. Frank Kermode, *The Sense of an Ending* (Oxford, 1967), 64.

hooliganism in the boulevard press, where it was first detected and defined; it also explores the reasons why the semisensational newspapers of the boulevard were the first to identify this fundamental form of conflict. Chapter 2 traces the escalation of hooliganism during the 1905–1907 Revolution; it analyzes the contribution hooligans made to the upheaval with their violent expressions of subterranean anger. Chapters 3 through 5 combine popular sources with those of the government and the intelligentsia to examine the ways hooliganism spread beyond the boulevard press and the St. Petersburg streets. Chapter 3 explores the diverse new forms hooliganism took after the 1905–1907 Revolution, when it appeared in the countryside and was adopted by avant-garde artists; it also surveys the debates hooliganism provoked among the educated and political elite. Chapter 4 returns to the streets of St. Petersburg to examine those who were taking practical steps to understand and eradicate the social and cultural sources of hooliganism: professional social workers and judicial experts. The lower-class youth culture these specialists uncovered, their efforts at "cultural improvement," and their interaction with poor youths illustrate the important role cultural categories played in dividing the privileged and the poor and structuring their responses to one another. Chapter 5 analyzes the growing fear that hooligan alienation was spreading among the lower classes as the persistence of poverty and cultural "backwardness" among the poor became better known, as hooligan crimes increased both in number and in violence, and as hooligan tactics were adopted by the labor movement during the upsurge in working-class unrest in 1912–14. The chapter culminates with an examination of the July 1914 general strike, which seemed to confirm this fear.

Three major motifs in this evolution of hooliganism provide a framework for understanding how people in St. Petersburg adjusted to living in a modern, industrial, transient, diverse, and politically volatile city. First of all, each phase in the development of hooliganism was characterized by changing perceptions and uses of public space. As migration inundated cities with peasants who then brought city ways back out to the countryside, public streets and squares throughout the empire became theaters for asserting and exhibiting contrasting cultures, styles, and behavior. The revolutionary display of mass power on the streets further undermined the ability of traditional social authorities and conventions to control the streets and dictate public behavior. After the 1905–1907 Revolution, violent hooliganism made public space increasingly unsafe for respectable pedestrians, a development that had profound consequences for social relations and perceptions. Much of the outrage over hooliganism was a reflection of the loss of the streets to the "many-thousand human swarm," as Andrei Bely evoked them in *Petersburg*, his great 1913 novel of the city.[9]

Second, as hooliganism appeared in new settings it revealed new expressions of hostility between classes and new fissures within existing social groups. Hooliganism, especially hooligan violence, revealed the depth of hostility smoldering among the urban poor, and it darkened society's perceptions of the lower classes as a whole. But the range of responses to the spread of hooliganism also paralleled the growing diversity of responses to all the issues of city life as educated society became more complex and the nineteenth-century intelligentsia began to lose its place as the sole leader of civil society.

Until late in the nineteenth century, the intelligentsia was a small enough group to be unified by its members' common European education and a shared set of values and cultural goals. Though they differed sharply on specific political positions, members of the Russian intelligentsia were more or less united in a commitment to the "cultural development" of the people and the cultural unity of the nation. This "culturalism" promoted the idea of a single culture, defined and embodied by the intelligentsia but accessible to everyone in a way that would allow the assimilation of the masses into a single, stable, and harmonious society.[10] But the Great Reforms of the 1860s and 1870s and rapid industrialization beginning in the 1890s eroded the unity and authority of the old intelligentsia by encouraging social diversity and cultural pluralism. The old intelligentsia and its didactic cultural project were challenged to varying degrees from many sides: the growing professional and commercial classes, the consumers of popular culture, and the artistic avant-garde all advanced their own ideas, tastes, and claims. By the 1910s, culturalism no longer dominated intellectual discourse. In fact, social fragmentation and the disintegration (or democratization) of the old cultural ideology spelled the end of the intelligentsia as a discrete social group. But while many people challenged the cultural program of the old intelligentsia, they simultaneously wished for the success of its mission. When hooliganism began to reveal the depth of society's failure to civilize the masses (or to impose

9. Andrei Bely, *Petersburg*, trans. Robert A. Maguire and John E. Malmstad (Bloomington, Ind., 1978), 11.
10. See Brooks, *When Russia Learned to Read*, 317–33, for a definition of Russian culturalism, which I adopt here, although I would add that often Russian culturalism included a heavy dose of Western Enlightenment rationalism and scientism, which is important in understanding perceptions of the "irrational" component of hooliganism.

cultural norms, depending on one's perspective), no consensus could be reached to explain the errors of the past or propose steps for the future.

Third, and overarching both the transformation of public space and diversification, hooliganism brought questions of culture out into the open. Explanations for hooliganism involved reevaluations of cultural difference, debates about the breakdown of "traditional" cultures, questions about the uses of cultural development projects for assimilating the poor into society, and doubts about the culturalist project. In this way, hooliganism reveals for us the centrality of cultural issues in late imperial Russia in shaping social policies and identities and in imagining a social and political future for Russia.

Thus while the symbolic discourse on hooliganism was dominated by images pitting respectable, cultured society against the uncultured and dangerous poor, it would be a mistake to view hooliganism purely as class conflict. The social and economic categories of class do not correspond neatly to cultural issues.[11] Neither the lower classes nor the middle classes (nor the intelligentsia as a class) were clearly defined in turn-of-the-century Petersburg. Nor is it a simple matter to identify the culture of respectability with some coherent middle class or to link hooliganism with a discrete lower-class social group. Hooliganism was first and foremost a cultural conflict and as such grouped people according to beliefs, values, and behavior as much as by status, occupation, and wealth. This is not to say that class differences played no role in hooligan behavior. On the contrary, the hooligan challenge was rooted in economic and social inequalities. But hooliganism was a special form of conflict that emphasized cultural issues. Hooligans expressed their antagonism in cultural forms; they used cultural weapons such as parody, mockery, and symbolic behavior; and even the more ordinary hooligan crimes were perceived as a threat to Russian culture. One of the central purposes of this book is to trace the outlines of a cultural landscape for St. Petersburg, within which social and political conflict—revolutionary class conflict—occurred. The point here is not to elevate culture above other categories but to establish its separate usefulness for understanding the critical developments in this period and to explore the way cultural categories intersect with issues of class and power.

But what is culture, and how is the concept used in this study?

---

11. Roger Chartier, "Culture as Appropriation: Popular Cultural Uses in Early Modern France," in *Understanding Popular Culture,* ed. Stephen Kaplan (Berlin, 1984); id., "Text, Symbols, and Frenchness," *Journal of Modern History,* vol. 57, no. 4 (1985).

③ Historical Approaches to Crime and Culture

At its most basic, culture consists of the shared values, practices, and codes of behavior, along with the means for enforcing codes and the forms for expressing them, that delineate a community.[12] Needless to say, the lines dividing communities are fluid: subcultures overlap (urban/rural, national/local, class/gender), and individuals can migrate between them. Culture is a less rigid ordering principle than legal or political structures, but it is more pervasive. Except during crises most people experience political or economic power intermittently, and as forces from without. But daily life is filled with the stuff of culture—language and religion, games and entertainment, fighting and rivalry, claims to justice, patterns of family interaction—all of which function in a multiplicity of ways. In relation to politics, culture can both reproduce and subvert power structures while translating power relations into everyday life. The economic reality of work is a necessity imposed from without and carried on according to rules someone else made up. But even in the workplace, economic conditions are perceived through cultural filters, through local practices and customs—colliding with, converging with, and circumventing officially imposed power. During periods of great economic and political transformation, when the old distinctions of the outer world no longer bind as tightly, people hang on to culture, especially its symbols, as a way of apprehending and functioning in the changing world. Culture, of course, is not static while the world around it changes, but at any one time enduring aspects of culture provide the materials for constructing our perceptions and for interpreting the new.

The social and cultural consequences of rapid industrialization, urbanization, and migration had become palpable in St. Petersburg by the first years of the twentieth century. Shared values, habits, and histories, recognizable practices, and similar interpretations of new experiences all helped bind people in alien surroundings by providing a framework for apprehending new political and economic arrangements.[13] In St. Petersburg

12. The best introduction to the history of the concept is Raymond Williams, *Keywords: A Vocabulary of Culture and Society* (New York, 1983), 87–93; see also A. L. Kroeber and Clyde Kluckhohn, *Culture: A Critical Review of Concepts and Definitions* (New York, n.d.).
13. Robert Darnton, *The Great Cat Massacre and Other Episodes in French Cultural History* (New York, 1985), 6; Daniel Brower makes a similar argument in *The Russian City*, 85–91; as does Leopold Haimson in "Civil War and the Problems of Social Identities in Early Twentieth-Century Russia," in *Party, State, and Society in the Russian Civil War*, ed. D. P. Koenker, W. G. Rosenberg, and R. G. Suny (Bloomington, Ind., 1989).

self-awareness about social position and its cultural markers was especially intense in new, emerging groups. Members of the urban work force were acutely conscious of features of dress, behavior, values, and ambitions that distinguished the skilled and settled urban worker-peasant from the "backward" peasant-worker. Surface differences in dress or slang symbolized deeper, less obvious distinctions in political consciousness or separation from the village left behind as well as more concrete distinctions, as in level of income and degree of workplace independence. Workers also displayed a sharp awareness of the ways in which they were perceived by people higher up the social ladder.[14] The semi-professional, semi-educated middle classes, ranging from those in the lowest white-collar positions to wealthy urban property owners, were also anxious to clarify their social position, to separate themselves from the "uncivilized masses," and to assert their own claims to the privileges of economic and educational superiority. Popular literature and newspapers were full of stories about people who had "fallen" from positions of privilege and status, as well as stories about success and upward social mobility.[15]

The anthropological concept of culture has been sifted out of the multiple meanings of the word only gradually. The concepts of coexisting cultures, of separate working-class or middle-class cultures, of culture as diverse, not universal, sets of values and conventions were not widely

14. For examples, see Reginald E. Zelnik, ed. and trans., *A Radical Worker in Tsarist Russia: The Autobiography of Semen Ivanovich Kanatchikov* (Stanford, 1986); id., "Russian Bebels: An Introduction to the Memoirs of Semen Kanatchikov and Matvei Fisher," *Russian Review*, vol. 35, no. 3 (1976) [Part 1]; vol. 35, no. 4 (1976) [Part 2]; Victoria Bonnell, ed. and trans., *The Russian Worker: Life and Labor under the Tsarist Regime* (Berkeley, 1983); P. Timofeev, *Chem zhivet' zavodskii rabochii* (St. Petersburg, 1909); Aleksei Buzinov, *Za nevskoi zastavoi* (Moscow and Leningrad, 1930); Ivan Babushkin, *Recollections (1893–1900)* (Moscow, 1957). On the worker intelligentsia see Mark Steinberg, "Consciousness and Conflict in Russian Industry: The Printers of St. Petersburg and Moscow, 1885–1905" (Ph.D. diss., University of California, Berkeley, 1987); Victoria Bonnell, *Roots of Rebellion: Workers' Politics and Organizations in St. Petersburg and Moscow, 1900–1914* (Berkeley, 1983); Allan K. Wildman, *The Making of a Workers' Revolution: Russian Social Democracy, 1891–1903* (Chicago, 1967). See also the profiles of "mass" and "conscious" workers in Tim McDaniels, *Autocracy, Capitalism, and Revolution in Russia* (Berkeley, 1988), 164–212.

15. Jeffrey Brooks, "Popular Philistinism and the Course of Russian Modernism," in *History and Literature: Theoretical Problems and Russian Case Studies*, ed. Gary Saul Morton (Stanford, 1986), 90ff. On the culture of upward social mobility within this group, see Brooks, *When Russia Learned to Read*, 269–94. On fears of falling and the "fallen," see Joseph Bradley, "'Once You've Eaten Khitrov Soup, You'll Never Leave,'" *Russian History*, vol. 11, no. 1 (1984); and chapter 5 below.

accepted anywhere in Europe during the period this study examines.[16] At the turn of the century culture was thought of as something to be achieved. Through a process of education, moral development, and refinement, people and whole nations might become cultured or civilized. When colonization brought Europeans into contact with other peoples, they did not immediately embrace the idea that the exotic customs they discovered were equally legitimate ways of living in the world. In fact they seized on those customs as further evidence of the superiority of European ways. For the same reason, many of the nineteenth-century exposés of lower-class urban life portrayed the poor as exotic savages, inhabiting distant and alien terrain.[17] In both cases a cultural hierarchy was implied: the strange customs portrayed were clearly inferior: "primitive," "uncivilized," "uncultured." Hooliganism appeared just when the concept of cultures in the plural was beginning to compete with the notion of one standard of judgment that situated peoples on a hierarchical scale ranging from uncultured to cultured.[18]

The hierarchical sense of culture did not consist solely of intellectual or aesthetic development or taste. Public behavior in Petersburg at the turn of the century was circumscribed by convention, as it was elsewhere in Europe at the time. Never mind that respectable people spat and blew their noses onto the street, members of the respectable classes who appeared in public (the aristocracy, of course, preferred to ride if they could afford it) took pains to adhere to conventions regarding public propriety. As a result, culture, or rather the acquisition and display of culture, represented a hierarchical dividing line in Russian society. Russia differed from the West both in the intensity of its obsession with rank and in its pro-

16. For a turn-of-the-century Russian view, see "Kul'tura," *Entsiklopedicheskii slovar' Brokgauz-Efrona*, vol. 17 (St. Petersburg, 1895), 6, where *kul'tura* is assumed to be a translation of the English and French "civilization." On the evolution of concepts of "culture" and their uses, see James Clifford, *The Predicament of Culture: Twentieth-Century Ethnography, Literature, and Art* (Cambridge, Mass., 1988), 92–114, 215–52; Marianna Torgovnick, *Gone Primitive: Savage Intellects, Modern Lives* (Chicago, 1990).
17. On the foreignness of the poor in Western Europe, see Gareth Stedman Jones, *Outcast London: A Study in the Relationship between Classes in Victorian Society*, 2d ed. (New York, 1984), 239–315; Gertrude Himmelfarb, *The Idea of Poverty* (New York, 1983), 307–70.
18. On the dawning recognition of working-class culture as separate and legitimate, see E. P. Thompson, "The Moral Economy of the English Crowd in the Eighteenth Century," *Past and Present* 50 (1971); Gareth Stedman Jones, "Working-Class Culture and Working-Class Politics, 1870–1900: Notes on the Remaking of a Working Class," in *Languages of Class: Studies in English Working-Class History, 1832–1982* (Cambridge, 1983), 182–83.

nounced emphasis on education as opposed to, or at least along with, wealth in determining social status. Furthermore, educated Russians were conscious of their country's position on the margins of civilization and its tenuous claim to have achieved a Western level of cultural development. Together these perceptions accentuated the need to acquire culture in order to achieve social status and magnified the conflicts that occurred between people on either side of the line dividing the cultured from the uncultured. Cultural difference, or the level of cultural achievement as it was understood at the time, was a major source of conflict in Russian society, and one that has been largely overlooked.

o   o   o

My conception of hooliganism as cultural conflict, social self-assertion, and an expression of popular values draws on recent trends in criminology and the social history of crime and popular culture. A new school of crime history emerged in the 1970s under the influence of works by E. P. Thompson, Eric Hobsbawm, George Rudé, and Louis Chevalier, who shifted historical attention from the criminals themselves to the societies that defined and regulated crime: crime became a *perceived* activity.[19] These historians and their followers rescued poachers, machine breakers, brigands, bandits, and others from the censure of their contemporaries and relabeled their acts "social crime".[20] This enabled historians to show a high degree of intentionality, rationality, and purpose in criminal acts. In sociology, at the same time, the "new" criminology took off in a similar direction, paying particular attention to the way language was used to define and punish behavior that threatened political and social powers.[21]

19. E. P. Thompson, *Whigs and Hunters: The Origins of the Black Act* (London, 1975); E. J. Hobsbawm, *Primitive Rebels: Studies in Archaic Forms of Social Movement in the Nineteenth and Twentieth Centuries* (Manchester, 1959); George Rudé, *The Crowd in the French Revolution* (Oxford, 1959); E. J. Hobsbawm and George Rudé, *Captain Swing: A Social History of the Great English Agricultural Uprising of 1830* (New York, 1968); Louis Chevalier, *Laboring Classes and Dangerous Classes in Paris during the First Half of the Nineteenth Century*, trans. Frank Jellinek (Princeton, 1973).
20. For a concise definition of social crime, see E. J. Hobsbawm et al., "Distinctions Between Socio-Political and Other Forms of Crime," *Society for the Study of Labor History Bulletin* 25 (1972).
21. Ian Taylor, Paul Walton, and Jock Young, *The New Criminology: For a Social Theory of Deviance* (London, 1975); Richard L. Henshel and Robert A. Silverman, eds., *Perception in Criminology* (New York, 1975). See also Howard S. Becker, *Outsiders: Studies in the Sociology of Deviance* (New York, 1963); David E. Kanouse, "Language, Labeling, and Attribution," in *Attribution: Perceiving the Causes of Behavior*, ed. Edward E. Jones (Morristown, N.J., 1971).

In both cases, scholars examined the ways that power, exercised by the state or a ruling class, could be used to control potentially dangerous sectors of the population by defining them as deviant.

In contrast, interest in cultural anthropology led other historians to explore crime and unrest for symbolic and ritual behavior that might provide clues to the mentality and values of popular cultures. Natalie Davis, Carlo Ginzburg, and Robert Darnton all showed the lower classes to be creative inventors of complex, dynamic, and changing cultures of their own, rather than passive recipients of diluted forms of elite culture.[22] The wide range of expressiveness found in popular culture was evidence of both popular cultural autonomy and the people's ability to interact on their own terms with elite culture in ways that produced sophisticated parodies of, and challenges to, what Antonio Gramsci meant by "cultural hegemony."[23]

Michel Foucault shifted the focus again and invigorated crime history by placing the construction of deviance at the center of the exercise of power. Foucault's conception of power, however, deemphasized the role of the state by showing how power can be exercised not only through oppression but through processes of classification and "normalization," which occur between groups throughout society. For Foucault, power consists of access to knowledge and language, which confer the ability to classify ideas, behaviors, and experiences and impose that classification, as norms, on others. Social groups create crime waves and moral panics, for example, both in order to define the unacceptable and to protect their own place in society by marking their own proper, normative behavior as superior. Access to the superior ranks depends on accepting social discipline and adopting the norms, which are, however, defined in such a way

---

22. Natalie Zemon Davis, *Society and Culture in Early Modern France* (Stanford, 1975); Carlo Ginzburg, *The Night Battles: Witchcraft and Agrarian Cults in the Sixteenth and Seventeenth Centuries* (London, 1983); id., *The Cheese and the Worms*, trans. John and Anne Tedeschi (New York, 1982); Darnton, *The Great Cat Massacre*; Peter Burke, *Popular Culture in Early Modern Europe* (New York, 1978). Inspiration for this group came from two directions: the work of Clifford Geertz, among which especially *The Interpretation of Cultures* (New York, 1973), and that of Mikhail Bakhtin, *Rabelais and His World*, trans. Helene Iswolsky (Bloomington, Ind., 1984).
23. This much-debated concept is discussed throughout Antonio Gramsci, *Selections from the Prison Notebooks*, ed. and trans. Quentin Hoare and Geoffrey Nowell Smith (New York, 1971), in particular 12–13 and, in reference to Russia, 238. For a view of Gramsci that outlines the strength of the model and shows Gramsci's understanding of cultural interaction, see T. J. Jackson Lears, "The Concept of Cultural Hegemony: Problems and Possibilities," *American Historical Review*, vol. 90, no. 3 (1985).

as to make them only partly within the grasp of the lower orders. In Russia, as we will see, hooliganism provided respectable society with a counterexample for defining the norms of respectability, both for its own self-identification and for "disciplining" the working classes.[24]

In contrast, Michel de Certeau explored how people conduct their lives outside of and in defiance of efforts to confine, oppress, or discipline them. He argued that for most ordinary people daily life is composed of creative acts that allow them to develop an autonomous sense of self and community despite superordinate power.[25] Certeau also showed how people continue to engage in these efforts to detach themselves from the "grid of power," even when self-assertion fails to erode the actual edifice of state power, because it is through such wilful actions that we construct a satisfying sense of our place in the world.

These studies emphasizing cultural dynamism and the power of culture, taken together with the evidence of the creativity and intentionality among people labeled as criminals, make it possible to understand the role hooliganism played, not just in the repertory of popular culture and politics but in the changing political and cultural relations of Russian society as a whole. The subjective, emotional, and value-laden observations of crime, which were often expressed in symbolic shorthand, can be more useful than other data for analyzing the class and cultural conflicts inherent in hooliganism. But, while hooligans, like the medieval *skomorokhi*, or minstrels, have been made known to us primarily "by their enemies,"[26] hooliganism was much more than a figment of the respectable society's imagination, and hooligans did what they could to escape being subjects of normalization. The repeated patterns visible in hooligan behavior reveal specific choices individual hooligans made, producing a "text" that can be read and interpreted. Hooligan acts may be treated as outward signs of inner values the same way ritual and other public behavior are analyzed by anthropologists for the meanings they convey to participants and ob-

24. Michel Foucault, *Discipline and Punish: The Birth of the Prison*, trans. Alan Sheridan (New York, 1977); and on the use of language and the control of knowledge for ordering social life, Foucault, *The Order of Things*.

25. Certeau, *The Practice of Everyday Life*, esp. 77–114. Other historians have studied specific ways that people use the paltry tools at their disposal to resist, subvert, or circumvent power; studies range from Richard Hoggart's examination of popular songs and newspapers in England in the 1950s, in *The Uses of Literacy* (London, 1957) to James C. Scott's treatment of "weapons of the weak," used in covert economic and political protest by peasants in Malaysia, in *Weapons of the Weak: Everyday Forms of Peasant Resistance* (New Haven, 1985) to Dick Hebdige's analysis of punk style as an expression of rebellion, in *Subculture: The Meaning of Style* (London, 1979).

26. My thanks to Bill Todd for pointing out the similarity.

servers. Hooligans used culture (both consciously and inadvertently) to transform everyday power relations on the streets of the city, the one arena where they could seize some power. The hooligans' self-assertion contributed directly to the disorders of the revolutionary era, and, more indirectly if more fundamentally, hooligans reordered the operation of authority on the city streets by challenging the power of respectable society to control street life. The construction of hooliganism and the conflicts it represented brought together issues of culture and power in ways that indicate the need for a broader notion of what constitutes power, what forces are able to challenge its authority, and what role culture plays in distributing power.

▤ The Boulevard Press and Other Sources

Hooliganism was first defined and publicized in the boulevard press—the commercial, semi-sensational tabloid newspapers that appeared at the end of the nineteenth century.[27] After 1905, hooliganism appeared in an ever-widening circle of publications, but the printed discourse on hooliganism was indelibly marked by its initial emergence in the boulevard newspapers because they were uniquely situated to grasp the cultural and class elements of hooliganism that made it so useful both as a tactic and as a symbol. Since the boulevard press created the model of hooliganism from which all other sources drew and since it is a prodigious but virtually untapped mine for historians, it merits more of an introduction than the other sources used in this study, whose genres are better known.[28]

The most popular of the boulevard newspapers, *Peterburgskii listok* (*The Petersburg Sheet*), and the similar, if somewhat less successful, *Peterburgskaia gazeta* (*The Petersburg Gazette*) both aimed at a broadly defined middle-class readership, though they attracted some aristocratic and some working-class readers as well.[29] *Peterburgskii listok* in particular occupied an important spot on the Russian cultural landscape. Other newspapers published information about cultural, political, and social life, but *Peterburgskii listok* was the first newspaper in Russia to concentrate all these aspects of daily life in one publication, devoted specifically to news about

27. For a general history of the boulevard press going back to its origins in the 1860s, see Louise McReynolds, *The News under Russia's Old Regime: The Development of a Mass-Circulation Press* (Princeton, 1991), 52–72; Brooks, *When Russia Learned to Read*, 117–23.
28. With the exception of the well-thumbed police department archive in TsGAOR (fond 102), archival sources on hooligan crimes were not made available to me.
29. Readership profiles will be discussed in chapter 1. It was not until after 1905 that boulevard newspapers specifically for lower-class readers appeared. Both *Peterburgskii listok* (*PL*) and *Peterburgskaia gazeta* (*PG*) had circulations of around 30,000 in 1900, approximately equal to the Petersburg edition of *Birzhevye vedomosti* (*The Stock Exchange News*), a moderate political and financial newspaper,

the capital. The boulevard press, however, was so roundly criticized by the Russian intelligentsia that its genuine merits were, and have been, overlooked.[30] According to B. I. Esin, the premier Soviet historian of journalism, the boulevard newspapers "cultivated apoliticism," proffering instead of serious news, "light reading, sensationalist rumors, incidents, vulgar jokes, patently indulging the prejudices of their subscribers."[31] This modern Soviet view echoes the ideas of the contemporary intelligentsia about the boulevard press, but in the case of *Peterburgskii listok* it gives a false impression of the contents and tone of the newspaper. Along with sensationalistic crime, scandal, and gossip, it was, in fact, a good source of news, information, and entertainment: in the words of its first editor, it was intended to be "an organ of everyday life."[32]

In contrast to the official government press and newspapers published for a national audience, *Peterburgskii listok* provided a wide range of information about culture, commerce, politics, and sports specifically for the capital's readers. In the early twentieth century, international and national news were squeezed in among the advertisements on the first two pages, followed by the comings and goings of Russian and foreign royal families and government dignitaries. The heart of the paper was made up of reports on local issues and events and the activities of various societies and trade

---

and Moscow's *Russkoe slovo* (*The Russian Word*), a national general-interest newspaper, and smaller only than the conservative *Novoe vremia* (*New Times*), and *Moskovskii listok* (*The Moscow Sheet*), at 40,000. But PL and PG were newspapers of the street, and more people bought PL on the street than through subscriptions. PL had the highest street sales of any newspaper, with about 10 million copies sold in 1905. *Peterburgskaia gazeta* sold 3.5 million copies on the street in 1905, and *Novoe vremia* just over 5 million. After the 1905–1907 Revolution increased the public's appetite for news and eliminated most censorship restrictions, circulations rose quickly, doubling, trebling, and in the case of *Russkoe slovo* increasing fivefold. *Gazeta-kopeika*, a new, cheap, working-class newspaper achieved a remarkable subscription of 250,000. *Peterburgskii listok*'s circulation and street sales remained steady, suggesting that it had found its audience before 1905. It neither acquired new readers from the growing mass of literate, urban readers nor lost readers to other, newly popular newspapers. (Figures cited were compiled by McReynolds, *The News*, Appendix A, Tables 4–6).

30. McReynolds treated *Peterburgskii listok* as an important cultural institution but emphasized the newspaper's "sensationalist" elements (*The News*, 140, 226, 237, 248); Brooks also treated the boulevard press seriously, but he used newspapers as a source for fiction rather than for news about life in the city (*When Russia Learned to Read*, 117–30). Brooks's characterization of *Moskovskii listok* as conservative and anti-Semitic should not be attributed also to *Peterburgskii listok*, which was neither.

31. B. I. Esin, *Russkaia dorevoliutsionnaia gazeta, 1702–1917: Kratkii ocherk* (Moscow, 1971), 47.

32. N. A. Skrobotov, *Peterburgskii listok za tridtsat'-piat' let, 1864–1899* (St. Petersburg, 1914), 3.

organizations, theatrical and artistic groups, and church and charity societies. Romantic adventure novels and thrillers (often dealing with crime and banditry) were serialized daily. A chronicle of "incidents," as they were called (*Dnevnik prikliuchenii*), reported crimes, accidents, suicides, and fights. Drawings lampooning local officials or commenting sardonically on the city's social problems or simply illustrating the day's stories were daily features by the turn of the century. Regular signed columns, feuilletons, and sketches commented (usually critically) on politics and social problems, with special attention to the St. Petersburg City Duma, the Petersburg district circuit court, and the Justice of the Peace courts; these columns also provided lighter fare with observations on the weather or the latest gossip from the lives of such popular celebrities as Sarah Bernhardt or Fedor Chaliapin. Occasionally probing and insightful, though equally often superficial and lighthearted, these columns provide an index to concerns of the newspaper's readers.

Peterburgskii listok also had a cultural mission, which, however, was never explicitly stated and only gradually established. The wide variety of genres, articles, and stories depicting the diversity of life in the capital—celebrating certain activities and deploring others—described the boundaries of acceptable behavior for its readers. *Peterburgskii listok* constructed a Russian variant of the culture of respectability that predominated in the "civilized" West. Respectability as delineated in the boulevard press was not socially exclusive; it was offered to all readers, of whatever class, provided they adopt the values and behaviors applauded as cultured. Examples of civilized respectable workers could be found in its pages, as could the occasional aristocrat. For this reason (among others already mentioned), I have usually avoided identifying the readers of the boulevard press and the consumers of hooligan images with a specific social class and have opted for the cultural category of respectability instead. Adherents of respectable culture in Russia (and readers of newspapers like *Peterburgskii listok*) tended to be members of the new middle classes rather than the unprivileged poor or the privileged rich, but what distinguished them were the values they shared and their reception of the cultural symbolism they found in the boulevard press.

Respectability, however, should be understood as a relative term. What passed for morality tales in the boulevard press earned only approbation from the established intelligentsia (radical wing included), who derided the newspapers and the commercial culture they purveyed as vulgar, sleazy, and crude. But while accounts of excessive violence and a lurid interest in private life deserve to be called sensationalistic, to dismiss such reporting because of its sensationalism is to slight the real services these newspapers provided their readers. If the news reporting was, at times, highly spiced with gossip and scandal, even Esin believed that it was usually accurate.[33] More important, emotive language and graphic description made the news digestible for readers whose interest in politics may have been eager but not necessarily profound. Moreover, sensationalistic reporting was not limited to attracting readers by engaging them emotionally, nor did it necessarily minimize the social and political features of crime or of any other issue, as some have argued.[34] The boulevard newspapers' reporting of scandalous crimes, outrageous behavior, and the private lives of public figures supplied engrossing reading but also offered readers unforgettable examples of improper behavior, defined the parameters of the acceptable, and reassured readers of their own superiority for never sinking so low. Furthermore, lurid crime and scandalous gossip was surrounded in the newspapers by other stories, and together these shaped the reading experience and resulting perceptions of the city. *Peterburgskii listok* presented a consistently solid quality and ample quantity of local, national, and international news, which countered its sensationalism and made it multidimensional.[35]

The boulevard press was not, of course, lacking in ideological biases, but there was considerable variation among the different newspapers. On national political issues *Peterburgskii listok* (and, to a lesser extent, *Peterburgskaia gazeta*) took moderately liberal positions, supporting the call for government based on the rule of law and, in 1905, for civil and political liberties. On local issues *Peterburgskii listok* was a consistent critic of City Duma policies. It regularly published articles reproaching the Duma for its indifference and inaction, especially in regard to the city's poor population. During the 1905–1907 Revolution *Peterburgskii listok* (and, again to a lesser extent, *Peterburgskaia gazeta*) wrote sympathetically about many working-class issues, especially economic exploitation, and published daily reports of strikes, rallies, and demonstrations.

Crime reporting in *Peterburgskii listok* followed simple conventions typical of the boulevard press of its day. It presented crime and violence both as serious social problems and as entertaining reading, though it should be noted that the treatment of crime before 1905 was often tame

33. Esin, *Russkaia dorevoliutsionnaia gazeta*, 50–52.
34. McReynolds, *The News*, 60, 143, 237; Brower, *The Russian City*, 177.
35. In this regard *Peterburgskii listok* compares favorably with its rival, *Peterburgskaia gazeta*. While *Peterburgskaia gazeta* generally avoided the blood-and-guts type of sensationalism, it provided much less "serious" news and analysis and fewer of the lessons in respectable culture that *Peterburgskii listok* offered: where *Peterburgskii listok* published outraged examinations of the origins of hooliganism, *Peterburgskaia gazeta* presented amusing and informative interviews with gang members.

and understated in comparison with the sensationalism and melodrama of post-1907 journalism. Crime reporting was a popular feature in the boulevard press, but, as a rule, before 1905 crime was neither prominently displayed nor graphically described even in the boulevard newspapers renowned for their sensationalistic reporting. Only in 1905 did some newspapers begin to highlight their daily crime reporting, emphasizing criminal violence with bold headlines, melodramatic language, and drawings or photographs.[36] Crime was covered in three kinds of stories: simple entries in the day's "chronicle," which listed crimes and other incidents; reports of trials held in the circuit courts and the courts of the Justices of the Peace, which appeared several times a week; and occasional separate articles, columns, or feuilletons about especially curious crimes. Most boulevard papers also published letters on crime from readers. The crime "chronicle" or column contained the most common and least digested reporting of hooligan offenses. Such chronicles of crimes and incidents appeared in almost every major newspaper regardless of its political profile or intellectual style.[37] They generally appeared in the middle pages, in a smaller typeface, and listed anywhere from three to as many as ten or twelve incidents daily. The chronicles were not entirely devoted to crime; side by side with robberies, pickpocketing, fistfights, and murders of passion appeared a variety of noncrime incidents, including traffic accidents, runaway horses, fires, drownings, suicides, abandoned children, and explosions. The crime entries in the chronicle were laconic and understated in comparison with the language used in separate articles. Even so, the language is suggestive, and along with the reporting of hooliganism elsewhere in the boulevard press it provides clues to the cultural significance of hooliganism.

The boulevard press undoubtedly played a role in forming popular perceptions of the city and its inhabitants, but determining the extent to which any text "reflects" or "shapes" the views of its readers is difficult,

36. All boulevard newspapers occasionally reported a bloody crime in lurid detail before 1905, but the contrast between the two periods is unmistakable in terms of both the number reported and the graphic language used after 1905, as is discussed in chapter 5.
37. The exceptions were the illegal newspapers of revolutionary parties, which focused almost exclusively on political theory, tactics, and local practice during this period. However, in the last few years before the outbreak of World War I, in an effort to win readers, even revolutionary party newspapers bent to capitalist market forces and conceded to popular taste by including crime columns and other information of a less explicitly political nature.

and newspapers present particular problems.[38] Newspapers always contain a variety of genres, and they are literally polyphonic, representing the decisions of a board of editors and publishers, the contributions of a newsroom full of writers, an assortment of advertisers, and a few letter writers from among their readers. It seems logical that newspaper portrayals of public issues had some impact on their readers' understanding of those issues by virtue of the language chosen, the images displayed, and the emphasis placed on a given subject. But newspapers cannot have an infinite power to shape popular perceptions for two reasons: first, people bring to their reading a range of previous experiences that allows a spectrum of interpretations; and, second, newspapers must appeal to readers' existing preconceptions in order to sell. Therefore, commercial newspapers use a number of strategies to control the symbiotic process of shaping and reflecting. Usually the newspaper's commercial character is seen as an impediment to accurate representation of reality: everyone knows that newspapers shape the news in a way that sells, probably distorting the real events.[39] But the distorted story has to reflect readers' expectations or no one will buy it.[40]

Newspapers are meant to be read quickly and thrown away, not pondered and analyzed; so they rely on cultural clues that reduce meaning to a limited repertory of perceptual categories that are comprehensible to a large number of people. Some variation in interpretation will always occur, of course, but newspapers are designed to limit variation. One way newspapers appeal to readers while restricting their interpretive choices is through the repetition of specific words, images, or symbols, which journalists use to convey ideas about complicated social phenomena in simple form, "without presenting the abstract argument."[41] Symbolic representations of reality may dilute and simplify the news, but for historians they provide essential evidence of cultural expectations, values, and beliefs. The images and symbols associated with hooliganism, and, more important,

---

38. For a discussion of the problems of "reflecting" and "shaping" for historians, see Michael MacDonald, "Suicide and the Rise of the Popular Press in England," *Representations* 22 (1988); and Reginald E. Zelnik, "From Felons to Victims: A Response to Michael MacDonald," *Representations* 22 (1988): 36–59.
39. It was not always so. For a history of the belief in newspapers' "objectivity" see Dan Schiller, *Objectivity and the News: The Public and the Rise of Commercial Journalism* (Philadelphia, 1981).
40. Steve Chibnall, *Law-and-Order News: An Analysis of Crime Reporting in the British Press* (London, 1977), 207 and passim.
41. Joseph Bensman and Robert Lilienfeld, "The Journalist," in *Craft and Consciousness: Occupational Technique and the Development of World Images* (New York, 1973), 209–10.

the endurance of hooliganism as a symbol, would not have been possible if the label had not struck a responsive chord among the newspapers' regular readers. When newspapers began to use various epithets—"savages," "beasts," "apaches"— to describe hooligans, they were shaping readers' perceptions of the phenomenon of hooliganism by clarifying, articulating, unifying, and reducing disparate meanings to a single symbol. But the symbol had to "ring true" by appealing instantaneously to preconceptions. The meanings a newspaper uses to *shape* reality have to *reflect* readers' prior experience.

These limitations on the interaction between newspapers and their readers make it possible to identify the language commercial newspapers used to clarify, articulate, and shape reality and to see in those language choices symbols that represented and reflected readers' cultural values and expectations. As a result it is easier for the historian to define a newspaper's "image" and the values it conveys. It is also possible to identify those values more directly with a newspaper's readers. Rather than evade the biases in the sources or simply corroborate their evidence with material from other sources, this study depends on the biases that shaped the news to elucidate the values that the newspaper conveyed and readers imbibed.

The tsarist censorship, of course, also shaped the way news was presented, but it seems to have had little impact on the quantity or type of crime news reported. The task of monitoring every newspaper in the Russian empire was too large for the agency established for that purpose, and there were numerous methods, both legal and illegal, to circumvent its prohibitions against reporting certain types of incidents.[42] The censors repeatedly harassed *Peterburgskii listok* for disobeying censorship guidelines, but financial and other penalties did not stop the newspaper from publishing crime reports even when they were illegal. In 1903 a censorship regulation was introduced that prohibited the publication of information about the "escapades of hooligans." In the same year *Peterburgskii listok* was taken to court for publishing drawings of hooligans and prostitutes.[43] But by the end of 1903 one journalist could write that hooliganism had become a topic that never left the crime columns.[44] Throughout this period

42. Benjamin Rigberg, "The Efficacy of Tsarist Censorship Operations, 1894–1917," *Jahrbücher für Geschichte Osteuropas* 14 (1966); id., "The Tsarist Press Law, 1894–1905," *JfGO* 13 (1965).
43. Circular dated November 22, 1903, cited in M. K. Lemke, "V mire usmotreniia," *Vestnik prava*, vol. 35, no. 7 (1905): 156; B. I. Esin, *Russkaia gazeta i gazetnoe delo v Rossii* (Moscow, 1981), 113.
44. Pchela, "Den' za den'," *PL*, November 10, 1903.

the press coverage of crime coincided with police and judicial crime rates, undeterred by the censors. Since this was true both before and after the virtual elimination of censorship in the reforms of 1905–6, it seems that censorship did not affect decisions to report crime.[45] On the other hand, the relaxation of censorship may have given writers freer rein to adopt the more graphic and melodramatic language that crept into the newspapers after the 1905–1907 Revolution.

o   o   o

As hooliganism (and awareness of hooliganism) spread, it was reported in newspapers popular with other readerships, each of which contributed its own class and political rhetoric to the hooligan question. Among such newspapers were *Gazeta-kopeika* (*The Kopeck Gazette*), also a boulevard newspaper but one that targeted a working-class readership; the conservative *Novoe vremia* (*New Times*); and the liberal *Rech* (*Speech*). Comparison of coverage in these publications will be used to corroborate some aspects of hooliganism, to show the range of interpretations hooligan behavior elicited, and to identify the features peculiar to the boulevard press. After 1907, hooliganism generated interest in the "thick" journals, which usually combined literature and political or social commentary; in the new journals devoted to modernist artistic works and manifestos; and in the professional legal journals, each of which provided additional perspectives on hooliganism.

Statistical data have been used here with some caution. There was a time when historians of crime would not touch official statistics, because they felt that instead of representing "real" crime rates, statistics could show only how much crime was detected by the police or prosecuted by the courts. It has now become clear that published crime statistics influenced much of what was written in the nineteenth century about crime. The annual publication of judicial statistics was cause for comment in popular newspapers and legal journals and thus had a considerable influence on perceptions of crime in Russian society as in the West.[46] Histori-

---

45. Charles A. Ruud, *Fighting Words: Imperial Censorship and the Russian Press, 1804–1906* (Toronto, 1982), 221–26; McReynolds, *The News*, 218–22.
46. M. N. Gernet, ed., *Prestupnyi mir Moskvy* (Moscow, 1924), xxii; S. S. Ostroumov, *Ocherki po istorii ugolovnoi statistiki dorevoliutsionnoi Rossii* (Moscow, 1961), 159–60, 240–41. Statistician A. Kaufmann wrote at the time that "the statistics of the Ministry of Justice constitute a branch in which Russia occupies, if not the first place, at least one of the first places among European states" ("Russia," in *The History of Statistics*, ed. John Koren [New York, 1970], 517).

ans have since turned back to crime statistics to see what careful use of them can produce. V. A. C. Gatrell and T. B. Hadden argued, reasonably, that although statistics could never represent the "dark figure" of crime—the number of crimes actually committed—they could be used to show long-term trends and fluctuations, assuming a certain level of consistency within institutions in treating and recording crime.[47] The rise in prosecution rates for hooliganism was a subject of public discussion among Petersburg judicial officials and in the press throughout the period under study, so the local crime statistics entered into the discourse on hooliganism. But statistics on hooligan crimes are complicated by the fact that hooliganism was never identified as a separate offense in the Russian criminal code.[48] When hooligans were arrested or came before the court they were indicted for other offenses already individually prohibited and punished by tsarist law. Armed robbery, for example, was against the law; it was also a misdemeanor to appear "in a drunken state" on the streets. But it was commonly understood that a hooligan drunk differed in some significant way from other public drunkards and that a hooligan with a dagger in his hand differed from other armed thieves. These distinctions, however, are not apparent in the aggregated statistics published by the Ministry of Justice. Fortunately, the local St. Petersburg court responsible for prosecuting petty crimes, the *mirovoi sud*, or Justice of the Peace Court, published lengthy commentary together with its annual statistics, which includes invaluable material for analyzing the statistics and assessing the importance of hooliganism in the capital.

Establishing the "real" level of crime took on new importance for historians questioning the seemingly universal assumption that urbanization and industrialization increase crime. This belief came under attack when historians realized that in urban, industrial settings more institutional attention was paid to controlling the concentrated lower-class population. The greater the attempts at control, the higher reported rates of crime rose, but the actual number of crimes may not have changed.[49] This ques-

---

47. V. A. C. Gatrell and T. B. Hadden, "Criminal Statistics and Their Interpretation," in *Nineteenth-Century Society: Essays in the Use of Quantitative Methods for the Study of Social Data*, ed. E. A. Wrigley (Cambridge, 1972).
48. Efforts to pass laws against hooliganism will be discussed in chapter 3. On laws against hooliganism after the revolution, see M. Isaev, "Khuliganstvo: Iuridicheskii ocherk," *Khuliganstvo i khuligany: Sbornik* (Moscow, 1929).
49. Abdul Quiyum Lodhi and Charles Tilly, "Urbanization, Crime, and Collective Violence in Nineteenth-Century France," *American Journal of Sociology* 79 (1973); Eric Johnson and Vincent E. McHale, "Socioeconomic Aspects of the Delinquency Rate in Imperial Germany, 1882–1914," *Journal of Social History*, vol. 13, no. 3 (1980); John R. Gillis, *Youth and History* (New York, 1981).

tion has particular relevance for early twentieth-century Russia, though from a slightly different perspective. Almost all social and labor historians have followed Leopold Haimson in arguing that urban society was undergoing a process of profound social destabilization that created difficult, if not unresolvable, problems for the tsarist government in the years before World War I.[50] In Haimson's view civil society was not only bitterly estranged from the state but was also profoundly split itself once workers and the educated elite lost the common ground that had united them against the tsar in 1905. This study of hooliganism shows that *perceptions* of social instability were at least as important as *actual* economic and social conditions in polarizing society and shaking its foundation. The chasm Haimson found between workers and the intelligentsia that was expressed in high culture and labor politics was echoed in less exalted but equally important places, in the boulevard press and on the streets, and the discourse on hooliganism reveals a city even more fragmented than Haimson imagined. Social fractures not only divided the middle and lower classes, but each was splintered internally as well.

The Revolution of 1917 shaped the way all historians have viewed late imperial history. Initially social historians were primarily concerned with groups having the most conspicuous political impact: the bureaucracy, the intelligentsia, the industrial working class, and more recently the nobility and the peasantry. But when we examine turn-of-the-century urban Russia as a society in transition rather than as a society preparing for revolution we find a myriad other groups in the population and we see that the political and economic conflicts they generated were often expressed in cultural forms. In other words, hooligans may well have hated respectable and privileged society on the basis of differences in status, class, wealth, power, or ideology, but they understood those differences through a filter of cultural artifacts and symbols: differences in dress and manners, in public behavior, in speech patterns or gestures, in entertainment tastes, and so on. The conflicts over culture illuminated by the discourse on hooliganism reveal sources of hostility and distrust that contributed to social instability in the years before World War I and hindered the building of consensus in postrevolutionary society as well. The history of hooliganism uncovers cultural conflicts that divided and demoralized urban society but at the same time gave urban inhabitants a language for creating and understanding the city and their place in it.

50. Leopold Haimson, "The Problem of Social Stability in Urban Russia, 1905–1917," *Slavic Review*, vol. 23, no. 4 (1964) [Part 1]; vol. 24, no. 1 (1965) [Part 2].

1 The Boulevard Press Discovers a New Crime

Do you want to hear a strange confession? When I read the murder scene in *Crime and Punishment*, I always want Raskolnikov to succeed in escaping, not to get caught. You too? . . . But reading about the same kind of incident in a newspaper, you, of course, want the criminal to be caught quickly. No, art is not at all a simple matter. It's a very ambiguous thing.

—Vsevolod Meyerhold

Early in 1901 a series of articles appeared in *Peterburgskii listok* bemoaning the recent and widespread disruption of peaceful street life. Lower-class boys and young men, referred to as gangs of "hooligans," were appearing on formerly tranquil streets and behaving rudely, sometimes threateningly. The earliest reports complained about groups of rowdy youths obstructing sidewalks, annoying passersby, shouting obscenities in the presence of ladies, whistling and singing loudly on the street, demanding money, and throwing rocks. Although the offenses were not new, they attracted attention because they were occurring with greater frequency and because they exhibited behavior that seemed unusual to their audience. Above all, the reports of hooliganism focused on the hooligans' demeanor. According to the reports, they acted with a special kind of bravado, with brazen arrogance, insolence, and defiance—all neatly contained in one Russian word—*nakhal'stvo*—a word that would continually recur in reports and discussions of hooliganism.[1] The hooligans showed no consideration for respectable pedestrians. Worse yet, they appeared to take pleasure in sowing alarm and aggravation among the peaceful passersby.

Interest in hooliganism was sparked at *Peterburgskii listok* when one of its writers received a collective, anonymous letter begging the news-

1. Sometimes *nakhal'* was used; a variant connoting less abstract, more immediate forms of the same behavior.

paper to call official attention to a situation raging out of control in their neighborhood. Signed only "Landlords of the Petersburg Side," it read:

> Dear Sir,
> You no doubt are not unaware of the existence of the gangs of rogues that go under the names of Gaida, Roshcha, and Koltovskaia. . . . The measures taken against them by the police have produced no results whatsoever. For the sake of public tranquility, I urge you to bring this terribly disturbing situation to the attention of those to whom responsibility for such matters belongs.[2]

The journalist, it turned out, was already familiar with the dangerous behavior of the "hooligans." He knew from personal experience that it had become impossible to walk at night along Bolshoi Prospekt, the central avenue of the district, "without meeting up with these rowdy types (*bezobrazniki*), swaggering along in crowds of up to a hundred."[3] But he was impressed that they had become such a serious problem as to move the landlords, "ordinarily such a complacent and indifferent group," to action. Intrigued and sympathetic, the writer set out to investigate.

He discovered (or, quite likely, knew all along) that one of the letter's authors was an acquaintance. "Mr. N." confessed that he had chosen anonymity to protect himself against hooligan reprisal. The street scene he described aroused contempt and moral outrage as well as irritation and fear. Armed with daggers, brass knuckles, and small weights on strings (*giri*) that were twirled menacingly, the hooligans eluded police control. Hooligans stood in knots all along the sidewalk and knocked people off their feet. They threw rocks through shop windows and not long before had destroyed a whole row of mirrors in one shop. Their swearing and coarse language "hung in the air," and they regularly disrupted events at the local "People's Hall" (*Narodnyi Dom*) with their boisterousness.

Many of the transgressions "Mr. N." described were not, in fact, crimes or acts prohibited in the criminal code, and the majority of them were more offensive and threatening than actually dangerous. What was most disturbing about the incidents was the hooligans' uninhibited presence in "respectable" neighborhoods and the ease with which they could take

---

2. A. V., "Grustnyi fakt," *PL*, February 25, 1901.
3. Ibid. *Bezobraznik* (the person) and *bezobrazie* (the offenses) were often used to refer to hooligans and hooligan behavior. The words convey both rowdiness and outrageousness, which do not combine well in any English equivalent. My translations emphasize whichever component seems most appropriate, but should be taken to imply both.

control of the streets. Both the "Landlords" and the journalist blamed the police and the courts for allowing these outrages to get out of hand.

Two months later another long article devoted to street crime appeared. It was now clear that the sphere of hooligan activity was not limited to the Petersburg Side but had grown and was continuing to grow. This article focused even more sharply on differentiating the new and old elements of the recent appearance of hooliganism. The pseudonymous author, S-i, emphasized that while the offenses committed by the hooligans were not new, they had occurred on a smaller scale and in a less obtrusive manner in the past. Previously their victims had been people "who for the most part belonged to the lower strata of the population."[4] In the past, rowdy youths and toughs armed with knives had confined themselves to the periphery of the city, where they preyed upon the poor and powerless, and there they were little noticed.[5] But then their "sphere of activities widened," as did their *nakhal'stvo*. "Now," the author observed, "we have come to such a pass that people are forced to endure every conceivable encroachment on the part of these unruly characters."[6]

The hooligans described in the article were a diverse lot ranging from pranksters and pickpockets to petty thieves armed with knives. On the streets, among pedestrians, they acted with "boundless insolence." They "bump into and badger women and young girls with unrestrained expressions and curses." Worst of all, though, was the danger after the sun set,

> when every passerby risks attack by hooligans. Demands for money and assaults on those who refuse to comply have already been reported in the [crime] chronicle. People are afraid to walk the streets alone. . . . Hooligans do not ponder consequences—if need be, they hasten to use their knives and other weapons.[7]

Even in the face of these very real dangers this author also chose to emphasize not the criminal or possible physical consequences of hooliganism, but the social and the moral. The most important element of the new hooliganism, the feature that most sharply distinguished it from

---

4. S-i, "Pogibaiushchie deti," *PL*, April 19, 1901.
5. Ibid. In this period the police rarely investigated crimes involving the city's poor population. This was the perception of the public and was admitted by the police department itself. See R. S. Mulukaev, *Obshcheugolovnaia politsiia dorevoliutsionnoi Rossii* (Moscow, 1979), 25. Robert J. Abbott makes the same case for the 1860s and 1870s in "Crime, Police, and Society in St. Petersburg, Russia, 1866–1878," *The Historian*, 40 (1977): 70–84.
6. S-i, "Pogibaiushchie deti."
7. Ibid.

earlier disturbances, was the manner in which the hooligans behaved, described here acidly:

> They act openly and in herds (*skopom*), loudly proclaiming their presence and exhibiting little concern about the possibility of punishment. These days hooligans "operate" everywhere. They "favor" us with their company on every street of the capital, at public meeting places and popular promenades where an abundance of "clients" can always be found.[8]

Furthermore, the author concluded, the harm hooligans did was not limited to "material loss and personal insult." They had a "corrupting" (*razvraiushchii*) influence on the children of the lower classes, and often middle-class children as well. The author feared that this wave of hooliganism had the potential to create an entire generation of depraved youth.[9]

By 1903, regular readers of *Peterburgskii listok* could not help but conclude that the capital had a serious crime wave on its hands. Other newspapers in the city also began to print reports of hooliganism. Popular legal publications, such as *Sudebnaia gazeta* (*The Judicial Gazette*) and the journal *Iurist* (*The Jurist*), included discussions of hooliganism in articles on the general rise of crime in the capital. In a series of articles on the role of village migrants in the growth of crime, N. Kontsev focused not on the "commonly heard" complaints about the police, but on the city's innate attraction for the most degenerate "good-for-nothings and cast-offs" of the village population. These peasants came to the city looking for excitement and entertainment as well as work, but, having no skills, they soon fell in with "their own kind" and began to prey on the innocent. Kontsev explicitly linked the propensity for crime with culture: the unsavory culture of the city and the low level of culture the peasants brought with them from the countryside combined to lure the migrants into the world of crime.[10]

The growing attention to hooliganism occurred in the midst of rising concern about crime in general. Newspapers, judicial figures, and police authorities all registered awareness of the increase in crimes of all sorts. Petty crime seemed especially troublesome. The House of Detention (the

8. Ibid. Quotation marks are in the original.
9. S-i, "Pogibaiushchie deti."
10. N. Kontsev, "O sudebnom proletariate," *Sudebnaia gazeta* [hereafter *SG*], August 11, 1902; id., "O prestupnom proletariate," *SG*, July 21, 1902. See also id., "O prestupleniiakh," *SG*, June 2, 1902; and K. A. Dvorzhitskii, "Khuliganstvo," *Iurist* 8 (1904).

prison for the Justice of the Peace Court) was overflowing (see tables 1–2 in the Appendix). One had to "stand in line" to serve a sentence of less than a week's duration. Most commentators agreed with Kontsev that rising crime was due to the increasing population of migrants and that the migrants represented the dregs of rural society. Police repression concentrated on public drunkenness, prostitution, passport offenses, and disturbing the peace. In 1899 the House of Detention annual report (summaries of which usually appeared in the commercial and government press) indicated significant increases in the detention of factory and casual workers (*chernorabochie*) of humble origin (*prostogo zvaniia*).[11]

Hooligan assaults on respectable street life multiplied in 1903 and 1904, to the point where one observer feared *samosud*, or vigilante lynchings, if repressive measures were not strengthened.[12] Not only was the number of hooligans and hooligan incidents mounting, but the hooligans' insolence seemed increasingly brazen, as well as increasingly hostile. Swearing, disturbing the peace, public drunken brawls, and harassment of passersby had become common occurrences. Numerous streets were reputed to be "hooligan hangouts," too frightening or too unpleasant for respectable pedestrians (see fig. 1). The Narva Gates and the Harbor Field on Vasilevskii Island were so described,[13] but as disagreeable as this was for local residents, the outcry grew decidedly louder when hooligans began taking over locations in the center of the city. At the end of August 1903 one letter to *Peterburgskii listok* complained that "with the return of the dark evenings, gangs of idlers have taken over some central parts of the city—Senate Square and Aleksandrovskii Park—making it unpleasant for peaceful bystanders, especially women."[14] A few weeks later the letter was echoed in the crime column: "Despite the severe measures taken against hooligans, these characters continue their outrages, and now in the very center of the city, [where] a group of good-for-nothings attacked some young fellows and, with noisy shouts, beat them up."[15] Hooligans of this sort almost always acted in groups, which caused more than

11. *S.-Peterburgskie stolichnye sudebnye mirovye ustanovleniia i arestnyi dom v 1897 god, Otchet* [hereafter *PMS*], 124–30; *PMS 1898*, 139–40; *PMS 1899*, 183–84, 192; F. "K perepolneniiu 'Kazach'iago,'" *PL*, April 23, 1902; Aborigen, "Stolichnyi den'," *PL*, March 20, 1901.
12. K. Asoskov, "Iz sudebnoi praktiki," *SG*, December 14, 1903.
13. "Vesti s okrain Peterburga," *PL*, September 10, 1903.
14. A. B-r, "Iz kipy zaiavlenii: 'Shalosti' lobotriasov," *PL*, August 31, 1903.
15. "Dnevnik prikliuchenii [hereafter *DP*]: Eshche khuligany," *PL*, September 13, 1903.

Герои нашего времени.

Хулиганъ (босяку). Ты да я,—насъ двое.

Figure 1.   Heroes of Our Time (October 19, 1903).
The hooligan to the hobo: "You and me—we're two of a kind."

one commentator to call them too cowardly for serious crime
(*krupnye 'dela'*).[16]

Hooligans seemed to be well aware of, and even motivated by, the effect
they had on their audience and victims. Obstreperous hooligans would
subject people to public verbal abuse and confront them with unpleasant
or violent behavior only to enjoy their shocked reactions. In 1906, a pair
of hooligans entertained themselves by unscrewing the bolts on benches
in Tauride Park. When the unsuspecting, out for a stroll, stopped to rest
and fell smack on the ground, the duo applauded "furiously" and emitted
hoots of exaggerated laughter, "in wild ecstasy," adding to the humiliation
of the unwitting victims.[17] A letter from a reader, appearing under the
headline "Hooligan Rowdiness on a Horse Tram," also emphasized the

16. Andron Sladkii [V. A. Popov], "Peterburgskie negativy: Khuligan," *PL*, October 13, 1903.
17. E. M. "Iz kipy zaiavlenii: Bezobraziia v Tavricheskom sadu," *PL*, July 27, 1906.

hooligans' apparent taste for the provocative, dramatic gesture. A woman getting on a horse-drawn tram was followed by a man who was singing and swearing and generally pestering her. This singing "shop-assistant type" had begun to bother another woman passenger when two more hooligans got on the tram. They offered the singer vodka, then seized him and started pouring it down his throat. The singer lashed out at one of the hooligans, and the scene turned nasty. The hooligans beat up the singer and finally pushed him off the car.[18] In this case, the author of the letter was outraged that women were made to suffer such abuse and condemned the hooligans for forcing the public to witness their brutal behavior. But what is most striking about the account is that the hooligans, including the original singer, all seemed aware of the effect they were able to produce and the power it gave them. The singer took obvious pleasure in shocking the women, and the hooligans offered the women their aid with a theatrical display of mock gallantry. On the enclosed stage of the moving tram, in front of a captive audience, all three rowdies seemed to revel in the power of their performance.

Commentators were particularly disturbed by incidents in which hooligans harassed women. Hooligans frequently shouted obscenities at women or in their presence and frightened them by grabbing their clothing or bumping into them (see fig. 2). In December 1905 two hooligans, dressed in black raincoats and masks, leaped out of bushes to frighten female passersby.[19] In September 1905 *Peterburgskii listok* readers learned that a sixty-year-old woman, walking along the Zhdanov Embankment, was knocked off her feet and had her leg broken by a hooligan.[20] The police received so many complaints about swearing on the streets that a campaign was waged to arrest those caught cursing and a voluntary society was formed to fight the decline of morals.[21] Hooligan morality was graphically illustrated during the summer of 1906 when Nevskii Prospekt was "overrun" with young boys selling pornography. They proffered postcards, "alphabet books," and other printed material, not in dark doorways or even kiosks but right on the sidewalk. Often they would run in front of

18. T., "Iz kipy zaiavlenii: Bezobraziia khuliganov na konke," *PL*, October 15, 1903.
19. "DP: Khuliganskii maskarad," *PL*, December 31, 1905.
20. "DP: Zhertva khuligana," *PL*, September 25, 1905.
21. "Listok: Bor'ba s skverisloviem," *PL*, September 7, 1904; "'Skvernye' vykhodki khuliganov," *PG*, August 3, 1906; and V. Avseenko, "Bor'ba s ulitsei," *PG*, August 14, 1911; "Na zloby dnia," *PL*, July 21, 1905.

Нападеніе хулигановъ на дѣвушку на Балтійской улицѣ.

Figure 2. Hooligans Attack a Girl on Baltic Avenue (May 26, 1905).

"ladies and gentlewomen," shove one of the books in their faces, and flip through its pages, "forcing them to hurry their steps."[22]

In some ways, the victimization of women represented the essence of hooliganism. Just as hooligans chose to act when and where state power was weakest, they often chose the most vulnerable victims to torment. Whether or not women consciously upheld the values of respectability more tenaciously than men, women's respectability was considered more likely to be damaged by exposure to such "vices" as public drinking, verbal taunts, and pornographic displays. The victimization of women clearly shows that hooliganism was first and foremost a struggle for power: the power to define street behavior and assert control over the streets. Pestering women was a relatively effortless display of hooligan power, and it had the added benefit of threatening the power of respectable men to protect their womenfolk from the dangers and vices of the public streets.

Hooligans had always provoked outrage for asserting themselves on the main streets of the city, but the cries of indignation reached an unquestionably higher pitch when hooligans invaded that last bastion of respectability, Nevskii Prospekt. Nevskii, in fact, had never been entirely free

22. G. B-n, "Bor'ba s pornografiei," *PG*, August 6, 1906.

from association with vice and prostitution, and it had long been crowded with pedestrians of all classes; yet it remained the symbol and measure of the civilization of the Russian empire. As a foreign observer remarked as late as 1913, "Nevsky Prospect is the pride and boast of St. Petersburg. . . . The patriotic Russian believes that nothing can exceed the grandeur of the buildings, the opulence and luxury of the shops, or the smartness of the people who throng this famous street."[23] Wealth, power, and fashion were on permanent display there. Even the crass commercialism that had appeared in its street-level shops could not diminish the magnificent, imposing facades of the palaces that lined the avenue. To promenade along Nevskii was still a central activity of Petersburg social life, especially for those who had only recently acquired the status, and the proper clothes, to do so.

Before 1905 it had been possible for respectable pedestrians to ignore the peasants, workers, and other representatives of the poor with whom they shared Nevskii Prospekt. But when hooligans began exhibiting their arrogance and disrespect there, this preserve of respectability was invaded by the most unruly and frightening representatives of the lower classes. Dressed in their greasy jackets and their distinctive caps, hooligans pranced drunkenly, escorted their prostitute friends, harassed respectable women, and robbed passersby. While no district of the capital was immune from hooligan assaults, the hooligans' appearance on Nevskii symbolized the dimensions and consequences of their challenge. The following episode from a 1905 crime column shows many of the elements that had surfaced on Nevskii during the previous year:

> On May 27 at 8:00 P.M. two extremely drunk hooligans were walking along Nevskii Prospekt. Every minute they knocked into a man or offended a woman. One of them, brandishing an iron pole, threatened to break open the skull of each passerby. The other was swearing unrestrainedly. On the corner of Nevskii and Pushkin streets they kicked a tiny young boy who was hawking the evening news, and ten steps up the road they spat into what was left of a street peddler's cucumbers. . . . Cries and demands that the scoundrels be taken to the police station came from all sides. Mocking the public's indignation, one of the hooligans spat right in the face of a well-dressed man.[24]

23. A. Maccallum Scott, *Through Finland to St. Petersburg* (London, 1913), 227–28.
24. "DP: Vozmutitel'nyi fakt," *PL*, May 28, 1905.

The nature of these offenses was not unusual by 1905, although the finale of this episode was more hostile than most. What marked this incident as distinctive was the fact that the hooligans chose to perform in front of a select audience and in an arena that was previously off-limits. This is not to diminish the hooligans' awareness of their transgression. After all, they chose to shake an iron pole at Nevskii's shoppers and promenaders rather than at workers on Shlisselburg Road. But, as in earlier cases, the writer did not express surprise at the demonstration of such behavior, but rather indignation that it now occurred openly and that the respectable public had become its witnesses and victims. The arrogance of the hooligans consisted in their leaving the slums of the city to appear on its central streets and confront the wealthy, the powerful, and the cultured, and those who aspired to wealth, power, and culture.

Hooligan acts, no matter how frightening they may have been, were often more shocking than physically threatening. The outrage they provoked was reinforced when hooligans were associated with two social problems considered to be more offensive than dangerous: public drunkenness and prostitution. These problems had irritated respectable Petersburg society since at least the 1860s, when the first major wave of lower-class migration to the capital provoked loud complaints about the decline of public morality.[25] The difference was that public drunks and prostitutes were portrayed in *Peterburgskii listok* as displaying their well-known deplorable immorality with a new degree of disrespect and hostility.

Alcoholism and public drunkenness were certainly not new problems in twentieth-century Russia, nor were they problems exclusively associated with lower-class life. Yet at the turn of the century they came to be associated with hooliganism, because in many cases public drunks displayed the same brazen insolence and disregard for the conventions of acceptable public behavior that distinguished other hooligan antics from non-hooligan crimes. According to police and judicial sources, drunks began to appear more frequently in the center of the city, and they acted with unexpected self-assertion (in part, just for appearing on those streets in that state). A highly publicized police campaign against public drunkenness culminated in a wave of mass arrests in 1900–1902.[26] Thus a per-

25. *Golos,* March 16 and 18, 1865, November 4, 1865; Reginald E. Zelnik, *Labor and Society in Tsarist Russia: The Factory Workers of St. Petersburg, 1855–1970* (Stanford, 1971), 240–82; James H. Bater, *St. Petersburg: Industrialization and Change* (Montreal, 1976), 150–212.
26. Public drunkenness was prohibited by article 42 of the *Ustav o nakazaniiakh, nalagaemykh mirovymi sud'iami,* the code of punishments for the Justice of the

ceived increase in rowdy public drunkenness coincided with the appearance of hooliganism at the turn of the century. Many observers, including some *Peterburgskii listok* writers, blamed hooliganism on alcohol abuse. Hooliganism frequently was identified with lower-class drunken sprees on paydays, holidays, and weekends. "On holidays," one reporter noted, "there are more loafers and drunks of all sorts on the streets, and therefore one is more likely to encounter, especially in the evening, a band of drunken hooligans."[27]

One of the rationales for the government liquor monopoly introduced in St. Petersburg in 1898 was to curb crime, although there was no consensus that it would do so. In bureaucratic and legal circles optimism ran high, but others closer to the scene argued that the monopoly would serve only to encourage illegal distillation, more public drinking, and degenerate hooligan behavior. One commentator wrote that "drinkers who previously remained hidden in various taverns and 'dens of drink' now exhibit their vice on the streets, which cannot help but have a harmful effect on the public, especially on children."[28] Illegal alcohol distillation and sales were widespread in Petersburg and were a central element of hooligan culture, as the following report, which features an underground vodka seller, or *sbiten'shchik*, shows:

> Three o'clock in the morning. Voznesenskii Prospekt. Hooligans stroll with their ladies. Squalling, quarreling, swearing, and, somewhere, dancing on the sidewalk to the accompaniment of a *gubak*. . . . Around the corner stands the *sbiten'shchik*. A few rare passersby and yard keepers are his only witnesses. A band of

Peace courts, issued as vol. 4 of the judicial reform statutes, *Sudebnye ustavy 20 noiabria 1864 goda* (St. Petersburg, 1864). For figures on arrests and detentions for article 42, see *PMS 1897*, 124; and *PMS 1902*, 133. These figures represent only a fraction of those arrested under article 42 (many were fined and released), and do not include those who were picked up by the police, spent the night in a precinct drunk tank, and were released without being tried. In 1901 in St. Petersburg, 54,940 persons spent the night in a drunk tank; in 1902, 52,490. Of a total population of approximately 1.4 million, this was an average ratio of 1:14. N. I. Grigor'ev, "Ustroistvo priiutov dlia vytrezvleniia p'ianykh," *Gorodskoe delo* 18 (1910): 1247.

27. Om, "Khuliganskii vopros," *PL*, April 8, 1903.

28. Dembitskii, "O primenenii st. 129 ust. o nak., nalag. m. s., i 1494 ulozh. o nak. k presledovaniiu ulichnogo p'ianstva," *SG*, May 27, 1901. For an optimist's position, see M. B. Starostin, "Vzgliad zakona na p'ianstvo," *SG*, August 26, 1901.

hooligans jokes about it. Clearly a regular occurrence in this neighborhood.[29]

Another feature of hooligan culture, more offensive to public morality than it was dangerous, was the hooligans' association with prostitutes.[30] In the cases of hooliganism discussed in *Peterburgskii listok* and other sources, female hooligans very rarely appear.[31] Women, of course, engaged in public rowdiness, drunken disturbances of the peace, petty theft, and other offenses that were considered acts of hooliganism when committed by men, but female offenders were rarely referred to as hooligans. One can assume only that even when women committed the same sorts of crimes hooligans were accused of committing they were not seen as equally threatening, or threatening in the same way. On the other hand, prostitution and open displays of sexuality by women *were* portrayed as threatening and offensive. Much of the moral opprobrium directed at hooligans was shared by their prostitute companions. One report noted that "the Narva Gates district has lately become a hangout for hooligans. On holidays one cannot walk there. . . . About ten women turned up recently on the other side of the gates and carried on indescribable debauchery right there on the street."[32]

In this context, in the pages and crime columns of newspapers like *Peterburgskii listok*, prostitution was the female equivalent of male hooliganism. Press descriptions of dangerous neighborhoods or hooligan haunts often made mention of hooligans walking with, flirting with, or fighting with their "sweethearts" (*damy serdtsa*) or their "fairies" (*fei*).[33] In 1903

29. Nash, "Kodiachiia 'kazenki,'" *PL*, July 23, 1906.

30. The fullest treatment of prostitution in tsarist Russia is Bernstein, "Sonia's Daughters"; see also Barbara Alpern Engel, "St. Petersburg Prostitutes in the Late Nineteenth Century: A Personal and Social Profile," *Russian Review*, vol. 48, no. 1 (1989).

31. Lists of people rounded up and fined for disturbing the peace occasionally included women. See "Nakazannye khuligany," *PL*, September 4, 1903. The only detailed case involving a female hooligan that I found in *PL* between 1900 and 1914 was "'Intelligentnye' khuligany," *PL*, October 1, 1906. The woman involved—"one Nikolaeva"—roughed up a seamstress to whom she owed payment for some linen. The only other specific case I found in the press was that of a woman tried in Tver' for disturbing the peace; she had been raising a ruckus in the courtyard of her building after being dismissed from her job. See K. Asoskov, "Iz sudebnoi praktiki," *SG*, December 14, 1903. In neither case was cultural challenge or shock value a motivating factor.

32. "Vesti s okrain Peterburga," *PL*, October 10, 1903.

33. Andron Sladkii, "Peterburgskie negativy: Khuligan," *PL*, October 13, 1903.

Peterburgskii listok ran a serialized novel called "The Hooligan" that featured a hooligan and his various prostitute companions as central characters.[34] In both real and fictional cases the men engaged actively in hooligan crime while the women were passive observers. Hooligans and prostitutes were portrayed as equally depraved morally, although in some cases the women were seen primarily as victims, at least at first, rather than as corrupting influences in their own right. And by all accounts, they were poorly treated by their hooligan companions, who sometimes functioned as their pimps and their exploiters.

Boris Bentovin, a doctor attached to the department that licensed prostitutes, portrayed the symbiotic relationship in unusually sympathetic terms:

> Recently, young apprentices, store clerks, and young factory
> workers have been swept into this turbid stream, keen for free sex
> and a high time, eager to sow their wild oats and to find an outlet
> for their youthful spirit. The joining of workers with pimps is
> new, but it undoubtedly occurs. The life of drink . . . soon leads
> these workers to become professional pimps—they become half
> pimp, half worker. What brings these fresh, able-bodied workers
> into the ranks of pimps and prostitutes? *Hooliganism*—which by
> now is entrenched among the older pimps, whose antipathy to
> work is infectious.[35]

In this account, hooliganism is not associated with specific acts but with an attitude toward work and the values of the dominant culture. Living parasitically off prostitutes was, in Bentovin's view, only a short step from rejecting other social strictures and acceptable legal behavior. The doctor's comments are interesting because he showed some understanding of the process by which the lives of young workers, who were lured at first by the appeal of high living, were transformed by habit and necessity into lives outside the law, where work was shunned and working held in contempt. Their brutal exploitation of prostitutes destroyed their own moral sense as well as that of the prostitutes. Hooligans, according to the doctor, were not born but bred.

34. S. Narskii, "Khuligan: Roman-khronika iz sovremennoi zhizni Peterburga," *PL*, June 30, 1903 (the first installment of a serial novel).
35. B. Bentovin, "Spasanie 'padshikh' i khuliganstvo," *Obrazovanie* 11–12 (1905): 345–46. The author based his portrait of hooligans on conversations with prostitutes.

All the forms of hooliganism discussed thus far have obvious social and moral overtones that link the different kinds of behavior. Each of the incidents cited was frightening and offensive, and in some cases the hooligans threatened peaceful passersby—but few of the offenses posed any real physical danger. But after mid-1903, genuinely dangerous forms of violent street crime were reported in increasing numbers in the *Peterburgskii listok* crime columns. Random hooligan pranks began to take a violent turn. In July 1905, for example, several adolescents let loose a wasp's nest on a suburban train. Another pair found it entertaining to throw cups of hot tea at pedestrians from the doorway of a tea shop on Sadovaia Street.[36] The most common form of hooligan violence, however, was the growing rash of back-street "muggings" and stabbings. Crime-column entries on these attacks were usually short and laconic, but by 1904 their titles rang with alarm: "Dikie nravy" (Savage Customs), "Nozhovaia rasprava" (Retribution by Knife), or even "Nozhevshchina" (The Rule of the Knife). The reports themselves developed their own regular formula: short, simple, and direct descriptions, including the time, place, number of attackers, and the damage done:

> At 3:00 P.M. in Sestroretsk a man was attacked by three strangers for no reason at all. Another stranger ran up and stabbed the victim, at which point they all ran off, leaving the victim on the ground.[37]

On May 5 three attacks were reported, including the following:

> On the night of May 4 a twenty-two-year-old *meshchanin*, Mikhail Mikhailov of Kartashikhinaia Street, was attacked on the Petersburg Side by a stranger. He suffered a deep knife wound.[38]

At the end of 1903 similar incidents appeared under such alarming titles almost weekly in the crime columns of *Peterburgskii listok*, and in 1904 at least one such incident appeared every four to five days. During the revolutionary years 1905 and 1906 the number of such attacks multiplied rapidly, with at least one reported almost every day. Typically these attacks occurred on dark or out-of-the-way streets, more often than not in

---

36. "DP: Khuliganskaia prodelka," *PL*, July 14, 1905; "DP: Dikie detskie nravy," *PL*, August 24, 1904.
37. "DP: Napadenie," *PL*, October 9, 1903.
38. *Meshchanin* (pl. *meshchane*), legally designated as "townsman," is sometimes translated as "petty bourgeois"; but *meshchane* might work in factory or nonindustrial labor, and many were poor. "DP: Nozhovaia rasprava," *PL*, May 5, 1903.

working-class neighborhoods on the outskirts of town, or in surrounding suburbs, such as Sestroretsk, or near stations along the railroad lines leaving the capital. These were not dramatic incidents staged for an audience of middle-class pedestrians. They were perpetrated by strangers on "the first passerby"—unarmed and unsuspecting pedestrians—and usually "for no reason at all." Victims were beaten or stabbed, occasionally for refusing to hand over their wallets or the few kopecks in their pockets.[39] Most of the victims were classified as peasants, workers, or *meshchane*. A railroad conductor surrounded by four hooligans on his way home from work was startled to hear them say: "Well, well brother, can you spare some change? You ought to treat us, you know." He replied: "What do you mean change? I'm a worker myself." So they grabbed his watch.[40]

Respectable pedestrians did not need to be the victims or observers of a crime for it to be labeled hooliganism. When hooligan attitudes infused incidents that occurred off the street or off the central streets, beyond the purview of respectable society, the distinctive characteristics of hooliganism were still noted. In one case,

> a wild, knife-toting good-for-nothing, feared by all who knew him, stabbed an acquaintance in a tearoom for refusing him the ten kopecks he needed for vodka. The wound was very serious; the victim spent four months in the hospital. At his trial, the hooligan denied his guilt and denied being in the tearoom until irrefutable evidence . . . was produced. Then he justified his behavior with the excuse that he was extremely drunk at the time of the attack.[41]

This incident lacked the element of public confrontation, but it was marked as hooligan by the pettiness, cynicism, and incomprehensibility of the perpetrator. The "good-for-nothing" hooligan disturbed the prevailing order of the tearoom for the paltry sum of ten kopecks, his violent response was out of all proportion to his acquaintance's act, and he cynically claimed drunken stupor (a common courtroom ploy at the time) when faced with his crime. Articles such as this elaborated the characteristics of the hooli-

---

39. Although *Peterburgskii listok* seems to have reported such attacks more regularly than other newspapers, similar hooligan attacks were reported in many other newspapers, including *Peterburgskaia gazeta* and *Vedomosti S-Peterburgskogo gradonachal'stva*; in the 1910s this sort of hooliganism was regular fare in newspapers running the gamut from the working-class *Gazeta-kopeika* to the conservative political newspaper *Novoe vremia*.
40. "DP: Napadenie na konduktora," *PL*, July 28, 1906.
41. "Iz zaly suda: Opasnyi khuligan," *PL*, October 8, 1903.

Къ появленію садовыхъ хулигановъ.

(Въ недалекомъ будущемъ).

— Ахъ, Марья Петровна, во что это вы нарядили вашего Колечку?!..
— Какъ во что? Въ самый модный спеціальный костюмчикъ для
гулянія въ городскихъ садахъ...

Figure 3. On the Appearance of Hooligans in Our Parks (Set in the Near Future) (April 24, 1903).
—My! Maria Petrovna, *what* is your little Kolia wearing?!
—What do you mean? He's dressed in the most fashionable little suit, especially designed for walking in our city's parks.

ganism phenomenon wherever it occurred. The fact that some hooligans stabbed other riffraff did not diminish the implied possibility that the whole city was at risk.

Public fears of hooligan violence were graphically displayed in *Peterburgskii listok* cartoons. In April 1903 a cartoon appeared under the title "On the Appearance of Hooligans in Our Parks" (fig. 3). The drawing shows a young child dressed in a collar with long, sharp spikes, longer than the child's arms, radiating out from his neck. In the caption one mother says to the other: "My! Maria Petrovna, *what* is your little Kolia wearing?!" "What do you mean?" Maria replies. "He's dressed in the most fashionable little suit, especially designed for walking in our city's parks." Another cartoon, published on the last day of the same year, is captioned "Hap . . . py New Year . . . to . . . You . . . !" (fig. 4). The drawing shows a man being stabbed in the back by a hooligan type (recognizable in distinctive cap and jacket) who punctuates his words with jabs of the knife, while a policeman runs belatedly toward them. The cartoon

По питерски.

— Съ пр... раздниюмъ в... васъ!..

Figure 4. New Year's Eve—Petersburg Style (December 31, 1903).
"Hap . . .py New Year . . . to . . . You!"

is entitled "Po Piterski" or, roughly, "Petersburg-Style," meaning "This is how New Year's Eve is celebrated in St. Petersburg."[42]

To some extent these fears of hooligan attack were exaggerated, since typical *Peterburgskii listok* readers were rarely the victims of hooligan muggings, even at the height of hooligan brazenness in 1905 and 1906. The jocular undercurrent in these two cartoons—unusual in the coverage of hooliganism—may have been partly a recognition of that fact; in any case, humorous treatment disappeared altogether by 1905. When newspapers began to expose their readers to daily reports of hooligan offenses, they created the impression of a city inundated by a new population of irresponsible, irreverent, and dangerous creatures. The knife-wielding mugger showed the same disrespect for law and order as the whistling and

---

42. *PL*, April 24, 1903, December 31, 1903. The idea for the spiked neck band may have derived from those illustrated in the London press in the 1860s during a scare concerning a similar crime known as garroting, in which criminals stole up behind unwitting victims and strangled them; see the *Punch* drawings reprinted in Pearson, *Hooligan*, 139.

swearing young tough loitering menacingly on a street corner. Further-more, the randomness of the attacks and the absence of comprehensible motivation attributed to many hooligans suggested that everyone was a potential victim. The similarities between back-alley violence and the outrageous, incomprehensible, and challenging demeanor hooligans displayed on central streets helped blur the distinction between genuine and imagined danger.

But in addition to differing in the degree of danger they posed, hooligan rowdiness and hooligan knifings were clearly different *kinds* of crimes. The blurring of those distinctions, the similarities newspaper writers and observers found in the disparate acts, are the central clues to hooliganism's cultural meaning and historical significance. Rowdy, defiant, dangerous acts on the part of physically intimidating lower-class men provided respectable society with the raw material for a discourse that not only explained the crimes but also delineated values and identities in an attempt to impose order on a city in flux. The formulas of crime reporting, in this case, not only featured repeated words, such as *nakhal'*, "savage customs," and "the first passerby." Crime reporting also repeated acts until they came to seem almost ritualistic. The threatening stare, the bump on the sidewalk, and the sudden knifing were repeated often enough, not to minimize their danger but to identify them directly with a type of person, distinguishing hooligans as a social and cultural group. The repetition of words and acts identified hooligans as a special social category, not exactly criminal (or not only criminal) but clearly Other.

It is a commonplace of some structuralist analysis to see culture as composed of binary oppositions: people learn who they are by constructing what they are not. "Bourgeois and crime are a true binary opposition," wrote Robert Nye in his study of crime and madness in *belle époque* France: "in linguistic and conceptual terms each notion is dependent on the other for the fullest meaning."[43] Whether or not this was a universal process, it was at work in the emergence of hooliganism in this period. But Russia was not France. A bourgeoisie was only just reaching critical mass in Russia at the turn of the century, and the middle classes were still undergoing a process of self-identification. As economic and social mobility intensified, the one relatively consistent element in social stratification was education and its public manifestations in culture. For Russian respectable society, to recast Nye's observation, "civilization" and hooli-

---

43. Nye, *Crime, Madness, and Politics*, 205.

ganism were the operative binary opposition. Russian readers of the boulevard press learned who they were, and then solidified their own place in
civilized society by construing the hooligan as the archenemy of civilization.

What, then, were the values inscribed in this "scourge of the capital?"
The appearance of lower-class rowdiness and back-street violence created
a new arena for class interaction, which called for a new vocabulary. The
first references to hooliganism in Russia usually made use of older native
terms such as *ozorstvo*, which conveys a prankish mischievousness, or
bezchinstvo, which includes defiance of rank. Most agree that the word
hooligan was introduced into Russian usage in 1898 by I. V. Shklovskii
in one of the monthly columns about life in England that he wrote for
Russkoe bogatstvo (Russian Wealth) under the pen name Dioneo.[44] Before 1900 the word was rarely, if ever, used in print, and the phenomenon
seldom noted.[45] Then in the first years of the century the word was quickly
absorbed into common usage, replacing the older, inadequate terms. No
attempt was made to define hooliganism systematically or legally until the
1910s, when proposals for outlawing the crime were circulated. Even then
the exact meaning of hooliganism as a social phenomenon and as a legal
category remained the subject of dispute. But even as early as 1901 it is
clear that when writers used the word *hooliganism* they fully expected
their audience to understand it. For the first few years, *hooliganism* was
occasionally still used interchangeably with *ozorstvo* or was linked with
gang activity. By 1903 it had developed resonances and an identity of

44. In London in the summer of 1898 there was a sudden upsurge in arrests for
disorderly and criminal public behavior. The perpetrators were dubbed "hooligans," and the word entered common usage in England as abruptly as it did in
Russia. Some British youngsters may have first used the word to describe themselves and their own rowdy antics, but the word caught on only when the press
gave it wide play after the 1898 disturbances. The word's Irish roots are obvious,
and its adoption by the British was probably connected with the recent migration
of Irish workers to London and British disdain for their rowdy ways. Shklovskii
described the London disturbances and their treatment in the British press in "Iz
Anglii," *Russkoe bogatstvo* 9 (September 1898): 128ff.; on the British origins of
the word see Pearson, *Hooligan*, 255–56 n. 3; and for some fanciful versions of
the etymology see Valery Chalidze, *Criminal Russia: Essays on Crime in the
Soviet Union*, trans. P. S. Falla (New York, 1977), 73.
45. P. Liublinskii, writing in the 1920s, claimed that the word *hooligan* was first
used by the St. Petersburg *gradonachal'nik* von Val' in 1892 and that the police
brought the word into popular usage ("Khuliganstvo i ego sotsial'no-bytovye
korni," *Khuliganstvo i khuligany: Sbornik* [Moscow, 1929], 38n). This is possible,
but I found no trace of the word in popular parlance or police documents before
1898.

its own, and *hooliganism*, the word, and hooliganism, the phenomenon, replaced other labels for and forms of lower-class rowdiness and petty crime in the forefront of public concern.

A major exception must be noted here. In the southern and southwestern cities of the Pale of Settlement, where Jews were legally required to live, the word *hooligan* came to be used almost exclusively in reference to pogromists—that is, young Slavic men who engaged in mass violence against Jews and their property or occasionally against students and intellectuals they associated with Jews. In these regions the hooligans resembled Marx's original "lumpenproletariat"—the street rabble who sided with the police in repressing radical demonstrations.[46] In the north, however, hooligans' involvement in the political process usually had the effect of subverting rather than supporting police aims, as will be discussed in the following chapter. For many among the educated elite, the bloody pogroms represented a prime offense against civilization, but violence against Jews was not an issue in the development of hooliganism in St. Petersburg.[47]

In *Peterburgskii listok* both violent and merely insolent hooliganism were presented as an affront to the same authority and values. Newspaper descriptions of muggings were comparatively plain and unembellished, and so they lack the cultural clues provided in descriptions of other forms of hooliganism: for example, the constant references to *nakhal'*, the hooligans' brazenness and bravado. The crime-column reports of the violent attacks, however, are not entirely opaque. The titles of the entries provide one clue for deciphering them. "Dikie nravy" (Savage Customs) not only rings of an anthropological discovery; it immediately connotes antonyms of "civilization." And "Nozhevshchina" (The Rule of the Knife) cannot help but summon up other dark and dangerous chapters from Russia's

---

46. On southern hooligan-pogromists see, for example, *Prikliuchenie odnogo khuligana* (Kiev, 1908); Charters Wynn, *Workers, Strikes, and Pogroms: The Donbass-Dnepr Bend in Late Imperial Russia, 1870–1905* (Princeton, 1992); Robert Weinberg, *The Revolution of 1905 in Odessa: Blood on the Steps* (Bloomington, Ind., forthcoming). Marx discussed the lumpenproletariat in "Manifesto of the Communist Party" (in *Political Writings*, vol. 1, *The Revolutions of 1848*, ed. David Fernbach [New York, 1974], 77) and in "The Class Struggles in France: 1848–1850" (in *Political Writings*, vol. 2, *Surveys From Exile*, ed. David Fernbach [New York, 1974], 52–53). *Odesskii listok* ran a regular column on hooligan offenses.
47. Laura Engelstein mentions that when street violence broke out between Black Hundreds and students, workers, or intellectuals, it was the students or workers rather than the Black Hundreds who were referred to as hooligans (*Moscow, 1905*, 140, 144).

history: in the early twentieth century "Pugachevshchina" still evoked fears of popular anarchy and violence. Similar to other offenses earlier labeled hooliganism, these dark-alley attacks were presented by *Peterburgskii listok* as more than simply a threat to person and property. They were also a threat to "civilization," to the orderly, proper, "cultured" world. What marked these crimes as a threat to "civilization" and what linked them to other forms of hooliganism were the alleged randomness and irrationality of the attacks. The entries endlessly repeated the refrain that muggings and stabbings occurred "for no reason at all," that the victim could have been anyone, "the first passerby," and that the attackers were strangers, or a "group of men unknown to the victim." These elements were implicit in the earlier nonviolent rowdiness of hooliganism, but they were brought to the surface here. Together they underlined genuine fears for personal safety on the streets and reinforced the fears that had surfaced earlier: that respectable society was losing control of the streets and that "civilization" was being threatened by "savages."

In this context, the obvious foreignness of the label *hooligan* served the dual function of distancing the reader from the offenders while at the same time making their presence seem even more frightening and inescapable: "a perpetual threat to everyday life, but extremely distant in origin and motives; both everyday and exotic."[48] The newspaper coverage enhanced the evocative power of hooligan images by its ambivalent presentation of hooligan news, alternating between the terrifying and the trivial. In a study of punk culture in Great Britain, Dick Hebdige noted that punks were treated as both "dangerous aliens and boisterous kids": demonized in reports of their scandalous antics, celebrated on fashion pages, treated solemnly in editorials, and ridiculed and domesticated in articles that tried to minimize their alienness (showing, for instance, that punks had mothers too).[49] Hooligans were also depicted in the press as trivial, irrational, and motiveless, committing crimes for no special reason and against random targets. But at the same time hooliganism was taken with the utmost seriousness—a challenge to authority, tradition, and civilization itself. In fact, the very pettiness of some hooliganism made the phenomenon that much more confusing and infuriating. The fact that hooligans could terrify passersby both with knives and with mockery multiplied the humiliation of their victims, confounded public responses, and made law enforcement extremely difficult.

48. Foucault, *Discipline and Punish*, 286.
49. Hebdige, *Subculture*, 92–99.

Hooliganism also helped clarify the changes taking place in the uses and conceptions of public space in St. Petersburg. Since the Great Reforms of the 1860s and 1870s the official imprint on everyday public life had been fading, diluted by the influx of people and commerce.[50] With the great wave of migration and increasing commercialization that began in the 1890s, streets and squares were more often given over to Bely's "great swarms of people" and to new activities, which inevitably introduced new conflicts. In the years before 1905, hooliganism highlighted the problems of control that had surfaced. The arrogance of the hooligans, their contempt for established rules of behavior, and the hostility they displayed toward respectable society betokened a subtle but unmistakable shift in the balance of power on the streets of the capital. The government seemed to be deaf to the threat, and the resulting anxiety was heard in the boulevard press in tones of fear and disgust. Hooligan confrontations did not mark the first encounters between members of respectable society and peasants and workers on the central streets. The older, central districts of the city had always had a socially and economically heterogeneous population. But that fact makes the horror with which *Peterburgskii listok* described the antics of the lower-class hooligans all the more striking; they were not strangers to the scene, but they were exhibiting new and strange behavior.[51]

Hooliganism was both a symbol of these changes and an agent of change. Whether it involved the petty harassment of middle-class pedestrians or a brutal stabbing and extortion, hooliganism occurred in public space. As a public crime, a public exhibition, and usually a public confrontation, it dramatized conflicting values and conventions. Similar public confrontations no doubt took place before they were described in the mass press, but when popular newspapers began reporting such events they transformed the meaning of the word *public*. Publication exposed even the private or distant indoor world of taverns, stairwells, and working-class suburbs to the gaze of the comfortable reader. By publicizing details of life in the slums, the boulevard press broke down barriers that had prevented Petersburg society from becoming familiar with the lives of the poor. Yet although the remarkable increase in the numbers of the poor and the

50. For an architectural perspective on the withdrawal of officialdom from public space see Blair A. Ruble, "From Palace Square to Moscow Square: St. Petersburg's Century-Long Retreat from Public Space," in *Reshaping Russian Architecture: Western Technology, Utopian Dreams*, ed. William Brumfield (Cambridge, 1990), 21–42.
51. On residential patterns, see Bater, *St. Petersburg*, 196–201, 373–80.

revelations in the press helped to demolish the old geographical and physical barriers separating classes, reporting on the lives of the poor did not erase social, economic, or cultural barriers. In fact, it had just the opposite effect. Familiarity created new boundaries. Knowledge and proximity produced new reasons for division and hostility, rather than assimilation. The newspapers brought the behavior, sounds, and smells of the urban poor into the homes of the respectable population. Rather than mollify fears of physical danger by showing that many, if not most, victims of hooligan attacks were themselves poor, the publicity hooliganism received served to reinforce the impression produced by actual street encounters—that the lower classes were increasingly dangerous, reckless, brazen, and hostile. The public element in boulevard-press reporting introduced one of the contradictions inherent in hooliganism: hooligans were both everywhere and far away, distant but dangerous.

Curiously, while the violence of hooligan incidents was terrifying, social fears took precedence over physical fears in *Peterburgskii listok* accounts of violent hooligan crimes. What linked the muggings with the aggravating but often harmless forms of rowdiness was the incomprehensible behavior of the hooligans themselves. That *Peterburgskii listok* linked the two did not make them identical but created connotations of similarity and showed that they were equally frightening. Linking them degraded the merely rowdy hooligans by associating them with truly dangerous criminals, but it also trivialized the violent by removing them from the ranks of hardened professionals. On the other hand, calling both hooliganism invested muggings with social and cultural significance and reinforced the threatening aspects of petty disturbances. Taken together, the disparate forms of hooliganism threatened the person, property, power, and culture of those who formerly enjoyed, or aspired to enjoy, social security and control.

o o o o

The preceding portrait of hooliganism illuminates some of the values and fears of respectable Petersburg, but what does it tell us about the social reality of hooliganism? The period in which hooligans appeared was an era of growing political unrest and lower-class activism. Perhaps hooligans were really ordinary factory workers whose shabby clothing and rough demeanor alone earned them the contempt of cultured society. Or, at the other extreme, perhaps they were professional criminals, a street-side tip of the criminal underworld. Did *Peterburgskii listok* fabricate hooliganism as a reflection of its readers' fears and aspirations, or did it accurately report the appearance of a phenomenon that, if not entirely new, reflected new attitudes and a new "language" of protest on the part of its perpetrators?

Police and court records from the period substantially support the accuracy of the *Peterburgskii listok* portrait of hooliganism. Tens of thousands of people were arrested, convicted, and incarcerated for offenses identified as hooliganism in the first four years of the century (see tables 3–4 in the Appendix). The steep rise in arrests and convictions for petty hooligan crimes after the turn of the century corroborates boulevard-press reports of a serious crime wave. The statistics on the rise of rowdy street crimes were also supported by annual commentary of Justices of the Peace.[52] Statistics on indictments and convictions for physical assault in the St. Petersburg Region Circuit Court also support the boulevard-press portrait of increasing violent street crime between 1900 and 1905 (see table 5 in the Appendix). The willingness and ability of hooligans to perform in public places during this period testified to both the weakness of police authority and the crumbling of social authority before 1905. Neither in this period nor later did hooligans take unnecessary risks. They were not daring adventurers, but they were quick to exploit a deficiency of power when they sensed it. Public alarm at the decline of control over street life was amplified by the popular perception that the police could do nothing to contain the hooligans and the courts could do little to punish them. The Petersburg Side landlords were not alone when they complained that the hooligans who roamed their streets were undeterred by fear of arrest. The hooligans knew that even if they were caught, they would be charged only with a minor infraction such as disturbing the peace. They would be tried in the *mirovoi sud* by a Justice of the Peace, who could sentence criminals to no more than three months in prison. Often when hooligans appeared in court, no questions were asked, and they would plead guilty to a minor charge, pay a three-ruble fine, and be released immediately.[53] Because there was no provision for hooliganism in the criminal code, most hooligans were charged with offenses that carried only light punishment. Armed muggers could be tried in the circuit court and did receive prison or exile sentences, but this did not seem to decrease the number of muggings. The Justices of the Peace were aware of the problem, as were the prosecutors in the circuit courts, but without a law referring specifically

---

52. See, for example, *PMS 1903*, 148.
53. A. V., "Grustnyi fakt."

to hooligan offenses, they had little power to punish most hooligans. During the interrevolutionary period it became increasingly clear that even the most violent hooligans, responsible for multiple knife assaults and heavily punished by the circuit court, were undeterred by punishment.[54]

As for the police, the writers and correspondents for *Peterburgskii listok* were relentless in their criticism of police efforts to control crime. In general, the police enjoyed little respect in Petersburg society. Outnumbered, ill trained, poorly paid, and barely motivated, the policeman on the street (*gorodovoi*) was no match for street crime. But the police administration was aware of the growing problem of hooliganism and active, in its own fashion, in attempts to curtail the crime. The capital's *gradonachal'nik*, or city governor, who was in charge of the police force, looked for a weapon against hooliganism in the security statutes passed in 1881 in the wake of the assassination of Alexander II. The statutes made it possible for the Ministry of Interior to issue "binding decrees" (*ob"iazatel'noe postanovlenie*), which allowed the police force to circumvent the judicial system and impose its own punishments, usually expulsion from the city, without trial.[55] Originally intended for use against sedition, several such decrees were implemented in 1901 to control street disorders and rowdiness: one forbade carrying knives and other weapons, and the other prohibited rowdy behavior on public streets.[56] The decrees were not terribly effective, because hooligans were notoriously difficult to catch, they far outnumbered police personnel, and these extra-legal measures came under attack from judicial authorities. New measures were instituted against hooliganism in 1903 when a new chief of the Criminal Investigation Division was appointed. Indeed, contrary to the popular perception,

54. The legal issues and the attempt to enact a law against hooliganism will be discussed in chapter 3.
55. Russia's notorious security laws operated in an extremely convoluted relationship to the legal system; see Samuel N. Harper, "Exceptional Measures in Russia," *The Russian Review*, vol. 1, no. 4 ([London], 1912); on the police and state authorities' differing legal approaches to sexual behavior, see Laura Engelstein, "Gender and the Juridical Subject: Prostitution and Rape in Nineteenth-Century Russian Criminal Codes," *Journal of Modern History*, vol. 60, no. 3 (1988); on the origins of the statutes see P. A. Zaionchkovskii, *Krizis samoderzhaviia na rubezhe 1870–1890 godov* (Moscow, 1964), 400–410; and Richard Pipes, *Russia under the Old Regime* (New York, 1974), 281–318.
56. December 9, 1901, and May 9, 1901, respectively. See *Prilozhenie k vsepoddanneishemu otchetu po S.-Peterburgskomu gradonachal'stvu za 1901 god* (St. Petersburg, 1902), 24–25; and *Otchet o deiatel'nosti S.-Peterburgskoi sysknoi politsii za 1903 god* (St. Petersburg, 1904), 7.

controlling hooliganism was a police priority. But the new measures were still unable to stem the tide.[57]

Police impotence was primarily due to a chronic shortage of personnel, a problem the police administration recognized but could not solve. Qualified recruits who were literate and morally desirable were in short supply. Salaries were low, as was funding generally for the regular police. But the main obstacle to effective policing was the outmoded operational structure of the police force. Patrolmen were required to stand at specified posts, except for regular inspection rounds of their district or when responding to a crime. This system made it impossible for patrolmen to deter crime by their general presence in a neighborhood, since their location was usually predictable.[58] At least, their presence was supposed to be predictable: station officers recorded a steady stream of complaints about patrolmen deserting their posts and disappearing into the nearest tavern.[59] Sometimes post patrolmen did manage to chase and apprehend hooligans after an attack, but more commonly the few hooligans who were chased were caught by nearby *dvorniki*, the omnipresent yard keepers who played such a noticeable role in urban social life. Regrettably, little is known about the *dvorniki* as a group, and their role in police work is beyond the scope of this study. Their capacity in apprehending hooligans, however, merits a few comments. Building owners employed at least one *dvornik* to serve as general custodian, handyman, and watchman; in large buildings, several *dvorniki* were employed. In addition, these men were required to perform specified functions for the regular police and some less explicit secret police duties as well. They were considered both indispensable and highly unreliable. In principle they were expected to fill the function a stationary post patrolman could not: to extend the presence of authority deep into each neighborhood. In practice, the *dvorniki* were a variegated lot; many had

57. *Otchet o deiatel'nosti*, 3–5, 11; *Alfavitnyi sbornik rasporiazhenii po S.-Peter-burgskomu Gradonachal'stvu i politsii, izvlechennykh iz prikazov za 1891–1901 gg.*, ed. I. P. Vysotskii (St. Petersburg, 1902), 450; "K obuzdaniiu stolichnykh khuliganov," *PL*, October 17, 1903. In 1903, 12,052 people were arrested under articles 38 (quarreling, fighting, brawling, or other rowdiness [*buistvo*] in public places) and 42 (public drunkenness). In the same year, 458 people were apprehended under the administrative order prohibiting carrying a knife or other weapon, and 238 under the binding decree prohibiting public rowdiness.
58. Robert W. Thurston, "Police and People in Moscow, 1906–1914," *Russian Review*, vol. 39, no. 3 (1980); Neil Weissman, "Regular Police in Tsarist Russia, 1900–1914," *Russian Review*, vol. 44, no. 1 (1985).
59. Vysotskii, *1891–1901*, 435–42, 642; *Alfavitnyi sbornik rasporiazhenii po S.-Peterburgskomu Gradonachal'stvu i politsii, izvlechennykh iz prikazov za vremia s 1902 po 10 iiulia 1904 g.*, ed. I. P. Vysotskii (St. Petersburg, 1904), 270.

allegiances closer to the crime world than to the police. Numerous instances of brutality, incompetence, and complicity in crimes made the role of the *dvornik* in police work a subject of unending debate. On the other hand, in most of the reports in the crime columns in which assailants were caught, they were caught by *dvorniki*, not patrolmen. Often the *dvorniki* took great physical risk in doing so. But since most reported hooligans managed to escape, it seems that few *dvorniki* were willing to take such risks. Most did nothing to prevent hooligan attacks and antics, some let apprehended hooligans in their charge escape on their way to the police station, and others engaged in hooligan acts themselves.[60]

The inability of the police to protect person and property, and comments to that effect in the boulevard press, contributed to the atmosphere of public fear in this period and helped undermine state authority as well. Hooligan intimidation of the police was noted by the earliest commentators: "They beat our *dvorniki*; the police run from them."[61] The image of a population beleaguered by hooligans and unprotected by police authority was a commonplace of the boulevard press by 1904. The outrage over hooliganism originated in the boulevard press because it represented the portion of the population left most vulnerable by the weakness of police protection.

▣ Readers of the Boulevard Press

We know what images the boulevard press disseminated regarding hooliganism, but except for the occasional letter from a reader we do not know much about who was reading these papers. Chance references in contemporary memoirs occasionally indicate preferences for particular papers and

---

60. On registration of *dvorniki* and the regulation of their work, see Vysotskii, *1891–1901*, 90–94, 161–63, 446–47; *1902–1904*, 270. On debate over *dvornik* police duties, see P. Mel'nikov, "Opasnaia sila," *Iurist*, December 12, 1904. See in particular a critique of police functions for *dvorniki* in Borivoi, "Dvornitskii institut," *PL*, February 6, 1905. On *dvornik* brutality and complicity in crime, see B. V., [untitled article], *Sudebnoe obozrenie*, March 13, 1905; "Iz kamery m. sudei: Nashi dvorniki," *PL*, April 5, 1905; "V kamere m. sudei: Dvornik-khuligan," *PL*, September 21, 1905; "Iz kipy zaiavlenii," *PL*, September 30, 1905; "Listok: Dvornik-khuligan," *PL*, September 5, 1913. On *dvornik* courage and success in catching hooligans, see "Sobytiia Peterburgskogo dnia: Pooshchrenie dvornikov v bor'be s khuliganstvom," *PL*, February 16, 1913. Abraham Ascher, *The Revolution of 1905: Russia in Disarray* (Stanford, 1990), 291, also reports that, inspired by revolutionary militance, a group of Petersburg *dvorniki* rebelled against their role as police spies in November 1905. They elected representatives charged with organizing a union for the *dvorniki*.
61. A. V., "Grustnyi fakt."

offer stereotypes about a newspaper's readers, but these are rare. Lacking readership surveys or subscription lists, we are forced primarily to deduce readership from "content analysis" of the newspaper's reporting and advertisements.

Peterburgskii listok's content was decidedly middle class. Its advertisements offered goods and services that middle-class Petersburgers desired and could afford. The values it promoted and reflected were those we commonly associate with bourgeois "respectability." Contemporaries' comments on the readers of *Peterburgskii listok* and similar newspapers consistently described them as members of the middle or commercial classes, with a few workers among them in the period before working-class newspapers were published. *Moskovskii listok,* a similar but more sensationalistic newspaper, appealed to "janitors and shopkeepers," store clerks, and "the less cultured merchants, businessmen, shopkeepers, and serving people."[62] Letters to *Peterburgskii listok* came from "landlords" and "respectable ladies."[63] The skilled worker Semen Kanatchikov related a friend's comments on stereotypical readers:

> I sat down, . . . took the newspaper *Petersburg Sheet* from the table and began to read, starting with the next-to-the-last page, where all kinds of local news and adventure stories were printed. . . . During my wanderings in and out of overnight hideaways and conspiratorial apartments, I had learned to determine the social position of the occupants by their newspapers. In this case there could be no doubt that the apartment dweller was a tradesman or an innkeeper.[64]

Judging from the announcements for meetings of workers' associations on the one hand and for philanthropic societies of interest to the capital's wealthier elements on the other, *Peterburgskii listok* attracted readers from the lower and upper classes as well. Kanatchikov also reported that in Moscow, before he became a "conscious" and politically active worker, he and his friends read *Moskovskii listok,* especially for the crime chronicles, the serialized novels, and the feuilletons.[65] However, it seems likely, judging from the content and tone of the reporting and advertising, that

62. Brooks, *When Russia Learned to Read,* 128; and Esin, *Russkaia dorevoliutsionnaia gazeta,* 47–49.
63. The column "Iz kipy zaiavlenii" printed letters from readers as well as comments from regular staff writers. When the readers identified themselves, they were always from the middle classes.
64. Zelnik, *A Radical Worker,* 323.
65. Ibid., 13.

workers in particular would have been a peripheral readership. The local news and adventure stories had a mass appeal, but much of the rest of the paper did not. Moreover, when *Gazeta-kopeika*, a newspaper published expressly for workers, was launched in 1908 it immediately attracted a huge readership without making a dent in that of *Peterburgskii listok*. The workers who did read *Peterburgskii listok* regularly were probably those who shared at least some of the respectable values and aspirations of the middle classes.

One problem in identifying the social origins of *Peterburgskii listok* readers is that we know very little about the social composition of the urban middle class in this period, and we know less about those who may have straddled the line between the middle class and the working class.[66] All we really know is that in terms of wealth and education there was a growing number of people who fell between the highly educated or noble elite and the barely literate poor. They worked for a living, but in commercial enterprises or government offices, not with their hands. At the turn of the century this class was a diverse and jumbled lot just beginning to sort itself out. It had become differentiated by occupation and stratified economically, but it was fused by a common sense of being set apart from the masses below and aspiring to the wealth and the values of those above. At the same time, at least one portion of this group, the growing professional classes, not only did not aspire to the values of the elite but was proud of its own practical, "modern" values.[67]

For many of these people the acquisition of culture in some form was a primary sign of status. In Russia, as elsewhere, the transformation of urban society included not only economic and demographic indicators; the sources and symbols of status were also in flux as new categories of identification appeared along with the variety of opportunities available to people with some education. In cultural terms, the rising middle class can be seen as a "new intelligentsia," described by Jeffrey Brooks as

66. What we do know has often derived from census materials in which legal categories obscured social and economic position. More detailed analyses have focused on the merchants; see Rieber, *Merchants;* Thomas C. Owen, *Capitalism and Politics in Russia: A Social History of the Moscow Merchants, 1855–1905* (Cambridge, 1981); Jo Ann Ruckman, *The Moscow Business Elite: A Social and Cultural Portrait of Two Generations, 1840–1905.* See also Orlovsky, "The Lower Middle Strata," 248–68; Michael Hamm, ed., *The City in Late Imperial Russia* (Bloomington, Ind., 1986); and Brower, *The Russian City*, 40–139.

67. This is a prevailing theme in E. W. Clowes, S. D. Kassow, and J. L. West, eds., *Between Tsar and People: Educated Society and the Quest for Public Identity in Late Imperial Russia* (Princeton, 1991); see pp. 46–49; 79–80; 97, 107; 110, 115; 146–48; 149–63; 183–98; 200–202, 211; 248–68; 273–87; 288–307.

a group that was poised uncomfortably between the less educated common people and the properly educated old intelligentsia. They formed the lower echelons of the infrastructure on which the industrialization and urbanization of prerevolutionary Russia depended, and during the late prerevolutionary period they made up the widest audience for serious belles lettres. They also had cultural pretensions. They wanted their tastes to be recognized as legitimate, and they wanted to be included in the cultural life largely dominated by the old intelligentsia.[68]

If we do not have the data to determine who this group was in social and economic terms, we do have material to talk about their culture. We know what they read, and, in regard to newspapers, we know what shaped their ideas about city life and their own place in urban society. Readership patterns have led some to the conclusion that it is best to associate a newspaper's readership with a "cultural milieu" rather than with a socio-economic class.[69] But while a newspaper's character can be defined in cultural terms—a readership can be identified with the values a newspaper represents rather than with the limiting notion of a particular class—it is equally important to remember that adherence or aspiration to a set of values shared across class lines does not obliterate preexisting conflicts and hostilities between classes. It is important to stress that workers who found some of their behavioral values best reflected in *Peterburgskii listok* would still find themselves at odds with members of the middle class over political and economic issues. And while some workers were frightened or disgusted by hooligan behavior, they did not necessarily share the outrage expressed in *Peterburgskii listok*. In fact, the reporting on hooliganism is itself telling evidence of the newspaper's class identification. When the working-class daily, *Gazeta-kopeika*, reported hooligan incidents, it ignored completely the insolent behavior, or *nakhal'stvo*, most closely associated in *Peterburgskii listok* with class and cultural challenge. *Gazeta-kopeika* reported only genuinely dangerous crimes as hooliganism and made it clear that hooligans often victimized the poor.

One must keep in mind, however, that the lines dividing groups in society were sometimes rigid and unyielding, and at other times porous

---

68. Brooks, "Popular Philistinism," 90–91. There was a considerable amount of social and cultural diversity within this group. It encompassed those who rose to the ranks of the cultured from the lower classes, those who joined in the culturalist crusade to bring the Russian classics to the people, as well as those whose claims to cultured status might include reading the boulevard press and dressing well, and it embraced many people in between.

69. Brooks, *When Russia Learned to Read*, 128–29.

and shifting. The worker whose story Kanatchikov related had no trouble reading a wide variety of newspapers or speaking with a wealthy engineer "about higher matters until late into the night," but he also insisted that he never felt at home anywhere except in a worker's apartment.[70] And the middle class itself was deeply divided by differences in cultural levels, ideas about social roles and social commitment, and literary or aesthetic taste.[71] The solution to understanding the social and cultural composition of the city, at least until more research appears, is not to substitute cultural categories for economic ones, but rather to remember that the two sets of categories overlap.

Newspapers like *Peterburgskii listok* helped create and define the new commercial culture of the capital in these years. While the commercial classes predominated among its readership, the newspaper was open to all who could afford the price of admission: literacy, the cost of the paper, and some cultural aspirations. The "new intelligentsia" was distinguished from the "old intelligentsia" by its lesser education, lower cultural attainment, and crass ways, but its members also lacked the characteristic trait of the "old intelligentsia"—a commitment to social and political reform. Stephen Graham, a British journalist in Russia who closely identified with the "old intelligentsia," described the new mercenary values of the emergent middle class in 1912:

> The new intelligent is of this sort; he wants to know the price of everything. Of things which are independent of price he knows nothing, or if he knows of them he sneers at them and hates them. Talk to him of religion and show that you believe in the mystery of Christ; talk to him of life and show that you believe in love and happiness; talk of woman and show that you understand anything about her unsexually; talk to him of work and show that though you are poor you have little regard for money and [he] is uneasy.[72]

Class and cultural self-consciousness made these "new intelligents" demand equal status for their tastes and values from the classes above, but they also had their eyes carefully trained on the masses below. It was equally important for them to rise above, and make manifestly clear that they had risen above, the "uncultured" masses. Here education and wealth

70. Zelnik, *A Radical Worker*, 322.
71. See, for examples, Edith W. Clowes, "The Moscow Art Theater," in *Between Tsar and People*, 271–87.
72. Stephen Graham, "One of the Higher Intelligentsia," *The Russian Review*, vol. 1, no. 4 ([London], 1912): 120.

were not enough to separate the "cultured" from the "uncultured." Since culture included, alongside aesthetic taste, a set of values and an adherence to a code of public behavior, the mastery of these marked one's arrival among the civilized or the cultured (the words were virtually interchangeable in this period). Their absence or weakness marked one as primitive or uncultured.

Judging from the attention *Peterburgskii listok* and the Sunday supplements to other popular newspapers paid to questions of decorum, etiquette, and fashion, proper public behavior in Petersburg was strictly defined. Petersburg's newly arrived middle classes were vigilant defenders of the symbols of their arrival. Cartoons and satirical farces made fun of social gaffes. In the winter and spring of 1901, for example, a major scandal electrified the pages of *Peterburgskii listok* when a fistfight broke out in a merchant society club. The parties involved blew the case out of all proportion. A prominent trial lawyer was retained by the defendant, which was very unusual in such petty cases.[73] The boulevard press followed the story avidly, commenting expansively on the "customs" and "morals" of club members. The articles covering the court trial and appeals bristled with disgust at such a display of "low culture" within the middle class. The moral of the story, and the point of all the publicity, was that securing a spot in the "new bourgeoisie" did not necessarily endow one with the manners appropriate to civilized society. *Peterburgskii listok* came out clearly on the side of manners and morals, roundly condemning the merchants' behavior in trial reports and commentary, without a trace of irony or humor. There was no attempt to deny the lapses of behavior among the middle class or to identify such behavior as typical of the lower class. Rather this was a display of acute sensitivity to the uncultured manners that still existed among their own kind.[74]

---

73. The case was tried in the Justice of the Peace Court, which was responsible for hearing petty criminal and civil suits. In civil cases the Justice of the Peace usually acted as sole mediator, hearing the particulars of the case from the parties involved. Even when attorneys were engaged, they were rarely lawyers of great prominence or stature.

74. Stories about the rough edges of the nouveau riche (especially if they are rock stars or live in Hollywood) are standards in the comic repertory of our contemporary popular culture. In 1901, as the press coverage of such scandals shows, the readers of *Peterburgskii listok* were not laughing; they were facing a genuine dilemma of self-definition and self-confidence. See "V kamerakh mirovykh sudei," *PL*, January 9, 1901; and Avgur, "Klubnye nravy," *PL*, January 14, 1901. The saga continued through February with weekly exposés of the mores of "club society." In March the case was appealed: "V s"ezde mirovykh sudei," March 8, 1901; and Aborigen, "Stolychnyi den'," March 9, 1901. In May the appeal was

Such a strict code of public decorum accompanied the values and conventions usually referred to as "bourgeois" (although their prevalence during this period among such antibourgeois elements as workers and those who would become the socialist architects of New Soviet Men and Women calls into question that class designation). Hard work, responsibility, and ambition; self-discipline and restraint in emotional and sexual expression; an abhorrence (at least in public) of activities considered vices—smoking, drinking, gambling, and so forth: these were esteemed as signs of *kul'turnost'*, of having become "cultured." What marked individuals as cultured, and what marked Russia as a civilized nation, along with adherence to such values, were education and a degree of aesthetic taste. There was more than a little hypocrisy in this public observance of polite values and behavior. Drinking, to mention only the most obvious, was prevalent among the middle classes, as it was among the poor and the elite. A cartoon to this effect appeared in *Peterburgskii listok* in 1903 (fig. 5). In the cartoon, captioned "Our Morals," a member of the intelligentsia points a finger at "the people," calling them "drunkard[s]." But as the cartoon points out, hypocrisy often sharpens the tongue of condemnation.

Such were the conventions that hooligans, with their rowdy behavior, trampled upon with abandon and obvious pleasure and challenged ever more threateningly starting around 1900. The outrage hooliganism provoked can be explained when we remember that the people who held to this vision of "civilization" clung to it with special tenacity and valued it so highly because they themselves had only recently acquired the right to consider themselves civilized. The reports of hooligan incidents in *Peterburgskii listok* reflect these feelings of pride and insecurity. During such a time of social transformation, when old social categories no longer provide a secure sense of identity, outward symbols take on added significance. To confirm their new economic status in society, members of this newly emerging middle class wanted to protect the outward symbols of privilege and cultural attainment, and they wanted to assert a certain amount of control over their immediate social environment. The extreme rank-consciousness of autocratic Russia made social differences matters of special significance and power in defining social relations.[75]

---

taken to the Senate: "V senate," May 13, 1901. In his column of May 13, 1901, "Stolychnyi den'," Aborigen noted that the case and all its publicity would probably not improve the deplorable "klubnye nravy."
75. On rank consciousness and working-class identification, see McDaniels, *Autocracy, Capitalism, and Revolution,* 166.

Наши нравы.

— «Иванъ кивастъ на Петра»... или «Я удавилась бы съ тоски, когда бы на нее хоть чуть была похожа»!..

Figure 5.   Our Morals (February 28, 1903).
"The pot calling the kettle black." An obviously drunken man, labeled a member of the "intelligentsia," is calling the man of "the people" a drunkard.

3 The Hooligans' "Text"

Peterburgskii listok undoubtedly amplified the dangers of hooliganism to reflect the fears of its readers. Yet hooligans were much more than passive instruments of middle-class fears. The tendency to describe hooliganism in lurid tones as an invasion of savages does not negate the reality of the hooligan presence or the genuine hostility of their acts. But since they chose actions, not words, as their weapons, we have to learn to read their behavior to understand their message. The hooligans' acts were filtered for us through the biases of the press, but the newspapers still relate basic facts about their behavior: what hooligans did; where and when they did it; their age, occupation, and gender. The conscious and unconscious choices embodied in these data offer keys to the hooligans' mentality and motives. As Iurii Lotman wrote in his study of the cultural milieu that produced the Decembrist rebels in the 1820s, "From the unconscious stratum of everyday behavior, the Decembrists constructed a conscious system of ideologically signifying behavior, complete as a text and permeated with higher meaning."[76] Lacking the literary or social models of the early nineteenth-century nobility, hooligans constructed a cruder text, but one equally complete and equally permeated with meaning. Hooligans made choices about actions that reveal underlying attitudes, which were rooted in their own social reality.

We know more about Russia's urban poor than about its middle classes, but we know little about those among the poor outside the industrial work force.[77] Sources on casual laborers or crowd behavior, which are available to historians of Western Europe, do not exist for Russia.[78] But, more important, hooligans are difficult to identify because they occupied an amorphous place in the social spectrum. They did not represent any particular constituency but were drawn from several social groups in the capital's lower-class population. Between the more clearly defined categories of respectable, urbanized workers and professional criminals were a large number of people who did not fit neatly into any established group. Just as peasants entering the city for the first time were difficult to label because they were only gradually and, typically, only partially transformed into workers, many people who worked did so in a variety of capacities. For the rougher element among the unskilled workers of the casual labor market, for whom the security of steady employment was a remote possibility, a little theft was a common answer to unemployment.[79] On the other hand, some unskilled or day laborers eventually made their way up into the ranks of the skilled, as memoirs of revolutionary workers attest. An individual's social identity was also a function of age. One's job as a teenager or young adult in the rapidly expanding (and contracting) economy did not necessarily determine one's status or economic identity for life. Nor did a bit of hooliganism as a young man mark one for a life of crime. Like worker identification, hooligan identification is suspended in the fuzzy areas between categories, caught in the changing dimensions of social mobility and aging. But if we keep in mind the fluidity of social

76. Iurii Lotman, "The Decembrist in Daily Life (Everyday Behavior as a Historical-Psychological Category)," in *The Semiotics of Russian Cultural History*, ed. Alexander D. Nakhimovsky and Alice S. Nakhimovsky (Ithaca, N.Y., 1985), 145.
77. What we do know comes primarily from Bradley, *Muzhik and Muscovite*; see also Bernstein, "Sonia's Daughters" (prostitutes); McDaniels, *Autocracy, Capitalism, and Revolution* ("mass" workers); Wynn, *Workers, Strikes, and Pogroms* (miners); Weinberg, *The Revolution* (dockworkers, salesclerks).
78. The classic study of the casual labor force is Jones, *Outcast London*.
79. "O prestupnom proletariate," *SG*, July 21, 1902; G. N. Breitman, *Prestupnyi mir: Ocherki iz byta professional'nykh prestupnikakh* (Kiev, 1901).

groups in turn-of-the-century St. Petersburg and the possibility of multiple identifications for all members of the lower classes, it is possible to decipher the press accounts of hooliganism and discern some social patterns there.[80]

When hooligans were arrested, some personal information—name, age, and sometimes *soslovie*—was given in the crime-chronicle entry. Descriptions of hooligans' social background include many categories of the lower-class population. Most references identify hooligans as young lower-class males, usually between the ages of eighteen and twenty-two, but sometimes much younger. S-i, cited earlier, bemoaned the "death of youth" in the depraved world of the urban poor: "Among the hooligans one can meet youngsters from nine to twelve years old who smoke and drink and carry on (*bezobraznichaiut*) just like adults."[81]

Only the very rare hooligan came from the privileged classes. In the pages of the boulevard press hooliganism was an exclusively lower-class phenomenon.[82] In 1913, when a colonel's wife called a student a hooligan for displaying insufficient respect, the colonel's wife was charged in the *mirovoi sud* with defamation (*oskorblenie*) and sentenced to seven days' detention. The student's lawyer argued that it is one thing if "fisherwomen" speak to one another that way, but the wife of a colonel should know better than to accuse a student of hooliganism. On appeal, all agreed—the Justice of the Peace as well as the reporter—that nothing gave the colonel's wife the right to call a student a hooligan.[83]

The greatest discrepancy in the sources centers on the question of the hooligans' connection with the working classes on the one hand and the criminal classes on the other. At one extreme, hooligans were identified as pimps and professional criminals or full-time thieves and knife-wielding

---

80. Most of the following portraits of hooligans come from the pages of *Peterburgskii listok*—primarily to maintain the consistency of the portrait. The point here is to identify the *PL* view of hooliganism and demonstrate its plausibility. However, the portrait given here is corroborated in the available published police sources, in the published records of the St. Petersburg *mirovoi sud*, and in the vast literature that appeared on hooliganism beginning around 1910, to be discussed in chapter 3.

81. S-i, "Pogibaiushchie deti"; Om, "Khuliganskii vopros."

82. I found only one case reported in *PL* between 1900 and 1914 of a hooligan identified as other than a worker, a peasant, or a *meshchanin*: the nineteen-year-old son of a nobleman who was caught attacking and wounding a twenty-seven-year-old peasant on Gorokhovaia Street (*PL*, September 2, 1905).

83. "Za slovo 'khuligan' 7 dnei aresta," *PL*, March 23, 1913; "Za slovo 'khuligan' 10 dnei aresta," *PL*, April 28, 1913. At the appeal the Justice of the Peace increased the sentence to ten days but with the possibility of substituting a forty-ruble fine.

toughs.[84] At the other, they were described as regular workers.[85] But most attempts to define hooligans as a group recognized the diversity of types who could be called hooligans at one time or another. The serialized novel "The Hooligan," which appeared in *Peterburgskii listok* in 1903, opens with a group portrait:

> They are a motley lot, and not only in external appearance. On the contrary, their social diversity is no less sharp. Here one finds everything: government scribes, telegraph clerks, post office and customs agents, metalworkers, printers, apprentices, tavern and café waiters.[86]

This melodramatic fiction was confirmed in nonfiction accounts. S-i, for example, noted that hooligan gangs ranged from factory workers to people who peddled "whatever they could find" to thieves and pickpockets.[87]

Within this "motley lot," however, there seems to have been a core of young men who fairly regularly crossed the hazy line between the factory and the street, and between the capital's periphery and its center. The majority of people arrested for hooligan acts had the least stable urban occupations: they were unskilled day laborers at factories or workshops (*podenshchiki* or *chernorabochie*).[88] Some left more steady jobs for life on the streets, either part-time or full-time.[89] The insecurity and unpre-

---

84. On thieves, see, for example, "DP: Tri zaitsa," *PL*, April 20, 1905, in which the attackers were recognized as three famous hooligans known as the "three hares"; and "DP: Opiat' khuligany na Ligovke," *PL*, August 22, 1905. On pimps as hooligans see "Vesti s okrain Peterburga," *PL*, September 11, 1903; Nash, "Khodiachiia 'kazenki,'" *PL*, July 23, 1906; "Bor'ba s 'khuliganstvom' (Iz besed)," *PG*, July 30, 1906.
85. A. V., "Grustnyi fakt"; "DP: Zhertva khuliganov," *PL*, September 14, 1903.
86. Narskii, "Khuligan," *PL*, June 30, 1903.
87. S-i, "Pogibaiushchie deti."
88. "DP: Napadenie na ulitse," *PL*, March 16, 1905; "DP: Nozhovaia rasprava," *PL*, July 26, 1906; Sladkii, "Peterburgskie negativy"; "Prodelka shaiki khuliganov," *PL*, October 6, 1906. That the core of hooligans in St. Petersburg was drawn primarily from the casual labor pool is supported by research on a group with similar characteristics in Odessa; see Robert Weinberg, "Workers, Pogroms, and the 1905 Revolution in Odessa," *Russian Review*, vol. 46, no. 1 (1987).
89. One infamous hooligan, who went by the name Ivan Ivanov, was known to have worked formerly as an unskilled transportation worker (as a *nosil'shchik* and a *gruzovshchik*) (*PL*, October 24, 1906). Another lengthy description of hooligan types identified hooligans as "members of the so-called 'free professions': typesetters, shop assistants, and hairdressers (*naborshchiki, prikazshchiki,* and *parikmakheri*)" (Sladkii, "Peterburgskie negativy"); when a group of hooligans that had been terrorizing pedestrians along Bol'shaia Grecheskaia Street were caught they turned out to be workers at a rolling mill (*zhelezo-prokatnyi*) ("Prodelka shaiki khuliganov," *PL*, October 6, 1906).

dictability of the casual labor market made the unskilled day laborers most likely to cross back and forth between the worlds of crime and work. The fact that hooliganism was identified as a "holiday" problem, that there were many more hooligans on the streets on weekends, confirms the suspicion that at least some hooligans became hooligans only on their days off.[90]

It seems safe to conclude that while many hooligans were sometimes also workers and participated with workers in some of the basic features of urban life, others were different from the majority of workers in some fundamental ways. Not only did they act differently, which was the reason for their notoriety, but they also dressed differently, and, judging from their sense of drama and their acute sensitivity to the response they provoked, they saw themselves differently.[91] Some individuals became hooligans only on the occasions when they committed hooligan acts (for instance, on payday), but there was a core of people who regularly exhibited hooligan attitudes and behavior and who formed a distinct subgroup within the urban lower class. Nonetheless, despite their distinctiveness, hooligans should be seen not as an entirely discrete social group but as a cluster of people situated along a continuum of lower-class groups. The line dividing hooligans from workers, especially casual workers, was never sharply drawn.[92] Many hooligans identified themselves as workers, either with specific occupations or as casual workers, when they were arrested.[93] Nor

90. Om, "Khuliganskii vopros."
91. On dress, see especially Sladkii, "Peterburgskie negativy." Cartoons and reports throughout this period depict the same distinctive features: flat "blini-like" caps, greasy jackets and trousers, jerseys instead of shirts, and patent leather boots. Hooligans were often not shabby but displayed a distinct sense of style.
92. For the social links between criminals, transients, and permanent residents of Moscow's most famous slum, the Khitrov Market, see Bradley, *Muzhik and Muscovite*, 275–81, 334–36.
93. The occupational categories recorded by the *mirovoi sud* House of Detention leave too many ambiguities to provide solid evidence for identifying hooligans, and the statistics on occupation were not broken down by crime; they are aggregates for all people imprisoned during a given year. However, only a tiny minority of the men imprisoned by Justices of the Peace during this period identified themselves as without any profession or a job, averaging between 3.5 and 5 percent of the men annually between 1900 and 1914. From one-quarter to one-third of the men imprisoned identified themselves as "unskilled or factory workers" (*chernorabochie i fabrichnye*), and about another one-third said they were "artisanal" (*remeslenniki*), which might indicate skilled workshop employees or skilled factory employees but also included the unskilled workers employed in shops and plants where skilled work was done. Another 10 to 15 percent worked as drivers or haulers, about 5 percent were servants, and the rest worked in some trading capacity or as professionals; see *PMS 1900–1914*.

should hooligans be seen as a class of professional criminals or a group totally outcast, living beyond the bounds of ordinary working-class life.[94] The majority of hooligans were tied to the world of work, at least part of the time, through self-identification and everyday interaction.

Thus the boulevard-press portrait of this group of hooligans offers some intriguing insights into a little-known segment of the urban lower class, the casual laborers. Because so little information has been available about casual laborers in Russia, and because labor activists tended to view the mass of workers with disdain, we have been accustomed to thinking of the Russian working class as composed of two layers. A thin elite stratum of skilled, literate workers was separated from the mass of workers, referred to as "grey" or "dark," who were believed to be backward or ignorant and to retain closer ties to the countryside. The casual workers who composed the core of hooligans fit neither category. The hooligans described here were often literate and clever, and while it is impossible to determine where they were born or how long they lived in the city, they were certainly well schooled in city ways. Yet while they were clearly urban creatures, their young age and their economic status afforded them little of the stability of the skilled proletariat. It is possible that this combination gave them, unlike the "grey" peasant-workers, the confidence and street savvy to engage in the kind of self-assertive but politically limited offenses for which hooligans were known, but neither the stability nor the commitment necessary for sustained radical labor activity. They also rejected certain of the labor elite's cultural ambitions. While many elite workers aspired to some features of bourgeois culture despite their antagonism to (and exploitation by) bourgeois power, hooligans remained antagonistic to the whole of the culture of the middle and upper classes and theatrically resisted attempts to impose that alien culture on them.

A number of the early articles on hooliganism associated hooligans with street gangs, although hooligan behavior had little in common with the

---

94. The trend in crime history is to minimize the existence of professional criminal classes. In a recent book George Rudé argues that criminals in nineteenth-century England never constituted a class; there were some professional criminals but not enough to form a class; the remainder were drawn from and integrated into the rest of society, especially among the lower classes (*Criminal and Victim: Crime and Society in Early Nineteenth-Century England* [Oxford, 1985], 123–26). David Philips also argued that in England only 10 percent of crimes committed involved professional criminals; most criminals held working-class jobs but stole, robbed, or fought on occasion (*Crime and Authority in Victorian England: The Black Country, 1835–1860* [London, 1977], 287).

usual activity of gangs in this period.[95] Unfortunately, virtually nothing is known about urban street gangs in the Russian empire. Although many of the published memoirs written by workers who lived in these neighborhoods mentioned recreational brawling as well as ethnic or regional hostility among workers, few offer any insight into organized gangs or neighborhood gang warfare.[96] The juridical and criminological literature is also more or less silent on the issue. The police knew of the existence of gangs and struggled to control them, but gang activity was not a high priority, and few descriptions of their activities or character remain.[97] Yet boulevard-press reports make it clear that, as in many other cities, gangs were a visible feature of the urban landscape.

In 1905, *Peterburgskaia gazeta* published a series of articles on gangs and hooligans that sheds some light on these issues.[98] These articles, based on interviews with a gang leader and eyewitness observations of the Gaida and Roshcha gangs at work and play, advanced a rather romantic view of the gangs. The unnamed gang "secretary" claimed in the interview that the original Gaida and Roshcha were themselves offended by the newer hooligans who sullied the name of the venerable, old gangs, with their arrogant self-assertion and self-advertisement. While the new hooligans committed social offenses and senseless outrages, the original Gaida and Roshcha lived according to a strict code of honor; they fought only each other, and only for specific, well-defined reasons. The gangs, he claimed, originated around 1900, when individuals who normally fought one another, usually over local girls, decided to band together to protect their turf from the boys of other parts of the city. They called themselves the Roshcha after the small grove on the Petersburg Side where they met. The "city" boys from across the river banded together into the Gaida, and

---

95. A. V., "Grustnyi fakt"; S-i, "Pogibaiushchie deti"; A. B-r, "Iz kipy zaiavlenii: 'Shalosti' lobotriasov," *PL*, July 31, 1903. See also "O prestupleniiakh," *SG*, May 26, 1902, on the growth of gang participation in ordinary crimes; and Om, "Khuliganskii vopros," who argued that, contrary to the common wisdom, hooligans did not operate in gangs.

96. Kanatchikov, for example, mentions that "after workers collected their pay, the [Nevsky Gate] area witnessed constant fights, scandals of all kinds, hooliganish gang-beatings of innocent passersby"; but this clearly does not refer to organized gang fighting; see Zelnik, *A Radical Worker*, 95.

97. *Vsepoddaneishii otchet po S.-Peterburgskomu gradonachal'stvu za 1901 god* (St. Petersburg, 1902), 24–25; *Otchet o deiatel'nosti*, 2–13.

98. Gaida, "Stolichnaia iazva: Ocherki iz zhizni Peterburgskikh khuliganov," *PG*, May 30, 1905; Nevskii, "Stolichnaia iazva," *PG*, June 5, 1905; Nevskii, "Stolichnaia iazva," *PG*, June 6, 1905. (Despite the different pseudonyms, the articles were written by one author.)

in the first two years of the century the two staged enormous brawls on the streets of the Petersburg Side. The conflict attracted a great deal of attention in the press, the courts, and police precincts. But by about 1903 the gangs had disintegrated under new pressures. Some of their members had become pimps, living off their prostitute girlfriends. The "true" Roshcha and Gaida both separated themselves from prostitution and ceased fighting one another. However, despite their avowed distaste for the new hooligans many gang members accepted the label hooligan for themselves.

This description of gang history and activities does not contradict earlier stories. It seems likely that hooligans were becoming increasingly brazen at the same time that the Roshcha and the Gaida were fighting openly on the streets of the Petersburg Side. Since both were new to street life and both involved young male workers and casual laborers (also corroborated by the Roshcha leader interviewed), it is not surprising that the local "Landlords" and *Peterburgskii listok* writers could not distinguish between them. To peaceable observers the hooligans and the street-fighting gangs seemed equally menacing: the hooligans, because they directly and intentionally irritated people on the street, and the gangs, for introducing massive brawls to formerly peaceful public places.

Just as the hooligans' origins straddled social categories, hooliganism as a phenomenon straddled categories of unrest. In part this was a problem of definition, because *Peterburgskii listok* stigmatized behavior that was acceptable in other contexts. But in part, the hooligans' offenses revealed new connections between social, political, and cultural forms of discontent.

Some rowdy public behavior was branded hooliganism in *Peterburgskii listok* because the cultural standards of urban respectability were being applied to behavior that was acceptable elsewhere. Public drunkenness, loud voices, and fistfighting, for example, were ordinary elements of working-class and peasant male culture. But regardless of the offenders' intent, such behavior affronted pedestrians when it occurred on the capital's central streets. It is also clear, however, that in many cases hooligans intended to offend their audience and victims, and that they took pleasure in doing so. The menacing looks, obscenities shouted "in the presence of ladies," rocks thrown through store windows, and drunken cavorting on central streets conveyed more than a simple clash of cultural standards. Hooligans clearly challenged the dominant conventions, all the more so when they openly laughed at the displeasure of their victims.

Hooligans of all kinds consciously chose their victims just as they chose to perform on fashionable streets. The unruly and the threatening among them chose to disrupt public life on trams, in central parks, and on major avenues rather than (or in addition to) making trouble in working-class quarters, far from the gaze of respectable society. Even through the prism of *Peterburgskii listok,* it is clear that hooligans took pleasure in shocking their middle-class audience and enjoyed the power they had achieved, however briefly, on the streets. Therefore, even without the *Peterburgskii listok* rhetoric about the decline of civilization, the patterns of hooligan behavior and the choices hooligans made show that many hooligans were indeed posing a challenge to their middle-class audience. Not only did *Peterburgskii listok* convey the fear that the values of respectability and the authority of civilization were being violated, but the hooligan acts themselves confirmed that fear. The hooligans' choices, however, also show that they viewed their challenge in different terms than their middle-class audience did.

Everything about hooligan behavior marks their acts as a challenge, but what kind of challenge? Based on what they did, where they took action, and who they were, we can apply insights derived from studies of similar episodes in other contexts to draw some conclusions about the hooligans themselves. These were not purely economic crimes committed for material gain. Therefore they seemed "motiveless" or "random" to their practically minded audience. They were not, however, without purpose. Order, propriety, and social authority were their targets. Self-assertion and a measure of control over street life were their goals. The hooligans not only dared to victimize their social betters; they attacked everything those social betters stood for. Yet hooliganism was not a "social crime" in the sense that the term is used by crime historians.[99] Although there is an obvious "social" component in hooligan confrontations, their acts were not committed in order to redress a perceived injustice by transforming the social order or abolishing some unjust law. Although hooligans challenged the middle-class right to social authority, they seemed more interested in self-assertion and seizing control, in expressing defiance, anger, and alienation, than in acquiring social authority for a constructive purpose. It makes more sense to see hooliganism as a demonstration of

99. The classic discussion of social crime is Hobsbawm, *Primitive Rebels.* Much has been written about social crime since then; critiques of Hobsbawm include Anton Blok, "The Peasant and the Brigand: Social Banditry Reconsidered," *Comparative Studies in Society and History* 14 (September 1972); and Temma Kaplan, *Anarchists of Andalusia, 1868–1903* (Princeton, 1977); see also John Brewer and John Styles, eds., *An Ungovernable People: The English and Their Law in the Seventeenth and Eighteenth Centuries* (New Brunswick, N.J., 1980).

popular culture, a nasty way for some lower-class men to proclaim that they would never adopt the respectable conventions of behavior necessary for admittance to society. Hooligan mockery and ritual humiliation were a deadly serious version of the "carnivalesque" Mikhail Bakhtin discovered in Rabelais, and which he believed existed in popular culture everywhere. Like early modern peasants at carnival, hooligans in St. Petersburg displayed exaggerated forms of ordinary, lower-class, coarse behavior in order to transgress social convention and declare the autonomy of their own "uncultured" way of life. By seizing control of the streets, they temporarily created a space free of hierarchy, similar to that provided by carnival, where they could invert the usual relations of power.[100] But hooliganism seemed dangerous and threatening rather than a harmless display of Rabelaisian fun, because hooligans were not performing only at carnival, where order was suspended temporarily and with everyone's consent. They were appearing repeatedly on everyday streets and before an audience unwilling to relinquish the social and cultural hierarchy.

There was no suggestion, however, that hooligans had any desire to transform the political order fundamentally or permanently. The hooligans' acts were too trivial or too self-contained to suggest that their aim was political power in any traditional sense. But there was a political issue here: the hooligans had in mind a new kind of power. Their actions suggest that they resented being told how to act properly; they wanted the right to act as they wished, where they wished. They made clear their intention to seize those rights by using a new weapon, which, in the context of social transformation, had acquired a new potency: the ability to shock and intimidate.

This interaction between hooligans and members of the middle classes on the streets and in the pages of *Peterburgskii listok* demonstrates the need to adopt a broader understanding of what constitutes "political" activity. Although hooligan acts did not reveal political motivation or political consciousness in any traditional sense, the hooligans' interaction with the middle classes was clearly a conflict over power, more specifically over the distribution of power in everyday life. The content of this conflict

---

100. "Carnival celebrated temporary liberation from the prevailing truth and from the established order; it marked the suspension of all hierarchical rank, privileges, norms, and prohibitions. . . . This led to the creation of special forms of marketplace speech and gesture, frank and free, permitting no distance between those who came in contact with each other and liberating from norms of etiquette and decency imposed at other times" (Bakhtin, *Rabelais*, 7, 10, 89–92 and passim).

was cultural—the definition of proper public behavior and the free expression of a cultural self-definition—but the object of the conflict was the power to determine whose cultural norms could be displayed on the streets. However misguided or destructive their behavior, the hooligans were expressing a form of class hostility that their audience understood as "politically" significant. Even the knife-wielding muggers, whose behavior had the least to do with direct assaults on respectability, were asserting their power to defy authority and were portrayed in the boulevard press as a threat to civilized public life. Hooligans made it clear that informal social authority would no longer be sufficient to control the public behavior of the lower classes. Hooligans not only challenged society's right to invoke informal authority but suggested that its instruments—respectability and cultural development—were irrelevant.

Although little understood at the time, aggressive hooligan displays of a swaggering, defiant street style were an assault on the prevailing conception of culture as a single standard to which all should aspire. Unlike the Russian nihilists of the 1860s, with their simple dresses, shorn hair, and blue glasses, hooligans were probably not self-consciously creating a counterculture. But their distinctive style of public presentation insisted just as powerfully on its own legitimacy as a rejection of respectability. In discussing the public relationship between British punks and their audience, Hebdige noted that countercultural styles are often used to communicate cultural difference in order to expose the efforts of mainstream cultures to represent their own values as normative and universal, which is what the Russian intelligentsia, old and new, had always assumed.[101] One of the reasons hooliganism worked as a symbol was that it appeared at a critical historical moment, when universal ideas about culture and consensus about what constituted civilization were breaking down both in Russia and in the West.

Since the eighteenth century there had been general agreement among the articulate sectors of European societies that civilization, based in reason, order, and progress, was the goal of society and that mass enlightenment of some kind was the means to reach that goal. By the end of the nineteenth century many European intellectuals were beginning to question those century-old ideals. At the same time, educated elites were losing their monopolies on articulated public opinion. The proliferation of the mass press and the masses' discovery of their ability to influence affairs

101. Hebdige, *Subculture*, 102.

of state and society gave voice to ideas and values that differed from those of the elite. Fin-de-siècle culture was remarkable for its questioning of the rationality and superiority of mainstream European culture. What is less well known is that a similar challenge was being posed from below. At the same time that fin-de-siècle intellectuals were exploring the newly discovered realms of irrationality, violence, and sexuality, hooliganlike waves of crime were presenting the same issues on the public streets. These challenges to the enlightenment ideal of civilization ensnared the socially and culturally mobile middle classes everywhere in Europe. In Russia, the spread of enlightenment ideals regarding cultural development had been the prime mission of the intelligentsia, old and, to a lesser extent, new. When these ideals came under attack the old intellectual elite were less worried about hooliganism than about the urban commercialization of culture and the aestheticism of avant-garde art, which together distracted educated society from its social and political mission. But the insecure new intelligentsia, with their questionable claims to civilization, felt the sting of hooliganism especially sharply. All these groups were reacting to (and participating in) the splintering of the educated elite, the fragmentation of society as a whole, and the corresponding diversification and democratization of culture, which the hooligans on the street symbolized in particularly aggressive forms.

This incipient rebellion against the concept of a universal cultural standard also accounts for the fundamental ambivalence embedded in hooliganism. On the one hand the flood of peasants into the city made it impossible *not* to notice the existence of profound cultural difference, yet the prevailing culturalist model assumed that everyone in Russia would eventually become civilized and assimilated into society through a single process of cultural development. In the face of social and cultural divisions no new unifying ideas arose to provide a pluralistic structure for incorporating difference. Hooligans were both terrifying and trivial, threatening and ridiculous, alien and everywhere, incomprehensible and familiar, because hooligans aggressively insisted on their difference and legitimacy, but their audience did not yet have categories for thinking about difference that refused to be inferior. Hooliganism worked as a symbol because it encompassed this ambivalence and enabled people to think about cultural difference before they could comprehend cultural multiplicity.

When in 1905 some of these social divisions were overcome in common opposition to the autocracy, hooligans continued to perform on the margins of the revolutionary upheaval as reminders of the fissures in society and the dangers unrest posed for Russian civilization. Hooliganism acquired additional meanings during the revolution as hooligans violently displayed the depths of their alienation and the bitterness of their rage. And although the Revolution of 1905–1907 was a watershed in determining political views and political alignments, it should be clear from this study of cultural conflict that critical problems of social interaction were already established before 1905.

2   From Under Every Rock
Hooligans in Revolution, 1905–1907

> The whole country is simply permeated with sedition and
> reeking with revolution, racial hatred and warfare, murder,
> incendiarism, brigandage, robbery and crime of every
> kind. . . . As far as can be seen we are on the high road to
> complete anarchy and social chaos.
>
> —W. H. Stuart, Acting U.S. Consul
> October 1905

The 1905–1907 Revolution was a major turning point in Russian history,
but while historians have studied the roles played by workers, government
figures, and liberal and socialist activists, we know little about the way the
revolution was experienced in everyday life. In hindsight it may seem
clear that the victory of October 1905 was a hollow one. Almost as soon
as the diverse opposition movements came together in the assault on autocracy that forced the tsar to promise a constitution and a parliament, the
balance of power began to shift back in favor of the government. Yet
during those years, especially during 1906, but right up until the coup
d'état of June 1907 that effectively restored the tsar's power, the outcome
did not seem assured. Immediately following the issuance of the October
Manifesto the country was beset by an unprecedented number of popular
disorders, which prolonged the crisis and disrupted society's cross-class
united front against the autocracy. One fact that often gets lost in the
social and political history of the period is that the revolutionary process
in 1905–7 was a *violent* one. It was violent in well-known, spectacular
(but intermittent) episodes, and it was violent every day on the streets.
By concentrating on the year 1905 alone and on the great achievements
of that year—the labor movement's mass general strikes and the liberation
movement's constitutional victory—historians have inadvertently minimized the role and scope of violence as it was witnessed from day to day.[1]

1. There have been some recent exceptions: John Bushnell, *Mutiny amid Repression: Russian Soldiers in the Revolution of 1905–1907* (Bloomington, Ind., 1985);
Wynn, *Workers, Strikes, and Pogroms*; Weinberg, *The Revolution*. Violence is

Sensational incidents of violence accounted for more than 15,000 deaths in terrorist assassinations, peasant revolt, pogroms, government punitive expeditions and executions, and the street battles of armed uprisings.[2] But such dramatic and significant occasions of violence were interspersed among other events of those tumultuous years. The ordinary inhabitants of Russian cities also witnessed an unprecedented rising tide of daily crime and criminal violence, both on the streets and in the newspapers that informed them about events beyond their immediate purview. Highly visible and widely publicized, the crime wave of the revolutionary years began accelerating in the middle of 1905, reached its crest during the summer and fall of 1906, and continued well into 1907, when police finally brought it under control. The spectacular incidents of political violence that punctuated the unfolding of the revolution occurred against a background of continual, everyday, personally threatening crime, street disorders, and public violence. Together these events shaped contemporaries' everyday experience of revolution and contributed to the uncertainty of its outcome. While the total number of victims pales in comparison with the death tolls of other revolutions, the violence of these years haunted public discussion during the course of the revolution, and violence was

---

recognized as important but with some limitations in Ascher, *The Revolution of 1905*; Gerald Surh, *1905 in St. Petersburg: Labor, Society, and Revolution* (Stanford, 1989); Engelstein, *Moscow, 1905*. Historians who study the countryside, on the other hand, have not neglected its violence: Robert Edelman, *Proletarian Peasants: The Revolution of 1905 in Russia's Southwest* (Ithaca, N.Y., 1987); Teodor Shanin, *Russia, 1905–1907: Revolution as a Moment of Truth* (New Haven, 1985).

2. Terrorist assassinations, on the rise since the turn of the century, killed 4,000 officials in 1906–7; see Paul Avrich, *The Russian Anarchists* (Princeton, 1967), 64. Between 1905 and 1907 approximately 7,000 peasant attacks occurred; in the fall of 1905 alone, peasants set fire to 3,000 noble manor houses, causing at least 40 million rubles of damage; see Shanin, *Russia, 1905–1907*, 94, 175. Government repression of the revolution was brutally violent, from Bloody Sunday through the December armed uprisings, which occurred in two dozen cities (in which, in Moscow alone, 1,000 workers and 100 government troops were killed), to the hanging executions of 3,000 activists in what were known as "Stolypin's neckties" (1,144 under illegal courts-martial and another 2,000 civilians executed by ordinary courts-martial) and the "punitive expeditions" against sedition in the countryside; see Hans Rogger, *Russia in the Age of Modernization and Revolution* (New York, 1983), 223; George Yaney, *The Urge to Mobilize* (Urbana, Ill., 1982), 186–92; Ascher, *The Revolution of 1905*, 323. In almost 700 fierce pogroms at least 3,000 Jewish men, women, and children were mutilated, raped, and killed in 1905. Pogroms between 1903 and 1906 destroyed 66 million rubles of Jews' property; see Shlomo Lambroza, "Jewish Responses to Pogroms in Late Imperial Russia," in *Living with Anti-Semitism*, ed. Jehuda Reinharz (Hanover, N.H., 1987), 268–69.

uppermost in the minds of contemporaries in later years as they strove to understand its meaning.

In 1905 and especially 1906 the St. Petersburg newspapers, from the staid to the sensational, spewed out a regular diet of social disorder, popular unrest, and street violence, *every day*. *Peterburgskii listok* and *Peterburgskaia gazeta* reported turmoil of all kinds. Throughout the year, mass rioting and brutal fistfighting broke out on the streets. The city "teemed" with "shady characters," beggars, vagabonds, prostitutes, and hooligans. Public drunkenness was epidemic. Even the prisons were unable to prevent rioting among prisoners. A typical crime column for those years included a daily roster of several hooligan street attacks, a murder and a couple of attempted murders, and several incidents of theft and armed robbery. Crime of every kind seemed to be out of control, and bloody government retribution, horrific as it was, could not bring about a return to order. Pchela, the Bee, a regular *Peterburgskii listok* columnist, wrote that violence was exceeding "acceptable" bounds: "Revolutions are bathed in blood. Freedom is bought with blood . . . , but Russia's victims are too numerous. . . . Some [violence] is politically motivated, but some is motivated by nothing at all."[3]

The disorders of everyday street life are important in this study because street crime and violence were linked with the hooliganism featured in the prerevolutionary boulevard press. Massive arrests of and publicity for people identified as hooligans occurred after every major revolutionary event, beginning with the Bloody Sunday massacre in January 1905. From the summer of 1905 until the fall of 1906 hooliganism never left the pages of the commercial press. By labeling as hooligan new sorts of public disorder, *Peterburgskii listok* and other newspapers were implying a connection between certain street disorders of the revolutionary years and the defiance and fears that characterized hooliganism at its inception. The escalation of disorders associated with hooliganism also made the phenomenon, and the word itself, known to people outside of the circle of boulevard-press readers. As a result of its acceleration, its association with new and more violent behaviors, and its appearance in new settings and in new publications—in other words, because it occurred in the revolutionary context—hooliganism took on greater, or, simply, more sharply defined political significance as well. After 1905, hooliganism was always associated with violence and with the potential for serious social disturbances.

---

3. Pchela, "Krovavyi pir," *PL*, July 20, 1906.

Hooliganism was the most prominent form of street crime and violence between 1905 and 1907. Contemporary publications are filled with references to hooligan attacks, hooligan degeneracy, hooligan brawls, and hooligan crime, but hooliganism's place amid revolutionary unrest has been largely ignored or misunderstood by historians. Western and Soviet scholars who concede its existence persist in seeing hooliganism as either anti-revolutionary, pogromist violence or as ordinary crime, entirely divorced from the revolution around it.[4] Nor did most contemporaries take hooligan violence seriously as a manifestation of social or political unrest. Radicals, following Marx, disparaged it as the work of lumpenproletarian "scum."[5] On the right, politicians and publicists dismissed it as the work of the criminal mob.[6] The government treated hooliganism as a crime problem created, according to various points of view, by poverty or by moral or mental deficiency. In most sources, hooliganism was presented as nothing more than an unfortunate by-product of revolution, to be controlled if possible but not worth serious political consideration. As a result, a significant element of popular animosity and popular protest has been overlooked. In all these sources, however, the cultural conflict displayed in hooligan behavior and the political significance that behavior accrued are apparent even if they went unrecognized at the time.

Hooligan violence in 1905–7 sprang from a pool of hostility toward the government and its representatives and toward respectable society in general. This hostility was not expressed in "conscious" or "disciplined" actions, and it had almost exclusively negative consequences, but it was expressed in forms that were neither aberrations nor short-lived creatures of revolution. Nor was hooliganism entirely distinct from other forms of unrest during those years. Brawling and rock throwing and other forms

---

4. Ascher rescued hooliganism from oblivion in his recent account of 1905, but he diminishes its importance by associating hooligan acts with either anti-revolutionary violence or ordinary crime (*The Revolution of 1905*, 93, 129–36). Surh cites hooliganism as "one clear marker" of the disintegration of order after 1900 (along with peasant riots, pogroms, labor unrest, and the growing political activism of the intelligentsia); he also includes cases of petty violence, such as window breaking or rock throwing, when they occur in connection with an explicit labor action (*1905*, 172ff., 313). Engelstein concentrates on street violence very similar to that discussed here but primarily during the "Days of Freedom," which followed the announcement of the October Manifesto (*Moscow, 1905*, 138–48). Illustrations from 1905–7 satirical journals show the preoccupation of educated society with the blood on the government's hands; see David Porter and Cathy King, eds., *Blood and Laughter: Caricatures from the 1905 Revolution* (London, 1983).
5. B. Utevskii, "Khuliganstvo v epokhu 1905–1914 gg.," *Khuliganstvo i khuligany: Sbornik* (Moscow, 1929), 20ff.
6. For example, A. E. Riabchenko, *O bor'be s khuliganstvom, vorovstvom, i brodiazhnichestvom* (St. Petersburg, 1914).

of street violence of the revolutionary period were rooted in traditions and rituals of Russian lower-class culture and, when brought to the center of the city, reflected long-standing lower-class discontent with subordination. Hooliganism in 1905–7 was a complex phenomenon, having close, if submerged, links with revolutionary events. While hooligan acts were indeed manifestations of ordinary crime, they continued to possess the elements of class and cultural conflict that had emerged before 1905. And while hooliganism differed significantly from revolutionary labor unrest, the two shared important features, including lower-class self-assertion in protest against powerlessness and the use of public space to press demands. In addition, the hooligans themselves, as primarily casual workers, were closely related socially to the workers whose discontent fueled the revolution.

Many of the sources historians have used to study popular unrest in the 1905–1907 Revolution share the dismissive bias of contemporary political actors. The published collections of documents that we rely on were selected and edited in the 1950s and 1960s by Soviet historians who were bound by a narrow, linear view of the development of class consciousness.[7] Consequently, these collections omitted incidents that did not serve as evidence of growing political awareness and sophistication among Russian workers or of their capacity for organization and discipline. They underrepresent the levels of street violence that actually occurred during the revolution and have given historians the false impression that popular violence disappeared, if it was ever significant at all, with the coming of class consciousness.[8] But while hooligans were not "conscious" workers,

7. *Vtoroi period revoliutsii, 1906–1907 gody,* 4 vols. (Moscow, 1957–1965); and volumes in the series *Revoliutsiia 1905–1907 gg. v Rossii: Dokumenty i materialy,* ed. A. M. Pankratova et al. (Moscow, 1955–1963), including *Revoliutsionnoe dvizhenie v Rossii vesnoi i letom 1905 g.,* 2 vols., ed. N. S. Trusova (Moscow, 1957–1961); *Vysshii pod''em revoliutsii 1905–1907 gg.: Vooruzhennye vostaniia, Noiabr'–Dekabr' 1905 goda,* ed. A. L. Sidorov (Moscow, 1955).
8. Until very recently labor historians have shared this bias by focusing primarily on "conscious" or "legitimate" forms of labor protest. Haimson recognized the importance of "spontaneous" antiauthoritarianism, but he placed such demonstrations in the 1912–14 period; see his "Social Stability"; Daniel Brower examined cases of lower-class violence in "Labor Violence in Russia in the Late Nineteenth Century," *Slavic Review,* vol. 41, no. 3 (1982). Critical replies to Brower in the same issue of the journal minimized labor violence: R. E. Johnson, "Primitive Rebels? Reflections on Collective Violence in Imperial Russia," 434; R. G. Suny, "Violence and Class Consciousness in the Russian Working Class," 439; and D. Koenker, "Collective Action and Collective Violence in the Russian Labor Movement," 445–46. The first monographic works to consider labor violence seriously focus on pogroms in Odessa and the Southern Industrial Region; Weinberg, *The Revolution;* see Wynn, *Workers, Strikes, and Pogroms.*

they were often workers nonetheless, working for wages at least some of the time. Their actions should be seen as emanating from the same social and economic milieu as the developed labor movement, even though hooligan actions were not a response to labor-management conflict. Hooligans did not express the same political consciousness as workers who engaged in strikes, nor was there solidarity between striking workers and rowdy hooligans. But hooligans lived in the same neighborhoods and experienced the isolation and animosity toward privileged society that contributed to working-class activism.

The role hooliganism played in the revolution has been hidden from history because it does not fit neatly into existing categories of popular unrest. Historians of labor unrest and popular violence categorize incidents according to such criteria as the participants' degree of political consciousness, the nature of their motives and goals, their level of organization, and their place in the social structure. Although historians have recognized gradations along these scales, this sort of categorization sets up a number of false dichotomies: political/economic, organized/spontaneous, radical/reactionary, proletarian/peasant. It also creates illusory distinctions between workers and criminals and between the respectable poor and the riffraff. To make the past comprehensible, categorization of some kind is necessary, but it suggests the existence of a world far more orderly than the fluidity of social reality. The impossibility of fitting hooliganism into the existing categories of crime, violence, unrest, and protest makes it clear that the whole picture of popular violence and lower-class unrest will come into focus only when we view organized labor protest as but one manifestation of lower-class discontent. We need to see the links connecting the remarkable acts of conscious workers with the unpalatable and destructive acts carried out by their less fortunate, less educated, and less disciplined brothers and sisters, and we need to understand the forms of unrest and protest in between these poles. We must look beyond the obviously political to see others forms of social and cultural conflict, which in the case of hooliganism had wide-ranging political consequences even if they had only minimal political motivation. We can see the hooligans' destructive rage on the streets as an essential part of the revolutionary experience, and we can see the importance of the cultural aspect of the workers' struggle for power in their own lives. We can also appreciate a wider range of fears that mass activism provoked during the revolution and after it subsided.

The boulevard-press portrait of the revolution in St. Petersburg differs in significant ways from that painted by modern social historians. In the pages of the boulevard press, Petersburgers witnessed diverse forms of unrest, including incidents of individual and collective hooligan violence alongside working-class strikes and political activism on all fronts. The press not only portrayed crime and violence as crucial ingredients in the revolutionary situation but also presented them as socially and politically significant. While hooliganism in *Peterburgskii listok* and *Peterburgskaia gazeta* bore only a tenuous relation to explicitly political unrest, it was implicitly portrayed as a manifestation of social and cultural conflict that had political repercussions, and as such was a part of the overall dynamic of revolution. This is not to say that *Peterburgskii listok* presented hooliganism sympathetically. On the contrary, from the beginning hooliganism was depicted in sharp contrast to "legitimate" labor protest, strikes, and working-class demands for political and economic improvements, which *Peterburgskii listok* consistently supported.

It should be noted that while other sources reported hooliganism in this period, it is not always clear how they used the term. *Peterburgskii listok* and *Peterburgskaia gazeta* were unusual in their use of consistent labels and categories to describe incidents of unrest. As they began to call new forms of disorder hooliganism, the connotations they popularized began to appear elsewhere, making their pioneering usage an influential standard.

Three kinds of incidents were labeled hooliganism during the 1905–1907 Revolution in the boulevard press. They were, first, the kinds of hooligan muggings, rowdiness, and displays of "immorality" that had appeared at the turn of the century but multiplied rapidly in 1905; second, massive public brawling, rioting, and destruction of property; and, third, violent attacks on policemen. These were all characterized by a lower degree of political motivation or consciousness than labor unrest but also by greater political content and consequences than ordinary crimes. If we view them all along a political continuum, we can see them strung out between labor unrest and ordinary crime. A continuum also allows us to keep in mind the fluidity of the lines dividing degrees of political consciousness and significance, social origin, and cultural conflict. *Peterburgskii listok* and *Peterburgskaia gazeta* specifically identified the differing degrees of political intention and significance implicit in them, and this underlined, in a way no other source did, the social and cultural dimensions of popular discontent as a whole.

▤ *"Masters of the Street"*

Beginning immediately after Bloody Sunday (January 9, 1905, when government troops ignited the popular revolution by shooting on a demonstration of unarmed workers) and escalating throughout 1905 and 1906, reports of hooligan rowdiness and back-street hooligan muggings rose dramatically in number, appearing more often than reports of other street disorders. Each day the newspapers reported at least one and usually as many as three or four different hooligan incidents (in addition to increased numbers of other crimes, including thefts, robberies, murders, and arson). Still, most commentators agreed that only a fraction of hooligan incidents were reported to the police or in the newspapers. It was estimated, for example, that only one-fifth of the incidents on the Peterhof Highway were reported, although hooligan robberies there had become a nightly occurrence.[9]

The rise in crime was widely acknowledged and discussed, which seemed to contribute to the general panic over the unprecedented visibility and danger of "shady characters" (*temnye litsa*) and pitiful or unsavory types.[10] *Peterburgskii listok* published a slew of serious articles analyzing the rise in crime and its relation to the revolution. It also publicized the anxious responses of city dwellers and journalists. "These 'lowlifes' (*shpana*) hold the local populace in terror," concluded the article about the Peterhof Highway, and a number of writers observed that "the license of the capital's hooligans [was] beginning to reach terrifying proportions for peaceful people" and "the hooligans' 'insolence' (*beztseremonnost'*) knows no bounds."[11]

After the government suppressed the militant labor movement in December 1905, radical workers ceased to pose a serious political threat to the government, and the focus of the political movement shifted from mass politics to the State Duma and from the city streets to the villages, where peasant rebellion was gaining momentum. But St. Petersburg remained in the grip of social turmoil that had been unleashed by the revolutionary upheaval, though the roots of the turbulence lay in the decades before 1905. Strikes, while diminishing in number, continued to interrupt the restoration of normal economic life during 1906 and 1907.[12] The city government was besieged by thousands of unemployed workers, locked out and blacklisted, who were well organized and vocal in demanding work

---

9. "DP: Nozhevshchina," *PL*, October 10, 1905.
10. In addition to *PL* and *PG*, see, for example, *Novoe vremia*, February 10, 1906; and police reports in TsGAOR, fond 102, delo 40, chast' 2, listy 9–26, July 19, 1905.
11. "DP: Napadenie khuligana," *PL*, September 22, 1905; "DP: Nozhovaia rasprava u Narodnogo doma," *PL*, September 6, 1906.
12. The latter years of the revolution have not received the attention that 1905 has received. On strikes in St. Petersburg in 1906 and 1907 see U. A. Shuster, *Peterburgskie rabochie v 1905–1907 gg.* (Leningrad, 1976). The second volume of Abraham Ascher's study appeared after this book went to press.

and food.[13] Many of the social ills afflicting the poor population that predated the revolution continued unabated and in the wake of the mass movement appeared in sharper relief. The legions of beggars who had always surrounded churches and government offices swelled with the rising number of unemployed and surged to the center of the city.[14] According to numerous sources, it was "not a rare phenomenon to see totally passed-out drunkards on the street"; not a new phenomenon surely, yet on a scale that shocked and irritated people in 1906.[15] Prison populations, now swelling with political offenders, never returned to pre-1905 levels, even after political and administrative prisoners had been transferred or released. Housing was, as always, scarce and expensive; so flophouses and other shelters—for vagabonds, beggars, young waifs, alcoholics, and the homeless—were filled far beyond capacity. In the summer, when nights were warmer, the streets and parks and the open fields on the city's outlying islands were alive with transients. The "shady characters" who had begun to make their presence felt on central streets a few years earlier now occupied whole neighborhoods. Everywhere in the city they behaved as they wished, exhibiting neither fear of arrest nor deference to respectable pedestrians.

Both the number of hooligan incidents and the brazenness of the hooligans reached new heights. Muggings occurred with a frightening regularity and an equally frightening inexplicability. On Easter in 1906, for example, victims of more than fifty hooligan attacks were treated in one city hospital alone. In September 1906, one "hooligan beast" stabbed a doorman who refused him entry to the "People's Hall."[16]

The typical attack in the revolutionary period resembled the back-alley muggings of previous years: an unsuspecting pedestrian, sometimes drunk, usually lower class, was ambushed by a group of young men:

> The peasant Feodosei Bezhurkin, a typesetter, age nineteen, was attacked by several youths while walking along Zakharevskaia Street and received one wound to the head. He fell. They ran off.

13. Their demands were widely reported in the press and followed conscientiously and sympathetically by *Peterburgskii listok*; see, for example, *PL*, April 14, 1906, April 15, 1906, May 4, 1906. See also Sergei Malyshev, *Unemployed Councils in St. Petersburg in 1906* (London, 1931); *Vtoroi period*, vol. III, pp. 83–88; Shuster, *Peterburgskie rabochie*, 206–9, 224–25, 251–56.
14. *Statisticheskii ezhegodnik S-Peterburga za 1905 g.* (St. Petersburg, 1906), 75; and *za 1906*, 58; "Gorodskie dela," *PL*, July 20, 1906.
15. N. S-n, "Gorod i alkogolizm," *PL*, August 5, 1906.
16. "DP: Napadenie khuliganov," *PL*, April 4, 1906. "DP: Nozhovaia rasprava u Narodnogo doma," *PL*, September 6, 1906.

A passerby grabbed one hooligan, but then he was knifed, and the hooligan got away.[17]

But as hooligan incidents increased, people began to take matters into their own hands:

On May 21, late in the evening, a pharmacy clerk was surrounded by about fifteen hooligans on his way home from work.
—Hey, big shot (*shliapa*), why don't you walk with us?
—Beat him up, boys. What are we waiting for?
—Hey, Mister, off with your clothes!
The noisy, threatening crowd began more "decisive" actions. Suddenly the victim produced a revolver.
—Watch out, you creeps (*Proch', merzavtsy*), or I'll shoot.[18]

As in earlier years the crime-column reports usually appeared without editorial comment. But when analysis did appear, even in reports of the most dangerous muggings and knife attacks, it still stressed hooligan *na-khal'stvo*—brazen, defiant insolence—as often as the physical danger of attacks. In the cases noted above, it was the "insolence" and "license," not the danger hooligans posed, that were most notable. Another entry in the crime column noted sarcastically that during the revolution hooligans had gained the temerity to attack in the light of day:

We have had more than one occasion to mention the exploits and heroic deeds performed by hooligan gentlemen on Nevskii Prospekt. At night the hooligans are in complete control. And now these gentlemen are not too inhibited to display their daring during the daylight hours, when Nevskii is teeming with people. The fourteen-year-old daughter of a nobleman was harassed on Nevskii by the type of person who wears multicolored scarves and his cap askew. He followed and stabbed her. The hooligan was the sixteen-year-old son of an artisan, Grigorii Ivanov.[19]

As before, nothing provoked as much outrage in *Peterburgskii listok* as the appearance of hooliganism in the center of town, where the hooligans

---

17. "DP: Napadenie na ulitse," *PL*, May 9, 1905.
18. "Buistvo khuliganov," *PL*, May 24, 1906.
19. "DP: Napadenie khuligana na Nevskom pr.," *PL*, April 10, 1906. See also "DP: Grabezh sredi bela-dnia," *PL*, July 16, 1906; "Iz kipy zaiavlenii: Khuligany u Vladimirskoi tserkvi," *PL*, October 30, 1905. Parks too had become dangerous according to complaints in many similar articles: *PL*, July 19, 1906, September 6, 1906, September 10, 1906; *PG*, August 8, 1906.

took increasing advantage of the breakdown of authority and the impotence of the police:

> On the Fontanka Embankment, next to the building of the
> Ministry of Communications and near a flophouse that is always
> filled with representatives of the hooligan "proletariat" and the
> dregs of society, among whom human blood is worth less than
> Neva water, two casual laborers (*chernorabochie*) sixteen and
> seventeen years old began fighting with each other. One stabbed
> the other in the back.[20]

Hooligan brazenness and the enormous upsurge in the number of hooligan incidents took on new political significance in the revolutionary context as powerful evidence of the breakdown of official police authority and the ebbing of informal social authority and control over neighborhood streets as well. During the revolution hooligans acted as if they thought the streets were theirs and control over their own behavior was a right they had won, a sign of their power. Evidence of the hooligans' newfound power was conveyed in dozens of *Peterburgskii listok* reports on neighborhoods where hooligans reputedly controlled the streets. " 'The hooligans have conquered,' cry the capital's inhabitants," is how one relatively sober analysis began.[21] Traditionally high-crime districts such as Smolensk and Harbor Fields on Vasilevskii Island or "Ligovka" (Ligovskaia Street) near the Nikolaevskii Station were "overrun" with hooligans and other "shady types" by late 1905.[22] According to another report, even the police preferred not to enter Smolensk Field, because it was "the hooligans' kingdom." "In some places," it was reported, "they simply own the streets, playing cards, passing around vodka, making love with their girlfriends right on the sidewalk."[23] Peski, a district several blocks from the Nikolaevskii Station across Nevskii from Ligovka, was the scene of repeated hooligan incidents, including mass gatherings, huge brawls, and individual harassment of the decreasing number of pedestrians who ventured onto its streets. According to one account: "Hooligans have completely taken over the square and with the air of victors they act far from humbly."[24] Even if such statements were exaggerated for dramatic effect,

20. "DP: Nozhovaia rasprava," *PL*, July 26, 1906.
21. P., "Pomoshch' khuliganam," *PL*, May 15, 1906.
22. "DP: Opiat' khuligany," *PL*, April 21, 1906.
23. A. S-v, "Khuliganskie zabavy," *PL*, August 30, 1906.
24. "Iz kipy zaiavlenii: Zavoevanie khuliganami skvera," *PL*, May 30, 1906. See also "DP: Khuligany na Peskakh," *PL*, June 29, 1906; " 'Khuliganskii' klub," *PL*, June 30, 1906; and N., "Tsentry khuliganstva (Iz besedy)," *PL*, October 13, 1906. *PG* ran an article about the Peski *dvorniki*, who claimed that they could not cope with the recent influx of hooligans and petitioned for additional post patrolmen; see "Listok: Khodataistvo dvornikov," *PG*, July 16, 1906.

they were repeated so often during the revolutionary years that they clearly reflected, and possibly helped create, a climate of fear on many of Petersburg's best streets. Whether or not the hooligans "controlled" the streets in any conventional sense, they were capable of making public life so unpleasant and dangerous as to keep people out of certain neighborhoods and off their own streets. In the eyes of the hooligans and their respectable neighbors this was de facto power, and it was a hooligan victory.

The police began to turn the tide against street crime only after St. Petersburg was placed under a state of Extraordinary Security in 1906.[25] In fact, court statistics for hooligan crimes actually decreased during the revolution, because the majority of hooligan cases were processed outside the law under binding decrees issued according to the state-of-siege provisions of the Extraordinary Security statute.[26] These decrees put teeth in the police campaign begun in 1905 to initiate a series of street sweeps (*chistki*) or roundups (*oblavy, obkhody*) to recover the public space in the center of the city from hooligans. According to *Peterburgskii listok* unofficial reports, approximately 16,000 hooligans and other "shady characters" were detained and expelled from the city under these decrees. This is in addition to the approximately 114,000 people convicted of petty hooligan offenses in normal court procedures in the period 1905–7 (see tables 3–6 in the Appendix).

Campaigns of this sort were not unprecedented, but they hardly made a dent in the crime problem in the capital. For decades the police periodically descended on well-known criminal haunts and flophouses. The search for "suspicious types" and their arrest or expulsion from the city (usually for lacking proper residence documents) were common newspaper items before 1905.[27] The first major street sweeps of the revolutionary period were

25. According to the security statute passed in 1881 after the assassination of Alexander II, a region could be placed under Reinforced Security, Extraordinary Security, or flat-out martial law. St. Petersburg had been under Reinforced Security since 1881 and was placed under Extraordinary Security between 1906–10 and after 1914; see Harper, "Exceptional Measures."

26. *PMS 1906*, 199; *PMS 1910*, 124; "Otnoshenie ot 11 minuvshego iiunia," from the Ministry of Justice to the Ministry of Internal Affairs, TsGAOR, fond 102, delo 40, chast' 2, listy 9–26, July 19, 1905. Surh recently argued that the Petersburg *gradonachal'stvo* had been lobbying for use of binding decrees against street crime and disorder since at least 1903, in order to enhance its dwindling authority in the city as much as to curtail street crime; the Ministry of Interior resisted these entreaties until 1906 ("The Police and the Lower Classes of St. Petersburg, 1895–1914" [unpublished paper]).

27. In 1904, *Peterburgskii listok* published a cartoon with the sardonic caption "For the 'shady' characters who sometimes find shelter in the 'flops,' a police

carried out during the summer of 1905, but the roundups ceased with the resurgence of political unrest that fall.[28] When they were renewed in 1906, most of the effort was directed at purging the central streets, but forays were also made into working-class neighborhoods and traditional criminal haunts to root out the problem at its source, as the police viewed it. In April 1906, *Peterburgskii listok* reported that 2,520 beggars, thieves, hooligans, and others were arrested in the capital. On one night, 150 people were arrested on the central streets between 11:00 P.M. and 4:00 A.M.[29] In July approximately 3,000 fell into the police net in one police district alone.[30] In another district (in the Narva borough) the police reported a surprisingly good catch when 250 hooligans were seized in one day.[31] During the second half of 1906 the roundups continued. In the beginning of August 3,150 hooligans were reported exiled from the capital, and approximately 1,200 additional hooligans were said to have been arrested in nocturnal roundups.[32] In September the newspapers reported the roundup of even larger groups. According to police figures, 2,916 people were seized on the Petersburg Side and another 795 in the Vyborg quarter.[33] After September, arrests and exiles decreased considerably, with *Peterburgskii listok* reports accounting for about 1,000 hooli-

---

roundup does not come as an entirely pleasant surprise." See "Politseiskii obkhod nochlezhnykh domov," *PL*, January 25, 1904; "DP: V nochlezhnykh priiutakh," *PL*, March 28, 1903; N. V., "Razgrom v nochlezhnom dome Makokina," *Iurist*, May 16, 1904. On searches in the Great Reform era see Bradley, *Muzhik and Muscovite*, 271–72.

28. "DP," *PL*, July 14, 16, 21, and 28, 1905, and August 4, 11, and 14, 1905.

29. "DP: Zaderzhanie khuliganov," *PL*, April 23, 1906, reported the 150 arrested on April 22. The others were arrested during the one-week period April 10–16, and included 205 thieves and burglars, 638 beggars, 313 who lacked proper passports, 286 for street disorders, and 888 picked up "for various reasons": "DP: Obkhod," *PL*, April 26, 1906. "Listok: Vysylka khuliganov," *PL*, April 10, 1906, added 40 "hooligan-recidivists" to the totals for April.

30. Several weekly reports of roundups appeared in July that emphasized the preponderance of hooligans among those seized; see "DP: Zaderzhanie khuliganov," *PL*, July 15, 1906; "DP: Aresty khuliganov," July 18, 1906; "Listok: 3000 arestovannykh khuliganov," *PL*, August 17, 1906. Similar reports were published in *PG*; see July 16 and July 30, for example.

31. "Proisshestviia: Massovyi arest khuliganov," *PG*, August 1, 1906.

32. "Listok: Vysylka khuliganov," *PL*, August 4, 1906; "Listok: 'Chistka' Peterburga," August 6, 1906; "Listok," August 7, 1906; "DP: Stolknovenie politsii s khuliganami," August 7, 1906; "Listok: Zaderzhanie khuliganov," August 9, 1906; "Listok," August 11, 1906.

33. "DP: Ochistka prestupnogo Peterburga," *PL*, October 11, 1906. Still other reports suggest even higher totals: "Listok," *PL*, September 12, 16, and 19, 1906; "DP: Ochishchenie prestupnogo Peterburga," October 5, 1906.

gans picked up in the three-month period between October and December.[34]

Peterburgskii listok seemed intent on celebrating the police effort to restore order. On August 1, 1906 an article appeared reporting that the *gradonachal'nik* had ordered the police, "under his personal responsibility," to take immediate steps to discontinue disturbances and eliminate prostitutes and hooligans from Nevskii Prospekt and other central streets.[35] A week later, in an article reporting the exile of 750 hooligans apprehended in tearooms, dives, parks, and elsewhere, *Peterburgskii listok* announced the firm intention of the police to purge St. Petersburg of "all these types," by no later than September 1.[36] Later in the month, *Peterburgskii listok* published an unsigned accolade to the belated police campaign. The author concluded that "in general the police are beginning to exhibit some energy in their effort to clean the capital of its filth. And none too soon."[37] *Peterburgskii listok*, however, does not seem to have made an effort to report arrests systematically, and on that account these figures cannot be considered reliable in any statistical sense. But if *Peterburgskii listok* was not overly concerned with providing precise indicators of police activity, the intent of the publicity was clear. Regular reports of successful police sweeps might have allayed public fears and public charges of official inaction and, perhaps most important, might have conveyed a sense of order returning to the city. But judging from the continued outcry over hooligan outrages and hooligan "control" of the streets well into 1906, it seems likely that the large number of detentions for street disorders may have only underlined the dimensions of the hooligan problem. Complaints about police laziness, cowardice, and impotence did not decrease.[38]

During the revolution loss of control and fear of assault—physical, verbal, and visual—intensified the anxiety that permeated the boulevard press. As before, these disparate forms of hooliganism had developed into a public battle over the control of street life. That this was a conflict over

34. "DP: Ochistka prestupnogo Peterburga," *PL*, October 12, 1906; "Listok: Vysylka khuliganov," November 28, 1906; "Listok: Vysylka khuliganov," December 8 and 14, 1906.

35. "Listok: 'Chistka' Peterburga," *PL*, August 6, 1906.

36. Ibid. Of the 750 arrested, about 300 were sent to their registered place of origin; the rest were sent to western Siberia where they were told that workhouses were being built for them.

37. "Ochistka prestupnogo Peterburga," *PL*, August 26, 1906.

38. "DP: Khuliganskaia rasprava," *PL*, May 17, 1906; N. S., "Gorod i nishchie," *PL*, September 2, 1906.

power is repeatedly echoed in press reports on street life. Despite the efforts of the police to clear the streets, the most common cry in the crime columns relayed the idea that "hooligans have captured the Petersburg streets and behave as if *they* were the masters there."[39]

▤ Brawling and Rioting

During the 1905–1907 Revolution the label hooliganism was expanded to include two forms of popular violence: massive public brawling and attacks on policemen. In terms of political motivation, brawling did not display any greater consciousness than rowdiness and mugging, but the boulevard press endowed it with greater significance because it was a more massive display of hooligan self-assertion and street power, and it was violently destructive on a much larger scale. Attacks on policemen, which will be discussed below, exhibited somewhat greater political intention and had more deeply resounding political repercussions.

Nothing better exemplifies the spread of hooligan violence and the powerful impression it left during the revolution than the massive public brawling and destructive riots that occurred during 1905 and 1906. Memoirs and police sources suggest that brawling had long been a favorite pastime among workers in Russian cities as well as villages.[40] But massive public brawls made a dramatic entrance onto the scene inhabited by the rest of the population in the spring of 1905. Beginning in March, public brawls and riots escalated in number and scale, reaching a peak in the summer of 1906 and continuing until the winter of 1906–7, when they began to taper off. Estimates of the number of people involved in these incidents ranged from a few dozen to 2,000. Destruction occurred in every Petersburg neighborhood, from solidly working-class districts on the periphery to the very center of Nevskii Prospekt. However, the majority of incidents reported in *Peterburgskii listok* and *Peterburgskaia gazeta* took place not in the distant industrial suburbs but in the mixed neighborhoods adjacent to the center of the city where the peaceful population had been feeling its control slipping away since hooligans had appeared at the turn of the century.

The most violent incidents took place during the spring and summer of 1906 and ranged from mass fistfights involving a few dozen men to full-

39. N. G-e, "Interesy dnia: Biolog o khuliganakh," *PG*, January 13, 1906.
40. Brower, "Labor Violence," 425–27; Zelnik, *A Radical Worker*, 13, 60; Chalidze, *Criminal Russia*, 17–19, 81–82, 136; Sula Benet, trans. and ed., *The Village of Viriatino* (New York, 1970), 143–45; V. Lebedev, "K istorii kulachnykh boev na Rusi," *Russkaia starina* 7–8 (1913): 332–40.

scale rioting lasting several days. Twice in June and July fierce and, to passersby, terrifying brawling broke out on the Anichkov Bridge, which was located right on Nevskii Prospekt.[41] Both fights on Nevskii prompted outraged complaints about the moral and civic decline of the city and the desperate need to restore order.[42] In August 1906, *Peterburgskii listok* reported that a brawl involving hundreds of people in the Vyborg district was averted by the police only at the last moment. Several other mass fights broke out on streets and in taverns throughout the city that month.[43]

On a number of occasions what started as mass fistfights evolved into full-fledged riots. One of these occurred on Vereiskaia Street, located in a relatively high-crime district near the Obvodnyi Canal, a neighborhood inhabited by workers in nearby factories and by petty criminals, beggars, and vagabonds who lived in the local flophouses. There was still enough of a "respectable" population, as the newspaper account put it, "to have been begging for ages and in vain to clean out the vice-ridden spots (*zlachnye mesta*)" along the street. These "dens of the lowest sort" were physically ravaged when a fight, which began between "various types of rowdies," led to a destructive rampage. The police could halt neither the fighting nor the destruction, and the crowd dispersed only after Cossacks arrived. Why did hooligans destroy the flophouses and taverns where they lived and worked? Curiously, the newspapers at the time did not wonder about this. But it was probably for the same reason that the local residents could not have the buildings shut down: they were owned by "rich" outsiders, who received a sizable income in rent.[44]

---

41. The hooligans apprehended during the first brawl managed to escape from the *dvorniki* who were accompanying them to the police station, prompting a letter from a reader who overheard passersby wondering: "How can it be so easy for these bandits of daily life to carry on their outrages?" "They're birds of a feather, of course. Vodka-drinking pals. Such manners on the Anichkov Bridge!" "Iz kipy zaiavlenii: Poboishche khuliganov," *PL*, June 10, 1906; "DP: Grandioznoe poboishche na Anichkovom mostu," *PL*, July 1, 1906.
42. "DP: Grandioznoe poboishche na Anichkovom mostu," *PL*, July 1, 1906. In this second case the article ended as follows: "It is long since time to devote serious attention to the outrages (*bezobraziia*) appearing on the Anichkov Bridge and the nearby Fontanka Enbankment."
43. "DP: Razgon khuliganov," *PL*, August 8, 1906; "Proisshestviia: Poboishche v traktire," *PG*, August 1, 1906; "Proisshestviia: Poboishche," *PG*, August 7, 1906, among others.
44. "Razgrom pritona," *PL*, April 4, 1906. *Priton* usually referred to a haunt or den but could also mean brothel. Here the meaning is unclear, but the fact that the article mentioned that it opened again for business suggests a brothel, a tavern, a flophouse, or some combination.

Extensive damage was done in several neighborhoods by brawling and rioting in June and July 1906. On three separate occasions, rioting lasted for three days, once in the working-class Kolomenskaia district and twice in mixed neighborhoods on the Petersburg Side. In Kolomenskaia in June, as in April, the rampage began as a mass brawl between "various groups of the city's lowlife (*podonki*)": rival bathhouse workers and other locals, the latter identified only as *bosiaki* (tramps) or hooligans. Apparently, the bathhouse workers began to beat up one of the hooligan "patrons" of the baths, and someone else began to beat up the *dvornik*, and then the whole local population, "everyone in the surrounding buildings," joined in the fray. At some point, men on both sides quit beating one another in order to vent their rage on the bathhouse itself. Within half an hour every window and door was broken, and the interior was thoroughly destroyed. The police appeared with their weapons drawn, which momentarily calmed the crowd, but then "stones started flying and all hell broke loose." The whole street was littered with hooligans, shouting, whistling, swearing, and breaking windows and walls. It was not until one o'clock in the morning that the police were able to pacify the crowd, estimated at about 2,000, but some fighting went on all night.[45] Two nights later the scene repeated itself, this time at a brothel, where a fight led to a riot that demolished the building and a nearby government liquor store.[46]

While hooligans were destroying property throughout the night in the working-class quarters southwest of the city center in late June, riots also raged for three days on the Petersburg Side. The same crime column that reported the "enormous brawl on the Anichkov Bridge" recorded the end of three days of rioting on the Petersburg Side.[47] On the same day *Novoe vremia* reported brawling and rioting in half a dozen locations, many of which, it pointed out, were spots frequented by respectable society—parks, squares, and theaters, including popular theaters and clubs.[48] Then, at the end of the month, rioting broke out again on the Petersburg Side, again lasting three days. Major streets in the neighborhood had become so dangerous that even the normally intrepid cabdrivers (*izvozchiki*) refused to drive there at night. Meanwhile, the police were "standing around in pairs at their posts," but doing nothing. The violence of the rioters and the

45. "DP: Razgrom zhukovskikh ban," *PL*, June 24, 1906; "DP: Razgrom ban," *PL*, June 25, 1906.
46. "Razgrom pritonov," *PL*, June 27, 1906; "Proisshestviia," *Novoe vremia* [hereafter *NV*], June 27, 1906.
47. "DP: Neudavshiisia razgrom," *PL*, July 1, 1906.
48. "Nochnye bezporiadki," *NV*, June 27, 1906.

passivity of the police allowed hooligans to destroy completely several taverns and shops and permitted these "knights of the night" (*nochnye rytsari*) to terrorize and extort money from anyone foolish enough to venture out on the streets.[49] In other isolated incidents during July 1906 hooligans wrecked a boardinghouse in the Okhta district and demolished two restaurants near the center of town, one close by the Marininskii Theater, and in the middle of July a crowd of young hooligans broke windows and wrecked storefronts along a whole block on Sadovaia Street near the Haymarket, including a tea shop run by the reactionary Union of Russian People.[50]

The attention paid to these incidents in the boulevard press suggests that they held more than simple human interest for readers, yet they are difficult to analyze and classify. Distinctions we would like to make or that have been made in other studies of collective violence—between political and nonpolitical violence, between primitive and conscious protest, or between preindustrial and industrial forms of protest—are blurred here. This is not only because the reports are incomplete but because the incidents themselves combine elements that have been seen as straddling traditional categories. The question to ask here is not, Why do these accounts omit the details we would like? but, Why did *Peterburgskii listok* consider these accounts full enough?

At first glance these brawls and riots seem entirely unconnected with the political events going on around them, suggesting that they were a classic example of the actions of a revolutionary "mob." The mob was a familiar feature of nineteenth- and early twentieth-century literature on collective violence, which portrayed the mob as representing the criminal dregs of society and depicted its actions as devoid of all reason, intention, and morality. Most historians now reject such characterizations as a reflection more of their authors' fears than of the actual composition and intent of violent crowds.[51] The majority of boulevard-press descriptions of hooligan mass violence also counter the classic depiction of the mob. In fact, the boulevard press tended to minimize the "irrational" elements of

49. Lesh, "Iz kipy zaiavlenii: Khuliganskii terror," PL, July 26, 1906.
50. "DP: Razgrom postoialogo dvora," PL, July 22, 1906; "Napadenie khuligan na restoran," PG, July 11, 1906; "Vcherashnyi den' v Peterburge: Razgrom restorana," PG, July 25, 1906; "Buistvo na Sadovoi ulitse," PG, July 10, 1906; "K buistvu na Sennoi," PG, July 11, 1906.
51. George Rudé first debunked such myths about the "mob" in The Crowd; Susanna Barrows has broadened the discussion of fearful images of the "mob" to include cultural conflict in her study Distorting Mirrors: Visions of the Crowd in Late Nineteenth-Century France (New Haven, 1981).

these incidents and to endow the brawls with meanings that implicitly linked them to the revolutionary movement. In most cases the authors of reports expected to find at least some reason for the mass street fighting and destruction of property, and they reported what motive they could discover. Although the damage done always seemed out of all proportion to the cause of the fighting, and this was portrayed as incomprehensible, the fighting itself was not dismissed as irrational or motiveless.[52]

At the same time, *Peterburgskii listok* never portrayed these incidents as politically motivated acts. The boulevard press consistently and clearly distinguished between revolutionary and hooligan destruction of property. Participants in these brawls were almost always identified as hooligans, lowlife, vagrants, and the like, not as workers; thus they were associated more closely with the criminal element of the lower classes than with the activist, revolutionary working class.[53] The boulevard press also distinguished carefully between what it considered to be hooligan vandalism and legitimate revolutionary violence. When hooligans ransacked shops, restaurants, and other enterprises in the cases discussed above, reports of the incidents appeared in the newspaper's daily chronicle of crimes, fires, and accidents. When destruction occurred in connection with events the newspaper considered politically legitimate the incidents were reported in the daily chronicle of revolutionary events, which included strikes, rallies, and demonstrations. In July 1906, for example, when dairy workers shattered the windows of their shops and vandalized their inventories, the report of the incident appeared among the day's political events and was not labeled hooliganism. The dairy workers' justification for resorting to violence was specifically labor related: they destroyed the shops after their employers refused to close up at the promised hour of 7:00 P.M., which resulted in their having to work overtime.[54] *Peterburgskii listok* sympa-

---

52. This was especially true of *Peterburgskii listok*. *Peterburgskaia gazeta* reports were more likely to ignore causes and focus on the amount of destruction or the scale of the brawl.
53. "Razgrom pritonov," *PL*, June 27, 1906; "DP: Razgon khuliganov," *PL*, August 8, 1906, for example.
54. "Vcherashnyi den': Razgrom slivochnoi lavki," *PL*, July 2, 1906. See also "Stolknovenie s prikazchikom" in the same issue. Throughout the spring and summer of 1906 *Peterburgskii listok* articles on the strike movement and the social disorders displayed intense sympathy for the plight of workers and no censure for the measures they took. "Zabastovki na zavode San-Galli," *PL*, July 16, 1906, sympathetically described the exploitation of unskilled workers and their difficulties in seeking redress during a strike. When frustration led them to dump their foreman in a wheelbarrow and escort him thus beyond the factory gates, this common bit of hooligan behavior appeared justified by events. See also "Malen'kie 'zabastovshchiki,' " *PL*, July 2, 1906; "Sredi remeslennikov," *PL*, April 10, 1906;

thized with the dairy workers' cause and presented their violence as a legitimate protest against economic exploitation, even though the dairy workers' violence was no different from the hooligans' destruction of the shops and taverns along Sadovaia Street and elsewhere. A similar distinction was made in a comparison in *Peterburgskii listok* between the capital's hooligans and the *bosiaki* of Odessa. The word *bosiak* comes from the Russian word for "barefoot" (*bosoi*) and is usually translated as "hobo" or "tramp"; but Odessa's *bosiaki* were rootless in a much more limited sense. They were the unskilled casual workers who performed the menial jobs in the city's mammoth ports, and in 1905 they were responsible for some of Odessa's most violent demonstrations.[55] Unlike hooligans, however, according to *Peterburgskii listok*, *bosiaki* were "serious" and "willing to work . . . , [and] so, when the port is working well, Odessa is calm."[56] Whatever the truth of these observations, *Peterburgskii listok* wanted to emphasize the logic and work ethic of the *bosiaki*, in contrast to the attitudes and actions of the hooligans, who shunned work and engaged in violence without a clear economic or political motive.

But while no radical motives were apparent, neither was hooligan violence portrayed as reactionary or anti-revolutionary in any way. Brawling hooligans were not implicated in the violence between workers who were reluctant to go on strike and the radicals imploring them to put down their tools, despite the fact that the boulevard press reported numerous incidents of this kind. The Petersburg boulevard press never associated hooligans with the reactionary Black Hundreds, known for their violent resistance of revolution activity, for violence against all suspected agents of revolution, and especially for violence against Jews.[57] In fact, one of the more destructive battles of the wild summer of 1906 occurred when hooligans

---

"Obshchee sobranie vybornykh," *PL*, April 16, 1906. *Peterburgskaia gazeta* was less consistent in this regard than *Peterburgskii listok* and was less willing to grant legitimacy to any acts of violence.

55. On *bosiaki* in Odessa, see also Weinberg, "Workers, Pogroms, and the Revolution."

56. M., "Chto takoe Odesskii bosiak," *PL*, June 29, 1905.

57. On fights between radical workers and Black Hundreds see "Sredi rabochikh: Izbienie chlena 'soiuza russkikh liudei,' " *PG*, July 5, 1906; "Proisshestviia: Osada doma chlena 'Soiuza russkogo naroda,' " *PG*, July 7, 1906; "Proisshestviia: Massovaia draka rabochikh," *PG*, July 20, 1906 (in this mass fight the parties facing each other were "conscious workers and Black Hundreds"); *Vtoroi period*, vol. II, pt. 1, pp. 227–28, 239–40; Shuster, *Peterburgskie rabochie*, 209, 238–39; Engelstein, *Moscow, 1905*, 112, 138–48; Surh argues that Black Hundreds groups were not very important politically in St. Petersburg during 1905 (*1905*, 195–96, 353–54, 362, 389–90).

attacked a Black Hundreds tearoom that had recently opened on Sadovaia Street.[58]

The distinction between hooligans and reactionaries is worth stressing because, as noted earlier, in the southern and western regions of the empire, especially in the Pale of Settlement, pogromists, who were also particularly active during this stage of the revolution, were frequently labeled hooligans. It is also worth stressing because hooligan violence was similar in some ways to pogromist attacks. Both were negative, destructive responses to social, economic, and cultural tensions that were triggered by the cultural conflicts of urbanization and the revolutionary breakdown of authority. In St. Petersburg, in the absence of one large ethnic minority that would make cultural differences eminently clear, hooligans were people who directed their hostilities (also profoundly cultural) against class rather than ethnic enemies. It may well be that some people engaged in hooligan riots as well as in fights with radical workers, and even in political demonstrations. But the boulevard press, which reported each kind of incident, made clear distinctions between them in 1905–7. When labor unrest was again on the upswing after 1912, such distinctions would not be drawn so sharply, but even in that period hooliganism would be implicated in labor radicalism, not in the popular anti-radicalism of the Black Hundreds.

It is possible, of course, that the boulevard press characterized brawling as hooligan violence instead of legitimate political protest in order to diminish its significance, just as elite nineteenth-century observers denigrated genuinely political collective action as the work of a mob. But the fact that the newspapers made careful distinctions among various kinds of violence and even singled out certain forms of violence as possessing a legitimacy equivalent to strikes suggests that this is unlikely. There are no hints in the boulevard-press reports or in any other sources to suggest that these brawls resembled Luddism or food riots or had any other political agenda, whether denied by contemporaries or hidden from historians.

The key to understanding the significance of street brawls and their place in the revolutionary upheaval is the boulevard press's labeling of this violence as hooliganism. By no means were all the forms of crime and violence that proliferated during the revolution referred to as hooliganism in the boulevard press. The identification of brawling and rioting with hooliganism links them with the prerevolutionary escalation of rowdy

---

58. "Listok: Otkrytie eshche odnoi chainoi-chital'ni 'soiuza russkogo naroda,' " *PL*, July 2, 1906; "Pogrom na Sadovoi ul.," *PL*, July 10, 1906.

and outrageous public hooligan offenses. Brawling and rioting resembled hooliganism in their ostentatious violations of public order and property, their contempt for legal and social authorities, the participants' assertion of their power to dominate street life, and their appearance in the center of the city. The identification of brawling with hooliganism is a reminder that street violence forced peaceful citizens off the streets they considered to be their own, and displayed, in a terrifying manner, the potential power of the lower classes when they chose to vent their rage. In the revolutionary context, hooliganism dramatized the dangers that seemed to be inherent in the awakening of mass public activism. By following on the heels of political events, by taking advantage of the breakdown of order and authority, by continuing to assert themselves in 1906–7 even after the labor movement had been crushed, hooligans represented the underside of popular political activism.

In a much more direct way violent public brawling and rowdiness accentuated the revolutionary breakdown of order. Hooligan violence undermined efforts to restore governmental authority and proved a serious problem for the local agencies of law enforcement. To suppress street fighting and violence the ordinary police continually needed special gendarmes and Cossack units as reinforcements. Curiously enough, the hooligans' ability to prevent the restoration of order did not provoke a reactionary campaign for "law and order" or a call for extra-legal solutions, at least not in the boulevard press.[59] On the contrary, judging from boulevard-press reports, the violence seemed to reinforce the popular loss of faith in authority that accompanied the revolution by exposing the weakness of the police, who proved almost totally ineffective against street violence. By the end of 1905 some Petersburgers, including workers, had become sufficiently disturbed by the danger of hooliganism and the absence of any protection from arbitrary attacks that they petitioned the City Duma with requests to establish a volunteer militia. Articles also appeared in *Peterburgskii listok* and other newspapers calling for the establishment of a militia or armed guard against hooliganism. One writer suggested "arm[ing] ourselves with Brownings," and workers in the Moscow Gates section of the city organized a neighborhood surveillance system to watch out for hooligans and vagabonds.[60] The City Duma approved the

---

59. *Novoe vremia*, the conservative newspaper, did respond to such disorders with calls for extra-legal methods of repression, as did much of the rural nobility during the interrevolutionary period, when similar disorders swamped the countryside. See, for example, "Nochnye bezporiadki," *NV*, June 27, 1906.

60. "Listok: V bor'be s khuliganami," *PL*, September 30, 1906; N. S., "Gorod i nishchie"; *Sudebnoe obozrenie*, no. 10, March 6, 1905, 238.

idea in principle, noting that the existing police force was incapable of performing the duties required of it, and a commission was created to set up a militia. Nothing, however, came of it.[61]

To deny hooligan violence conscious political intent is neither to diminish its significance in the urban unrest of the period nor to suggest that the hooligans were nothing but mindless ruffians. Despite a lack of political goals, hooligan rioting and the conscious labor movement drew from similar sources of hostility. Even though brawling pitted members of the lower classes against one another, their refusal to remain within the boundaries of their own neighborhoods and their ability to seize public spaces and intimidate the rest of society conveyed a broadly defined challenge to authority that paralleled the "legitimate" working-class protests against political, social, and cultural authority in the workplace at a time when workers also moved en masse into public view for the first time. Furthermore, the hooligans' choice of targets may not have been as irrational and self-destructive as it appears. Though hooligans patronized the flophouses, brothels, taverns, and liquor stores they destroyed, it is quite possible that all these buildings were, like the Vereiskaia Street flophouse, owned by outsiders who were perceived as wealthy, condescending exploiters. It seems likely that the hooligans did not feel that they had any particular stake in the maintenance of someone else's property. This is not to argue that hooligan rowdiness, brawling, and rioting were identical with workers' protests in strikes and demonstrations, nor is it to argue that workers sympathized with or supported hooligans; many did not. But the two groups should not be seen as entirely distinct—they occupy different points on a single continuum of lower-class responses to powerlessness.

The consequences of hooligan violence are hard to discern because they do not fall easily into established categories. The boulevard press portrayed hooligan street violence as criminal, apolitical events and as an unfortunate but simple result of the revolutionary upheaval. But we can see that while brawling and rioting displayed no clear political motives or goals, they did represent something more than simple, motiveless destruction. In exhibiting their violence on Nevskii Prospekt or destroying rows of shops in their own neighborhoods, hooligans were asserting their authority over the

---

61. "O peredache v vedenie goroda politsii bezopasnosti i ob uchrezhdenii gorodskoi militsii," *Izvestiia St. Peterburgskoi gorodskoi dumy* [hereafter *ISPGD*] 28 (1905): 518–22; "O priniatii mer k ograzhdeniiu naseleniia stolitsii ot nasilii so storonu ulichnykh ozornikov i khuliganov," *ISPGD* 29 (1905): 719–22. Ascher notes that in other cities the establishment of militias to control hooliganism and crime was also discussed (*The Revolution of 1905*, 131).

streets and venting the rage of people with no other means of expression. They had an impact because they contributed to the breakdown of order, they added an attack on property to the assault on government authority, and they continued to demonstrate their anger long after both the government and the opposition leadership (liberal and radical) thought popular unrest should subside. These characteristics of hooligan violence are even more apparent in the hooligans' ambushes of the police.

▤ *Attacks on the Police*

The police force was incapable of controlling street crime even before 1905, and it bore much of the blame for the proliferation of crime and violence during the revolution.[62] As ordinary policemen were commandeered to help the political police root out subversion, and as criminal and political violence escalated, public faith in the ability of the police to protect person and property, much less halt the decline of public morals, diminished (see fig. 6). But if, in fact, the policeman on the street was reluctant to confront hooligans, he had good reason. Beginning in 1905 and accelerating in 1906, armed attacks on policemen became common and dangerous.[63]

Soviet document collections and Soviet historians have recognized confrontations with the police only when they could be construed as evidence of working-class militance. The incidents that appeared in these works showed workers and policemen in conflict after rallies or strikes at which revolutionary party orators have spoken, revolutionary songs have been sung, and red banners have been unfurled.[64] Even on the rare occasions when hooligan "types" appeared at such events, their presence was explained, though without substantiation, in politically positive terms—as

---

62. One *Peterburgskii listok* reader was understandably outraged when a policeman explained to her that *dvorniki* and policemen were afraid to interfere with what they called "hooligans' rights as citizens"; see Emilia Meier, "Iz kipy zaiavlenii: Torzhestvo khuliganov," *PL*, July 8, 1906. Criticism of the police was too common to cite here in full; see, for example, Pchela, "Politseiskoe bezsilie," *PL*, August 16, 1906; P., "Pomoshch' khuliganam," *PL*, May 15, 1906; "Iz kipy zaiavlenii: Zavoevanie khuliganami skvera," *PL*, May 30, 1906; M., "Iz kipy zaiavlenii: Khuliganskaia idilliia," *PL*, July 30, 1906; A. S-v, "Khuliganskie zabavy," *PL*, August 30, 1906.
63. By September 1905, attacks on policemen had become serious enough for the *gradonachal'nik* to issue an order imposing special punishment on those caught assaulting policemen; see "Prikaz S.-Peterburgskogo gradonachal'nika," *PL*, September 25, 1905.
64. For example, *Vtoroi period*, vol. II, pt. 1, pp. 228, 602 n. 161; *Vserossiiskaia politicheskaia stachka v oktiabre 1905 goda*, ed. L. M. Ivanov. (Moscow and Leningrad, 1955), 356, 371, 381; Shuster, *Peterburgskie rabochie*, 240, 246.

Полицейское усердіе.

— Городовой!.. Грабятъ!!!..
— Не кричи, дьяволъ!!!.. Тутъ никакъ сицилистъ идетъ,—спугнешь!
—а ихъ хватать велѣно!..

Figure 6. Police Diligence (July 2, 1906).
The policeman is ignoring the robbery taking place at his feet, claiming that he has orders to arrest the Sicilian heading down the street.

testimony to the spread of political consciousness.[65] *Peterburgskii listok* and *Peterburgskaia gazeta* reported a far greater number and variety of clashes with the police (and with soldiers and other authorities) and as a result presented a fuller and more complex picture of the lower-class challenge to authority during the revolution.

The newspaper reports on street attacks pose problems of analysis similar to those encountered for reports on brawling. It is never entirely clear who was participating in the attacks or to what extent they were motivated by political or other considerations.[66] Certainly, working-class animosity

65. *Vtoroi period*, vol. II, pt. 1, p. 228; Shuster, *Peterburgskie rabochie*, 246–47, 257. In all fairness to Shuster there are hints in his own statements that the violence of 1906 was something less than a sign of developed class consciousness. He described the situation as "complex and fluctuating" during the summer of 1906, and he conceded that the Bolshevik party could not control spontaneous reactions to events; he concluded, however, that even spontaneous actions and even the presence of nonworkers did not detract from the political militance of the working class during this period.
66. Robert Thurston briefly discussed newspaper reports of attacks on the police in Moscow during 1906–7. He saw the attacks as politically motivated and as a residue of the social and political hostilities of 1905 ("Police and People in Moscow," 330, 329–32).

toward the police has been well documented,[67] but far from all the attacks that occurred during the revolution were motivated by political militance. Violent confrontations with the police took a variety of forms that represented the whole spectrum of street violence seen during these years. If one views these attacks as part of the larger phenomenon of street violence during the revolution, one comes to the conclusion that the attacks were motivated by a wider set of causes, and that they were not simply evidence of the hostility of 1905 lingering into 1906 and 1907, but part of a broader and more long-term wave of social disorder, with a more complex composition, that crested only in 1906.

Some attacks were clearly associated with conscious political activity or followed closely on the heels of political events. In one case, workers leaving a government warehouse after their shift broke out singing the "Marseillaise." When a policeman demanded that they stop they threw rocks at him. In another case, workers using their fists and rocks to persuade cab drivers to go on strike were interrupted by policemen who shot into the crowd. The workers responded by hurling their rocks at the police; one unfortunate policeman was caught, disarmed, and "beaten half to death." The boulevard press also included numerous examples of violent confrontations after police and troops tried to break up rallies or demonstrations.[68]

Other attacks were associated with ordinary crime. A twenty-seven-year-old baker, "in a violent mood," was pestering people on the street, yelling and shoving, until he finally attracted the attention of a policeman. Irritated at being stopped, the baker attacked the policeman and tried to swipe his revolver. Shouting "Comrades, to the rescue!" he was quickly joined by a group of friends who tried to free him. More policemen arrived to disperse the crowd and take the baker off to the precinct.[69]

---

67. Zelnik, *A Radical Worker*, 96; McDaniels, *Autocracy, Capitalism, and Revolution*, 175; Brower, "Labor Violence," 428–31.
68. "Stolknovenie rabochikh s politsiei," *PG*, July 12, 1906; "Vcherashnyi den' v Peterburge: Stolknovenie rabochikh s politsiei," *PG*, July 25, 1906.
69. "DP: Napadenie tolpy na gorodovogo," *PL*, June 29, 1906. On clashes with professional criminals see "DP: Napadenie vorov na gorodovogo," *PL*, September 19, 1906; I. K-ov, "Prestupnaia kommersiia," *PL*, August 18, 1906. Cases of criminals attacking policemen to free their comrades were reported frequently in *PL* before 1905 as well. Soldiers had also become common victims of hooligan attacks, much to the horror of *PL* writers, who viewed this as yet another sign of the decline of morals. In 1905 a general just back from Port Arthur was attacked by hooligans on Nevskii Prospekt: "DP," *PL*, March 1, 1905. However, soldiers might also be involved in hooligan violence as perpetrators. For example, one of the mass brawls of 1906 was begun by drunken soldiers: "Razgrom pritonov," *PL*, June 27, 1906.

The great majority of cases, however, fall in between overtly political and criminal situations. They did not occur in connection with revolutionary events and do not seem to have been motivated by a conscious, politically determined hostility toward the police; yet they seem to possess more in the way of rebellious content than the personal animosity or immediate material incentives that marked other attacks. The following two reports are typical of these incidents. The first was reported in a separate, but unsigned, article entitled "Attack on a Policeman Conducting Prisoners":

> A policeman was attacked for the purpose of freeing the prisoner he was conducting to the precinct station, a hooligan who had been arrested in connection with a row (*debosh*) he had started in the tavern "Peking" near the Triumphal Gates. The policeman was taking him to the station of the Fourth Narva Precinct when about ten people—unemployed and loafers (*bez opredelennogo zaniatii*)—standing not far from the station began throwing stones at him. The policeman held the hooligan's arm tight. Suddenly a shot came from the crowd. Five bullets all missed him. Then one hooligan slashed his ear and shoulder with a knife. [The policeman] took out his revolver just as other policemen arrived (attracted by the sound of shots), and the crowd dispersed. On the street lay a bootmaker, famous here as Isaac the Ataman, his head bleeding from a gunshot wound.[70]

The second comes from the crime column and is headed "An Attack on a Policeman":

> At 10:00 P.M. on June 27th, an enormous crowd assembled along Zabalkanskii Prospekt, near the Novomoskovskii Bridge on the Obvodnyi Canal. Disorder was provoked when drunken hooligans and workers attacked a policeman who was trying to disarm them. The policeman suffered a knife wound but managed to draw his sword and wound his attacker. Then some other workers came to the aid of the policeman. They fetched more police, who were able to disperse the crowd.[71]

The first thing to notice here, as in the case of brawling, is that *Peterburgskii listok* did not dismiss either of these as the work of an irrational "mob" composed exclusively of criminals or social outcasts. These events were portrayed as even more goal-oriented than the hooligan brawls. In the first example the goal was to free a comrade, a fairly common cause of

70. "Napadenie na gorodovogo s arestantom," *PL*, September 3, 1906.
71. "DP: Napadenie na gorodovogo," *PL*, June 28, 1906.

attacks even before the revolution, and in the second case to avoid surrendering weapons. Neither is, strictly speaking, a political act (the "comrade" under arrest had been picked up for a civil disorder—raising a ruckus in a bar). Yet it is the targets not the goals of the attacks, and the profusion of assaults on policemen during this period, that give this form of street violence deeper political overtones than brawling or other forms of hooliganism.

As with the incidents of brawling and destruction one must ask whether these clashes were in reality some kind of revolutionary political protest that had been attributed in the boulevard press to a criminal element to diminish their importance. But again placement of the reports and the language used in describing the incidents show that the boulevard press was able to grant legitimacy to events it considered politically motivated, while still distinguishing between clearly criminal acts and the murkier incidents of hooligan violence. The first hooligan incident cited above was published as a separate article of special interest, the other in the crime chronicle. Confrontations with the police with clear (or clearer) political connections, such as those involving the public singing of revolutionary songs, were reported in the daily list of revolutionary events.[72] Hooligan attacks on the police differed from other lower-class actions, such as strikes and demonstrations, in both goals and methods, in much the same way that hooligan rioting differed. Striking workers called for economic improvement and political reform in a system *Peterburgskii listok* also regarded as deplorable; thus these acts were endowed with a certain legitimacy. The lack of such goals and the use of violence against authorities for comparatively trivial reasons deprived hooligan attacks of that legitimacy. On the other hand, hooligan attacks were not prompted by criminal or purely material gain. Both the incidents cited here demonstrated a willingness to confront and resist authority; both displayed a conflict with authority that had specific and rational goals. Thus, while maintaining distinctions among various forms of street violence, the boulevard press placed these examples in between the activities of the revolutionary labor movement and the work of "mobs" or criminal gangs. In terms of political content they stand closer to legitimate protest than hooligan brawling does by virtue of their direct attack on figures of authority.

That hooligan violence against the police straddled traditional categories of politics and crime is even more apparent when we look at the partici-

72. For example, "Vcherashnyi den'," *PL*, July 2, 1906; "Zabastovki," *PL*, July 16, 1906.

pants in the attacks. Again the key to understanding these incidents is their identification as hooliganism and the identification of some attackers as hooligans. In the two cases cited above the participants were described as a combination of hooligans and workers. Isaac the Ataman combined the two in a single identity: he was a shoemaker, a worker, but his nickname was a typical one among the leaders of hooligan youth gangs and professional criminal gangs. In contrast, participants in labor actions were always identified as workers, and participants in massive brawling and destruction were almost exclusively referred to as hooligans. Perpetrators of ordinary crimes were usually identified with their crimes rather than with a social group: thief, murderer, drunkard. Clearly some care was taken in the boulevard-press sociology of lower-class unrest to classify participants, but we can be more specific than this, and even more so in this period than in the years before 1905.

When participants in lower-class unrest were identified by occupation in the press reports they were almost exclusively from the ranks of marginal and casual workers—*chernorabochie, podenshchiki* or "former workers," "loafers," "people without specified occupation."[73] These were all people on the bottom lower-class rung of the social ladder, whose hold on economic security was tenuous even in the best of times. Under revolutionary conditions, the insecurity of the casual labor population was intensified. Strikes and lockouts increased the number of unemployed through closures and blacklisting and generally limited the opportunities for gainful employment. Moreover, with the forces maintaining law and order "vanishing into thin air" the opportunities for illegal or semi-legal activities increased in scope. Casual laborers and unskilled workers were the most likely to cross back and forth between the worlds of work and crime. Thus the majority of people likely to engage in the forms of street violence that straddled criminal and revolutionary mass actions were drawn from a social group that also allowed crossover between two worlds. It also stands to reason that many people who participated in hooligan actions enjoyed a bit of brawling or rabble-rousing in the evenings after a hard day at work or a long day of looking for work, or a day of choosing not to look for work. But it is important to remember that these were people who participated, however tangentially, in the working-class world. Their responses to their own economic problems, to revolutionary agitation, and to the revolution itself were assertive, dramatic, destructive, and

---

73. "DP: Napadenie na ulitse," *PL*, March 16, 1905; "DP: Nozhovaia rasprava," *PL*, July 26, 1906; "Prodelka shaiki khuliganov," *PL*, October 6, 1906.

misogynist, but these response were forged in the same neighborhoods that produced labor's heroes. Given these connections with the working class, hooligan attacks on the police should be considered as related to the workers' movement. Since the revolution unleashed a torrent of such hooligan demonstrations, they should be considered a part of the revolutionary experience. But how was hooliganism related to revolutionary acts and relevant to an understanding of the revolution? What are the politics of crime and violence?

▣ A Politics of Hooliganism

The relationship between political and criminal or "mob" collective action, especially when such acts involve violence, has long been recognized as problematical. The basic dilemma was neatly formulated by William Rosenberg and Diane Koenker in their comparison of two main theoretical models. In Louis Chevalier's work, the "laboring classes" came to be identified with the "dangerous classes," and real differences between the two were ignored. Marx and Engels, on the other hand, categorically distinguished the proletariat from the lumpenproletarian "scum," a view that overlooked not only the real social milieu of the lower classes, in which workers mingled with "the poor, pickpockets, street hawkers, and deserters," but also the fact that individuals could cross boundaries between the various worlds of work and crime. I would add that more recent historical works cannot resolve the problems this relationship raises, because they focus on forms of collective violence, such as food riots or agrarian revolts, that have much more easily recognizable political origins and can more clearly be identified with existing categories of political action.[74] Hooligan violence, however, and hooligans themselves do not fit into either of these models.

As the kinds of violence discussed here indicate, attempts to distinguish between political and criminal violence have been troublesome because the categories have been too rigidly defined, leaving little room for events that fell outside them. Individuals might engage in both kinds of activities, and some behavior, like hooliganism, can share characteristics with each. It is even possible that the marginalization of the labor movement in 1906 and 1907 may have pushed some workers across the line that separated

---

74. William G. Rosenberg and Diane P. Koenker, "The Limits of Formal Protest: Worker Activism and Social Polarization in Petrograd and Moscow, March to October, 1917," *American Historical Review*, vol. 92, no. 2 (1987):305–6; see also Louise Tilly, "The Food Riot as a Form of Political Conflict in France," *Journal of Interdisciplinary History* 2 (1972).

organized labor activism from undisciplined expressions of rage. The suppression of the labor movement in December 1905 and the subsequent lockouts and blacklisting made everyday life much harder for thousands of workers, and that made "legitimate" labor actions more difficult to organize, opening the door to frustrated and explosive displays of anger.

Hooligan violence makes it clear that it is time to address popular unrest in less narrowly political terms. The politics of crime and violence in 1905 and 1906 shows that struggles for power take less overt and less constructive forms among people with limited access to the beneficial weapons of the strong, such as literacy, education, relative financial security, and hope. Social and cultural rebelliousness can be an expression of protest on the part of the marginal, inarticulate, and hateful. Is that protest political? Hooligan challenges during the revolution had little to do with constitutional politics or labor politics, but hooligans' assertion of power on the streets was political in two ways. First, hooligans who brought their rowdy, dangerous, and destructive actions to the central streets were engaged in a politics of everyday life, which involved negotiating for control over public behavior and symbols of control. Second, the hooligans who were lashing out at symbols of authority or authority figures themselves were protesting their powerlessness in a society that oppressed them as members of the lower classes. The same political and social milieu can spawn both people drawn to organized and disciplined movements for change and those who engage in ugly, self-destructive, and unsympathetic attacks on individual strangers, property, and symbols of authority. We need to recognize that lower-class struggles against the autocracy, the police, or respectable society's cultural authority can take a variety of forms, from the unsavory to the heroic. In his work on resistance to racism among Blacks in Great Britain, Paul Gilroy describes the ways that social and political structures limit the protest options of the dispossessed: the unemployed, for example, cannot organize and go on strike even if they perceive the economy to be the cause of their troubles. Gilroy goes on to say that when anarchic or destructive actions result societies deflect responsibility for them by denying the political significance of violent destruction or rioting and calling it crime.[75] We need to resist the temptation to dismiss hooligan violence, as most did at the time, as motiveless

---

75. Paul Gilroy, *"There Ain't No Black in the Union Jack": The Cultural Politics of Race and Nation* (Chicago, 1991), 32–34, 153–222. Gilroy's epigraph quotes the writer June Jordan, who wrote: "If you make and keep my life horrible, then when I can tell the truth, it will be a horrible truth; it will not sound good or look good, or God willing, feel good to you either."

or incomprehensible. In so doing, Russians closed their eyes to a critical form of lower-class hostility.

Rather than view hooliganism as a phenomenon entirely distinct from the labor unrest of 1905–7, it makes more sense to see both as variants of lower-class protest against diverse forms of oppression. Despite the many significant differences between the hooligans' mentality and that of radical working-class demonstrators and despite the differences between the acts they engaged in, their hostility to society sprang from similar sources of powerlessness and defiance. The revolution brought out other connections. Hooligans' assaults on respectable culture resembled conscious workers' political demands for control over their lives and cultural demands for respect. All forms of hooligan activity and working-class protest were performed in public by members of the lower classes, all were marked by a historically unprecedented willingness to confront established authorities directly, all were perceived as signs of social or class hostility, and all exhibited, on a mass scale for the first time in Russian history, the novelty of lower-class visibility and power.

Hooligans also shared with workers an abiding hostility toward certain aspects of the culture of the middle and intelligentsia classes. Many different forms of this antagonism existed, although it only gradually became apparent to Russian civil society. Political studies of 1905 have shown that, despite the alliance of workers with liberals during the fall of 1905, workers distrusted the liberal intelligentsia, whose social condescension was never entirely hidden by political support.[76] The social gulf was often symbolized by cultural differences—in manners, education, and expectations of submission—as well as by political differences. After the liberation movement's constitutional victory in October 1905, politics and culture were entwined in the increasingly pessimistic discussions of the relations between the intelligentsia and the people that permeated the liberal press around the time of the election campaign for the First Duma. M. I. Fridman, for example, writing in *Rech* in April 1906, believed that the Kadets had the most to offer the workers as a political party, but he feared that "the workers' distrust of the intelligentsia . . . had created insurmountable barriers against [our] enlightenment (in the broadest sense of the word) work among the property-less and 'dark' strata of the population."[77] This

76. Surh, *1905*, 379–82, 411 n. 3; Emmons, *Political Parties*, 359–78; Shuster, *Peterburgskie rabochie*, 242–43; William G. Rosenberg, "Kadets and the Politics of Ambivalence," in *Essays on Russian Liberalism*, ed. Charles E. Timberlake (Columbia, Mo., 1972), 145–46.
77. M. I. Fridman, "Rabochie i partiia narodnoi svobody," *Rech'*, April 1, 1906. See also E. Grimm, "Povorot," *Rech'*, April 4, 1906.

hostility bears some similarity to the well-known tensions that arose between conscious workers and the radical intelligentsia before 1905.[78] The boulevard press noticed exactly this form of cultural conflict and social animosity in the behavior of hooligans even before the 1905–1907 Revolution. Some of the same issues that drove a wedge between workers and radical intellectuals and workers and liberals were the issues at stake in the street war between hooligans and respectable pedestrians: manners, hegemony, and submission.

In all of these cases, class differences and political tensions were experienced and recorded in explicitly cultural terms. Semen Kanatchikov repeatedly felt humiliated before his middle-class acquaintances by his inability to match their manners and poise. Liberals and radicals alike dazzled, irritated, amused, and infuriated the earnest young worker-*intelligent*, and these experiences formed a backdrop for the main themes in his tale of coming to consciousness. Visits to the homes of well-off, fashionable liberals in St. Petersburg or socialist bohemians in Saratov often included confusing and embarrassing moments when Kanatchikov and his friends faced mysterious behavioral norms and "alien way[s] of life and thinking."[79] On one occasion Kanatchikov was mortified when he misunderstood and mispronounced an unfamiliar word and on another when his nervousness intensified his unrefined table manners.[80] These blunders left Kanatchikov forever ambivalent toward the social elite, but, unlike those who became hooligans, he was simultaneously determined to master the "proper" behavior and culture of the intelligentsia. Most important, cultural difference contributed to his determination to establish an autonomous workers' movement for genuine change.

Hooligans reported the same pressures but were affected differently by them and drew different conclusions from them. Aleksei Svirskii, a writer of popular sketches of the city, who himself began life in a working-class family, recorded the "burning shame" of a nineteen-year-old hooligan, who told the following story to explain why he abandoned the life of a respectable, if poor, youth:

> I remember how I became friends with one of the boys in my class. His name was Trikartov. He was a strong boy and fearless, which was why I liked him. He was also rich, while my father was a poor, simple man, a saddle maker. Once Trikartov invited me to

78. Wildman, *Workers' Revolution*; Zelnik, "Russian Bebels"; McDaniels, *Autocracy, Capitalism, and Revolution*, 208–30.
79. Zelnik, *A Radical Worker*, 105.
80. Ibid., 90–92, 102–10, 189–96, 382–84.

his house, and I went. When we arrived, it turned out that he lived in a private house with a fancy doorman and coachman. I wanted to run off in the other direction, but it was too late. . . . When his mother came up to us in rustling silks . . . I bowed my head and stuck out my hand. . . . Then we were called to the table, and that is where my torment began. I didn't know what, how, or with what to eat. I got confused and blushed. After dinner Vitenka took me to his room, where we played, wrestled, and read until it got dark. As I got ready to go home Vitia led me to the stairs, but on the landing he stopped me and said, "Zhenia, you are going to be offended by what I say, but I want to give you some advice. You should never eat fish with a knife. It is not done. And also when a lady greets you, never be the first to proffer your hand." I didn't walk down the stairs but rolled down like a ball. In my burning shame even tears came to my eyes. Oh, God, you could never understand. A year went by, and still I remembered everything. At night I would lie in bed and suddenly recall how I ate my fish at the Trikartovs', and I would see it lying in a pool of blood. That's how ashamed I was.[81]

Zhenia's response to the experience was to seek revenge. With two robberies and one attempted murder on his record, he never outgrew the particular pleasure of shocking ladies and girls on the central streets of the city. "It's amazing," he said, "how cowardly people can be. I can frighten a whole streetful of people all by myself."[82] In contrast, Kanatchikov's response to his embarrassment produced satisfactions of a more enduring nature, but in both men's lives, intense emotional experiences of their cultural shortcomings played major roles in shaping their consciousness. In retrospect we can see the political potential of this sort of cultural conflict as an indication of the polarization to come.

Even in 1905 at the height of class unity in opposition to the autocracy, between the *verkhi*, or upper classes, and the *nizy*, or lower classes, the euphoria of political alliance could not efface social and cultural tensions. The boulevard press portrayed social tensions along with social unity, and during the revolution awareness of a generalized lower-class animosity was also dawning among educated elite. Even among liberals, who were far less prone than conservatives to dismiss lower-class violence as mob lawlessness, fears of a jacquerie or *Pugachevshchina* were never far from the surface. Significantly, some recognized the cultural content and the

81. A. [I.] Svirskii, "Peterburgskie khuligany: Ocherki," *Peterburg i ego zhizn'* (St. Petersburg, 1914), 264–65.
82. Svirskii, "Peterburgskie khuligany," 266.

power of symbols in the social tensions. In an article on the liberals' dilemma, E. N. Trubetskoi, an eminent Kievan professor of philosophy, warned radicals against encouraging an armed uprising. The article was written after the October Manifesto and after the waves of hooligan, peasant, and pogromist violence that followed during the "Days of Freedom," but before the armed uprisings of December:

> The wave of anarchy that is advancing from all sides, and that at the present time threatens the legal government, would quickly sweep away any revolutionary government: the embittered masses would then turn against the real or presumed culprits; they would subject to destruction the *entire intelligentsia*; the masses would begin indiscriminately to slaughter all who wear German clothes [i.e., the well-dressed]—conservatives, liberals, revolutionaries.[83]

This is not a simple dismissal of all mass action as mob irrationality; it is an acknowledgment of the depths of the social chasm in Russia and the bitterness of lower-class hatred. It is also a statement that would make no sense if one's perception of 1905 excluded hooliganism. What is important here for understanding the role hooligans played in the revolution is Trubetskoi's recognition of a generalized hatred for all the *verkhi*, and its expression in cultural terms. He specified that the masses would slaughter not the wealthy or the educated or the powerful, but the well-dressed, wrapped in foreign ways.

As the "organ of everyday life" it claimed to be, *Peterburgskii listok* recorded the everyday experience of the revolution and devoted much attention to analyzing the sources and content of hooligan hostility. Again and again one hears the same two refrains in the chorus of outrage over the hooligan question. First, hooligans had only contempt for respectable society and its values. As a biologist put it in an interview in *Peterburgskaia gazeta*, "They spit on everything."[84] Second, they refused to act properly—that is, submissively, as tradition and their social status dictated—something no civilized Western European capital would permit.[85] What had been implicit in the prerevolutionary boulevard press, that hooliganism challenged established authority and threatened Russia's march toward civilization, now became explicit in the revolutionary context. In

83. E. N. Trubetskoi, "Dve diktatury," *Russkie vedomosti*, November 16, 1905; quoted (with emphasis and bracketed material) in Ascher, *The Revolution of 1905*, 296–97.
84. N. G-e, "Interesy dnia."
85. Nevskii, "Stolichnaia iazva (Ocherki iz zhizni Peterburgskikh khuliganov)," Part 1, *PG*, May 30, 1905; "Nochnye bezporiadki," *NV*, June 27, 1906.

May 1905, one of *Peterburgskii listok*'s regular columnists wrote in reference to hooliganism that

> cars and trams run along the streets, women appear in the latest Parisian fashions, but look at humanity and you see that civilization is no farther along than our ancestors in the Bronze Age. . . . As always in times of transformation, from under every rock crawls some dark, anti-social being.[86]

As for the hooligans themselves the revolution did not create hooliganism or its challenge to social authority and respectable culture, but it provided the environment for hooliganism to multiply "with the speed of a microbe," as one hooligan put it a few years later.[87] Hooliganism coincided with social and political unrest, but it did much more than simply coexist with revolution. It was an integral part of the upheaval that occurred in Russia as the old regime began to disintegrate and people of all kinds pressed their claims. Hooligans, unlike activist workers, lacked the skills, motives, and courage needed to initiate a serious assault on government power, as discussed in the previous chapter. They surfaced where authority was already vulnerable, but, unlike the Black Hundreds or other reactionary groups, Petersburg hooligans were neither reacting to changes they found distasteful nor attempting to preserve the status quo. And their actions before 1905 make it clear that they were also no mere by-product of revolution. Hooligans were expressing their bitterness at their position in society with the only tools available to them. The visibility, assertiveness, and increasing discontent of politicized workers, the absence of police authority, and respectable society's inability to exert social control all gave hooligans license for increasingly defiant exhibits of rage. They, in turn, pushed the revolution in new directions, sapped official strength when it was badly needed, created new rifts between social groups—rifts along social and cultural rather than exclusively political lines—and took the revolution along "the high road to complete anarchy and social chaos."[88]

The connections between hooligans and labor are not meant to demonstrate that hooliganism was a form of nascent labor protest. Clearly, hooligans and hooliganism were different in many ways from activist workers and their movement. Nor are the links between the two meant to attribute

---

86. Pchela, "Odichanie," *PL*, May 16, 1905.
87. Svirskii, "Peterburgskie khuligany," 258.
88. W. H. Stuart, Acting U. S. Consul, Batum, letter dated October 13, 1905; quoted in Ascher, *The Revolution of 1905*, 132.

some incipient heroism to the hooligans or to justify their obnoxious behavior and terrifying violence. But the history of hooliganism does show that hooligan violence was an integral feature of the revolutionary experience, with strong social and cultural ties to the labor movement and important political repercussions. It shows that destructive acts can originate in the same environment and spring from some of the same impulses that motivate constructive ones. It also demonstrates that even the most senseless violent crimes can express a form of rage that societies ignore at their own risk.

In these respects the portrait of revolutionary violence that appeared in the boulevard press differs substantially from models of collective violence elaborated by historians of Western Europe. Hobsbawm, Rudé, Thompson, and Tilly, to name only the most eminent, each presented a historically linear model of collective action in which "primitive" or "premodern" forms of collective violence gave way to "conscious" or "modern" forms that were characterized by politically evolved motives, methods, and goals. In each of these models, earlier forms of protest were displaced by the more advanced forms, as the working class developed "class consciousness." But linear models do not fit the Russian revolutionary situation. This is not to deny that a portion of the Russian working class did develop a conscious political outlook, eschew violence, and engage in disciplined activity, or that this conscious element dominated and led the working-class movement. However, conscious workers were only a small portion of the work force, not to mention of the entire lower-class population. Their actions did not displace less politicized collective violence but rather coexisted with it.[89] Street violence did not disappear or even diminish with the arrival of the conscious labor movement. Both movements increased in scope and scale beginning in 1905, and they did so in tandem.

Hooliganism was as much a product of Russia's rapid industrialization and government intransigence as the radical labor movement was. The breakdown of informal mechanisms of social authority that maintained control over the public behavior of the lower classes was a problem that arose everywhere in Europe with the appearance of modern industrial cities, and that remains in the postindustrial age. The specific anxieties street crime provoked, the social interaction it represented, and the political consequences it entailed are all associated with the kind of cultural conflict and class interaction that occurred when massive urban in-migration pro-

---

89. On the telescoping of industrialization in Russia and its consequences for the Russian labor movement see Bonnell, *Roots of Rebellion*.

duced new interclass experiences and perceptions and a new balance of power on city streets. By shifting our focus from economics to culture we can see that hooligan street violence was not a "primitive" or "premodern" conflict but a quintessentially urban and modern one. Recently historians have argued that more generalized forms of anti-authoritarianism did not appear in Russia until the resurgence of labor protest in 1912, following the government massacre of striking workers at the Lena Gold Fields in Siberia. This discussion of hooliganism shows that such unrest began much earlier and was recorded in the boulevard press, whose audience was especially sensitive to it, but that it began to be noticed by the old intelligentsia and educated elite only after 1912.[90]

Yet while hooligans shared much with workers—in many cases they were workers—hooligans were not workers acting qua workers. Their demonstrations were not labor-management disputes, they pressed no demands to improve their positions as workers, and their political significance was not manifested in actions against the state. In some respects, hooliganism bears a stronger resemblance to peasant forms of mass action and specifically to the peasants' revolutionary movement of 1905–7, with which it coincided. Like peasants, hooligans felt their subordination acutely and with resentment, yet they had little confidence in their ability to transform the social order. But if neither peasants nor hooligans were capable of mounting an independent assault on state or social power, they were both willing to exploit a power vacuum when they found one. John Bushnell made a similar argument for another "special case of Russian peasant rebellion": the mutinous soldiers of 1905–6. Under normal conditions, when the government's power seemed intact, the soldiers did their duty, but "when they believed the regime's writ had expired, soldiers mutinied."[91]

It is no accident that hooligan violence, like peasant rebellion and soldiers' mutinies, escalated in late 1905 and continued into 1906. In 1905, major hooligan surges often peaked in the aftermath of events that displayed the government's weakness. In the days following the Bloody Sunday massacre an eyewitness wrote, and not in the commercial press, that "whatever disturbances occurred after Sunday evening were due to hooligans and [the] worst elements of the town, who recognized the moment

90. Leopold Haimson and Ronald Petrusha, "Two Strike Waves in Imperial Russia, 1905–1907, 1912–1914," in *Strikes, Wars, and Revolutions in an International Perspective*, ed. Charles Tilly and Leopold Haimson (Cambridge, 1989).
91. Bushnell, *Mutiny*, 226, also 45–48.

as favorable."[92] Another great wave of hooligan violence began during the backlash that followed the issuance of the October Manifesto, and continued throughout 1906, peaking in the summer when political crises followed hard on each other's heels. During that period, from late 1905 through the summer of 1906, the political atmosphere was saturated with violence and discussions of violence. From October to December 1905, radical newspapers openly encouraged violence and openly debated the efficacy of armed uprising. Until December the government seemed too weak to respond.[93] Then in June and July 1906, when rumors about the dissolution of the Duma circulated amid contrary rumors about the creation of a liberal cabinet, political instability enabled the least politicized elements of society to assert themselves again. Demonstrations of political unrest often "spilled out from the factories onto the streets," mingling hooligans and conscious workers, despite efforts by the radical intelligentsia and the militant workers to separate themselves from less reputable elements.[94] The peasant rebellion also peaked, as is well known, in the summer of 1906. Activism among the least skilled workers and the unemployed was on the rise at the same time.[95] In addition, hooligans may have provided links between urban and rural revolution. Even the police conceded that when hooligans were expelled from the capital, they had no trouble making their way back to the city from their villages. And as we will see in the following chapter, rural authorities, from this period on, complained about the disruptive influence of hooligans in the countryside.

While hooligan behavior can exist independently of revolution (as it did in Western Europe at this time), hooliganism in some form also seems to be an inevitable companion of revolutionary strife. The kind of anti-authoritarian hostility that hooligans exhibited, with its destructive eruptions and symbolic cultural content and targets, is a common denominator in modern cities. The conflicts inherent in the city's mixed and transient populations and the inevitable presence of the utterly dispossessed guarantee a measure of alienation and bitterness. This hostility may not be capable of leading to conscious revolutionary or even reform movements, but in times of uncertainty and vacillating authority it is an inescapable, desta-

92. Sir Charles Hardinge to Lord Landsdowne, January 27, 1905; quoted in Ascher, *The Revolution of 1905*, 93; Surh, *1905*, 171.
93. On the atmosphere of violence, see Surh, *1905*, 335, 342–44; Ascher, *The Revolution of 1905*, 293, 307.
94. Shuster, *Peterburgskie rabochie*, 246; "Arestovannyi miting," *PL*, July 2, 1906.
95. Shuster, *Peterburgskie rabochie*, 246–47.

bilizing factor in urban social life. In times of transformation (such as 1900–1905) it manifests itself, and in times of revolution (such as 1905–7) it can rage out of control.

The newspapers of the street were committed to reporting everything happening on the street, and that included escalating crime, rioting, and the ambush of police authority, along with explicitly revolutionary activity. The boulevard press shaped its readers' perceptions of the revolution by distinguishing categories of unrest and labeling them. But while these categories neither exhausted the variety of lower-class behavior during the revolution nor fully explained it, the boulevard newspapers reported disturbances that most other sources were only beginning to acknowledge. Consequently the boulevard press gives us perspective on a kind of discontent that has been ignored by historians but was certainly not fabricated by the press.

The raw rage of the marginal poor became an inescapable fact of life in Russia during the 1905–1907 Revolution, and it was a harbinger of things to come. The origins of class hostility and social polarization that became clear in 1914 were already in operation at least as early as 1905. Even before 1905, hooliganism was an early warning sign of lower-class responses to respectable culture and to the power of the privileged classes. The everyday experience of the 1905–1907 Revolution introduced hooliganism, in its most violent forms, to Russian society at large. In the years that followed, hooliganism erupted in new settings, and, in a society haunted by memories of revolutionary hooliganism, it evolved new forms and meanings.

3 Ripples Spread
To the Village, the Law, and the Arts

From every corner of Russia, from Arkhangelsk to Yalta and from Vladivostok to Petersburg, fly reports of the horrors of the new, mass, motiveless crime that prevents people from living and growing and breathing in peace. The countryside is seized with terror. The city is in a panic.

—V. I. Gromov
Journal of the Ministry of Justice, 1913

The public spectacle of revolutionary power, exhibited by the masses and educated society alike, made manifest the changes that had occurred in Russian society in the previous decades. The organized assault of liberal forces on the autocracy demonstrated the existence in Russia of a "public sphere," a space for civil society to develop a public discourse and public opinion (implicitly a plurality of opinions) independent of the government, which in turn allowed society to effect democratic political change.[1] But the evolution of a public sphere had concrete visual and physical effects as well as social and political ones. The sudden visibility of the lower classes, their undeniable power when united, and the violence of revolutionary events made it clear that power in the public space was changing hands. During and after the revolution a larger audience in locations all over the empire was becoming aware of the lessons learned earlier by St. Petersburg's respectable pedestrians and readers of the boulevard press—that the massive influx of lower-class migrants had transformed social relations on the streets.

It was in this context that hooliganism evolved from an essentially urban phenomenon into a broad cultural category useful in a remarkable variety of situations. The diverse examples discussed in this chapter—rural hooliganism, the legal debates over regulating hooliganism, and avant-garde artists' use of hooligan tactics—each developed for specific purposes,

---

1. Jürgen Habermas, *The Structural Transformation of the Public Sphere*, trans. Thomas Burger (Cambridge, Mass., 1991); for applications of Habermas to Russian society see McReynolds, *The News*, 3, 12, 29, 288; Brower, *The Russian City*, 94, 172.

but all shared a number of characteristics. All represented negotiations concerning the uses, control, and definition of public space. All were agents of and responses to the erosion of traditions brought about by migration, commercialization, and the diversification of life in city and village alike. And all represented attempts to assimilate social change after the 1905–1907 Revolution diminished expectations of lower-class subordination and deference. In each case hooliganism expressed tensions that arose as cultural diversity developed and consensus was breaking down—in rural society (both among the peasantry and between peasant and noble) and within the educated elite.

The discourse on hooliganism begun in the commercial press and embellished during the revolution provided handy images for capturing and understanding all these changes. After the peasant revolution was brutally suppressed by punitive expeditions and the government regained its control of rural society, there remained a residue of popular unrest that took forms associated with urban hooliganism. As hooligan behavior spread, discussion about it also reached beyond the pages of the boulevard press to appear in professional legal circles and elite "thick" journals, sensationalistic novels, and daily newspapers of all political stripes. Hooliganism became the subject of debate in the highest government bodies as it entered discussions about judicial and police reform. As the ripples spread, a wide range of voices was heard, from the shrill, hysterical outcry of frightened provincial landowners to the precise juridical distinctions of legal discourse. In this spectrum of responses to hooliganism one finds explicit confirmation of the views implied in the boulevard press's prerevolutionary coverage of hooliganism, but one also hears new explanations for the phenomenon and new propositions for eradicating it. When cultural diversity took hooligan forms among avant-garde artists, the same publications that had decried the hooligan assault on tradition and civilization were horrified by the futurists' challenge to classical Russian culture and to the ability of the old intelligentsia to determine cultural standards. Every society has rebels who attack the authorities to assert their own vision, and everywhere defenders of tradition cry out to protect what they cherish, but as modern societies become increasingly complex and diverse, the struggles multiply. Such battles may not be powerful enough to topple a state, but they reveal the forces that hold societies together or tear them apart.

⧈ *Hooliganism in the Countryside*

The insolence and defiance associated with urban hooliganism were first detected among Russian peasants amid the revolutionary wave of destruction that began in 1905. In her study of the provincial nobility, Roberta Manning noted that "landowners and local officials were surprised to see the resentful and rebellious faces when peasants dropped their deferential, self-abnegating masks."[2] After the revolution, hooligan insolence remained and the landowners' fears did not subside. One recalled that by the summer of 1908 "something essential, something irreparable had occurred and it was within the people themselves."[3] Animosity replaced the "peasants' previous courtesy, their friendliness, bows and willingness to pull off the road [upon encountering the vehicle of a local nobleman]."[4] In the following years rural hooliganism swelled to epidemic proportions in some provinces, leading many among the provincial nobility to consider it "the main scourge of the countryside."[5] By 1913 the Ministry of Internal Affairs felt the need to convene a special commission, under the chairmanship of A. I. Lykoshin, to study its impact and devise measures for its eradication.[6] The proliferation of hooliganism in the countryside makes clear that both the behavior and the conceptual categories identified earlier in the city were useful in a new context. But because the rural scene was no longer so isolated from city life, hooliganism also became one of the main symbols of the growing interaction between city and countryside.

Rural hooliganism took many of the same forms seen in the city, including the disparate range of offenses it encompassed, which made rural hooliganism equally difficult to define precisely. As in Petersburg, rural definitions of hooliganism shared an emphasis on the way in which the acts were carried out: the hooligan's display of insolence or defiance—*nakhal'*—or, in some cases, the very fact that behavior previously circumscribed by noble authority was now openly flaunted. The literature on rural hooliganism was characterized by outraged reports of hooligan incidents, ranging from annoying pranks to terrifying physical assaults,

2. Roberta T. Manning, *The Crisis of the Old Order in Russia: Gentry and Government* (Princeton, 1982), 147.
3. Quoted in Manning, *The Crisis of the Old Order*, 146.
4. Quoted in Manning, *The Crisis of the Old Order*, 147.
5. I. Zhilkin, "Provintsial'noe obozrenie," *Vestnik evropy* 2 (1913): 365–66 and passim; and 4 (1913): 363 and passim.
6. In his article on rural hooliganism, "Rural Crime in Tsarist Russia: The Question of Hooliganism, 1905–1914," *Slavic Review*, vol. 37, no. 2 (1978), Neil Weissman relied primarily on the documents of this commission. Some Lykoshin Commission documents, including provincial governors' reports and the final report, are also to be found in "Ob obrazovanii pri zemskom otdele Osoboi mezhduvedomstvennoi Komissii dlia vyrabotki nekotorykh meropriiatii pri khuliganstve," TsGAOR, fond 102 (Department of Police), delo 14, chast' 21a and chast' 21b (2-oe deloproizvodstvo).

in which hooligans displayed disrespect for traditional authorities or traditional values. Even more than city officials, rural authorities were shaken by such exhibitions of popular disrespect and defiance. Not only noble landowners but government representatives, priests, peasant parents and elders, and especially the women of these groups were victims of hooligan offenses. A survey of marshals of the nobility produced "practically identical" answers to questions evaluating hooliganism: "Hooliganism takes the form not only of pranks, drunkenness, swearing, and disrespect for parents, elders, and women, but not uncommonly also of blasphemy, arson, and the destruction of public and private property."[7] P. P. Bashilov, the governor of Ufa, compiled massive and detailed data on hooliganism in his province. Among hooligan acts he included manifest disrespect for parents, elders, clergy, and other authorities; throwing rocks at passersby; breaking windows; tearing up trees, flowers, and vegetables but not for use; petty theft of edibles for use; demanding money from passersby; disturbing the peace; singing "uncensored" songs; swearing; yelling; carrying illegal arms; torturing animals; beating passersby; brawling; pestering women on the streets with verbal and physical abuse (up to and including rape); and numerous forms of destruction of property.[8] Such acts were proliferating, Bashilov thought, because the laws prohibiting them did not take into account the new attitudes hooligans exhibited, and the old laws prescribed punishments too lax to deter them.

Two of the most disturbing characteristics displayed by rural hooligans were their level of maliciousness and their special victimization of women. V. Ivanov, a reliable witness and usually straightforward commentator, reported the following as a typical case of village hooliganism:

> In the village N., a young noblewoman was calmly walking down the road when a hooligan, well known to everyone, approached and began to pester her, asking for her handkerchief. When she refused him, he threw her to the ground, held her down with his knee on her chest, took off her dress, and stripped her entirely. As a crowd gathered he shouted, "Look, guys, at the *intelligentka*." After this, he got up, hit her on the back of the head, and walked away as if nothing had happened.[9]

Such incidents were seen by many as a result of the "decline of morals" that afflicted rural society. But, whatever cultural transformation was in-

7. Cited in M. D-ii, "Bor'ba s khuliganstvom," *Rech'*, February 12, 1913.
8. P. P. Bashilov, "O khuliganstve kak prestupnom iavlenii, ne predusmotrennym zakonom," *Zhurnal ministerstva iustitsii* 2 (1913): 222–24.
9. V. Ivanov, *Chto takoe khuliganstvo?*(Orenburg, 1915), 8.

deed taking place, both in terms of a relaxation of strictures on female behavior and a decline in lower-class subservience, increased hooligan attacks on women can only partly be attributed to it. Certainly a loosening of moral constraints was evident in city and village alike. But it seems equally likely that hooligans, whose offenses were primarily exhibitions of power, chose female victims in the countryside for the same reasons they did so in the city: because women were perceived to be weaker and therefore easier targets. Just as hooligans attacked policemen when the vulnerability of the police was apparent to one and all, here, elite and educated women, who lacked the physical power to resist attacks, were easy marks. Women might have remained more secure from hooligan attacks if traditional morality had not also been challenged, but it was the combination of cultural transformation and perceptions of female weakness that appealed to hooligans seeking to assert their power in social life. Still, this hooligan's cry, identifying the noblewoman as a member of the intelligentsia, suggests that class and culture, alongside gender, played a part in the attack. It is impossible to know how much meaning the hooligan attributed to his chosen words, but it is worth remarking that the hostility he expressed was directed against the woman's cultural status as much as her privileged position.

The belief that rural society was disintegrating under the pressure of hooligan violence and insolence was nourished by the publication and immediate popularity of I. A. Rodionov's potboiler *Our Crime* in 1909.[10] The novel begins with a gigantic, bloody, and brutal brawl and continues with an enumeration of every possible hooligan outrage. Rodionov portrayed village life as a world reeling under the effects of unremitting, senseless violence and animalistic savagery. The novel was a success among the rural nobility, who found it expressed their fears as well as their general estimation of the peasant population. One especially histrionic observer commented that the author "was exactly right" about the current state of rural life, and he added that a judge in his district "shed tears" while reading the book.[11]

Liberal and socialist opinion, however, tended to dismiss the picture portrayed in *Our Crime* and the consensus it claimed to represent. D. Zaslavskii, writing in *Sovremennyi mir* (The Contemporary World), protested that the nobility's view of hooliganism was nothing more than "hysterics, malicious lies, and ordinary, common ignorance." "The nobil-

10. I. A. Rodionov, *Nashe prestuplenie (Ne bred a byl')*, 1st ed. (St. Petersburg, 1909).

11. K. I. Fomenko, *Khuliganstvo* (Kiev, 1913).

ity," he declared, "is least of all qualified to judge peasant life. The slander of the landowner-writer Rodionov is no more convincing for being repeated by a thousand voices."[12] Many contemporary commentators charged the frightened nobles with exaggerating the hooligan threat, calling in the police for minor offenses that previously would have gone unreported and forgotten.[13] Since statistics on rural crime are even less reliable than those on urban crime, it is difficult to evaluate such accusations.[14] Both sides, however, saw hooliganism as something more than ordinary petty and violent crime. All observers combined petty crimes with brutal battery and rape in discussing hooliganism and found this mix a significant factor in the major political, social, and cultural changes taking place. And as hooliganism spread, definitions of hooligan behavior and its effects became more concrete, more politicized, and more contested.

The divergence in views of hooliganism was partly political and partly due to differences in perspective between rural and urban dwellers. Many leftists felt that the rural nobility, supported by central government figures, exaggerated the hooligan threat in order to enforce extra-legal repressive measures in revenge for the peasant uprising of the revolution. These writers accused nobles of applying the label hooligan indiscriminately, to all peasants and to all criminal offenses, based on class prejudice.[15] They saw rural hooliganism as a legacy of serfdom, of the peasants' ongoing discontent with the settlement of the land question, and of their relentless poverty—in other words, an almost inevitable response to centuries of harsh treatment.[16] Zaslavskii thought that only urban hooliganism could be considered a senseless criminal offense. Rural hooligans, he thought, were "ordinary *muzhiks*," and rural hooliganism, "the result of the unbreachable rift between landowners and peasants, about which discussion could no longer be calm and objective."[17] A. Petrishev, the

---

12. D. Zaslavskii, "Bor'ba s khuliganstvom," *Sovremennyi mir* 1 (1913): 125.
13. A. Petrishev, "Khronika vnutrennei zhizni: O khuliganakh," *Russkoe bogatstvo* 1 (1913): 334–39; Manning, *The Crisis of the Old Order*, 145; Zhilkin, "Provintsial'noe," *Vestnik evropy* 4 (1913): 362.
14. There is no doubt that crime *rates* were rising rapidly, but, it bears repeating, rising rates signify increased prosecution of crime. On crime rates in this period, see A. P. Mel'nikov, "Kolebaniia prestupnosti v tekuschchem stoletii," *Zhurnal ministerstva iustitsii* 5–6 (1917): 61–63, 113; S. S. Ostroumov, *Prestupnost' i ee prichiny v dorevoliutsionnoi Rossii*, 2d ed. (Moscow, 1980), 168–70.
15. Petrishev, "Khronika," 340–41, 346; V. Brusianin, "O khuliganakh i khuliganstve," *Novyi zhurnal dlia vsekh* 4 (1913): 147–48; S. I. Elpat'evskii, "Bezchinstvo," *Russkoe bogatstvo* 5 (1912): 86; Zaslavskii, "Bor'ba," 122–24; Weissman, "Rural Crime," 231.
16. Petrishev, "Khronika," 343, 346–47; Zaslavskii, "Bor'ba," 127.
17. Zaslavskii, "Bor'ba," 126–27.

political commentator for *Russkoe bogatstvo* and a vocal critic of the provincial nobility, regarded elite behavior as anything but a model of *kul'turnost'*, observing that "the ruling classes are on the same level [as the hooligans] in regard to morality, self-constraint, and respect for others." In his opinion they should be punished for their own displays of disrespect.[18]

These writers, however, never dismissed hooliganism, and they shared with their opponents on the right considerable common ground in their understanding of what hooliganism was. Although they interpreted behavior and its causes differently, they all recognized genuine changes in peasant behavior that indicated a new defiance in peasant mentality. Petrishev, for example, began by claiming that many of the petty offenses labeled hooliganism were nothing more than instances of the "injured vanity of rural petty tyrants": a peasant forgets to remove his hat, and he is punished as a hooligan. Petrishev was incensed by a case of alleged hooliganism in which a child, standing in the road, shook a stick at a general driving along in his carriage. Beside himself with fury, the general saw to it that the child's mother was severely punished. In fact, according to Petrishev, what happened was that when the general's carriage came charging down the road a group of mothers and children scattered except for one frightened child, whose stick was thrown at the horse in confusion. "Who is the hooligan here?" Petrishev asked rhetorically.[19] But, although he thought too many such "offenses" were punished as hooliganism, Petrishev went on to define hooliganism in much the same terms that one found in reactionary provincial publications, with emphasis on the cultural and class aspects of hooligan behavior:

> A person throws off the social bridle, and moral and religious constraints; "divine threats" do not frighten him, he doesn't fear society's opinion of him or the judgment of the courts because he is sure he will not be held responsible or punished; he emits the cry of a wild animal, with base instincts and motives: "I do what I want to do."[20]

There was a clear but unspoken (and probably not fully recognized) consensus that what marked hooliganism as special, new, and frightening was the hooligans' *nakhal'*, their willingness to exhibit publicly their lack of respect for traditional authorities and conventional social and cultural con-

18. Petrishev, "Khronika," 354.
19. Ibid., 334–35, 342–45.
20. Ibid., 352.

straints and their disregard for existing forms of social control. The critical difference here is that on the left publicists viewed hooliganism as a dangerous but understandable response to poverty, land hunger, and noble oppression, which demonstrated the bankruptcy of the old order. On the right, hooliganism was seen as violence for the sake of violence. There was some disagreement on the right over whether the acts were motiveless and aimless or whether they represented concerted attacks on authority, but in either case they signaled a deplorable disrespect for rural authority.

Thus analyses of rural hooliganism, on both the left and the right, connected it much more explicitly with disrespect and class hostility than the Petersburg press coverage of hooliganism in the first years of the century had done. The cultural conflict that had been vaguely perceived by boulevard-press writers was clearly evident in the countryside after 1907. In many cases, rural hooligans in this period openly declared their hostility toward the elite, as in the case of the assaulted *intelligentka* cited above. In cases of vandalism, the destruction of everything from windows and fences to grave-site crosses and manor houses was evidence that the formal strictures of rank and the informal mechanisms of social control no longer constrained behavior. The hooligans' willingness to engage in such behavior was almost universally taken as a sign of popular protest rather than as a purely criminal act:

> The hooligan reacts like a bull to a red flag when confronted with symbols of power, intelligence, and material wealth. By making open, public attacks on those who possess these, he seeks to express his hatred for them, and this gratifies his depraved and brutal nature.[21]

Village hooligans confirmed such impressions by strolling around late at night singing songs like these:

Я гуляю по ночам	At night I strut around,
Не поддаюсь богачам	And rich men don't get in my way.
Я любому богачу	Just let some rich guy try,
Рыло на бок сворочу	And I'll screw his head on upside-down.

21. M. A. Goranovskii, *Khuliganstvo i mery bor'by s nim* (Grodno, 1913), 6.

Мы гуляем по ночам	We strut around at night,
Не уважим богачам	Doing what we please.
Кулаки свои распустим	We just let our fists fly
Богачей гулят не пустим	To keep the rich in line.[22]

Мы ребята-ёжики	We are the Porcupine Boys.
По карманам ножики	Knives in every pocket,
По три гири на весу	Rocks on ropes to swing at you,
Револьвер на поясу	Revolvers in our waistbands too.[23]

The pronounced class aspect of rural hooliganism supports arguments, made on both the left and the right, that it was a substitute for more overt political actions, which had become too dangerous by 1907. Unlike politically motivated and organized actions of the revolutionary period, hooligan acts were rarely premeditated or organized, and hooligans did not press a political program of any kind.[24] Yet the links are also striking and should not be overlooked. The difficulty of pinning down the precise political content (like other aspects) of rural hooliganism lies in the very diversity of its forms. Looking at rural hooliganism in the context of its urban roots, we can see that it fell somewhere between direct political protest and ordinary crime. It bore a strong resemblance to what James C. Scott has called "everyday resistance."[25] Scott's "weapons of the weak"

---

22. Vasilii Kniazev, "Sovremennaia derevnia o sebe samoi: Chastushki Peterburg-skoi gubernii," *Sovremennik* 4 (1912).

23. A. Sh-v, "Khuliganstvo v derevne i ego 'poeziia,'" *Vologodskii listok*, June 23, 1913. As is typical of folk songs, these examples exist in many versions. "The Porcupine Boys" was a widely recorded song, preserved in numerous versions from different regions, including this Tver' version: "My rebiata ezhiki/ U nas nozhiki litye/ My otchaianny, otpety/ Iz otchaiannykh otchaianiia/ Kolotili, bu-khali/ Kolotit' nas khoteli//My rebiata ezhiki/ U nas v karmanakh nozhiki/ My Sibiri ne boimsia/ Iz Sibiri ubezhim/ Kupim nozhiki podol'she/ Vsekh liudei pere-svezhim." See V. I. Simakov, *Sbornik derevenskikh chastushek* (Iaroslavl', 1913), 561–64. Simakov's and Kniazev's books were cited and reviewed widely in the urban press as part of the public discourse on hooliganism; for example, *Gazeta-kopeika* published one version of "The Porcupine Boys" in its December 16, 1912, issue.

24. Weissman, "Rural Crime," 238–39; Weissman found that another similarity to the revolutionary disorders was the "strong evidence" suggesting that there was considerable sympathy for hooligans among the peasants, but there is equally strong evidence of peasants' fear and disgust for at least some hooligan offenses, including such widespread practices as drunkenness and violent brawling. See "O bor'be s narusheniem obshchestvennoi tishiny i poriadka," TsGAOR, fond 102, delo 14, chast' 21b, list 258; Riabchenko, *O bor'be*, 11, applauded peasant *samosud* for hooliganism.

25. Scott, *Weapons of the Weak*.

can include everything from flight to indirect confrontations, such as nighttime pilfering, to direct confrontations, such as using unacceptable language and deceit. Similar forms of protest on the part of the inarticulate and powerless had been weapons in the Russian peasants' arsenal since before the era of enserfment. Such acts became more significant in the interrevolutionary period for three reasons. First, the 1905–1907 Revolution made the privileged classes aware of their vulnerability to the new forces of lower-class power and violence. Thus sensitized, the rural elite found it harder to dismiss forms of "everyday resistance" as peasant laziness or sullenness. Second, hooliganism surfaced in the wake of other social and economic changes. Migrant labor, the intrusion of industry into the countryside, the Stolypin land reforms, the October Manifesto (even with its limitations), all served to shake the social and cultural foundations of rural life. Since hooliganism also attacked the local emblems of established social authority and property, it came to be associated with everything wrong with village life in the wake of those changes. Third, hooligan offenses had in fact become more numerous and more violent. The combination of rapid change and revolutionary experience made observers more aware of the habitual "everyday resistance" of the rural population, but peasant actions had also taken on a new aggressiveness. Hooligans, of course, stopped short of organized assaults on manor houses. They chose their targets somewhat more randomly—the lone woman on the road, the unprotected vegetables in a garden, markers on graves, stolen or defaced "for no reason at all"—but their acts were attacks on privilege, education, wealth, and power. Like the urban phenomenon, rural hooliganism was characterized by a contradictory combination of direct attack on authority figures or symbols and seemingly random acts, such as attacks on public property and the almost insignificant pilfering of vegetables, which were indirect signs of the breakdown of informal mechanisms of social control. This accounts for the confusion among rural observers who saw hooligans simultaneously as motiveless animals and as challengers of authority. As in the city, hooligans in the countryside chose specific targets for their convenience. In this they also resembled the military mutineers of 1905 and 1906, whom Bushnell described as "sensitive to fluctuations in the forces that controlled them" and willing to take advantage of any perceived weakening of restraints.[26]

Almost all rural commentators, and many others as well, believed hooliganism to be linked in some way to the revolutionary politics of 1905–7,

---

26. Bushnell, *Mutiny*, 47.

and saw in hooliganism a challenge to authority. Yet, for all the explicit class hostility expressed by rural hooligans, provincial authorities tended to view hooliganism in the narrowest of political terms. In general, provincial landowners felt relatively secure in their control of political institutions by 1912, after the elections to the Fourth Duma, but these institutions and their noble personnel had virtually no popular support. The empty power of rural political institutions was a primary weakness of the late tsarist government and made noble political power something of a sham.[27] The local hysteria over rural hooliganism, and the seriousness with which hooliganism was viewed by government figures, is a measure of just how small the sphere over which nobles could exercise their authority was. It is also a sign of how little credence they were willing to give to the political content of the hooligans' defiance; for, despite their recognition of the class hostility hooligans expressed, most rural authorities viewed hooligan insolence and violence in primarily cultural terms. Hooliganism was seen as both a symptom and a symbol of the world that modernity had ushered in. This balance of political and cultural factors and the fragility of noble authority in this period can be seen clearly in the public discussion of the causes of hooliganism and the measures recommended to resolve it.

By the time hooliganism had been discussed in "every provincial newspaper" and "never left the pages of the capitals' press" the central government was finally ready to open its own discussion in the national arena. In July 1912, the Ministry of Internal Affairs sent a circular to provincial governors, noting that hooliganism was beginning "to make rural life impossible," and requesting information on hooliganism in the provinces.[28] Several governors published their responses, and the reports as a whole formed the core of materials consulted by the Lykoshin Commission. In 1913, Minister of Justice I. G. Shcheglovitov published a legislative draft consisting of proposed new laws defining, prohibiting, and punishing acts of hooliganism.[29] The minister submitted the proposal to the State Duma for debate and sent it out to provincial and district *zemstvo* leaders, local judges, and Justices of the Peace for their comments. The publication of the proposal called forth a flood of responses from the legal

27. Leopold Haimson, ed., *The Politics of Rural Russia, 1905–1907* (Bloomington, Ind., 1979).
28. The circular and questionnaire are in TsGAOR, fond 102, delo 14, chast' 21 (no list).
29. "K voprosu o merakh bor'by s khuliganstvom," *Zhurnal ugolovnogo prava i protsessa* 4 (1913).

profession as well as from the rural and urban authorities and popular publications. The government's intent was to elicit definitions of hooliganism and suggestions for combating it, including evaluations of the existing punitive measures.[30] It got much more than that: a nationwide debate on the conditions of social and moral life in Russia. The appearance of a national forum for discussion revealed, among other things, that hooliganism was not exclusively urban or rural, but it linked the two in ways that served to increase the growing antagonism between city and village.

Although there were significant differences between left and right, and rural and urban, discourses on the causes of hooliganism, most people by the 1910s had come to believe that hooliganism was rooted not only in culture, but in recent and profound changes in the cultural climate. Conservatives tended to see change as "moral degeneration" or a "decline in morals."[31] These attitudes may not have been noticed for the first time, but in the environment of interrevolutionary society they mattered in new ways, loosening constraints on public behavior, permitting hooligan rowdiness, self-assertion, and violence, and destroying the cloak of inviolability in which traditional authorities had been clothed.

Although most conservatives associated hooliganism with the lower classes (whether rural or urban), a significant minority noticed hooligan attitudes among members of the elite as well.[32] In this debate elite hooliganism took on a special cast, quite different from that perceived by observers on the left, and revealing of the ways hooliganism focused attention on larger social issues. M. A. Goranovskii blamed hooliganism on the "decline of religious-moral principles in the family," and since he found the same moral decline among the urban intelligentsia and the dark and ignorant peasants, hooligans could also be found among both groups. Goranovskii's elite hooligans were urban creatures, the children of "egotistical, intelligentsia mothers who practiced so-called free love." These blighted children, rather than receiving "maternal tenderness, [were] obstacles to their mothers' selfish aims." Lower-class children might also become hooligans through parental neglect, he thought, but in their case the cause was economic need, not self-indulgence.[33]

30. "K voprosu," 103–4; also "Khronika," *Pravo* 27 (1913): col. 1665.
31. "O bor'be s narusheniem," TsGAOR, fond 102, delo 14, chast' 21b, list 259; P. A. Blagoveshchenskii, *O bor'be s khuliganstvom: Iz eparkhial'noi zhizni* (Petrograd, 1914), 3ff.; Riabchenko, *O bor'be,* 5, 11; Goranovskii, *Khuliganstvo,* 11.
32. The Lykoshin Commission described hooliganism as "not limited to any one class or environment"; "Zhurnal obrazovannogo pri MVD Osobogo Mezhduvedomstvennogo Soveshchaniia po voprosu o merakh bor'by s khuliganstvom v sel'skikh mestnostakh," TsGAOR, fond 102, delo 14, chast' 21b, list 361.
33. Goranovskii, *Khuliganstvo,* 11–12.

On the left, commentators sought to explain hooliganism as a natural result of social change. Mensheviks like Zaslavskii and liberals like the *zemstvo* physician and publicist S. I. Elpatevskii and N. N. Polianskii, a well-known jurist and Moscow Justice of the Peace, saw the cultural changes taking place as more promising. Polianskii argued that hooligan offenses became a problem only when a sufficient proportion of the population had become "cultured" enough to be bothered by hooligan crudeness and rowdiness. The cultural development of some made the depravity of the riffraff at the bottom stand out in sharper relief. Polianskii went so far as to claim that hooliganism was not actually on the increase as everyone believed, but that with the rise in the cultural level of society, behavior that once went unnoticed "now irritates the eye."[34] With insight rare for the time, Polianskii hit upon one of the main features of hooliganism that attracted so much attention to it, but his explanation fails to account for the more serious crimes associated with hooliganism, and it ignores the motivation of the hooligans themselves.

From a broader perspective Elpatevskii argued that major upheavals transform society, first and foremost, by destroying what traditionally constitutes "propriety" (*prilichie*). He used the word "propriety" to stand for the codes of conduct governing public behavior and the consensus that determined and enforced them. Political unrest on top of long-term economic and social change shattered the rules governing public behavior. The result was increased opportunity for improvement for those who could take advantage of it, and Elpatevskii believed that some members of the lower classes were exhibiting a higher degree of "culture" and were moving closer to, not farther away from, "the cultured strata." But revolution also increased opportunity for negative forms of self-assertion, in public rowdiness, crime, and seemingly aimless manifestations of malice. Negative manifestations, however, were not the monopoly of the poor and weak: the "expropriations" and armed robberies of the revolutionary era, carried out by radicals from the privileged classes, he argued, ought to be included in any understanding of hooliganism.[35]

Arguments on both left and right linking hooliganism with radicalism and other elite behaviors were never fully developed, leaving the impression that they were either politically motivated or only vaguely understood, or both. Yet there were, in fact, similarities between lower-class

34. "X s"ezd russkoi gruppy mezhdunarodnogo soiuza kriminalistov," *Pravo* 10 (1914): col. 817.
35. Elpat'evskii, "Bezchinstvo," 87; see also A. Mertvyi, "Khuliganstvo," *Utro Rossii*, November 11, 1912.

hooliganism and armed "expropriations" and cultural decadence, though perhaps not the same similarities that contemporaries perceived. In the case of the radicals' armed robberies and terrorist assassinations as well, there can be no doubt that revolutionaries and anarchists felt free to carry out such acts because they had lost respect for the government's authority—not necessarily its power, but its moral authority.[36] As for the new morality of the interrevolutionary period, the practitioners of "free love" did pose a challenge to the traditions of Russian culture: both to the moral straitjacket of the bourgeoisie, including its constraints on public behavior, and to the didactic, purposive cultural practices of the nineteenth-century intelligentsia. The renewed legitimacy of aesthetic inquiry and the savoring of the artistic act rather than art's social or political purpose challenged the very foundation of Russia's intellectual heritage with methods quite similar to those hooligans used to challenge conventional behavior on the streets, as will be discussed in more detail below.

Wherever one stood on the benefits of cultural transformation, evidence of change was everywhere, to judge from responses to official inquiries, publicistic literature, and the popular press. For Goranovskii and most other observers, the destruction of authority in the family was central to understanding the origins of hooliganism. Traditions were breaking down within families, and parents and elders felt that they were no longer able to command respect or control the activities of their children.[37] In part these changes resulted from the economic independence and geographical distance from parental control that migrant workers achieved. Kanatchikov conveyed well the loosening of family bonds that occurred the longer he lived in the city, far away from the relatively homogeneous culture of the village and from the moral authority of his father.[38] The changing role of women was considered by at least one writer to be the key element in the declining state of the rural family. E. Militsyna saw women both as victims and as perpetrators of the decline of morals in the countryside.

---

36. Norman M. Naimark, "Terrorism and the Fall of Imperial Russia," University Lecture, Boston University, 1986; Avrich, *The Russian Anarchists*, 48–50, 61, 67–68. Avrich described groups of anarchists who called themselves *Bezmotivniki* (the Motiveless) and who engaged in violent terrorist acts directed against not the state but the whole of bourgeois society by assaulting its random representatives. Among their favorite tactics was hurling bombs into theaters and restaurants, the prime gathering places, and symbols, of the middle classes.
37. In addition to Goranovskii, *Khuliganstvo*, 11–12ff. see Riabchenko, *O bor'be*, 14, 22–23; Blagoveshchenskii, *O bor'be*, 5; "O bor'be s narusheniem," TsGAOR, fond 102, delo 14, chast' 21b, listy 257–58.
38. Zelnik, *A Radical Worker*, 1–75 passim; esp. "The Beginning of My Apostasy," 27–36.

All day long, she wrote, women had to listen to the nasty songs and incoherent speeches of the heads of their households, "who can think of nothing other than quenching their burning thirst." Either they would begin to sell vodka illegally themselves or they would in any case see it all around them, making decent family life impossible.[39]

Alcohol abuse, not surprisingly, was cited more often than any other factor, on the left and the right, as a sign of social decay and a cause of hooliganism. The Lykoshin Commission claimed alcohol was "not only the irreplaceable companion of hooliganism but practically its primary source."[40] A detailed survey of leading Orthodox clergymen in the countryside, carried out by the Holy Synod, produced unanimous agreement that alcoholism and the illegal production of liquor contributed to the growth of hooliganism.[41] Elite authorities were not the only ones complaining about drunkenness. In at least one province, peasant assemblies protested frequently that drunkenness was encouraging hooliganism and that young people drank whatever they could find, wherever they could find it.[42] Some observers saw further evidence of the "decline of morals" in widespread disrespect for the clergy and the church. This connection was made most often on the right, but even among the clergy such disrespect was considered far from the most important factor in the rise of hooliganism.[43]

All the factors contributing to the "decline of morals"—the disintegration of the family, rampant alcoholism, lack of respect for religion—were themselves viewed only as symptoms of another long-term problem: the migration of peasant-workers back and forth between city and village. Implicit in much of the urban literature on hooliganism, especially in the boulevard press, was the assumption that hooligans brought to the city the low level of culture associated with the peasant way of life. The degeneration that allowed them to display their crude and violent ways may

---

39. E. Militsyna, "Derevenskaia 'khuliganka,'" *Rech'*, April 6, 1913.
40. "Zhurnal Osobogo Soveshchaniia," TsGAOR, fond 102, delo 14, chast' 21b, list 372.
41. Blagoveshchenskii, *O bor'be*, 8. The survey was carried out by the Holy Synod in March 1913 "in the wake of" the inquiry of secular officials carried out by the Ministry of Internal Affairs.
42. "O bor'be s narusheniem," TsGAOR, fond 102, delo 14, chast' 21b, list 258.
43. The Holy Synod survey cited alcoholism, the weakness of law and the judicial system, and the influence of the city and its revolutionary propaganda as more important causes. Blagoveshchenskii, *O bor'be*, 4–9. See also Fomenko, *Khuliganstvo*, who cited hooligan mockery of priests walking on the streets; also "O bor'be s narusheniem," TsGAOR, fond 102, delo 14, chast' 21b, listy 257–59; Riabchenko, *O bor'be*, 11.

have occurred in the dives and slums of the city, but many of the forms it took—public drunkenness, brawling, coarse rudeness, and violence—were seen as peasant in origin. Somewhat contradictorily, urban observers tended to believe that hooliganism was primarily a city problem. Socialist Zaslavskii and conservative V. I. Gurko both argued that the city alone provided fertile ground for genuine hooliganism, while in the countryside it appeared in only "weak and insignificant forms."[44] Conversely, in the countryside hooliganism was depicted as a disease spread by migrating workers. In the clerical responses to the Holy Synod survey, "labor transience" ranked first among the causes of rural hooliganism. The clergy saw the city as a magnet drawing off the best of village youth—some cited "whole districts where, with only the rarest exceptions, not one peasant had not spent part of his youth in a city."[45] One cleric complained that if the money at least made its way back to the village, all might be forgiven, but it was all too often spent in the city on restaurants, taverns, prostitutes, and revolutionary propaganda.[46] This lack of differentiation between cultural and political artifacts of the city was typical. One group of rural authorities described the deleterious influence of labor migration as enabling "familiarity and friendship with hooligans from other places [and] the reading of left-wing newspapers and especially of boulevard crime novels."[47] Returning to the village, the young men enjoyed showing off their city clothes and city habits, which attracted admiration and "set the countryside smoldering, needing only a spark, like 1905."[48]

These perceptions of hooliganism support the view proposed earlier that hooliganism was a phenomenon of people and places in transition. Just as urban hooligans were shown to be those on the margins of the working class—casual workers and apprentices—who had the least sense of permanence in either culture, in the countryside hooligans were also

44. Gurko quoted in Zhilkin, "Provintsial'noe," *Vestnik evropy* 4 (1913): 362–63; Zaslavskii, "Bor'ba," 127.
45. Blagoveshchenskii, *O bor'be*, 6.
46. Ibid., 6, 9–10.
47. The authors of this "harmful literature" were thought to be insulting and mocking authority while glorifying crime and making criminals sympathetic; see "O bor'be s narusheniem," TsGAOR, fond 102, delo 14, chast' 21b, list 259.
48. Blagoveshchenskii, *O bor'be*, 6. "O bor'be s narusheniem," TsGAOR, fond 102, delo 14, chast' 21b, list 259. See also "Zhurnal Osobogo Soveshchaniia," TsGAOR, fond 102, delo 14, chast' 21b, list 361; Goranovskii, *Khuliganstvo*, 1; [A. I. Mosolov,] *Doklad chlena Postoiannogo soveta A. I. Mosolova po voprosu o razvitii khuliganstva* (St. Petersburg, 1913), 4; M. P. Chubinskii, "O khuliganstve," *Izvestiia S.-Peterburgskogo politekhnicheskogo instituta* 21 (1914): 187; Brusianin, "O khuliganakh," 145, 154.

those on the periphery of rural life. If observers exaggerated the importance of crime novels and taverns in producing hooligans, they were consistent in attributing importance to features of their culture that were clearly in flux. The Lykoshin Commission emphasized the gradual transformation of the "conditions of life" in the countryside with the penetration of industry into the village: "The growth of hooliganism is dependent on contact with concepts of [a social] order different from that of the village."[49] This understanding of rural hooliganism adds a new dimension to the analysis of cultural conflict. Not only were hooligans reacting to the imposition of alien codes of conduct associated with their social superiors, but hooliganism was also produced by conflict between two different lower-class cultures. Much has been written about the political consequences of the Russian workers' explosive mix of peasant and proletarian elements.[50] In their continual migration between city and village many peasant-workers were unable to identify clearly with either culture. Migrants had just enough new experience to be both admired and deplored in their native villages, but not enough to either leave the old world behind or have sufficient stake in the new world to channel their hostility into disciplined forms.

The publicistic discourse on hooliganism also makes clear the extent of interpenetration of city and village by the 1910s and suggests that the gap between city and village may have been widening as awareness of each other introduced new reasons for distrust.[51] In the village, hooliganism was portrayed as an invasion by the worst features of city culture, and in the city hooliganism was associated with the low level of peasant culture, an obstacle to the spread of civilization. In both city and village hooligans were symbols of alien ways, which cast into doubt long-held beliefs.

What role did the 1905–1907 Revolution play in the spread of hooliganism into the countryside? By stressing the appearance of hooliganism before the outbreak of the revolution I have tried to emphasize the impor-

49. "Zhurnal Osobogo Soveshchaniia," TsGAOR, fond 102, delo 14, chast' 21b, listy 361, 368; also Weissman, "Rural Crime," 230–32.
50. Theodore Von Laue, "Russian Labor between Field and Factory, 1892–1903," *California Slavic Studies* 3 (1964); Haimson, "Social Stability"; Zelnik, "Russian Bebels"; id., "The Peasant and the Factory," in *The Peasant in Nineteenth-Century Russia*, ed. Wayne S. Vucinich (Stanford, 1968); Robert E. Johnson, *Peasant and Proletarian: The Working Class of Moscow in the Late Nineteenth Century* (New Brunswick, N.J., 1979).
51. In discussing the role of literacy in urban culture, Michael Hamm also suggests that the gap between city and village was expanding; see his "Continuity and Change in Late Imperial Kiev," in *The City in Late Imperial Russia*, 110.

tance of long-term social, economic, and cultural changes. Most writers of the 1910s agreed. Some of the more hysterical among them took the short view, claiming that the revolution had shown that authority could be attacked with impunity and that now "all is possible."[52] The majority, however, on both left and right saw the revolution as a catalyst, bringing to the surface problems and tensions that had been simmering for years.[53] The most direct result of the revolution was the exile of thousands of urban workers to their native villages, at just the time when rural revolutionary unrest was on the rise. But one should also not discount the impact of more diffuse aspects of the revolutionary experience on the activities and perceptions of contemporaries. The violence and self-assertion of the lower classes on the one hand and the violence and weakness of the tsarist government on the other produced strong impressions that faded slowly.

That the most thoughtful observers sought explanations of hooliganism both in long-term developments and in the basic structures of late imperial society suggests the seriousness with which hooliganism was viewed as something other than a crime problem. It is also evidence that while this period is often characterized as one of widespread political apathy and cultural individualism, at the local level significant social and cultural conflicts continued, and considerable thought was given to social problems. In the countryside, most of that thinking was backward looking and predictable, at least in regard to hooliganism. Rural nobles and some peasants as well saw their way of life seriously threatened by what they considered to be influences from the outside: modern industry, land reforms, radical propaganda, and lower-class violence. They lamented the weakening of traditional authorities and social structures but had little understanding of the forces at work in their own villages that undermined tradition. This becomes even clearer in the debates over efforts to eradicate hooliganism, in which the majority of vocal rural nobles called for immediate, extra-legal punitive measures and criticized those in favor of longer-term cultural solutions aimed at ameliorating the destabilizing effects of economic and social change.

▤ *National Debates on Punishment and Prevention*

For all the divergence of opinion over the diagnosis and cure of hooliganism there was, at first, wide agreement that existing laws and court

52. Fomenko, *Khuliganstvo*; Riabchenko, *O bor'be*, 5; "Zhurnal Osobogo Soveshchaniia," TsGAOR, fond 102, delo 14, chast' 21b, list 362.
53. Goranovskii, *Khuliganstvo*, 2–3; Mertvyi, "Khuliganstvo," 2; Elpat'evskii, "Bezchinstvo," 97; Blagoveshchenskii, *O bor'be*, 6.

practices could not even begin to treat the illness. Observers across political lines thought that cultural conflicts had festered into serious crime problems because of the weakness of Russia's legal structure. Beyond this point, agreement ended. There was little consensus on the issue of law reform, and most of the debates divided along political lines. Minister of Justice Shcheglovitov, Governor Bashilov of Ufa, A. I. Mosolov of the United Nobility, and the members of the Lykoshin Commission agreed that hooliganism was spreading because the laws were not strong enough to deter it.[54] Liberal jurists and observers emphasized the weakness of institutional authority and judicial practices rather than the failure of law or legal powers. As early as 1901, complaints were voiced about the lenient prosecution of hooligans. The pettiness of the offenses and the heavy caseload of the Justices of the Peace meant that many hooligans were only assessed small fines and released.[55] As Asoskov noted in *Sudebnaia gazeta*,

> It is not surprising that cases of disturbing public peace and tranquility, assault, blasphemy, cursing, and other forms of rowdiness increase from one day to the next in our streets and courtyards. One should not be surprised by all this, because such persons, both male and female, have every reason to hope that they will go unpunished.[56]

Others on the left argued that hooliganism was encouraged primarily by the authorities' own low regard for law and their *proizvol*, or arbitrary abuse of legal power. M. P. Chubinskii, a prominent jurist, wrote:

> It is difficult to teach respect for the law where one finds examples of *proizvol* at every step and where belonging to a privileged group (such as the Union of Russian People) protects law breakers from punishment, something that for some time has occurred with the highest degree of cynicism and unabashedness.[57]

---

54. Shcheglovitov cited in I. [V.] Gessen, "Vnutrennaia zhizn'," *Ezhegodnik gazety Rech' na 1913 god* (St. Petersburg, 1914), 31–32; see also "K voprosu," 103–4; Bashilov, "O khuliganstve," 224; [Mosolov] *Doklad*, 5; "Zhurnal Osobogo Soveshchaniia," TsGAOR, fond 102, delo 14, chast' 21b, list 362.

55. *Ustav o nakazaniiakh nalagaemykh mirovymi sud'iami* (St. Petersburg, 1864), articles 35–58; "Po vysochaishim otmetkam na otchet za 1909 SPb gubernii," TsGAOR, fond 102, delo 20, chast' 1; A. V., "Grustnyi fakt."

56. K. Asoskov, "Iz sudebnoi praktiki," *Sudebnaia gazeta*, December 14, 1903; also A. V. Likhachev, "Ob usilenii nakazanii dlia khuliganov," *Zhurnal ministerstva iustitsii* 5 (1913): 83; "Zhurnal Osobogo Soveshchaniia," TsGAOR, fond 102, delo 14, chast' 21b, list 362; Blagoveshchenskii, *O bor'be*, 4–5; "Khuliganstvo," *NV*, April 9, 1913.

57. Chubinskii, "O khuliganstve," 207.

Even Blagoveshchenskii, the priest who compiled the Holy Synod survey on hooliganism, decried the government's abuse of legality, which he called "hypocrisy" and "fertile soil for the growth of hooliganism."[58]

The legislative draft proposal devised by the Ministry of Justice and published in 1912 did nothing to improve the government's reputation for respecting legal norms. Fundamental to the ministry's proposal was the concept that hooliganism was not a crime sui generis but a circumstance (*ottenok*) that could characterize or be associated with any crime. Since any crime might be committed with these characteristics, the proposal conceded that precise legal definition was not possible. The ministry, therefore, proposed guidelines for a definition of hooliganism to be used in establishing whether a crime had been committed "in the hooligan manner." It would be the court's responsibility to determine the degree to which these characteristics were present, thereby requiring harsher punishment. A crime was to be considered hooliganism if it was characterized by any one of three aggravating circumstances:

> particular maliciousness or licentiousness on the part of the guilty party or a manifest lack of correspondence between the motivation of the guilty party and the criminal act undertaken or intent on the part of the guilty party to violate in a crude manner the personal rights of the victim.[59]

These guidelines, which were based on responses to the ministry's preliminary inquiries, drew vociferous criticism. On the whole the proposal is remarkable for its view of law as something rather more flexible and subjective than the Russian legal system, or other modern, Western legal systems, allowed. The interpretive power that would have been necessary to implement the ministry's proposal was a feature normally restricted to customary law.[60] Every aspect of the draft was subject to attack, and not all the criticism came from jurists on the left. The conservative newspaper *Novoe vremia* numbered among those who called for a more precise definition of hooliganism, one that would stand up in court.[61] Most of the

58. Blagoveshchenskii, *O bor'be*, 11.

59. The original text is "ob osoboi zlobnosti ili raspushchennosti vinovnogo, libo o iavnom nesootvetstvii pobuzhdenii vinovnogo s predpriniatymi prestupnymi deistviiami, libo o namerenii vinovnogo grubo nadrugat'sia nad lichnost'iu poterpevshego" ("K voprosu," 106–7).

60. Some interpretive latitude was also granted to the Russian Justices of the Peace; see Joan Neuberger, "Popular Legal Cultures: The St. Petersburg *Mirovoi Sud*," in *The Great Reforms*, ed. John Bushnell and Ben Eklof (Bloomington, Ind., forthcoming).

61. "Khuliganstvo," *NV*, April 9, 1913.

legal profession agreed with *Novoe vremia* that the guidelines offered by the ministry were too vague to apply in court. Some argued that the proposal excluded too many hooligan offenses. Others pointed out that it included crimes that had nothing in common with hooliganism. One writer cited a celebrated murder case in which a student mutilated and sliced up the body of a fellow student, an act that exhibited all three of the ministry's characteristics but could under no circumstances be considered hooliganism.[62] Others maintained that no new laws were necessary because provisions already existed for increasing the punishment for a crime if it were accompanied by aggravating circumstances similar to those associated with hooliganism. Some jurists simply argued that hooliganism could never be defined precisely enough to apply in court.[63] The Moscow Council of Justices of the Peace criticized the ministry proposal on all fronts. The Moscow JPs objected that the proposal's definition of hooliganism "suffered from an extreme lack of precision," violated basic principles of the system of punishments, and displayed a fundamental ignorance of judicial practice.[64] The concept of "particular maliciousness" came in for the most criticism. The Moscow JPs contended that no court could distinguish degrees of malice.[65] V. V. Krumbmiller, a Kharkov Justice of the Peace agreed, pointing out that the capacity to distinguish between maliciousness and particular maliciousness is not to be found among judges but more properly should be the province of psychiatric specialists. In his own experience, what often appeared at first to be dissoluteness frequently turned out to be full-fledged mental illness.[66]

On practical grounds both the St. Petersburg and Moscow Justice of the Peace councils argued against establishing guidelines for defining aggravating circumstances that would increase severity of sentences. The Petersburg JPs objected to harsher penalties because they would neither prevent nor control the crime. Some crimes, they argued, are not affected by increased repression. Reflecting on its disastrous experience with in-

---

62. Ivanov, *Chto takoe*, 2.
63. For a survey of professional legal opinions of the draft proposal see the minutes of the 1914 conference of the Russian Group of the International Association of Criminologists, *Otchet X obshchego sobraniia russkoi gruppy mezhdunarodnogo soiuza kriminalistov, 13–16 fevralia 1914 g.* (Petrograd, 1916). The speeches and discussions on hooliganism were reprinted in *Pravo* 9–11 (1914).
64. "Otzyv Moskovskogo stolichnogo mirovogo s"ezda o ministerskom zakonoproekte o merakh bor'by s khuliganstvom," *Iuridicheskii vestnik* 3 (1913): 229–31, 237–38.
65. "Otzyv Moskovskogo," 230.
66. V. V. Krumbmiller, *Zlobodnevnyi vopros: Khuliganstvo i bor'ba s nim. Po povodu proekta Ministra iustitsii* (Khar'kov, 1913), 3–4.

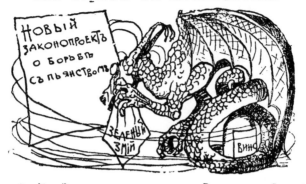

Къ борьбѣ съ пьянствомъ.

«Зеленый змій».—Эхъ, вспомнишь старинку: вся Русь не могла безъ меня «быти»; отовсюду, бывало, почетъ, уваженіе и на всѣ торжества приглашенія!.. А теперь—всюду брань, поношеніе, да протоколы о выселеніи! Эхъ, самъ, кажись, запью съ горя!..

Figure 7.   On the Campaign against Drunkenness (February 20, 1914).
Russians hallucinate green serpents when they get too drunk, just as Americans of earlier generations saw pink elephants. This green serpent is reading a "Legislative Proposal for the Campaign against Drunkenness" and mourning the days when drinking was revered rather than condemned. He quotes the famous words of the medieval Grand Prince Vladimir, who declared that Russians could not live without drink, and he announces that he must "drown his own sorrows."

creased prison sentences for public drunkenness in the mid-1890s and in 1900–1902, when the police arrested as many people as they could lay their hands on for appearing drunk in public, the Petersburg JPs argued that the habitual alcoholics who comprised the majority of those tried under article 42 were anything but cured by a stint in prison, and the police campaigns had not had any noticeable effect on alcoholism or on public drunkenness.[67] (See fig. 7 for a wry comment on anti-alcohol campaigns.) Hooliganism, they argued, would be similarly impervious to massive police campaigns. In general, however, the St. Petersburg Council responded more positively to the ministry's proposal than its Moscow counterpart. The Petersburg JPs expressed no objection to the ministry's definition of hooliganism or its general formulation of the legislative draft. Their main objection was that the ministry had neglected offenses that constituted common forms of hooliganism in St. Petersburg: assault, brawling, and disturbing the peace, all of which occurred frequently on the streets of the capital. The Petersburg JPs also implied a larger criticism in their discussion of the police campaign against public drunkenness.

67. PMS 1913, 277–78.

They suggested that the causes of hooliganism, like the causes of alcoholism, lay outside the sphere of activity influenced by the court. The court could judge and punish illegal actions only, but punishment would not necessarily diminish or deter the crimes that were rooted in deep social and cultural problems.

On the question of motive, some observers agreed with the ministry that hooliganism was typically motiveless or aimless, but the proposed legal formulation of this aspect of hooliganism did not satisfy legal professionals. Krumbmiller noted that, according to accepted legal practice, if will and reason are not in evidence, a person cannot be held legally responsible.[68] The Moscow Justice of the Peace Council pointed out that the lack of correspondence between motive and act is recognized by both judicial and psychiatric authorities as the most important feature of the mental condition that *acquits* defendants of criminal responsibility. As such it could hardly be the basis for increasing punishment.[69] Governor Bashilov tried to sharpen the issue by proposing an examination of the prior relationship between victim and accused, suggesting that a crime should be considered hooliganism if the victim in no way provoked attack. Such a formulation, he argued, would not need to be decided by a psychological expert.[70] But others pointed out that from a psychological point of view unmotivated maliciousness simply could not exist.[71]

The emphasis on psychological analysis in these comments was not unrelated to contemporary juridical theory and practice. The role of medical and psychological expertise at criminal trials was a subject widely discussed throughout Europe in the late nineteenth and twentieth centuries. Russian jurists and criminologists were thoroughly integrated into the international juridical community and would have been familiar with the issues of forensic psychology as they were understood at the time. Nonetheless, although mental incompetence as a factor in assessing criminal responsibility had been introduced into Russian criminal law, it remained a controversial issue within the legal profession.[72] The psychological fea-

---

68. Krumbmiller, *Zlobodnevnyi vopros*, 4.
69. "Otzyv Moskovskogo," 230.
70. Bashilov, "O khuliganstve," 226–27.
71. Chubinskii, "O khuliganstve," 190–92; A. Makletsov, "K voprosu o iuridicheskoi otsenke khuliganstva," *Iuridicheskii vestnik* 2 (1913): 237.
72. See A. I. Iushchenko, *Osnovy uchenii o prestupnike, dushevnobol'nom i psikhologii normal'nogo cheloveka* (St. Petersburg, 1913); A. F. Koni, "Psikhiatricheskaia ekspertiza i deistvuiushchie zakony," *Vestnik evropy* 2 (1910); V. Bekhterev, "Ob"ektivno-psikhologicheskii metod v premenenii k izucheniiu prestupnosti," *Vestnik evropy* 8–9 (1909).

tures that could be introduced as evidence were still being debated, but it was generally agreed that their purpose was to establish competency, not culpability. The draft's emphasis on motive and intention, as opposed to psychological competence, introduced features of crime that were normally beyond the court's role to decide. Ordinarily the law required a court to decide whether a crime had been committed by the person charged—not how, why, or how nasty the criminal. A. N. Trainin, a Moscow criminologist, Justice of the Peace, and outspoken critic of the government's efforts to combat hooliganism, challenged the ministry's use of psychological factors for defining hooliganism, arguing that "there was a logical blunder in the very attempt to give hooliganism a juridical definition." Unlike other crimes, Trainin said, hooliganism had "no objective content." It was rather a reflection of "the world of inner psychological turmoil," and therefore outside the range of psychological factors that the court was to take into account.[73]

The legislative proposal, in fact, was not much more than a rendering of popular opinion into legal language. The Ministry of Justice captured the popular definition of hooliganism as insolent self-assertion in the absence of traditional agents of social control, but this definition proved difficult to translate into law. Discussions in the State Duma of the draft proposal provoked harsh criticism from the left: "*This is philistinism! . . . This project is juridically illiterate, cannot withstand legal criticism, and has no rationale other than the protection of the nobles' own social interests.*"[74]

As the tsarist government whittled away at the rights guaranteed in the Fundamental Laws issued in 1906, anger and concern about government arbitrariness understandably increased.[75] The opposition to the ministry's proposed law against hooliganism reflected these fears and attracted the interest of eminent legal experts. The inclusion of three reports on the hooliganism question at the Tenth Conference of the Russian Group of the International Association of Criminologists in 1914 testifies to the authenticity of concern about hooliganism and the law among Russia's

73. A. N. Trainin, "Khuliganstvo," *Pravo* 10 (1914): col. 748 (transcript of Trainin's speech at the Tenth Conference of the Russian Group of the International Association of Criminologists [hereafter RGIAC]).

74. Gosudarstvennaia duma, *Stenograficheskii otchet* [hereafter *GDSO*], 4-yi sozyv, 1-aia sessiia, chast' II, zasedanie 38 (April 29, 1913), cols. 637–38.

75. On late imperial Duma politics, see Geoffrey Hosking, *The Russian Constitutional Experiment: Government and Duma, 1907–1914* (Cambridge, 1973); on the political crisis of confidence see Hans Rogger, "Russia in 1914," *Journal of Contemporary History*, vol. 1, no. 4 (1966).

most distinguished jurists. Most of the members of the Russian Group were liberals; many were prominent Kadets—V. D. Nabokov was president at the time. A few members were non-Marxist socialists. The issues raised at the conference concerning legal measures to combat hooliganism show that the left's motives for rejecting various law proposals were not based on a denial of the severity of the hooligan problem but rather on an insistence that hooliganism be treated as an ordinary legal problem with standard legal solutions. These jurists viewed hooliganism within the context of criminal law rather than as a manifestation of social or political conflict.

The conference of criminologists rejected the ministry's draft proposal in near unanimity. Individual members, however, presented various and even contradictory reasons for this. Trainin aroused the greatest controversy by claiming that hooliganism was not on the increase, but he won consensus in arguing that hooligan offenses were all already prohibited by existing law and that the proper role for the court was to decide whether an offense was committed by the person accused, not what the motives or attitudes of the perpetrator were.[76] Nabokov spoke against the ministry's draft proposal and against another set of proposals offered at the conference on the grounds that their definition of hooliganism and the laws based on it were not legally practical. He added, however, that events of recent years had demonstrated the need for reform of laws concerning personal inviolability. All were agreed that any new law had to be precise in its definition of hooliganism and had to refrain from impinging on the legal rights of both victim and criminal.[77]

Jurists at the conference were particularly outspoken in their rejection of extra-legal methods. Most of Trainin's speech, and, indeed, many of the other speeches at the conference, centered on the pernicious use of binding decrees and extra-judicial administrative measures employed by the police and central government against hooliganism.[78] Among such measures, Octobrists had introduced a proposal in April 1913 in the Fourth

---

76. Trainin, "Khuliganstvo," *Pravo* 10 (1914): cols. 747–49; "X s"ezd," *Pravo* 10 (1914): cols. 817, 819, 820. Trainin's argument about the decrease in hooligan crimes was based on an incorrect and incomplete reading of local *mirovoi sud* statistics on hooligan offenses. Among other things his figures stop before 1912, when the upsurge in hooliganism became indisputable; see "Otzyv Moskovskogo," 232–35.

77. V. D. Nabokov, "Desiatyi s"ezd kriminalistov," *Pravo* 9 (1914): cols. 658–62; "X s"ezd," cols. 815–16; Chubinskii, "O khuliganstve," 183–90.

78. Trainin, "Khuliganstvo," *Pravo* 10 (1914): cols. 755–57; and *Pravo* 11 (1914): cols. 857–62.

Duma for appointing an official with special judicial powers similar to those land captains had wielded. It should be noted that in 1912 the government had finally finished its reform of the local court system, a central feature of which had been the extension of legal rights to the peasantry and the abolition of land captains.

Duma opposition to proposals of administrative measures for hooligans was vigorous, eloquent, and frustrated. The Kadet F. I. Rodichev charged that the original introduction of land captains brought massive repression, but to no good purpose.[79] An Octobrist and supporter of the proposed judicial officers, Count Kapnist, argued in contrast that land captains were essential because the peasant (*volost'*) courts refused to prosecute hooligans for fear of revenge, a charge supported by evidence elsewhere.[80] Rodichev responded to these and other claims by referring to the new legislation on local court reform just passed. He insisted that what was needed was "court, gentlemen, court, court, court," not new land captains, not new binding decrees.[81] The Octobrist delegate who introduced the motion reinstituting land captains argued that Russian society should not have to wait for the implementation of new courts while hooliganism was multiplying with each passing day.[82] By the spring of 1913, enough Duma liberals deserted Rodichev to approve the measures.[83] A binding decree for use against hooliganism was issued in February 1913, and it was applied widely thereafter. Duma Kadets argued, but to no avail, that such administrative measures violated the provisions of the statutes on Extraordinary Security, which were supposed to be used only against sedition. More persuasive to the government no doubt was the positive response of the St. Petersburg *gradonachal'nik,* who claimed within a few months that the new binding decree made a significant impact in helping to control hooligan crimes.[84]

Conservatives generally called for repressive measures, not worrying too much about the legal means employed to impose them. It was widely believed that hooliganism had proliferated because legal punishment was

79. *GDSO*, 4-yi sozyv, chast' II, 1-aia sessiia, zasedanie 38 (April 29, 1913), col. 627.
80. Ibid., col. 655. On local fears of hooligans see the exchange of letters published by "Skitalets" in his regular column in *Gazeta-kopeika* for December 12, 1912, January 6, 1913, and January 7, 1913.
81. *GDSO*, cols. 642–43.
82. Ibid., col. 632.
83. Ibid., cols. 650–59. See also Weissman, "Rural Crime," 234–35.
84. Report of the St. Petersburg *gradonachal'nik,* TsGAOR, fond 102, delo 14, chast' 21b (no list).

limited, and hooligans regarded prison as a vacation. The absence of serious deterrence, it was thought, further eroded both formal and informal authority.[85] There was also wide support on the right for the ministry's proposal to reintroduce corporal punishment. At the IX Conference of the United Nobility, speaker after speaker called for a return to corporal punishment and longer prison terms for hooligans.[86] When Gurko tried to propose cultural and educational improvements as preventive measures he was shouted down.[87] When another speaker, Prince Unkhtomskii of Kazan, presented a resolution to force hooligans to pay for damage they caused, the audience responded "coldly," viewing such measures as too soft. When Unkhtomskii maintained that the nobles' fear of hooligans might be exaggerated and that hooliganism was rare in his province, someone shouted: "Lucky for you! You should stand for a while in our shoes."[88] Applause and cheers greeted Mosolov when he stood to defend himself against charges of exaggerating hooliganism. Mosolov called for steps insuring immediate relief: "At such an acute time, it is impossible to speak of various educational measures. . . . Hooliganism is a filthy wave flooding all of Russia. . . . We need urgent and decisive steps. We cannot wait twenty or thirty years while enlightenment takes effect."[89]

The portrait of hooliganism painted by the rural nobility matched its portrayal in the most sensationalistic pages of the boulevard press. This vision produced an atmosphere of terror and established the pretext for the revival of corporal punishment and other harsh punitive measures, just as the left feared. Governor Bashilov opposed corporal punishment in principle (on humanitarian and political grounds), but he believed that it was the only form of punishment appropriate to the hooligans' own cruel behavior.[90] Tsar Nicholas himself supported the revival of corporal punishment. In response to a proposal to construct workhouses for hooligans in the annual police report for 1909, Nicholas wrote: "Yes, or better yet, the rod, as is done in Denmark."[91] Goranovskii argued that hooligans were so debased and vicious that only the most brutal punishment could have any effect on them. Prison would only encourage their natural lazi-

85. [Mosolov], *Doklad*, 5–6.
86. Zhilkin, "Provintsial'noe," 361–66; [Mosolov,] *Doklad*, 4–6.
87. Zhilkin, "Provintsial'noe," 362–63.
88. Ibid., 363.
89. [Mosolov,] *Doklad*, 6 and passim; Zhilkin, "Provintsial'noe," 363–64.
90. Bashilov, "O khuliganstve," 229–30.
91. "Izvlechenie iz vsepoddaneishego otcheta za 1909 g. o sostoianii S.-Peterburgskogo gradonachal'stva," TsGAOR, fond 102, delo 20, chast' 17, list 1.

ness, and workhouses could not reverse their moral degeneration; so, he maintained, "corporal punishment should not disturb our consciences." The only way to control hooligans, he believed, was to make punishment severe enough to frighten them "the way an animal is frightened." He observed that "when what distinguishes human beings from animals is lacking, the only possible response [on our part] is an animal one."[92] It was this sort of writing, more than the conservatives' analyses of hooligan crimes, that most angered jurists on the left.[93] They did not deny that hooliganism was a serious problem, only that the criminal should not be viewed as a subhuman species outside the scope of human law. The liberal view struck conservatives as too abstract to cope with reality. A. E. Riabchenko complained that the measures necessary to combat hooliganism were obstructed by "cheap liberals among the bureaucrats, who philosophize and quibble over the legality and the efficacy of physical reprisal."[94]

Noble representatives, however, were not unanimous in calling for corporal punishment. Governors' reports to the Lykoshin Commission showed that the rod was favored by thirteen governors, seven provincial assemblies, six provincial bureaus, and eleven *zemstvo* assemblies.[95] This was a sizable portion, to be sure (especially for a measure that had been largely abolished with serfdom in 1861), but far from the majority. The Lykoshin Commission itself was divided on the issue.[96]

Objections to corporal punishment within the legal establishment were unequivocal. At the Conference of the Russian Group of the International Association of Criminologists in 1914, Nabokov spoke for all his colleagues when he rejected corporal punishment out of hand.[97] The volume of support for corporal punishment, however, compelled other opponents to argue in more detail. One *Peterburgskii listok* columnist reminded his readers that under serfdom corporal punishment had proven to be the "least effective, most degenerate" form of punishment. "The stick has two ends," he wrote, suggesting that the cure might be worse than the

92. Goranovskii, *Khuliganstvo*, 20, 22–23.
93. M. N. Gernet spoke effectively on this issue at the RGIAC conference; see "X s"ezd," col. 819.
94. Riabchenko also referred to the Fourth Duma as "our more than liberal Duma" (*O bor'be*, 10–11, 21).
95. N. F. Luchinskii, "Mery bor'by s prazdnoshataistvom i khuliganstvom," *Tiuremnyi vestnik* 3 (1915): 576.
96. "Zhurnal Osobogo Soveshchaniia," TsGAOR, fond 102, delo 14, chast' 21b, listy 361, 373ff. According to the report on the survey of marshals of the nobility, marshals from northern provinces tended to support the revival of corporal punishment more than southern marshals; see D-ii, "Bor'ba s khuliganstvom."
97. "X s"ezd," *Pravo* 10 (1914): col. 819.

disease, since it would give the government one more opportunity to abuse its power.[98] Many believed that corporal punishment would harden offenders, especially young offenders, in their anti-social attitudes, making them more likely to enter the ranks of professional criminals. Unlike those who saw hooligans as depraved animals, Ivanov and others believed that hooligans could be rehabilitated. Their social instincts could be reborn and their souls healed, he argued, but only by genuinely humane treatment.[99]

This position rested on the belief that hooliganism was a cultural and social problem that required cultural and social cures rather than physical punishment and retribution.[100] In place of extra-legal sanctions and corporal punishment, liberals and other leftists recommended measures intended to raise the cultural level of the people as well as their respect for law and individual rights. Universal education, "healthy" entertainment to lure people away from alcohol, economic relief to prevent women and girls from turning to prostitution, and better care for orphaned and abandoned children were among the most commonly proposed measures. Not incidentally, those who argued for cultural rather than punitive steps tended to be the people least threatened by hooliganism directly. They also understood least of all that in many cases hooliganism was a defiant rejection of such cultural development projects. And while right-wing observers tended to favor the immediate benefits of extra-legal sanctions, several of them also supported long-term cultural measures as well.[101] If culture could not rehabilitate inveterate hooligans, it was expected to prevent the development of hooliganism in the future. Many liberals and criminologists also pleaded eloquently for a uniform legal system, for equality of all before the law, and legal guarantees for individual rights in order to instill the respect for law and order needed for a stable and secure society.[102] They tended to see government arbitrariness and popular violence as mutually reinforcing. I. V. Gessen, a leading Kadet jurist and publicist, argued that society's indifference to legal political activity, and its widespread disillusionment with Duma politics, precluded the possibility of compelling the government to obey its own laws. The result of

98. V. P-v, "Kak borot'sia s khuliganstvom," *PL,* August 16, 1913.
99. Ivanov, *Chto takoe,* 11–12.
100. Ibid., 11.
101. "Zhurnal Osobogo Soveshchaniia," TsGAOR, fond 102, delo 14, chast' 21b, listy 373–82; Zaslavskii, "Bor'ba," 122–23.
102. Chubinskii, "O khuliganstve," 185, 189, 207; speeches of S. K. Gogel', P. I. Liublinskii, G. Krugliakov, and V. D. Nabokov in "X s"ezd," *Pravo* 10 (1914): cols. 818–19, 821, 828.

official disregard for the law was the encouragement of anarchy and violence, "the most threatening signs of which" could already be observed:
"Contempt for the principles of legality has taken on monstrous proportions and, in connection with [Stolypin's land reforms], has born terrible
fruit. Hooliganism has become a serious social problem."[103]

The legal debate over hooliganism displays typical responses to a pressing social issue in late imperial Russia. Those who argued that sufficient
laws already existed for prosecuting hooliganism in the present and that
cultural measures would eradicate it in the future were expressing the
most sanguine view of the crime to be heard in Russian society. By placing
hooliganism in a purely legal context they removed the shadow of political
subversion and social disintegration that darkened government and right-
wing arguments and colored commercial-press portraits. In doing so they
removed the justification for employing extra-legal methods, but they also
showed themselves insensitive to the genuine cultural and social conflicts
involved in the hooligans' challenge to authority.

Much has been made of the tsarist government's eagerness to resort to
extra-legal procedures for immediate, repressive solutions to long-range
problems. The case of hooliganism is no exception. Various central institutions, individual noblemen, and local organs of administration and police
called for, and instituted, extra-legal sanctions repeatedly, beginning with
the Petersburg police ruling against rowdy street behavior announced in
December 1901. While it is undoubtedly true that legal norms were regularly violated without scruple or constraint for political, repressive reasons,
it is important to recognize the motives in operation. Liberal jurists assailed the right for its wilful disregard of law, but the writings and speeches
of the conservative nobility and government officials reveal a mentality
less vengeful than shortsighted, ignorant, and impatient. After all, officials
had good reason to argue that the law was failing to deter hooliganism
and was incapable of providing effective punishment for hooligan crimes.
Even the more frantic among the gentry displayed a greater sense of
urgency than narrow self-protectionism. It is clear that they viewed special
administrative rulings and provisions for administrative justice as stopgap
measures necessary in a crisis situation. It is equally clear that supporters
of such measures had little understanding of the effects of bending the
law, to say nothing of the hostility engendered by such measures, not
only among those convicted for such crimes but within the surrounding
community as well. Indeed, the residue of hostility deriving from prior

103. I. [V.] Gessen, "Vnutrennaia zhizn'," *Ezhegodnik gazety Rech' na 1913 god*
(St. Petersburg, 1914), 31–32.

treatment was in large part responsible for the crisis in the first place. That hostility was undoubtedly not eased by the nobles' expression of their view that the common people deserved to be treated no better than animals.

Liberals were understandably skeptical of crisis justifications for skirting the law, given the state's extended use of the "temporary" security statutes instituted in 1881; they were still in place in the 1910s. From the conservative perspective, however, there was equal reason to doubt the effectiveness of the long-term solutions proposed by the liberal intelligentsia. Liberals had been speaking about "raising the intellectual and moral level" of the people at least since the Great Reform era. Clearly, the broader cultural measures proposed by liberal jurists incorporated greater respect for individuals and gave greater consideration to certain aspects of the socioeconomic origins of hooliganism. But while liberals may have displayed some awareness of the social roots of hooliganism, their rational legalism either ignored or misconstrued the depth of the social conflict that lay at the root of the problem and the power hooligans possessed to destabilize society. Furthermore, however humane and equitable liberal proposals appeared on the surface (and, of course, with regard to lifelong exile or fifty lashes there could be no comparison), the liberal conception of culturalism may also be construed as a form of cultural tyranny. Those features of culture so enthusiastically espoused by liberals often appeared utterly alien to some members of the Russian lower classes, who tenaciously resisted being culturally "improved."

The national debate concerning the origins of hooliganism and the campaign against it provide a case study of the place of law in a society with an ambivalent commitment to the rule of law. Historically, conservatives have been more prone to advocate repressive measures for dealing with criminals, while liberals have favored preventive measures. The proponents of administrative justice, of corporal punishment, and of extra-legal methods for dealing with hooligans were, for the most part, shortsighted, terrified, and brutal in their own disregard for the principle of individual rights. Their opponents, the supporters of legal integrity and long-term culture projects, were certainly more humane and were deeply committed to the importance of upholding the rule of law. But their purely legalistic view of hooliganism blinded them to the genuine conflict and challenge to traditional authority that animated the majority of hooligan crimes. In taking such a view they contributed to the continued weakness of judicial institutions and judicial authority, which allowed hooliganism to proliferate. Ironically, it may have been the refusal of the liberal jurists to support any law prohibiting hooliganism that enabled several provinces and cities to implement binding decrees allowing them to bypass the judicial system altogether.

This national discourse reveals from a new perspective the animosity between the haves and the have-nots in late imperial Russia. It shows that the breakdown of authority occurring in the countryside, as in the city, had roots in the cultural changes taking place alongside the better known political discontent. The discussion concerning measures to control hooliganism reveals a lack of support for the cultural measures proposed by judicial professionals and intelligentsia groups. Conservatives doubted the effectiveness of cultural improvement projects because they saw all around them an increase in the number and brutality of the "uncultured." At the same time, the cultural project of the old intelligentsia was besieged by members of the artistic community, who in the past had shared a belief in cultural progress and improvement. During the 1910s some of these cultural challenges closely resembled hooliganism. The avant-garde extended the hooligans' challenge, further undermined intelligentsia culturalism, and contributed to the social and cultural fragmentation of the period.

⑧ Hooliganism and Modernism

In the years after 1905, elite avant-garde artists used shocking behavior and offensive public pranks in the same way hooligans had: to attack old authorities, advertise an alternative set of values, attract attention to themselves, and assert their own power. The futurists in particular found hooligan tactics useful, inspiring, and amusing, but artists of the first rank from outside futurist circles also incorporated hooligan behavior, values, and images in their work. A full study of the hooligan motifs in Silver Age culture is beyond the scope of this study, but some mention must be made of the links between street hooliganism and the "hooligans of the palette" to show how central hooligan discourse had become in the 1910s and how fragmented the intellectual elite, and to establish the broader social and cultural context in which the Russian avant-garde, and indeed all urban society, operated.

Like hooligans, futurist poets, painters, musicians, and dramatists were rebellious, confrontational, self-consciously crude or "anticultured," and unabashedly self-promoting. Futurists chose to perform in public spaces where they could make their message heard and felt most sharply. And like hooligans, they embedded a serious message in their prankish behavior. The serious aesthetic challenge they dramatized was to the great artists and artistic traditions of the past. They used hooligan tactics to proclaim that the Russian and European classics had no relevance for the present. On the contrary, their power to influence succeeding generations had become a stultifying straitjacket. The futurists offered themselves in place of the dead past. Their most notorious manifesto called for "Pushkin, Dostoevsky, Tolstoy, etc., etc., to be thrown overboard from the ship of modernity."[104] In addition to past masters, the futurists assailed (what they imagined to be) the bourgeoisie, because they saw the fetters of traditional aesthetic authority symbolized in the philistine commercialization of culture, in the superficial, unreflective reverence for the great works of the past, and in the equally deadening restrictions on behavior embodied in bourgeois respectability.[105] The futurists' attacks on Pushkin and bourgeois philistinism originated in the same impulse as the hooligans' invasion of Nevskii Prospekt. Benedikt Livshits, the astute if eccentric chronicler of futurism, captured the invasion well in his depiction of the painters Ekster, Goncharova, and Rozanova: arriving from the provinces, these "Scythian riders" galloped into Moscow and Petersburg to challenge the pretension, refinement, and Westernism that reigned there,[106] not unlike the hooligans who infiltrated the main streets of the capital from their outposts on the city's periphery.

The futurists were hardly the first artists to challenge or reject past models of artistic achievement. But rebellion and iconoclasm take forms specific to time and place. In Russia in the 1910s the most important form of artistic rebellion—futurism—was hooliganistic. The futurists' most famous public pranks were designed to "shock the philistine," as Livshits put it, or to "throw a bombshell into the joyless, provincial street of the generally joyless existence" of conventional life, in Vasily Kamenskii's words.[107] Shocking the public both symbolized and attracted attention to their more serious aesthetic iconoclasm. Like hooligans, they used the

104. First published in the futurist collection of the same name, *Poshchechina obshchestvennomu vkusu* (Moscow, 1912), the manifesto has been translated and republished numerous times; see Vladimir Markov, *Russian Futurism: A History* (Berkeley, 1968), 45–46.
105. Benedikt Livshits depicted the futurists' disgust with bourgeois commercialization and propriety: "We were choking in a sea of well-intentioned, legalized triviality, and the energy with which a handful of people were trying to clamber out of this putrid mess of necrotic conventions was already prompting the legitimate suspicions of the powers that be" (*The One and a Half-Eyed Archer*, trans. John E. Bowlt, [Newtonville, Mass., 1977], 148).
106. Livshits, *The One and a Half-Eyed Archer*, 128–29; M. N. Yablonskaya, *Women Artists of Russia's New Age, 1900–1935*, ed. and trans. Anthony Parton (London, 1990), 117.
107. Livshits's phrase referred to the futurists' manifesto "A Slap in the Face of Public Taste" (*The One and a Half-Eyed Archer*, 121); Kamenskii's to the futurist publication *Sadok sudei*, variously translated as "A Trap for Judges" or "A Hatchery for Judges," cited in Markov, *Russian Futurism*, 9; this iconoclastic spirit was apparent in all futurist productions.

streets in new ways to create and seize a new kind of authority. They freed art from institutional control by exhibiting paintings and reciting poetry right on the streets.[108] Mikhail Larionov, Natalia Goncharova, Vladimir Mayakovsky, David Burliuk, and others strutted about Moscow in 1912 and 1913 (and later in provincial capitals) with painted faces and with wooden spoons or radishes in their lapels. Their outrageous clothes and their faces painted with flowers, letters of the alphabet, and abstract designs drew crowds of speechless onlookers, whom they tried to shock and entertain by declaiming poetry, reciting nonsense, or advertising that evening's public reading or lecture.[109] In one of the many manifestos futurists produced, Larionov and Ilya Zdanevich claimed: "We paint ourselves because a clean face is offensive, because we want to herald the unknown, to rearrange life."[110]

In a more serious vein, futurists defied artistic convention and "shocked the philistine" at the same time by creating serious works of art that appropriated elements of the culture that society considered "uncultured." They rejected the realism and social didacticism of the nineteenth century and the ethereal aestheticism of their symbolist contemporaries. The futurists invaded the territory of "proper art" with the coarse, crude, primitive, childlike, blasphemous, and erotic, all previously considered inappropriate in the realms of high culture, and they relished the discomfort they caused.[111] To cite but one example, here is Livshits's description of Burliuk's response to a reading of Rimbaud, which celebrates the primitivism and destructiveness in Burliuk's creative method:

> In front of my very eyes Burliuk was devouring his own god, his momentary idol. That's a real carnivore! The way he licked his teeth, the aping triangle on his knee: "The whole world belongs to me!" Could the Makovskys and Gumilevs withstand a folk-giant

108. Camilla Gray, *The Russian Experiment in Art: 1863–1922* (New York, 1962), 114.

109. Markov, *Russian Futurism*, 133–38; Livshits, *The One and a Half-Eyed Archer*, 141–42; Gray, *The Russian Experiment*, 115, 186; Edward J. Brown, *Mayakovsky: A Poet in the Revolution* (Princeton, 1973), 43–44; Ilya Zdanevich and Mikhail Larionov, "Why We Paint Ourselves: A Futurist Manifesto," in *Russian Art of the Avant-Garde: Theory and Criticism, 1902–1934*, ed. and trans. John E. Bowlt (New York, 1976), 79–83.

110. Zdanevich and Larionov, "Why We Paint Ourselves," 83.

111. Gray, *The Russian Experiment*, 106–8, 137; John E. Bowlt, "David Burliuk, The Father of Russian Futurism," *Canadian-American Slavic Studies*, vol. 20, nos. 1–2 (1986): 17, 29; Markov, *Russian Futurism*, 33–35, 42; Patricia Carden, "The Aesthetic of Performance in the Russian Avant-Garde," *CASS*, vol. 19, no. 4 (1985): 375.

like this! . . . And how tempting is this predatoriness! Wherever you look, the world lies before you in utter nakedness, around her tower beskinned mountains, like bloody chunks of smoking meat. Seize it, tear it, get your teeth into it, crush it, create it anew—it's all yours, yours![112]

Primitivism in modernist art had numerous sources, but here one cannot help but see the hooligan with his impudent grin (or the real knife in his hand) lurking behind Burliuk. Other painters, Goncharova and Larionov, for example, took pleasure in shocking audiences with their use of simple folk motifs to portray exalted subjects. The hooligan's defiant swagger can be seen behind Goncharova's peasantlike saints or Larionov's common soldiers and barbers. These gestures perfectly adapted the dualism inherent in the boulevard-press discourse on hooliganism—its coarseness in the face of propriety and tradition, its seriousness and prankishness, its pettiness and its genuine challenge to cultural verities.

The futurists' most famous synthesis of artistic statement with attack on artistic tradition and bourgeois culture was the manifesto with the hooligan gesture for a title, "A Slap in the Face of Public Taste." Issued in 1912 and signed by Burliuk, Mayakovsky, Aleksei Kruchenykh, and Velimir Khlebnikov, the manifesto combined a challenge to the authority of past literary masters (this is where they threw Pushkin, Dostoevsky, and Tolstoy overboard) with an attack on the superficial philistine standards of artistic merit that seemed to determine a work's success:

> And if *for the time being* the filthy marks of your "common sense" and "good taste" remain in our lives, nevertheless, *for the first time* the lightning flashes of the New Future Beauty of the Self-Sufficient word are already on them.[113]

The manifesto also promised the coming of a radical new art, but it was the futurists' rejection of the established masters that created a sensation.[114]

No one was more successful at fusing the playfulness and seriousness of futurism, at refusing the authority of traditional aesthetics while retaining a respect for its achievements, and at rejecting realism's social didacti-

---

112. Livshits, *The One and a Half-Eyed Archer*, 42; see also Markov, *Russian Futurism*, 33–34.
113. Reprinted in Markov, *Russian Futurism*, 46.
114. Elizabeth Kridl Valkenier disagrees, arguing that the futurists achieved public prominence only after Repin blamed the futurists' iconoclasm for indirectly inciting a mentally deranged icon painter to deface a Repin painting ("Il'ia Repin and David Burliuk," *CASS*, vol. 20, nos. 1–2 [1986]:55–57).

cism while addressing pressing social themes than Mayakovsky. In his poem "We Also Want Meat" Mayakovsky reversed conventional roles (celebrating a soldier's license to kill) and welded lyricism to violent, brutal imagery rejecting poetic tradition:

> Soldiers I envy you!
> You have it good!
> Here on a shabby wall are the scraps of human brains, the imprint of shrapnel's five fingers. How clever that hundreds of cut off human heads have been affixed to a stupid field.
> Yes, yes, yes, it's more interesting for you!
> You don't need to think that you owe Pushkin twenty kopecks and why does Yablonovsky write articles.
>
> . . . .
>
> For us—the young poets—Futurism is the toreador's red cloak, it is needed only for the bulls (poor bulls!—I compared them to the critics).
>
> . . . .
>
> Today's poetry—is the poetry of strife.
> Each word must, like a soldier in the army, be made of meat that is healthy, of meat that is red!
> Those who have it—join us!
> Never mind that we used to be unjust.
> When you tear along in a car through hundreds of persecuting enemies, there's no point in sentimentalizing: "Oh a chicken was crushed under the wheels."[115]

It is not hard to understand why the boulevard press responded to futurism the same way it did to hooliganism: with outrage at such exuberant desecration of cherished values of human life and military heroism.

The futurists' varied artistic experiments and public extravaganzas had in common an attempt to create a new realism capable of conveying the fragmentation and cultural complexity of the modern industrial city: in their own words, "to join art to life."[116] The chaotic, violent, and materialistic world ushered in by urbanization and the trauma of the 1905–1907 Revolution required a new kind of social message—one that reflected a new understanding of the complexity of society, a cynicism about traditional cultural and political methods for change, and yet a continued faith in the possibility of transformation. The message also required a new

115. Originally published in *Nov'*, November 16, 1914; here translated by Helen Segall in *The Ardis Anthology of Russian Futurism*, ed. Carl Proffer and Ellendea Proffer (Ann Arbor, Mich., 1980), 187–88.
116. Zdanevich and Larionov, "Why We Paint Ourselves," 81.

language that transcended the debasement of language in the ubiquitous commercial press and that recognized the failure of traditional realism to capture the fragmentation of daily life and the modern psyche. With typical realism, cynicism, and optimism Larionov redefined the achievements of civilization: "We declare the genius of our day to be: trousers, jackets, shoes, tramways, buses, aeroplanes, railways, magnificent ships—what an enchantment—what a great epoch unrivalled in world history."[117] Larionov wanted to join art to life, but he meant a life unfettered by social conventions and free from philistine expectations. He celebrated the simple material objects of everyday life, but not with the venal acquisitiveness of the crass bourgeoisie. He wanted trousers and shoes to be infused with a higher, spiritual, aesthetic meaning. This dual goal was at the heart of the basic contradiction in futurism: on the one hand, its attraction to popular or mass culture and its belief that art has a genuine social purpose, and on the other, its arcane aestheticism. Art historian Camilla Gray condemned the futurists as "rude," "ludicrous," "twisted," and "naive," but she found in their "frantic desire for self-advertisement . . . the social conscience that has always been so active in the Russian artist."[118] Yet the futurists' rejection of their middlebrow audience and their search for pure forms in abstract painting, *zaum* (transrational) poetry, and dissonant music isolated them from a mass audience and from the street spirit that inspired them. And their aestheticism and modernist social sensibility differed radically from the "social conscience" of the old intelligentsia.

In practice "joining art to life" often meant staging a theatrical confrontation between art and life. This is not the contradiction it seems. The futurists' confrontations with bourgeois respectability served to illustrate a contrast between the dead emptiness of propriety and the genuine vitality of the futurists' crude manners and spontaneous nonsense. Futurist public performances always included a lively interaction with the audience, whether in a theater, a lecture hall, a cabaret, or on the street. In public readings and lectures the futurists went beyond the theoretical attack of their manifestos and insulted their audience directly.[119] At a 1913 lecture performance, "The First Evening of the Speech Creators," Mayakovsky offended and provoked the audience when he addressed the military offi-

---

117. Quoted in Gray, *The Russian Experiment*, 136.
118. Ibid., 106–7, 116, 137.
119. The manifestos also became more offensive. "Go To Hell," the manifesto in *Futurists: Roaring Parnassus*, consisted largely of personal insults without theory to justify them. The symbolists, for example, became "crawling little old men of Russian literature" (Markov, *Russian Futurism*, 168).

cers in the front rows as "folds of fat in the stalls." He went on to attack a young man (and by extension all respectable society) with "You men, you all have cabbage stuck in your mouths," and he condemned the artificiality of respectable society by pointing at a young girl and proclaiming: "You women, the power is thick upon you. You look like oysters in shells of objects!" Soon, however, the whole audience, according to Livshits, "learn[ed] a rapid lesson in *budetlianin* (futurist) good taste" and settled in for the fun of the repartee, trading insults with the speakers.[120]

Despite the generally good humor that greeted many of their performances, the futurists reveled in their role as outsiders, much as the hooligans at times seemed to take pleasure in theirs. Kruchenykh claimed that his *zaum* poem "dyr-bul-shchyl" was "more Russian than all the poetry of Pushkin," and he was frequently heard to declare that he had "a sensual longing to be booed." It was Kruchenykh who initiated the futurist convention of throwing tea at the audience, adopted later by Mayakovsky, Burliuk, and Kamenskii on their seventeen-city provincial tour of futurist performances.[121]

Public reactions to futurist street theater ranged from disgust to amusement.[122] The boulevard newspapers responded with derision and outrage to everything the futurists produced (fig. 8, for example). But the futurists' critical audience—the literary press and "thick" journals—tried to ignore futurism.[123] The more sophisticated members of the futurists' audiences came to their performances for the fun of the scandal and participated with bemused detachment. The performances were well attended by the fashionable world of the capitals; so at least some portion of the audience must have shared the futurists' distaste for respectable culture. For the most part, it was understood that an attack on "Pushkin, Dostoevsky,

120. Livshits, *The One and a Half-Eyed Archer*, 150–51. Although it is hard to imagine a contingent of officers at a futurist reading (as spectators, not guards), they appear regularly in descriptions of such audiences. See K. Tomachevsky, "Vladimir Mayakovsky," in *Victory over the Sun*, trans. Ewa Bartos and Victoria Nes Kirby, in *Drama Review*, vol. 15, no. 4 (1971): 99–100.

121. Markov, *Russian Futurism*, 138; Livshits, *The One and a Half-Eyed Archer*, 150–51; Brown, *Mayakovsky*, 44–46. Throwing tea became a regular event at futurist evenings and a symbol of the futurists' insolent challenge to their spectators, closely associated with the movement after the provincial tour in 1913.

122. For examples, see *PL*, January 19, 1914, and March 18, 1914, on the withdrawal of "blasphemous" paintings from a futurist exhibition.

123. To some extent the futurist challenge was a generational one: the young rebels against the art establishment; see Tomachevsky, "Vladimir Mayakovsky," 98; Viktor Shklovsky, *Vladimir Mayakovsky and His Circle*, trans. Lily Feiler (New York, 1972), 52.

Футуризмъ въ архитектурѣ.

Футуристъ. — Я до всего дойду! И до архитектуры доберусь! Весь её фасадъ по своему раздѣлаю! Знай, значитъ, идіота-футуриста Глупыш-кина!..

Figure 8.   Futurism in Architecture (January 19, 1914).
The Futurist is proclaiming that he will do whatever he wants to do; he wants to remake the entire facade of classical architecture, so that his name, Stupidman, will be known worldwide.

Tolstoy, etc., etc.,'' was an attack on philistine reading habits and the constrictions inherent in canonization rather than an attack on the artists themselves. Even Livshits, a futurist and a great fan of futurist performance, was uncomfortable with the belligerent tone and style of ''A Slap in the Face of Public Taste.'' ''I slept with Pushkin under my pillow,'' he wrote, ''and who didn't?''[124] This clearly seems to have been the case at the futurists' most ambitious undertaking, the tandem performances on alternating evenings of *Vladimir Mayakovsky: A Tragedy* and *Victory over the Sun* in December 1913. Mayakovsky later claimed that ''they cat-called like hell,'' and at one point during *Victory over the Sun* spectators shouted: ''You're an ass yourself,'' and some ''heavy fruit buzzed by [one actor's] ear,'' but for the most part the audience responded to Kruchenykh's nonsense libretto, to Kazimir Malevich's extraordinary modernist sets and costumes, and to Mikhail Matiushin's cacophonous music with good-natured, though vocal, amusement and appreciation.[125]

124. Livshits, *The One and a Half-Eyed Archer*, 121.
125. Ibid., 161; Markov, *Russian Futurism*, 146–47; Tomachevsky, ''Vladimir Mayakovsky,'' 100.

For the futurists, the role of society's misfits provided an important source of creativity. As outcasts they could transcend conventional behavior and thought, which allowed them to challenge the standards that defined them as misfits. Just as hooligans challenged conventional behavior in order to "act as they pleased" in public, to quote one young hooligan,[126] the escape from convention freed the futurists from traditional aesthetics and enabled them to exercise their creativity in new directions. The spontaneity of street theater, the use of "inappropriate" elements of popular culture, collaboration with one another and with their audiences: these were the building blocks of the futurists' imaginative achievements.

The freedom of the outcast was also explored by artists who were not futurists but who shared the futurists' fascination with hooligan behavior. Aleksei Remizov, for example, was intrigued by and identified with outsiders and socially marginal characters (such as minstrels [*skomorokhi*] and holy fools) and was well known among his friends as an irreverent prankster. Pranks and imaginative play created a theater in which he could cross the boundaries of socially acceptable behavior and free himself to imagine alternative worlds. Viktor Shklovsky, who participated in Remizov's group "The Great Free Order of Monkeys" (a "theater without makeup and masks") and who parlayed the futurists' verbal experimentation into one of the basic tenets of Russian formalism, claimed about their group that "we play holy fools in order to be free."[127]

Fascination with some form of hooliganism entered the work of some of Russia's most prominent writers. Alexander Blok was unusual in his sensitivity to the divisions between the cultured and the uncultured in late imperial society, but he also believed that some hooligan characteristics—iconoclasm, blasphemy, vulgarity, drunkenness, and profligacy—were "an essential if contradictory part of the Russians' spiritual nature," that is, of Russian culture as a whole.[128] In so thinking, Blok chose to view the intelligentsia's alienation, creativity, and political opposition as akin to hooligan alienation and defiance. But of course that view assumed that there had long been something to challenge: an entrenched conservatism or the weight of tradition. Blok thus declared his identifica-

---

126. Svirskii, "Peterburgskie khuligany," 252.
127. This material on Remizov, including the quotations, is from Greta Nachtailer Slobin, "The Ethos of Performance in Remizov," *CASS*, vol. 19, no. 4 (1985): 419–25.
128. The quote is Chukovsky's formulation; see Kornei Chukovsky, *Alexander Blok as Man and Poet*, trans. and ed. Diana Burgin and Katherine O'Connor (Ann Arbor, Mich., 1982), 136–37.

tion with the hooligans rather than with the traditional or philistine commercial classes whom the hooligans assaulted. But he also understood that hooliganism represented a destructive force and, because educated society (himself included) had virtually no understanding of the common people, an unpredictable one as well.[129] The action in Blok's great poem of the revolution, "The Twelve," revolves around the paradoxically (and hooligan) creative potential in violence, death, and destruction. Stylistically, too, Blok provocatively brought together his own contribution to the great poetic tradition with folk rhythms, *chastushki*, and the harsh, foul language of the streets (while he leaves the bourgeois stranded forlornly on a windswept corner with his tail between his legs).[130]

Sergei Esenin's attraction to hooliganism was less abstract than Blok's and more personally troubling, as well as more artistically stimulating. Esenin adopted a hooligan persona in his poems "Hooligan" and "A Hooligan's Confession," but he also engaged in public hooligan acts: he boasted about chopping up icons for firewood to heat tea, and in 1919 he painted blasphemous and obscene verse on the walls of the Novodevichi convent.[131] Adopting the public pose of a crude, brazen hooligan allowed Esenin to reenact his own crossing of both cultural (especially religious) and class boundaries in his journey from peasant to poet. "A Hooligan's Confession" captivatingly alternates lyrical self-knowledge with vulgar self-assertion. Andrei Bely also employed a hooligan pose to explore serious, even spiritual issues. His short poem "A Little Hooligan's Song" depicts a jaded and ironic indifference in the face of death by joining the light singsong of a nursery rhyme with a violent hooligan's cynical disregard for the value of others' lives.[132]

It is not that these writers condoned hooligan crimes but that they saw hooliganism as representative of an attitude that resonated throughout

---

129. Blok's essays on these subjects span the period between 1908 and 1918: "Narod i intelligentsia," *Zolotoe runo* 1 (1909); "Ironiia," *Rech'*, December 7, 1908; "Stikhiia i kul'tura," *Nasha gazeta*, January 6, 1909; "Intelligentsia i revoliutsiia," *Znamia truda*, January 19, 1918; these and other essays were republished together as *Rossiia i intelligentsiia* (Petersburg, 1919).
130. "Dvenadtsat'" was originally published in *Znamia truda*, February 18, 1918.
131. The painted lines included "Look at the fat thighs/ Of this obscene wall./ Here the nuns at night/ Remove Christ's trousers," quoted in Gordon McVay, *Esenin: A Life* (New York, 1976), 119–20. Esenin's hooligan poems were originally published as "Khuligan," *Znamia* 5 (1920); and "Ispoved' khuligana," *Poeziia revoliutsionnoi Moskvy*, November 1920.
132. Andrei Belyi, "Khuliganskaia pesenka," *Korabli* (Moscow, 1907), reprinted in *Vecherniaia zaria*, May 7, 1907.

Russian culture in the 1910s. They recognized in the hooligans' behavior the same challenge to respectability and to the old intelligentsia's culturalism that the boulevard press recognized, only the artists embraced those challenges as a source of creativity—or as purifying destruction necessary for some kind of rebirth. The hooligan persona appealed to writers and artists of this period for the same reasons Rabelais's "carnivalesque" intrigued Bakhtin later on. Futurist performances, appearing like carnival in a "theater without footlights," allowed writers to stand outside the cultural establishment and look to the streets for "support in the struggle against the official culture." Acting as hooligans, the Russian modernists could throw off the weight of tradition, they could hurl tea at the seriousness with which Russian culture viewed itself, and they could revitalize Russian culture by mocking and destroying the old and starting anew. Bakhtin's "popular-festive carnival spirit" was, in the same way, profoundly ambivalent: at once degrading and transcendent. Carnival freed people to bring vulgar behavior out into the open, to mock authorities, and to invert hierarchies of power—to laugh at everything serious—but this "destruction and uncrowning are related to birth and renewal" in Bakhtin: "The death of the old is linked with regeneration; all the images [of carnival] are connected with the contradictory oneness of the dying and reborn world."[133]

③ Cultural Diversity and Social Fragmentation

Obviously there is a world of difference between young thugs throwing tea out a doorway at unsuspecting pedestrians and artists throwing tea on spectators who are expecting scandal and paying for the privilege. However, the manifold differences in class, purpose, context, danger, and audience cannot efface the importance of the similarities. The two phenomena were both responses to and agents of the same cultural changes then taking place in Russian society. The simple fact that hooliganism was appearing in new contexts was evidence of its cultural significance and its wide evocativeness. The similarities between futurism and rural and urban hooliganism show why hooliganism was evolving into a broad and enduring cultural category, able to convey important messages to many audiences. Specifically, the appearance of hooliganism in new settings demonstrated the general importance of cultural issues in Russia in the 1910s, the breakdown of consensus about them, the value of the public street as an arena

133. Bakhtin, *Rabelais*, 7, 11–12, 75, 217, 273–75.

for enacting the cultural conflicts involved, and the inability of the law to regulate such behavior.

The similarities between hooliganism and futurism began with the comparable public responses they provoked. The critics who attacked one attacked the other, and those who dismissed one dismissed the other, often in the same terms. Significantly, those who paid these criminals and rebels the least attention were also those who failed to appreciate the cultural challenge inherent in their ill-mannered public behavior. The boulevard press portrayed futurist artists much like hooligan ruffians, as incomprehensible, uncultured savages out to destroy civilization and its classic achievements. The established intelligentsia, professional art critics, and legal specialists tended to minimize the importance of both hooliganism and futurism. Among artists, although some attention was given to the futurists' publications and productions, their public antics were ignored in most serious literary circles and journals. Notably, the artists were often dismissed as "hooligans." Vasily Kandinsky repudiated "A Slap in the Face of Public Taste" as "hooliganism," and Burliuk was known as "a hooligan of the palette."[134] The disparaging implication here was that just as hooliganism was no real crime, Burliuk was no real innovator, and "A Slap in the Face" no more than irritating public rowdiness. The futurists' wild exhibitionist behavior was perceived as purposeless and unnecessary self-indulgence, just as hooliganism was seen as motiveless, petty self-assertion.

Time has proven the philistine boulevard press, despite its outraged tone, to have been more astute (if less sympathetic) than the guardians of law and high culture. In retrospect it is clear that the cultural conflicts embodied in the hooligans' and futurists' mockery of bourgeois respectability and traditional authorities and their challenge to the cultural standards of the old intelligentsia represented a genuine and deep-seated hostility toward the power of elite culture.[135] The increasing fragmentation and complexity of Russian social and cultural life was more readily acknowledged, though not explicitly and certainly not approvingly, in the boulevard press than among the country's political leaders, including opposition liberals and radicals, with their continued faith in the intelligentsia's mission to civilize the Russian people. The futurists recognized changes in

---

134. Markov, *Russian Futurism,* 392 n. 26; Bowlt, "Burliuk," 25.
135. That hostility erupted during and after the 1917 revolutions, as Richard Stites has shown, in similar forms of iconoclasm ("Revolutionary Iconoclasm," in *Revolutionary Dreams: Utopian Visions and Experimental Life in the Russian Revolution* [Oxford, 1989], 59–78).

the urban context that required a new language, new behavior, and new skills. But their abrasive behavior, their incomprehensible utterances, and their own didacticism won them little support in late imperial society.[136]

Both hooligans and futurists used public space in innovative ways, changing the quality of street life. Art and literary historians have long perceived the futurists' public behavior—their street theater and stage antics—as a component of their aesthetic message. As cultural products these public acts expressed the futurists' aesthetics, their values, their response to the social environment, and their demand for recognition of an alternative to the culture of the status quo. The hooligans' public behavior should be seen in the same light, as a cultural product. Although they were not making an aesthetic statement, their rowdy and crude behavior expressed their values, their response to the world around them, and their demand for attention. Both hooligans and futurists understood (though again not necessarily consciously) the power of public performance and the cultural significance of public behavior. They both adopted street theater as a medium because they were aware of the ways in which behavior (like clothing or manners) defined people and identified them with a set of values. Hooligans found behavior a useful weapon in part because they lacked a sophisticated political language; for futurists, dramatic behavior filled the gap left by a literary language that inadequately captured their message. For both, the seizure of public space attracted immediate attention, and their public performances created new kinds of power.

Hooligans and futurists used their new powers to invade the "cultured" world with rowdiness and blasphemy and to "shock the philistine," in order to challenge the elitist, purposive, rationalist cultural ideology of the nineteenth-century intelligentsia and the forms it took when adopted by the new intelligentsia. The futurists' attack on bourgeois philistinism and the old intelligentsia's culturalism was articulate and explicit: they claimed that nineteenth-century aesthetics were outdated, and they provided their own alternatives. The hooligans' challenge to culturalism was implicit in their attack on the respectable bourgeoisie. Hooligans openly refused to accept the role of cultureless objects who could be transformed with a

136. Many in the new generation of professional and commercial circles were also more aware of the need for new solutions to urban problems and were proud of the practical skills they might contribute, contrasting themselves with the old intelligentsia. But Bowlt argues that the merchant patrons of the avant-garde artists of the 1890s and 1900s were repelled, or at best amused, by the futurists' antics in the 1910s; see West, "The Riabushinskii Circle," 43, and Bowlt, "Moscow Art," 127–28, in *Between Tsar and People*.

simple infusion of what educated society, playing Pygmalion, considered culture. Whether people celebrated or deplored it, the spread of hooliganism in its multiple forms convinced a significant portion of the educated population—including important cultural figures, prominent urban political activists and commercial-press journalists, and reactionary defenders of the regime—that Russia's capacity to assimilate its people into a single cultured society and become a civilized and politically unified nation was diminishing with each passing day.[137]

These similarities force us to reconsider the designation of any cultural artifact as a product solely of class. Hooliganism and futurism were not devoid of class issues, but the futurists' use of hooligan tactics indicated that class was only one component of the conflicts in question, and that cultural politics crossed class lines. When one views each as part of a broader cultural movement one can understand why a rash of petty crimes and a series of silly public displays gained extraordinary prominence.

Just as hooliganism in St. Petersburg before 1905 advertised the existence of cultural diversity while most of society was still attached to universalist ideals, rural and modernist hooliganism represented forms of cultural pluralism their audiences only partly perceived. Together modernism and hooliganism not only dramatized the breakdown of traditional authority (which had assumed the submissiveness of the young, the poor, and the unpublished) but also revealed the collapse of cultural consensus and the rise of alternative ideas about behavior, values, and traditions. When writers from Zaslavskii to Goranovskii to commentators in *Peterburgskii listok* wrote about the hooligans of the privileged classes they were not associating Mayakovsky with the nameless knife wielder in a back alley or claiming that throwing rocks at pedestrians was identical with wearing radishes in buttonholes. They were defining a broad cultural environment in which the dominant motifs were diversity and challenge. Paradoxically, the similarities between hooligans and futurists across classes reveal the extent of cultural diversity and social fragmentation in Russia. In the context of simmering political discontent, the multiplication of cultures and the erosion of the power of culturalism to unify educated society contributed to the overall fragmentation and instability in Russia at the end of the old regime.

Andrei Bely articulated this fragmentation and its consequences better than anyone in his great symbolist novel *Petersburg*, and he used hooligan motifs (among many other techniques) to do so. Set in October 1905,

---

137. Further discussed in chapter 5.

Petersburg captured the bewildering insecurity and uncertainty of public life, partly through continual shifts in tone and perspective, but also by describing a city whose open spaces had become dangerous, unfamiliar, and ominously swollen by the "human myriapod." The Petersburg streets "transform passersby into shadows," Bely wrote, and even when one can escape indoors, "the street flows in your veins like a fever."[138] The forces that threaten the city expand or flow out into its streets: the "swarm" of workers from the factories encircling Petersburg and the Mongol or Asiatic hordes hovering on Russia's borders. The novel's plot pits Nikolai Ableukhov, a student intellectual, against his father, Apollon Ableukhov, a high government official, after the son is recruited by shadowy radicals to assassinate his father. But when the revolutionaries' bomb finally explodes, no one is hurt and nothing is destroyed except the already frayed relationship between father and son. For Bely the key conflict in Russia was not the obvious one enacted in 1905 between the intelligentsia and the state, which he depicted as father and son, embattled but essentially members of one family. More fundamental was the clash between the obsolete forces that had structured Russian society since the time of Peter the Great and the multiple forces of disorder threatening to destroy Russia. Though the state and the intelligentsia had once been creative, responsible for Russia's great achievements, both had become stuck in a lifeless, abstract, dogmatic, overly rational, and cowardly rut, protected from the anarchy of the streets but also cut off from their vitality.[139] Both father and son are terrified of life on the streets, in open spaces, in the "immeasurable expanses" of their country. Apollon feels safe only when he has retreated behind walls: in his carriage, "cut off from the scum of the streets by four perpendicular walls," or better yet deep inside his house, in his bathroom. Nikolai feels safe only outside, wearing a mask and a costume.[140]

But in this novel of shifting perspective, even these divisions are meant to be partial and overlapping. Peter the Great is both Creator and Anti-Christ, "authoritarian father figure and rebellious son."[141] Nikolai is an enervated intellectual, but he is also a hooligan. He agrees to murder his

---

138. Bely, *Petersburg*, 14, 17, 22, 51.
139. What follows is based partly on a discussion of Bely's article "The Line, the Circle, the Spiral—of Symbolism," in Robert A. Maguire and John E. Malmstad, "Petersburg," in *Andrey Bely: Spirit of Symbolism*, ed. John E. Malmstad (Ithaca, N.Y., 1987); Vladimir Alexandrov, *Andrei Bely: The Major Symbolist Fiction* (Cambridge, Mass., 1985); David M. Bethea, *The Shape of Apocalypse in Modern Russian Fiction* (Princeton, 1989).
140. Bely, *Petersburg*, 10, 12, 82, 122, 248.
141. Bethea, *The Shape of Apocalypse*, 125.

father for hooligan reasons (not for ideological or philosophical ones), his "clownish stunts" evoke "loathing and horror," and he sulks about the city disguised in a red domino, alternately amusing and terrorizing people (and getting noticed in the crime chronicle). Bely's Petersburg is a nightmare carnival, where the freedom from structure does not offer a temporary release into subversion and parody but a permanent plunge into contingency. Nothing in the novel is grounded: motives and even events are murky, all knowledge and meaning is conditional and contested, and the city itself floats in and out of focus, rising behind a scrim of dust and fog: all that is solid melts into air. In *Petersburg*, Russia's crisis is not a struggle between one or another ideology or even one or another vision of Russia, but fragmentation itself. Peter the Great thunders his bronze steed through the streets of the novel (still capable of terrifying people), but his vision for Russia has run its contradictory course; it is being swamped by the weight of its own divisive legacy and by Larionov's trousers and tramways. The popular revolt of 1905 (portrayed—and dismissed—in the novel as spontaneous turmoil punctuated by isolated sputtered slogans) could challenge the moribund old powers but held out slim promise for reunification or renaissance. The old forces for progress in Russia, whether reform from above or intelligentsia culturalism, could not cope with the multiple new problems of the modern city or face the challenges to their authority from seemingly every direction, and new alternatives seemed to promise only more contention. Bely portrayed a thoroughly divided and rudderless society marked by aimless and fruitless, but often destructive, challenges to authorities. He used the fractured, symbolic forms of his novel to convey the irreversible fragmentation of social and intellectual life in Russia, to reject the optimistic, rationalist realism of the old intelligentsia and the revolutionary movement, and to represent the ominous (but possibly creative) forces swelling the streets. Bely's apocalypticism has been read, in part as a transcendent, unearthly vision, but it was, at the same time, rooted in the everyday street life and historical reality of the city. The social coordinates of Bely's Petersburg correspond to the issues raised by the discourse on hooliganism: the seizure of public space, the challenge to traditional authorities, the fragmentation of society, and the discord over cultural issues. The prominence of these themes in the greatest Russian novel of this period helps explain why the boulevard-press battle with hooliganism could spread such wide and powerful ripples.

4 Nobody's Children
Juvenile Crime, Youth Culture, and the Roots of Hooliganism

Children of the streets, *Nobody's Children*, *bezprizornye*
children: this is the contingent, and it is enormous, from
which issue the depraved children and the criminal children.
— N. A. Okunev
1913

During the years when hooliganism was becoming a symbol of disorder, degeneration, and iconoclasm, hooligans posed an everyday practical problem for judicial officials, criminologists, and social workers. While the State Duma and the national "thick" journals were debating the finer points of the law by focusing on broad social and cultural developments, the local judicial communities in St. Petersburg and Moscow were undertaking detailed investigations into the specific causes of hooliganism and considering the immediate, practical steps necessary to prevent its further growth. Unlike their nationally prominent colleagues, the local jurists took hooliganism more seriously as a manifestation of urban instability. They saw hooligans as alienated from society in ways that had dangerous social and cultural consequences. Hooligans, they believed, never developed an inclination to work or take part in respectable working-class society, they were fatalistic about their position in the world, they were hardened by life on the streets and in prison, and they were becoming increasingly aggressive. Unlike *Peterburgskii listok* and the observers discussed in the previous chapter, the judicial experts viewed hooliganism as a genuine and serious but curable problem. Because the jurists and criminologists saw hooliganism as rooted in the values that shaped a hooligan's mentality and way of life, they sought an understanding of its causes in lower-class culture. And because they concentrated on prevention, they looked for its causes in childhood and in the institutions where the values of youth culture were formed: in the family and on the streets.

Assumptions about hooliganism led these specialists in crime and law to a sweeping examination of the lower-class family, lower-class youth culture, and juvenile crime. Their concern about the rise of hooliganism induced the Petersburg Justices of the Peace and a small band of social workers to fight an aggressive campaign against juvenile crime (with little in the way of government support or funding), which culminated in a significant reform of the local juvenile judicial system. Similar anxieties about lower-class families, youth, and juvenile crime and similar reform projects appeared throughout Western Europe and the United States during this period.[1] But the Russian experience was deeply influenced by concerns that young criminals would evolve into mature hooligans. When the Petersburg Justices of the Peace fought to establish a special court for juveniles, they did so not only to accommodate the needs of young offenders better, but explicitly to prevent the alienation that led hooligans to attack society.

It was not that most hooligans were young or that their rebelliousness was viewed as a function of youth—that discourse, perhaps surprisingly, is missing here.[2] Discussion of hooliganism as youth rebellion, as a temporary phase in the lower-class life cycle, as the result of a difficult transformation from youngster to adult, did not appear in the press or in the publicistic or legal literature in Russia.[3] Children and youths were often mentioned in press and professional discussions of hooliganism, but usually as an additional evil, a supplementary shock, or a potential problem. The professional criminologists and jurists did not see hooliganism as a youth problem; they saw juvenile crime as a breeding ground for grown hooligans.

Although some specialists stressed social and economic factors, which they believed produced juvenile crime and hooliganism, most saw hooliganism as a mentality or a moral propensity generated within lower-class culture.[4] Their investigations into the family, youth culture, and the

---

1. See, for example, Gillis, *Youth and History*; Derek S. Linton, *"Who Has the Youth, Has the Future": The Campaign to Save Young Workers in Imperial Germany* (Cambridge, 1991); Lenard R. Berlanstein, "Vagrants, Beggars, and Thieves: Delinquent Boys in Mid-Nineteenth-Century Paris," *Journal of Social History*, vol. 12, no. 4 (1979).

2. Compare with Robert Nye's discussion of Parisian apaches, Christopher Stone's of New York vandals, Stephen Humphries' of London hooligans; see p. 3 n. 4. The overwhelming majority of people arrested for hooligan crimes in St. Petersburg were seventeen and over; see tables 1, 2, 5, and 8 in the Appendix.

3. These theories derive from post–World War II studies of youth crime and gang activity; see Richard Cloward and Lloyd Ohlin, *Delinquency and Opportunity: A Theory of Delinquent Gangs* (Glencoe, Ill., 1963); Rose Giallombardo, ed., *Juvenile Delinquency: A Book of Readings* (New York, 1976).

4. This is in contrast to the professional discourse on crime in the 1860s, another period of heightened concern about crime, when, as Reginald Zelnik argues, there had been broad agreement based on an application of enlightenment social science that crime and the "debauchery and depravity so reviled by the police" were rooted

origins of hooliganism are often thoughtful, thorough, and sympathetic, and, as such, they provide another perspective on hooliganism as well as a new source for examining the lives of the youngest and the poorest of the poor in the Russian industrial city. However, the judicial experts studied lower-class culture in isolation from the rest of society, which seriously skewed their analysis and doomed to failure the projects they generated. This is particularly ironic because social and cultural interaction were at the heart of their reform program. At the national level discussed in the previous chapter, the "cultural measures" liberals clamored for rarely evolved beyond rhetorical statements and policy recommendations, but at the local level, cultural improvement projects were devised by a host of charitable organizations and municipal institutions. Indeed, the cultural improvement of the lower classes was considered essential for social assimilation and stability. As such it was a primary feature of the *obshchestvennost'*, or civic-mindedness, that dominated professional and middle-class activism and identity in the early twentieth century.[5]

The judicial community involved on the local level in the observation, analysis, and prevention of juvenile crime and hooliganism was typical of the post-1907 generation of social observers and activists. They were middle-class, well-educated professionals committed to eradicating some of the social problems that the revolution brought out into the open. For all they shared in the way of dedication they represented a somewhat diverse range of social, political, and educational levels. They included schoolteachers who volunteered as social workers and "guardians" for convicted juveniles on probation, university professors carrying out serious sociological research, prison officials, and Justices of the Peace actively engaged in judicial practice and research and in adapting the judicial and penal systems to contemporary needs. The journalists who reported on juvenile crime and hooliganism and who saw themselves as shaping public debate might also be included here. At times these individuals spoke to a national audience, but their primary concerns were with local problems and conditions. As a whole, this group tended to be liberal politically, with a sprinkling of socialists; they were primarily men, but there were a few women among them. They shared an optimistic view of the prospects for social assimilation and stability, believing that education and cultural development, as

---

in social and economic conditions rather than in moral deficiencies; see Zelnik, *Labor and Society*, 279–80. See also *Golos*, April 4, 1865, for example, where the recent increase in public drunkenness was described as a "social misfortune."
5. On related views expressed by other middle-class and professional groups see essays in *Between Tsar and People*.

they called it, would allow the lower classes to enter the ranks of respectable—though not necessarily middle-class—society. Like other members of the intelligentsia, these observers and activists were animated by a sense of public duty, including a mission to bring culture to the lower classes. The Justices of the Peace, for example, saw themselves not only as officials of the state, but as teachers, protectors, and benefactors of the desperately poor and culturally deprived.[6] They perceived the discontent so visibly displayed during the 1905–1907 Revolution as a sign of the urgency with which they needed to address long-standing social problems. And as professionals they believed that they differed from the old intelligentsia in their possession of powerful new tools for effecting social and cultural improvement, for carrying out the historic mission of educated society on a new, practical level.

These attitudes shaped the measures they designed for resolving Russia's social problems, but class interaction for them was strictly a one-way affair. They knew what they might offer the poor and uncultured, but they had little understanding of how they and their mission of cultural improvement might be received. As the mostly middle-class Justices of the Peace attempted to instill a rudimentary work ethic and a sense of respectable ambition in poor children in order to correct the deficiencies of lower-class culture and lure these children away from the streets, the Justices invariably ran into resistance. Although they achieved some success, these reform projects may have ultimately deepened the hostility of the city's poor youth toward the culture of respectability by trying to impose cultural improvement without also offering the possibility of concrete social and economic betterment. Thus the projects offer a case study in the developing relations between the professional middle classes and the urban poor, giving us insight into the interactive process of social self-identification. And no matter how slanted their conclusions, these studies provide an extensive look at life in the lower depths.

▤ *The Lower-Class Family,* Bezprizornost', *and Juvenile Crime*

There was a broad consensus in the capital among jurists, criminologists, and journalists representing a wide spectrum of newspapers that the children and adolescents who committed crimes were from troubled working-class families. These children had been deprived of the proper family su-

---

6. For a discussion of the mission of the Justices of the Peace, see N. N. Polianskii, "Mirovoi sud," in *Sudebnaia reforma*, ed. N. V. Davydov and N. N. Polianskii (Moscow, 1915); and Neuberger, "Popular Legal Cultures."

pervision and "moral upbringing" necessary to instill a proper work ethic and a healthy respect for other people, their property, and the law. They were *bezprizornye*—literally: uncared-for, untended, unsupervised, uncontrolled. Lacking family support and deprived of the concerned, watchful eyes of parents, these children were left to grow up "on the streets." Exposure to the dangers and immorality of the streets destroyed the children's moral fiber, alienated them from the world of respectable work, destroyed their hopes for the future, and set them outside of and against society. As a result, it was thought, they stood a good chance of developing into hooligans, in whom such characteristics became more or less engrained.

Historically, *bezprizornost'* has been associated with the social chaos of the 1920s, when millions of parentless, homeless children were seen roaming the Russian cities and countryside "in packs, robbing and killing in the brutal need to survive," as one historian put it.[7] Many starved or were themselves killed, but just as in prerevolutionary cities, stories about the most violent or dangerous *bezprizorniki*, as they were called, were publicized, while their less conspicuous cohorts fell by the wayside. Despite the astronomical increase in the number of homeless children after 1917 and despite their visibility and the impact they had on society as a whole, *bezprizorniki* and the problem of *bezprizornost'* were not a product of revolution and war: *bezprizornost'* was first recognized as an acute social ill at least a decade before 1914. In 1908, at the VII Congress for Representatives of Russian Juvenile Correctional Institutions, the criminologist and working-class advocate D. A. Dril' noted that while *bezprizornost'* had been mentioned more or less in passing at the previous congress in 1904, it had by 1908 become "the most important factor" in juvenile crime and hooliganism, and "an extraordinarily important problem for state and society."[8] So although the *bezprizorniki* of the Soviet period were more

---

7. Roger Pethybridge, *The Social Prelude to Stalinism* (New York, 1974), 55. The best recent studies of *bezprizornost'* in the Soviet period are Wendy Z. Goldman, "The 'Withering Away' and the Resurrection of the Soviet Family, 1917–1936," (Ph.D. diss., University of Pennsylvania, 1987); Peter H. Juviler, "Contradictions of Revolution: Juvenile Crime and Rehabilitation," in *Bolshevik Culture*, ed. Abbott Gleason, Peter Kenez, and Richard Stites (Bloomington, Ind., 1985); Jennie Stevens, "Children of the Revolution: Soviet Russia's Homeless Children (Besprizorniki) in the 1920s," *Russian History* 9 (1982); Alan Ball, "The Roots of Besprizornost' in Soviet Russia's First Decade," *Slavic Review*, vol. 51, no. 2 (1992).
8. D. A. Dril', "O merakh bor'by s prestupnost'iu nesovershennoletnikh," *Trudy sed'mogo s"ezda predstavitelei russkikh ispravitel'nykh zavedenii dlia maloletnikh, Okt. 1908 goda* (Moscow, 1909), 14–15.

numerous and desperate, and the society in which they operated more unstable and chaotic, the Soviet waifs were the heirs to a set of circumstances, to customs and patterns of existence, and to attitudes—both their own toward society and society's toward them—that developed earlier. The historical context of the rise of hooliganism—mass urban migration, economic transformation, and revolution—also enveloped the appearance of *bezprizornost*. Both were accompanied by a significant shift in the place children held in urban society.

Children were becoming a more visible presence in the capital as their numbers grew in proportion to the rest of the population. The city government was entirely unprepared to absorb large numbers of children into the population and unwilling to expend scarce resources on their behalf.[9] But the children of the poor also posed conceptual problems for middle-class and professional society, because the youths forced the middle classes to confront unresolved contradictions in their views of lower-class family life. Lower-class youths did not fit easily into established social categories. On the one hand childhood for them was deferred by the necessity of working for wages from a very young age. And at the same time, the economic realities of urban life postponed some of the responsibilities of adulthood because city boys commonly delayed marriage or left their wives and children in the countryside. Both situations led to the need for a community outside of family and a tightening of ties with peer groups.[10] The loosening of family bonds suggested here was not necessarily as drastic as it sounds or as it seemed to contemporary observers. It should be kept in mind that in many respects middle-class culture defined family life, family responsibilities, and the stages of maturation far more rigidly than the lower classes did. Whether by necessity or desire, lower-class families and lower-class culture were more loosely structured, and adult duties fell upon children at different ages than in middle-class families. Furthermore, when parents were unavailable, other responsible social institutions, such as groups with common village ties (*zemliachestva*) or

9. Everywhere in the empire City Dumas were controlled by members of the middle classes, who used city funds to improve the services and enhance the quality of life in their own neighborhoods and in the central districts primarily used by the elite and respectable population. On city fiscal policies in St. Petersburg and other major cities see the essays in Hamm, *The City in Late Imperial Russia*; Robert W. Thurston, *Liberal City, Conservative State: Moscow and Russia's Urban Crisis, 1906–1914* (New York, 1987).
10. Diane Koenker, "Urban Families, Working-Class Youth Groups, and the 1917 Revolution in Moscow," in *The Family in Imperial Russia: New Lines of Historical Research*, ed. David L. Ransel (Urbana, Ill., 1978), 283–87.

work units (*arteli*) or relatives, may have stepped in to fill the gap. But to middle-class observers of lower-class life the growing population of urban youth was living in an unregulated, unstructured environment, burdened by work when too young and unconstrained by responsibilities to their own children when already in their twenties. As a result, many youths were left free to wander the streets, creating a new set of problems for the city. These anxieties about the sprawling presence of poor children and youths shaped professional observers' interpretations of juvenile crime and its role in propagating hooliganism.

In 1903, the anonymous compiler of the annual St. Petersburg statistical collection interrupted his otherwise straightforward account of that year's events to express a sense of moral outrage. "As is well known," he declared, the increase in juvenile crime "testifies to the moral decline of our capital."[11] The statistical collections published by the St. Petersburg city administration were not known for personal interjections of opinion, but this anonymous indignation was typical of the heated response juvenile crime was provoking in St. Petersburg. The annual compilations of the Petersburg Justice of the Peace Court, which had jurisdiction over all petty crimes, showed the number of juvenile crimes committed to be on a sharp incline. The absolute number of convictions rose from 1,113 in 1900 to more than two-and-a-half times that number in 1910, when 2,848 juveniles were convicted. However, the actual ratio of juvenile crimes to all crimes was tiny. Before World War I juvenile convictions in St. Petersburg never reached 4 percent of the city's total convictions.[12] The empirewide statistics on juvenile crime also seemed alarming at the time. In his review of the period 1901–10, the leading statistician in the Ministry of Justice, E. N. Tarnovskii, argued that juvenile criminal convictions in the empire as a whole had risen at a rate of 111 percent (while total criminal convictions had increased by only 35 percent) and that the rate of increase far outstripped rates everywhere in Western Europe (see tables 7–9 in the Appendix).[13] However, while Russian rates of increase rose much more quickly than those in major Western European countries, the absolute number of juveniles (ten through sixteen years old) convicted in Russia

11. *Statisticheskii ezhegodnik S.-Peterburga za 1903 g.* (St. Petersburg, 1903), 127.
12. There was a short-lived decline in 1906–7 that paralleled total convictions and occurred for the political reasons discussed in chapter 2.
13. E. N. Tarnovskii, "Dvizhenie chisla nesovershennoletnikh (10–17 let) osuzhdennykh v sviazi s obshchim rostom prestupnosti v Rossii za 1901–1910 gg.," *Zhurnal ministerstva iustitsii* 10 (1913):45ff.

during these years remained small: under 4,000 through 1907, and in 1910, only 7,483. The percentage of youths convicted never exceeded 5 percent of the country's total convictions.[14] In comparison, in 1910 in Germany 51,315 juveniles were convicted of crimes, and in 1909 in Austria 8,945 juveniles were convicted. Even if we add the number of cases Tarnovskii estimated were tried by land captains and in village and Justice of the Peace courts—the figures cited above included only major crimes tried in the circuit courts—we still arrive at only approximately 25,000 convictions.[15] In light of the enormous differences in general population size, Russia's relative juvenile crime problems shrank still farther. In 1910 Germany had a population of approximately 64.9 million people, Austria 28.6 million, and Russia more than 160.7 million people.[16]

At first glance, it would seem that the agitation over these figures was exaggerated out of all proportion to the actual scale of the juvenile crime. The absolute numbers were small, and their comparison with those of other cities and countries remained favorable. But the statistics tell only part of the story. If the analysts were responding to the heightened visibility of youngsters in the city and the largely negative impressions those children left, then their reaction to the statistics makes more sense. There was, at the turn of the century, a dramatic increase in the sheer number of children residing in the city, and while the population of all age groups in Petersburg grew by leaps and bounds between 1900 and 1910, the proportion of children under seventeen years old grew most sharply.[17] Furthermore, the "dark figure" of actual crimes committed was undoubtedly much higher than the prosecution data suggest. Juvenile crime, in particular, is notoriously underprosecuted; so the impact of youth's increased visibility on the streets was intensified by the fact that they were

14. Tarnovskii, "Dvizhenie chisla nesovershennoletnikh," 49–55.
15. Ibid., 77.
16. Carlo M. Cipolla, ed., *The Fontana Economic History of Europe* (London, 1973), 747.
17. The only two groups in the population to increase as proportions of the whole were children up to the age of ten, and ten- to fifteen-year-olds. The total population increased by 32.8 percent between 1900 and 1910 while the number of children under the age of ten grew by 50 percent between 1900 and 1910, from 16.1 percent of the total population to 18.4 percent; the number of ten- to fifteen-year-olds increased by 34 percent, slightly more than the overall rate, and proportionally from 7.7 percent of the total to 7.9 percent. The proportion of all other groups to the total dropped. E. E. Kruze and D. G. Kutsentov, "Naselenie Peterburga," in *Ocherki istorii Leningrada*, vol. 3, ed. B. M. Kochakov (Moscow and Leningrad, 1956), 109; in Moscow in the same period the ratio of children to women also increased; see Bradley, *Muzhik and Muscovite*, 222.

unconstrained by the police. As we will see, popular and professional views of juvenile crime were influenced by these impressions of street life and anxieties about encroaching disorder at least as much as by the increase in convictions. Here again, hooliganism became a useful image for ordering perceptions of a troublesome social problem as observers sketched a correlation between the unsupervised child, the unruly adolescent, and the ultimately amoral and incorrigible hooligan.

o   o   o   o

Links between full-fledged hooliganism, juvenile crime, and childhood *bezprizornost'* were described by experts on both juvenile crime and hooliganism. In 1904, penologists and criminologists at the VI Congress for Representatives of Russian Juvenile Correctional Institutions were particularly disturbed by a rise in crimes that seemed distinctly hooliganistic. A. A. Fidler introduced these problems of juvenile crime as "so broad, complex, and difficult" that he thought the delegates could only begin to discuss them, having first to decide "What steps to take? Which ones are our responsibility?" Fidler said that "ruined" children

> are first of all pranksters and practical jokers (*balovnikov, shalunov*), but their pranks and jokes are different from ordinary pranks and jokes, which are more or less natural for all children, . . . but thanks to a bad example, thanks to *bezprizornost'*, and to the evil influence of their families, these pranks and jokes take on a bad and often immoral character. As a prank, these children torture animals; as a prank, they ruin or break anything that comes into their hands; as a prank, they beat their pals and often beat them brutally . . . ; it even happens that for the sake of a prank they commit arson, and there was a case where for the sake of a prank they committed murder.[18]

"In general," he went on, "ruined children seem fully unbridled; they recognize no authority other than physical strength, and not always even that." Their moral sense, he thought, was undeveloped, and their sense of responsibility for their actions was nonexistent.[19] The VII Congress of

---

18. A. A. Fidler, "O merakh bor'by s detskoiu prestupnost'iu," *Trudy shestogo s''ezda predstavitelei russkikh ispravitel'nykh zavedenii dlia maloletnikh, Mai 1904 goda* (Moscow, 1904), 417–19.
19. Ibid., 420.

the same group, meeting in 1908, devoted a number of sessions to the connections between juvenile crime, *bezprizornost*, and hooliganism.[20] And in 1911, at the VIII Congress, Fidler acknowledged that what he had been describing in 1904 had become well known as hooliganism.[21]

The belief that juvenile criminals were *bezprizorniki* who turned into hooligans was not confined to criminologists, however. Journalists from the boulevard press as well as the conservative, official press saw *bezprizorniki* turn to crime and then to hooliganism as early as 1903. In that year, one *Peterburgskii listok* article on the hooligan problem concluded that most hooligans were "children of the working class, free to wander untended around the streets and squares of the capital . . . [and] children who have served time in juvenile prisons (who had entered prison not entirely despoiled, but emerged as hooligans)."[22] The following year, *S.-Peterburgskie vedomosti* published an "open letter" that explicitly blamed the working-class family for leaving poor children uncared-for and unwatched:

> Who then are our hooligans? They are the majority of children who, from the first days of their existence, find themselves, for a variety of reasons, without parental care. Deprived of such refuge they grow up in the terrible environment of the slums. . . . In place of love, motherly concern, even pity, they know only hunger and cold in their terrifying situation. They know only abuse and coldheartedness; their pitiful little bodies are beaten and mutilated to arouse pity when begging. They become accustomed to lying and thievery, acquainted with bad language and all sorts of amoral talk and depravity. . . . All this, at a certain age, will bear fruit, and when that fruit has been discarded by human society, when it is hungry and has no reason to respond to kindness, it becomes depraved and malicious—a hooligan with nothing to lose.[23]

In 1914, when an audience of eminent Petersburgers crowded into the auditorium of the Kalashnikov stock market to hear a public discussion on the "campaign against hooliganism," the main speeches concerned juvenile crime. State Duma delegate M. M. Novikov exclaimed that the only

20. *Trudy sed'mogo s''ezda*, 189, 195–204.
21. A. A. Fidler, "Ob organizatsii shirokoi pomoshchi bezprizornym, zabroshennym i t. p. detiam," *Trudy vos'mogo s''ezda predstavitelei russkikh vospitatel'no-ispravitel'nykh zavedenii dlia nesovershennoletnikh, Okt. 1911 goda* (St. Petersburg, 1913), 280.
22. "K obuzdaniiu stolichnykh khuliganov," *PL*, October 17, 1903.
23. M. I. Mikhel'son, "Otkrytoe pis'mo gr. V. Bobrinskoi," *S.-Peterburgskie vedomosti*, January 18, 1904.

possible way to prevent hooliganism was to provide day shelters for the city's *bezprizornye* children. Professor S. K. Gogel, a liberal criminologist with a special interest in the poor, argued that the rise in juvenile crime was a harbinger of society's "decline of morals," and he called for society as well as the state to play a role in caring for the needs of *bezprizornye* children. Other speeches by political figures and professional jurists called for more rehabilitation institutions, deplored the contagiousness of hooliganism, the deleterious influence of alcohol abuse, and the general social disintegration associated with juvenile crime and hooliganism.[24]

All these people shared the belief that hooliganism grew out of juvenile crime, which itself was produced when children, growing up in the dangerous city, lacked parental guidance, supervision, and control, and so failed to develop a moral sensibility. Neither the young age of the criminals nor youthful rebelliousness nor a myriad of other possible explanations rooted in poverty, city life, or the individual personality were seen as primary issues. All were secondary to the absence of moral development due to *bezprizornost'*—the lack of parental care.[25] Disapproval of the lower-class family as the source of childhood suffering permeated public discussion of the problem.

The lack of parental care took two related forms: neglect and abuse. In regard to neglect, an annual survey of juvenile crime in the liberal and comparatively sympathetic *Pravo* concluded that

> the family, which alone is capable, as a social cell, of providing protection for a child in the early years, instead offers poverty and ignorance, and no possibility—and in some cases no desire—to provide care. It is here that the social pathology of crime has its origins. It can be explained by the destruction of the family as a social cell; it is clear that from the sick cell it is but a short step to children's court.[26]

How then was the protective "social cell" of the family destroyed? First of all, it was destroyed quite literally: parents did not live with their children; children did not live with their parents. Out of the 1,155 Peters-

24. "Vlast' ulitsy i khuliganstvo," *PL*, March 21, 1914.
25. There were exceptions to this ordering of causes—those who placed social and economic causes before moral ones—and they will be discussed below, but even these "structuralists" viewed poverty and social subordination in connection with the absence of proper supervision and upbringing in the dysfunctional lower-class family.
26. S. K. Gogel', "Detskaia prestupnost' v S. Peterburge v 1910 godu, po dannym popechitelei detskogo suda," *Pravo* 20 (1911): col. 1175.

burg juveniles under court supervision in 1910 (the first year the Special Juvenile Court system was inaugurated; see below), 73 percent lived in "broken homes." The largest number, 440, lived independently of their parents; 410 lived with either a mother or a father; and 150 had both parents somewhere in the countryside.[27] In another study of juvenile offenders, this time in Moscow, N. N. Makovskii found that 620 out of 2,500 children lived in a variety of situations excluding parents (in workshops, with relatives or guardians, or with others), and 1,319 did not specify where they lived. Only 601 said that they lived with their parents, and Makovskii suspected that this figure was exaggerated by the number of children who wished to present their lives as more stable than they were.[28] Data on the parental occupations of girls convicted of crimes in St. Petersburg in the 1910s suggest that only a small number of these girls lived with one or both of their parents. One-quarter of the girls' fathers and mothers subsisted on agriculture, probably living in the village. Of the rest, the majority had parents who worked at the lower end of the industrial sector. More than 35 percent of their fathers worked in trade or commercial shops, or as servants or casual laborers. Thirty-one percent of their mothers worked in similar occupations or as laundresses (see table 10 in the Appendix).[29]

There is little concrete evidence available for use in testing whether the judicial perceptions of neglect in the lower-class family were accurate or whether children who did not turn to crime had more stable family environments.[30] We know that the juvenile population of the capital rose during the period of rapid urbanization, but it is hard to tell how many children (not just juvenile delinquents) lived with one or both of their parents. An increasing number of children were being born in the capital between 1900 and 1910, which (even accounting for illegitimate children) suggests that there were more two-parent families, but again it is not clear how representative they were among the lower classes.[31] Barbara Engel

27. Gogel', "Detskaia prestupnost'," col. 1175; N. A. Okunev, "Pervyi s"ezd deiatelei po voprosam suda dlia maloletnikh," *Uchitel' i shkola* 3 (1914): 45.
28. N. N. Makovskii, "Sotsial'no-ekonomicheskie faktory detskoi prestupnosti v Moskve," in *Deti-prestupniki*, ed. M. N. Gernet (Moscow, 1912), 239–41.
29. E. I. Chichagova, "O prestupnosti devushek za piatiletie ot 1910 g. po 1915 g. po dannym osobogo suda po delam o maloletnikh v Petrograde," *Osobyi sud po delam o maloletnikh* [hereafter *OSDM*] 6 (1915): 13.
30. Part of the problem is that most of the research on the Russian family or marriage focuses on adult family members to the neglect of their offspring.
31. *S-Peterburg po perepisi 15 dekabria 1900 goda, Naselenie*, vyp. 1 (St. Petersburg, 1903), 3–4, 17; *S-Peterburg po perepisi 15 dek. 1910 goda, Naselenie*, Part II, vyp. 1 (St. Petersburg, 1912), 37.

reminds us that even though the number of cohabiting couples in St. Petersburg was increasing in the early twentieth century, they were still rare.[32] Only the most stable and well-off male workers could afford to bring their wives from the countryside or marry in the city, not because wives were expensive, but because the nearly universal implication of marriage in the early twentieth century was reproduction, and children were expensive and required unpaid care. A non-wage-earning wife provided a male worker with cooking, housekeeping, laundry, and other services, and she looked after their children, but she did not bring home an income. On the other hand, many workers apparently aspired to establishing a family in the city, and where families did live together they lived better, which seemed to confirm reformers' assessments.[33] From the 1900s on, workers increasingly married even when both spouses' wages were necessary to maintain a household; in which case children had to be sent to a relative in the countryside or looked after by a non-wage-earning woman, an older sibling, or by no one in particular.[34] This suggests that workers shared with respectable society a faith in the value of family life, though it is difficult to know if they valued families for the same reasons.

In many cases, the poorest children found themselves neglected out of sheer economic necessity. However rare the working-class family was in St. Petersburg, a significant number of the capital's married women with children worked for wages. Even when parents and children lived together, if both parents worked, they rarely saw their children. For others, living together might be prohibited, as for mothers who worked as servants and could not bring their children to live with them.[35] Even when both spouses worked in the same city, they might live apart if they worked in separate

32. Barbara Alpern Engel, *Between the Fields and the City: Women, Work, and Family in Russia, 1861–1914* (Cambridge, forthcoming). In Moscow as well only 7 percent of the city's male workers were living with their wives and children in 1897; 44 percent of married women were "living as a family"; see Bradley, *Muzhik and Muscovite*, 219–29.

33. Engel, *Between the Fields and the City*.

34. One 1912 survey showed that when men earned over 600 rubles a year only 6.6 percent of their wives worked for wages. But when men earned 225 rubles or less, 58.3 percent of their wives went out to work; Engel, *Between the Fields and the City*.

35. Roughly 50 percent of the women living in St. Petersburg and Moscow worked for wages in the 1910s. Domestic service was the largest single employer of women, with around one-quarter of all female wage earners. In 1908 about half the women working in factories were married and in peak childbearing years, and so probably had young children at home; see Rose Glickman, *Russian Factory Women: Workplace and Society, 1880–1914* (Berkeley, 1984), 59–61, 96.

factories or distant regions of the city.[36] Not surprisingly, the worst off among families with children were those headed by women without a male wage earner. Women who were abandoned, widowed, or married to an unemployed worker and mothers of illegitimate children were compelled to support their children on low female wages as well as to provide all or most of their own housekeeping services. According to Rose Glickman, such mothers were "not exceptional."[37] If their children were not themselves working or in school (a great rarity), they were free to spend their time wandering the streets, without adult supervision.

Some children lived entirely independently of their families. Often, in these cases, the neglect associated with *bezprizornost'* took terrible forms. One of the social workers appointed by the court as a guardian recalled the devastating sight of

> little children (four, five, six years old), completely abandoned, uncared-for, totally left on their own, alone amid a million and a half people in the capital. They were forced to spend their days on the streets or in tearooms, legally or illegally finding themselves something to eat. Then at night, like little animals, they crawl into the dung heaps in kitchen gardens, or onto hay barges, under bridges, and so forth.[38]

Some *bezprizorniki* did indeed live on the streets. Children slept in garbage bins, tar pits, and the pools of city fountains.[39] They found shelter in board-covered ditches or piles of leaves, in entryways, behind piles of firewood or bricks, and inside water pipes at construction sites.[40] In his study of the economic conditions in which poor children were living, Makovskii published two pitiful photographs of the shelters children found: one a "shed" (*kamorka*) filled with cots, laundry, and trash in the Khitrov Market, Moscow's worst slum, notorious for its desperate poverty and its criminal havens; the other even more depressing—a wooden garbage bin about a foot high and perhaps five feet long, in which juveniles apparently lived.[41] Vasia B., who found his way to a Moscow workhouse, wrote that

36. Engel, *Between the Fields and the City*.
37. Glickman, *Russian Factory Women*, 129.
38. V. V. Kimental', "Deiatel'nost' popechitelei (Ocherk godovoi raboty popechitelei)," *Osobyi sud po delam o maloletnikh: Otchet S.-Peterburgskogo stolichnogo mirovogo sud'i N. A. Okuneva za 1910 god* (St. Petersburg, 1911), 102.
39. S. V. Bakhrushin, *Maloletnie nishchie i brodiagi v Moskve (Istoricheskii ocherk)* (Moscow, 1913), 47.
40. T. E. Segalov, *Deti-prestupniki: Iz vpechatlenii vracha pri detskom sude* (Moscow, 1914), 5.
41. Makovskii, "Sotsial'no-ekonomicheskie faktory," 239–41.

when begging did not provide enough kopecks for a cot in a flophouse, and there was nowhere else to spend the night, "you lié down and sleep like a dog." Misha T. described fighting over a barrel to sleep in.[42] Many *bezprizorniki* in St. Petersburg supported themselves by begging. Always a common sight in Russian cities, begging became a major police concern after the turn of the century. Between 1905 and 1910 an average of approximately 15,800 beggars and homeless vagrants were picked up each year by the capital's special commission on begging. Between 1907 and 1910 about 1,700 of these each year were juveniles, between the ages of ten and seventeen.[43]

Yet even children who lived with their families did not always receive a moral education or upbringing; so, in addition to neglect, *bezprizornost* referred to parental abuse and harmful parental influence as well. At a 1914 congress on juvenile justice, *bezprizorniki* were described as

> children who find themselves in situations that have a pernicious influence on their morals and their health, . . . who engage in begging or prostitution as well as vagabondage; children whose parents or guardians are inclined to depraved or criminal ways; children who are ill treated by their parents or guardians; children whose parents have served prison sentences; and children whose morality and health have been threatened by their parents' criminal life.[44]

Many children were beaten by their mothers or fathers. Others discovered early that they could not depend on their parents to feed and house them.[45]

---

42. Ibid., 260–61.
43. *Statisticheskii ezhegodnik S.-Peterburga za 1905 g.* (St. Petersburg, 1906), 75; . . . *za 1906 g.* (St. Petersburg, 1907), 58; "Deiatel'nost' osobogo prisutstviia po razboru i prizreniiu nishchikh za 1908," *Predvaritel'nyi svod statisticheskikh dannykh po g. S-Peterburgu*, 20; "Deiatel'nost' osobogo prisutstviia po razboru i prizreniiu nishchikh za 1909 g.," 23; ". . . za 1910," 45; ". . . za 1911," 58; ". . . za 1912," 45; ". . . za 1913," 46.
44. *Pravo* 1 (1914): col. 47. A similar definition can be found in the draft proposal for a law to strengthen surveillance over such children and remove them from their parents; see "Zakonoproekt o merakh popecheniia nad bezprizornymi maloletnimi i o lishenii roditel'skoi vlasti i ob"iasnitel'naia k nemu zapiska. (Priniatyi Pervym Vserossiiskim S"ezdom Deiatelei po voprosam Suda dlia Maloletnikh, sostoiavshimsia v Petrograde v dekabre 1913 goda)," *OSDM* 4 (1915): 3.
45. Makovskii described many such cases in "Sotsial'no-ekonomicheskie faktory," 248–51; as did Dril', "O merakh bor'by," 16–17; V. P. Semenov, *Bytovye usloviia zhizni mal'chikov* (St. Petersburg, n.d.), 7ff.; and A. I. Zak, "Kharakteristika detskoi prestupnosti," in *Deti-prestupniki*, ed. M. N. Gernet (Moscow, 1912), 116–17.

One young recidivist was the son of an absent alcoholic father and an abusive mother, who subsisted on begging. Mother, son, and daughter usually slept on the street, resorting to flophouses only when forced off the street ("Why pay for it if you don't need to?"). Since early childhood the boy had been badly beaten; sometimes his mother forced him to lie on the floor while she struck him as many as seventy times with a rubber club (*rezina*). After two stints in prison the boy switched roles. Now he boasted that he repaid his mother for her "lessons," as she had called them, with his fists.[46] Alcohol abuse was considered to be a primary cause of childhood abuse and neglect. N. A. Okunev, the Justice of the Peace who founded the first Special Juvenile Court, placed particular emphasis on parental drinking, and he linked it explicitly with *bezprizornost'*: "Children with parents who drink cannot have good supervision, and from *bezprizornost'* is born juvenile crime."[47]

Parental abuse linked with *bezprizornost* might lead even more directly to juvenile crime. Dostoevsky's Marmeladovs, who sent their eldest daughter into prostitution and their little ones to beg on the streets, had hundreds, if not thousands, of real-life heirs in the Petersburg slums by 1900 who were recorded by the court and reported by criminologists during the first two decades of the twentieth century.[48] Parents persuaded their children to steal food or to beg to help support the family, while girls were encouraged or forced into prostitution. Some children committed crimes as their parents' accomplices. Cases of parental recruitment also

---

46. Semenov, *Bytovye usloviia*, 12; Makovskii, "Sotsial'no-ekonomicheskie faktory," 248–50; Dril', "O merakh bor'by," 16–17; and Zak, "Kharakteristika," 116–17.

47. N. A. Okunev, "Bezprizornost' maloletnikh, kak posledstvie voiny," *OSDM* 1 (1914): 10–11; see also Dril', "O merakh bor'by," 14, 16–17; I. [M.] Diomidov, "Alkogolizm, kak faktor prestupnosti nesovershennoletnikh," in *Deti-prestupniki,* ed. M. N. Gernet (Moscow, 1912); id., "Rol' alkogolizma v etiologii prestupleniia nesovershennoletnikh," *Trudy sed'mogo s"ezda predstavitelei russkikh ispravitel'nykh zavedenii dlia maloletnikh, Okt. 1911 goda* (Moscow, 1909), 1–2; Gogel', "Detskaia prestupnost'," col. 1173. For boulevard-press views on drinking see Zanoza, "Vstrechi i rechi," *PL,* October 18, 1903; and "P'ianstvo sredi detei v Peterburge," *PL,* March 20, 1914.

48. Semenov, *Bytovye usloviia*, 10ff.; E. I. Chichagova, "Otchet popechitel'nitsy," *Osobyi sud po delam o maloletnikh: Otchet S.-Peterburgskogo stolichnogo mirovogo sud'i N. A. Okuneva za 1910 god.* (St. Petersburg, 1911), 245ff.; Zak, "Kharakteristika," 117; Bakhrushin, *Maloletnie nishchie,* 36; I. T. Tarasov, untitled speech in *Trudy sed'mogo s"ezda,* 190–91; on masters who taught their apprentices to drink, see "K obuzdaniiu stolichnykh khuliganov," *PL,* 17 October 1903.

made their way into the popular, commercial press. In 1909 *Gazeta-kopeika* reported that the police had apprehended a gang of juvenile thieves—three girls, ages nine, ten, and twelve, and a thirteen-year-old boy who had been operating in Gostinnyi Dvor, the main shopping arcade in the capital, located on Nevskii Prospekt. The girls, it turned out, had been "sold" to thieves by their parents, who also were now acting as their fence.[49]

For many children the neglect and abuse of *bezprizornost'* were found in a surrogate family: the artisanal workshop with its patriarchal master/ father and coworker/siblings. Since apprentices were young children removed from their own families by the need to earn a living, the workshop was legally required to act as a substitute family, providing not only training for skilled work, but also a protective environment that offered a familial atmosphere, moral upbringing (*vospitanie*), and parental supervision and control.[50] Such was the ideal. Criminologists, Justices of the Peace, and police officials unanimously agreed, however, that the workshops failed miserably in providing shelter and a healthy environment for the young children who labored in them. Instead they offered rigid hierarchy, long work hours, isolation from the outside world, little opportunity for ambitions of upward mobility, and physical brutality meted out by artisanal masters for minor infractions.

Apprenticeship began at an early age, often as young as eleven or twelve, and the life was rigidly stratified and insulated, leaving young children subject to the power of all those above them. Isolation from any external authority or relief fostered the arbitrariness and brutality from which children fled to the streets. Perhaps even more important, the abusive authority and rigid hierarchy of the workshop prevented the development of respect for authority generally and gave some young children a reason to rebel against all authority. It is not clear exactly how many of the capital's street children were apprentices or former apprentices, though it appears to have been a considerable percentage, and dozens of sources cite bad experiences in workshops as a major cause of hooliganism.[51] The

49. *Gazeta-kopeika* [hereafter *GK*], May 28, 1909. In an untitled speech at the 1908 Congress of Juvenile Corrections Institutions, I. T. Tarasov proposed a law that would impose harsh penalties on parents for encouraging any sort of criminal act (*Trudy sed'mogo s"ezda*, 189–91).

50. "Novoe ubezhishche dlia mal'chikov," *S-Peterburgskie vedomosti* [hereafter *SPV*], October 3, 1902; "Printsipy raboty popechitelia," *Osobyi sud po delam o maloletnikh: Otchet S.-Peterburgskogo stolichnogo mirovogo sud'i N. A. Okuneva* (St. Petersburg, 1911), 104.

51. Makovskii's study of 2,540 juvenile offenders found 27.9 percent listed themselves as "artisanal," but many of those described as factory workers may also

police believed that the majority of juvenile hooligans were or had been apprentices.[52]

For some apprentices, the trials of artisanal work provided a source of solidarity, though not of the sort hoped for by respectable society or the police. In her study of Moscow and Petersburg labor organizations, Victoria Bonnell argued that workers who started out as young apprentices were best able to develop a positive sense of themselves as urban workers identified with a specific trade and "to find themselves inducted into the adult subculture of the factory or shop."[53] But workshops varied. For at least some apprentices, workshop culture failed to promote class solidarity, pride in work, or other positive aspects of proletarian identity; it was a nightmare to endure or escape.

Many children fled apprenticeship to escape purely physical brutality. Makovskii cited scores of examples of children who were beaten or tortured as apprentices, and he was not alone in reporting such abuse. One twelve-year-old was hit so hard on the back of his head that he poked himself in the eye with the cobbler's needle in his hand. An eleven-year-old, found unconscious under a snowdrift by a *dvornik* in the workshop courtyard, had been beaten and literally thrown out of the shop for ruining a shoe, though he had not yet been taught the skills to make it properly. One tailor made his eleven- and twelve-year-olds work until midnight and then get up again at 4:00 A.M. Apprenticeship was so intolerable for some children that they committed suicide.[54] Among the street children S. V. Bakhrushin studied were those who had fled from fear of beating and horrible conditions and those who had fled out of laziness. Some were dismissed for being ill or clumsy (breaking a teapot) or inexperienced (for

---

have been apprentices in factory workshops ("Sotsial'no-ekonomicheskie faktory," 237). Of the 767 girls indicted by the St. Petersburg Juvenile Court between 1910 and 1915, 25 percent (190) were apprentices; see Chichagova, "O prestupnosti devushek," 11; Zak, "Kharakteristika," 113; Bakhrushin, *Maloletnie nishchie*, 42.

52. "K obuzdaniiu stolichnykh khuliganov," *PL*, October 17, 1903. See also Zanoza, "Vstrechi i rechi," *PL*, October 18, 1903. In 1903, St. Petersburg *gradonachal'nik* General Kliegels called apprenticeship the "mainspring of hooliganism." Kleigels's comments were based on a report written for him by State Councillor Kobyletskii, "O meropriatiiakh k iskoreniiu ulichnykh besporiadkov v S.Peterburge," TsGIAL, fond 569, opis' 17, delo 1662, listy 2–8; cited in Surh, "The Police and the Lower Classes."

53. *The Russian Worker*, 9; id., *Roots of Rebellion*, 48–52, 62–69.

54. Makovskii, "Sotsial'no-ekonomicheskie faktory," 239–40; V. K. Khoroshko, *Samoubiistvo detei* (Moscow, 1909); "Novoe ubezhische dlia mal'chikov," *SPV*, October 3, 1902. Segalov indicated that malnutrition was also common; see his *Deti-prestupniki*, 5.

taking counterfeit money from a customer) or because of a recession. Others were fired for swearing, drinking, or stealing.[55] Makovskii believed that fugitive apprentices often turned to crime out of desperation. Once children were out on the street, having escaped from their workshops, they had nowhere to turn; so they were forced to steal or commit other crimes in order to survive.[56] Even children with parents in the city frequently avoided returning home, either from fear of their parents' anger or simply because the family could not support them in the first place.[57]

Gazeta-kopeika considered the apprentices' plight a problem for the whole society. When the police uncovered a gang of runaway apprentices stealing from trains, the journalist blamed their former masters. The apprentices had been

> poorly fed, brutally beaten, taught nothing, and burdened with
> inordinately difficult work. The children refused to stand for this
> "hard labor." They preferred the calamity of a vagrant's life to
> their doleful existence in apprenticeship.

Such runaways, he concluded, became society's problem not because they stole from transport vehicles but because their masters "rob society of useful workers."[58] In response to such charges, artisanal masters often claimed that only strict methods could forge experienced workers. Even when the courts began convicting workshop employers for abusing their apprentices, the masters defended their right to use harsh treatment.[59]

A few sources suggested that at least some apprentices who fled their workshops were not the victims of ill treatment but eagerly chose the freedom of the streets. V. P. Semenov, a former *zemstvo* teacher who worked as a court-appointed guardian for convicted juveniles, knew one young boy who "wanted to go out into the world and live the easy life . . . on 'easy money' (*legkogo khleba*)." He supported himself by stealing firewood and beer bottles.[60] Bakhrushin claimed that the life of "excessive work and violence" in the workshop destroyed respect for authority and respectable work and aroused a

55. Bakhrushin, *Maloletnie nishchie*, 42.
56. Stephen Humphries makes the same argument for the young hooligans who committed petty crimes in England around the same time (*Hooligans or Rebels?* 150–73).
57. Makovskii, "Sotsial'no-ekonomicheskie faktory," 239–40.
58. A., "Delo vsego obshchestva," *GK*, January 9, 1909.
59. Neuberger, "Popular Legal Cultures"; I. A. Pushnov, "Vvedenie mirovykh sudebnykh ustanovlenii," *Petrogradskii mirovoi sud za piat'desiat' let* (Petrograd, 1916), 40ff.; "Novoe ubezhische dlia mal'chikov," *SPV*, October 3, 1902.
60. Semenov, *Bytovye usloviia*, 5; see also Segalov, *Deti-prestupniki*, 5.

thirst for forbidden pleasures that lures youths out onto the streets. At first it is the cinema and cheap theaters, hotels, sweets, cigarettes, and a desire to obtain whatever they fancy—an accordion, or later liquor. These lead first to petty theft and then to the necessity to run away from home.[61]

One *Peterburgskii listok* writer visited a flophouse that young hooligans were known to frequent in order to verify the stories he had heard about runaway apprentices. Here he found not frightened, beaten-down children, but arrogant ruffians, bragging about their exploits, proud of having escaped the workshop. According to one flophouse denizen, a cranky old grey-haired worker, the boys enjoyed their lives of freedom, smoking and drinking, and making trouble. The journalist concluded: "With my own eyes I saw the future die for these children."[62] These observations supported the argument that a propensity for hooliganism was born in the workshop and the flophouse just as it was born in the working-class family.

Just as parents might abuse or neglect their children, many workshops provided instruction in "immoral" behavior. Bonnell cited memoirs of artisanal workers that describe some of the rituals of drinking and the participation of even very young apprentices in drinking sprees. For the criminologists seeking the moral origins of crime, workshop drinking was a major source of the corruption of morals that led children to commit crimes. Bonnell saw these rituals as one of the channels of induction into the adult world of the shop that made up for the cruel treatment suffered at the hands of employers—and surely they were, at least for some apprentices.[63] For others, however, drinking often provoked the violent abuse that made apprenticeship unbearable and made escape to an uncertain future on the streets preferable.[64]

It is difficult to determine why some apprentices found the community they needed in workshop life, while others fled. For our purposes it is important to understand that crime specialists of various kinds saw the artisanal workshop as another form of the dysfunctional family. Its abusive surrogate parents and the unsavory influence of its adult workers were seen as another kind of *bezprizornost'*, leaving apprentices without proper moral supervision and instruction. The long hours and deplorable material conditions of apprentice work were rarely cited by themselves as

61. Bakhrushin, *Maloletnie nishchie*, 42, 47.
62. K. G., "Pitomniki khuliganov," *PL*, August 28, 1903.
63. Bonnell, *Roots of Rebellion*, 51–52.
64. Makovskii, "Sotsial'no-ekonomicheskie faktory," 239–40; Iakov Berman, "Retsidiv v detskoi prestupnosti," in *Deti-prestupniki*, ed. M. N. Gernet, 311–12.

reasons children might have sought escape to the precarious freedom of the streets. In both the workshop and the working-class family *bezprizornost'* failed to provide children with the necessary moral upbringing or respect for authority, and both allowed children to escape the control and care of adults to roam the streets of the city. But alone *bezprizornost'* was not enough to turn the uncared-for youths into hooligans: it left children without the moral strength to resist contamination from all the wicked temptations they encountered once they were free to wander the streets.

▩ Bezprizornost', *Contamination, and Street Culture*

For the principal specialists writing on juvenile crime during this period, crime was primarily a moral issue, but their view of moral development was firmly embedded in a social context. In her denunciation of official efforts to curtail crime, I. Karpinskaia wrote that "the main (and unlimited) source of beggars, juvenile criminals, fallen women, and alcoholics, it has long been recognized, is the street—this university of all the sciences that corrupt the younger generation."[65] Semenov noted that a good family—"strong, ambitious, moral, and thrifty"—could "relatively easily guide a youth on an honest path," but freedom to wander the streets, as another social worker put it, left children with "no instructor in life to protect them from evil and direct them to the good."[66] There was broad consensus that exposing children to the destructive dangers of the streets turned relatively innocent youths into hooligans.[67] Life "on the streets" summoned up for these observers a world beyond the purview of respectable society, which lured children and then contaminated them with the immoral and illegal behavior on open display. The result, it was argued, was the alienation, idleness, and aggression associated with hooliganism.

65. I. Karpinskaia, *Bor'ba s ulitsei* (Moscow, 1906), 3.
66. Semenov, *Bytovye usloviia*, 11; Kimental', "Deiatel'nost' popechitelei," 102.
67. Segalov, *Deti-prestupniki*, 4–5, for whom moral development was explicitly connected with the lack of "cultural instruction" for the children; A. P. Udris, "Vospitatel'no-ispravitel'nye zavedeniia," *Osobyi sud po delam o maloletnikh: Otchet S.-Peterburgskogo stolichnogo mirovogo sud'i N. A. Okuneva za 1910 god.* (St. Petersburg, 1911), 141–43; Diomidov, "Rol' alkogolizma," 1; N. A. Okunev, *Trudy pervogo s''ezda deiatelei po voprosam suda dlia maloletnikh*, SPb. Dekabr 1913 (Petrograd, 1915), 10; Zak, "Kharakteristika," 116–17; Dril', "O merakh bor'by," 22; P. L. "VII S''ezd predstavitelei russkikh ispravitel'no-vospitatel'nykh zavedenii," *Zhurnal ministerstva iustitsii* 2 (1909): 220–21. The idea that children were malleable and therefore needed to be guided and organized to protect them from temptations developed elsewhere in Europe in the late nineteenth and early twentieth centuries; see John Gillis, "The Evolution of Juvenile Delinquency in England, 1890–1914," *Past and Present* 67 (1975): 97; id., *Youth and History*, 150–55; and Linton, "Who Has the Youth," 2–11.

"Once a village boy has passed through the school of the flophouse, the tearoom, and the police station," Semenov commented, "he will adapt to their invariable characteristics—cards, billiards, *vypuski*, movies, the tearoom, the park, the tavern."[68]

At the time, *bezprizornost'* was viewed almost exclusively as an urban problem. The city, it was thought, provided both the social and economic conditions for *bezprizornost'* to appear and the cultural institutions for its pernicious influence to flourish and infect the innocent. The streets deplored by reformers were obviously city streets, and they were often presented in contrast to an idealized village. According to one criminologist (but implicit in the works of many), a lack of adult supervision in the village was "unimaginable": everyone in the village worked in some productive capacity, men in the fields, women in the hut, and children, even when they left their huts and wandered around alone, were always looked after, because everyone knew everyone else. In the city, in contrast, fathers, mothers, and older brothers and sisters all worked away from home. The high cost of living either forced small children to find work as well or left them alone and untended. Even those children lucky enough to go to school would still be unsupervised for much of the day.[69] However accurate a picture of city life, this common image of the village was, to say the least, surprisingly uninformed. As historians have demonstrated, family life in the village was undergoing a process of transformation just as destabilizing as that being experienced by families in the urban working class.[70] Others have shown that direct supervision of children, even infants, was virtually impossible during the demanding periods of agricultural labor when women and men were at work in the fields. Kanatchikov started the chronicle of his life with the "outstanding" fact of his having survived the common perils of a peasant infancy, which included being "abandoned without any care during the summer harvest season."[71] In addition, given the widespread transiency of the working population between factory and field, many of the problems of family separation and fragmentation noticed

68. Semenov, *Bytovye usloviia*, 6.
69. N. A. Okunev, "Osobyi sud po delam o maloletnikh," *Petrogradskii mirovoi sud za piat'desiat' let, 1866–1916* (Petrograd, 1916), 728–29; Gogel', "Detskaia prestupnost'," cols. 1175–76.
70. Christine Worobec, *Peasant Russia: Family and Community in the Post-Emancipation Period* (Princeton, 1991); Barbara Engel, "The Woman's Side: Male Outmigration and the Family Economy in Kostroma Province," *Slavic Review*, vol. 45, no. 2 (1986); Moshe Lewin, *The Making of the Soviet System: Essays in the Social History of Interwar Russia* (New York, 1985), 49–56, 72–87.
71. Zelnik, *A Radical Worker*, 1; David Ransel, "Infant-Care Cultures in the Russian Empire," in *Russia's Women: Accommodation, Resistance, Transforma-*

in the city were common to both workers and peasants; indeed many of the families involved must have been one and the same.

This is not to argue that city and village poverty were identical or that transiency for both had the same effects on children or on family life. But by the time these issues were being discussed in the 1910s, the countryside had been the scene of various manifestations of social, not to mention political, instability, including the challenge to traditional authorities and the widespread hooliganism discussed in the previous chapter. Excessive drinking, wife beating, child abuse, hunger, and poverty were hardly unknown. Moreover, in almost any other context village social life would be criticized for much the same cultural backwardness and low moral development that criminologists and journalists deplored in city life. Ignorance of the village does not automatically disqualify the urban criminologists from understanding urban problems, but it is, among other things, a startling reminder of just how isolated many urban social reformers were from the lives of the majority of Russia's people, including the peasant portion of the population that produced the urban poor. More important, the contrast set up by urban criminologists between the pathology of the city and the health of the village allowed specialists to dwell on specifically urban facets of life, while neglecting others, such as endemic poverty, social immobility, and cultural transformation, that affected people in both settings.[72]

Many of the young offenders who began life in the countryside also idealized the village and were nostalgic or homesick for their village homes. The boys Semenov worked with often "forgot" that they had left the countryside because there had been nothing to eat or because their stepmother had thrown them out of the house or their father had drunk away all the family's possessions ("even the icons"). Even so, those who had come alone felt uprooted and lacking cultural moorings or emotional support.[73] The overwhelming majority of juvenile offenders, however,

tion, ed. Barbara E. Clements, Barbara A. Engel, and Christine D. Worobec (Berkeley, 1991), 116–17.

72. Most theories on the causes of modern crime start with the assumption that crime rates were closely correlated with urbanization and industrialization. Recent challenges are few and far between but include Gillis, *Youth and History,* 176ff.; Lodhi and Tilly, "Urbanization," 296–318; Johnson and McHale, "Delinquency Rate," 384–402.

73. Semenov, *Bytovye usloviia,* 1–2, 6. Kanatchikov, too, reported feeling homesick during his first weeks in the city, for the "village, for the meadows, the brook, the people who were near and dear to me." "Here in the hostile world of Moscow," he confessed, "I felt lonely, abandoned, needed by no one" (Zelnik, *A Radical Worker,* 8).

were either city-born or had been living in the city for a considerable
length of time. In 1910, approximately half of those convicted for petty
crimes had been born in the capital. Only 6 percent had been living in the
city for less than a year before their arrest.[74]

Bezprizornost' was viewed as an urban problem not only in contrast to
the situation in an idealized village family, but because the city provided
the economic, social, and cultural soil for the moral consequences of *bezprizornost'* to take root. T. E. Segalov, Semenov, Okunev, and others
believed that the city presented new and difficult situations for migrants.
The economy of the industrializing city required new skills and new sacri-
fices, which were hard enough to meet even with the support of a family.
Industrial work called for intellectual abilities and moral qualities—a capacity for work, the intelligence to learn new skills, and "an understanding
of property relations and the proper standards of behavior"—in order to
compete in the daily struggle for survival. Without the family's guidance
(often, in fact, eliminated by the economic demands of city life), *bezprizornye* children could not master these conditions; so they simply ceased
working and took up a life of crime.[75] Almost all commentators mentioned
a few purely economic factors connecting city life with *bezprizornost'*, but
only a few writers saw social and economic factors as the decisive ones in
producing juvenile offenders. Most believed that urban poverty was not
an evil in and of itself, but that it contributed to the problems of *bezprizornost'* by depriving poor children of constant and competent parental care
and leaving them vulnerable to the dangers and vices that congregated in
the city.

The fear that a hooligan mentality was contagious was not a new one
in this period, nor was it unique to Russia, but the medical metaphor was
employed widely during the 1900s and especially the 1910s to explain how
untended youths were changed into hooligans. Moreover, descriptions of
the environment that contained the hooligan "bacteria" often conflated
truly dangerous settings and activities with relatively harmless or even
beneficial ones for the children involved, seen as they were through the
prism of middle-class respectability. Even the most sober and scholarly
writers released torrents of moral outrage in describing this disreputable
side of lower-class culture. Dril's speech to the VII Congress for Represen-

---

74. Gogel', "Detskaia prestupnost'," col. 1174.
75. Segalov, *Deti-prestupniki*, 3–5; also Okunev, "Osobyi sud," 726–28; Semenov, *Bytovye usloviia*, 2–3, 7, 11.

tatives of Russian Juvenile Correctional Institutions was typical in its cultural bias and its melodramatic rhetoric:

> Thrown out onto the streets, into the "wide, wide world," the child or youth completes his education . . . when he encounters various misfortunes that undermine his still developing, embryonic physical stamina. He falls in with other abandoned, *bezprizornye* comrades, among whom many have already become almost full-grown professional hooligans, who live at the society's expense and to its horror. He encounters the company of veteran tramps, beggars, vagrants, prostitutes, thieves, and horse thieves. At every step he is irresistibly drawn to the temptations of crude, filthy pleasures that gradually erode all of his best human feelings, all necessary bases for positive actions. He encounters life in slums, dives, and flophouses; he finds games, cards, and billiards; vodka, drunkenness, early spiritual debauchery, masturbation, homosexuality, idleness, lies, deception, crime, and the other forms of instruction available on the street that further develop and strengthen the original education he received in his shattered family life.[76]

Dril's description here was not based on a reading of the boulevard press, despite the stylistic similarities (see fig. 9), but on his own experiences among working-class youths and his research on patterns of criminality among them. Because specialists set out to find the causes of hooliganism, they tended to emphasize the amorality, bravado, and disregard for proper, conventional behavior typical of hooliganism that they found in analyzing the cultural world of juvenile criminals. In a study of the links between film going and juvenile crime, A. I. Zak claimed that the movies cast a kind of addictive spell over children, which compelled them to steal the money for tickets. What on the surface appears to be primarily an economic argument in fact rests on current ideas about *bezprizornost'*. Zak's reports of individual cases stressed the youths' lack of supervision, their unquenchable and implicitly illicit desire to see movies, and their cunning persistence in overcoming obstacles to fulfill that desire. In these specific examples we can see the ways that experts wove together the conditions that they believed produced hooliganism: the modern city with its unsupervised streets, its poverty, and its popular entertainments that prevented proper development, while providing models of disorderly, dishonest, and disrespectful behavior. Eleven-year-old Liza, Zak reported, was growing up without much parental supervision, and after once going to the movies, she yearned to go again. But she had no money; so she turned to begging,

---

76. Dril', "O merakh bor'by," 17–18.

Пьянство среди дѣтей въ Петербургѣ.

Figure 9.   Drunkenness among Children in St. Petersburg (March 20, 1914). This drawing accompanied a news story about the young children who could be found almost every day drinking on the streets in the outskirts of the city. The article described their "abnormal" lives and claimed that "the majority of adults respond with indifference" to the children's drinking: "Only in rare cases does some old auntie or grandma" come along to punish a young girl drinking along with the boys.

using all kinds of clever methods to extract money from passersby. When her mother found out, she beat Liza, who, undeterred, stole a shirt to sell for ticket money. Tatiana, thirteen years old, showed no inclination toward criminal behavior until she moved to Moscow from the countryside. One visit to the movies got her hooked, and she went whenever she could, stealing money to pay for tickets. She too was punished—by being locked in her room—but she escaped by climbing down a drainpipe. When asked why she was not afraid to disobey her parents and risk the dangerous descent, she replied that people did such things all the time in the movies and survived.[77]

77. A. I. Zak, "Kinomotograf i detskaia prestupnost'," *Zhurnal ugolovnogo prava i protsessa* 4 (1913): 17–22. Vladimir Mayakovsky discovered his love for the movies in the same years, but as if to prove that interpretations of cultural influence vary according to class, the poet's sister remembered that "for lack of money, Volodya sometimes sneaked in[to the movies] without paying and not infrequently got into trouble, but for the cinema, Volodya sacrificed everything" (cited in

The overcrowded apartments where poor children resided and the flop-houses where a homeless child might be able to afford a cot also exposed children, it was thought, to contamination and eroded whatever moral upbringing their parents had succeeding in passing along. Conditions in Russian flophouses and slums are relatively well known.[78] Although in some cities a substantial number of regular workers with steady jobs shared the flophouses with beggars, vagabonds, prostitutes, and habitual criminals, respectable society viewed the flops primarily as "seedbeds of crime" where immoral and illegal behavior ran rampant. Describing the flophouses of Moscow's Khitrov Market for her readers in *Zhenskoe delo* (*The Woman's Cause*), E. Vystavkina complained that "drunks, petty thieves, and prostitutes of the lowest variety crowd before the children's eyes from morning until night, and they are not the least bit shy about [the children's] presence."[79] Even when children lived with their parents or relatives, they often shared overcrowded apartments with "unsavory" people, which made a moral upbringing impossible. Semenov described "corner" apartments in the Haymarket, where each corner of a room was rented to a different family, including one "as crowded as a flophouse," with fifteen cots, some of which were shared by as many as three adults. The denizens of another apartment that Semenov visited "glared at each other like wolves and hurled nasty and malicious curses." Their willing-ness to behave so crudely in Semenov's presence left him wondering how much worse they must have carried on when no social worker was around.[80]

Even those writers and criminologists who sympathized with the juve-nile offenders and who believed crime to be rooted primarily in social and economic conditions rather than in the moral failings of the working class could not resist condemning what they saw as corruption and sexual laxity reigning in the flophouses and overcrowded working-class housing. Mi-khail Gernet, a socialist university professor and the leading proponent of a social theory of criminal motivation, wrote in an early study connecting

---

Elizabeth Henderson, "Shackled by Film: The Cinema in the Career of Mayakov-sky," *Russian Literary Triquarterly* 7 [1973]: 298). What was criminal tendency for a child of the slums was artistic self-sacrifice for the poet.

78. Bater, *St. Petersburg*, 225–27; Bater's primary source on flophouses in this period is K. B. Karaffa-Korbut, "Nochlezhnye doma v bol'shikh russkikh goro-dakh," *Gorodskoe delo* 10 (1912): 627–42; also Bradley, *Muzhik and Muscovite*, 206, 287.

79. E. Vystavkina, "Bezprizornye," *Zhenskoe delo*, December 1, 1914, p. 10; see also Zak, "Kharakteristika," 114.

80. Semenov, *Bytovye usloviia*, 9–10.

housing conditions with crime that children were corrupted at a very young age in the "dark hovels" that were never "dark enough to hide coarse drunkenness and open debauchery." He found that the correlation between tight living conditions and crime against the person was especially strong because living in such close quarters destroyed respect for others as individuals. Who is more likely to commit crimes against peace and order, he asked, than those who grew up where peace and order were missing?[81] But Gernet's question raises others, which he failed to address. Why do only some poverty-stricken inhabitants of such neighborhoods become criminals? Why did small living space in village huts fail to produce similar kinds of crime? By 1909, when P. V. Vsesviatskii examined the connection between living conditions and crime based on Moscow court cases, these questions still had not been raised. Vsesviatskii made the same argument Gernet had: children in the slums were exposed to crime and sexual depravity, which destroyed their modesty, their respect for others, and their morality in general. Accordingly, these conditions explained why the most crimes were committed in the most crowded neighborhoods of the city.[82]

The pioneering work of these early social scientists exposed the horribly substandard and overcrowded living conditions of the Petersburg slums and established a crucial connection between social conditions and crime, but their assumptions about how that connection functioned were rooted in ideas about respectable morality and culture that ignored the larger social context. Despite the fact that Vsesviatskii and Gernet sought social rather than moral, individual, or biological causes of crime, their analysis rested on the primacy of moral influence and the exposure of slum children to behavior from which middle- and upper-class children were shielded. In arguing that exposure to these conditions produced criminal behavior they presented the youths as primarily passive beings, incapable of responding consciously or actively to their surroundings. Moreover, they failed to take into account the slums' position within the larger society—at the bottom of the social structure—which provided its own reasons for lawbreaking, rebellion, and alienation. This sort of analysis is contradicted by the personal characteristics of the juvenile criminals and hooligans, whose very acts displayed the youths' active nature.

81. M. N. Gernet, "Prestupnost' i zhilishcha bedniakov," *Pravo* 42 (1903): cols. 2396–98.
82. P. V. Vsesviatskii, "Prestupnost' i zhilischnyi vopros," *Pravo* 20 (1909): cols. 1264, 1268–73.

The contrast between passive images of juveniles as victims of contamination and their lively, daring, or desperate exploits is particularly striking in discussions of female crime and of the institutions of youth culture. Concerns about the plight of poor youths, while thoroughly justified in the majority of cases, may also have disguised fears about the freedom from control boys and girls enjoyed on the streets. The autonomy that they obtained in the absence of adult supervision made them acquire values and seek out forms of association other than those approved by respectable society. Thus *bezprizornost'* signified not only the absence or brutality of parental upbringing. The word also came to represent a whole network of social relations, experiences, and values, in the context of which poor children existed independently of any authority.

For the most part, the jurists and criminologists concerned with juvenile crime ignored girls altogether. When girls did raise concern, it was almost always prostitution that attracted the most attention, even though only a small percentage of female juvenile offenders were arrested for illegal prostitution.[83] Juvenile prostitutes were uniformly represented as victims of a criminal milieu into which they had fallen. In all too many cases, young girls were genuine victims of kidnapping, seduction, and recruitment by men who employed them as domestic servants and shopworkers or by unscrupulous agents who organized "white slavery" rings in Petersburg and throughout the empire.[84] But many others offered their services for purely economic reasons, and of their own accord (though the choice was made from a limited range of options). Like male hooligans and young criminals, many of them may have been the least passive and most enterprising girls. However, while juvenile prostitution provoked a public and professional outcry, its apparent threat to society ranked lower than that of almost any category of male criminality, and so it elicited even less action than male juvenile crime and hooliganism.[85] There were fewer shelters built for girls, fewer criminologists interested in female criminality and child prostitution, little interest in the differences between male and female juveniles, and as a result much less contemporary research.[86]

83. *PMS 1911*, 236; Chichagova's report is primarily taken up with comments about prostitution, even though only 13 of her 144 charges were prostitutes ("Otchet popechitel'nitsy," 254ff.).

84. Richard Stites, *The Women's Liberation Movement in Russia: Feminism, Nihilism, and Bolshevism, 1860–1930*, 2d ed. (Princeton, 1990), 184.

85. The publication of M. K. Mukalov's *Deti-ulitsy* in 1906, for example, caused a sensation in the commercial press. On the regulation of prostitution see Bernstein, "Sonia's Daughters."

86. V. I. Gal'pernin, "Detskaia prostitutsiia," in *Deti-prestupniki*, ed. M. N. Gernet (Moscow, 1912); at the 1914 congress on Special Juvenile Courts, a report on

As for the institutions of youth culture, when observers referred to the contamination of the streets, the process they had in mind took place in a specific setting: the cultural institutions of lower-class urban life where people of all ages gathered, relaxed, and entertained themselves. *Bezprizorniki*, boys and girls alike, gravitated toward precisely those urban institutions respectable society deplored: flophouses and taverns or, in Gogel's words, "street life and street friends, taverns, tearooms, excerpts from semi-literate stories about various heroes of the criminal world, which are sold at an affordable price on every corner, and finally gambling, billiards, etc."[87] Eventually, most specialists agreed, it was in these same taverns that contaminated youths turned into full-fledged hooligans.

In fact, however, evidence provided by the same observers suggests that the actual number of youths who actively engaged in these activities, while high, was lower than one might expect and far from universal. Of the juveniles convicted by Justices of the Peace and assigned to court supervision in 1910, 40 percent admitted spending time in taverns, 17 percent confessed to gambling and playing billiards, 53 percent to drinking, and 46 percent admitted reading cheap crime novels.[88] Of the 2,540 youths Makovskii analyzed only 19 percent described themselves as unemployed or beggars. Ninety-one percent of the juvenile recidivists that Iakov Berman studied had "some sort of job."[89] Among the girls E. I. Chichagova worked with between 1910 and 1915 fewer than 4 percent either begged or lived with their parents; the rest were working. Of the 255 boys and girls she worked with in 1911, 4 lived with their parents, 2 begged, and 12 would not say how they supported themselves, but the rest worked as apprentices, servants, factory workers, or "occasionally" as prostitutes.[90]

And yet other than tearooms and taverns there was hardly anywhere to go. There was little public entertainment for children in St. Petersburg

---

child prostitution was given by Karmina, who suggested that child prostitution was spreading because patrons were not prosecuted; see *Pravo* 1 (1914): cols. 49–50; M. K. Mukalov, *Deti ulitsy* (St. Petersburg, 1906); untitled article in *PL*, January 23, 1901. *Gazeta-kopeika*, July 20–24, 1912, ran a series on juvenile prostitutes that emphasized the tragedy of the girls' "fall" and the importance of reeducation but also included a letter sent to the newspaper from a young prostitute sneering at the idea that she was a victim, claiming that she enjoyed her "jolly life" and had chosen it voluntarily.

87. Gogel', "Detskaia prestupnost'," cols. 1175–76.
88. Ibid., col. 1176.
89. Berman, "Retsidiv," 310.
90. Makovskii, "Sotsial'no-ekonomicheskie faktory," 238; Chichagova, "O prestupnosti devushek," 12; id., "Otchet popechitel'nitsy," 245.

and less still accessible to the poor.[91] Even a child of the cultivated nobility was forced to carry on his social life in the dusty corners of the Russian Museum, as the writer Vladimir Nabokov recalled years later, and of course, few *bezprizorniki* were likely to have availed themselves of the same opportunity.[92] The worker Kanatchikov claimed that there was nothing to do when he arrived in St. Petersburg from Moscow (in the late 1890s) *except* go to the tavern or play billiards. In the Nevskii Gates region, where he and 60,000 other workers lived, Kanatchikov complained that there were only two "shabby" theaters, which, he concluded in agreement with the middle-class observers, helped explain why so many workers occupied their time with fighting, rowdiness, and hooliganism. Kanatchikov, however, believed that such activities were filling up the prisons as a result of boredom and isolation, not because of moral contamination.[93] Several youth clubs were established at this time, but they tended not to attract the poorest children. One popular club, which was built expressly to provide migrants from the provinces with "defenses against the pernicious influence of the thousand temptations of the big city," was visited primarily by white-collar workers: clerks in banks, offices, government agencies, stores and factories, and railroad offices.[94] In 1905 there were all of ten working-class clubs in St. Petersburg, and only ten more appeared between 1907 and 1914.[95] Public readings organized by literacy societies became fairly popular among workers, but these were for adults, not children, and they required that the audience exhibit some degree of decorum.[96] Scanning the pages of *Gazeta-kopeika* for these years one finds announcements for readings as well as for sporting events, plays, and the like. "People's Halls" (*Narodnye doma*) were constructed in Petersburg and Moscow to provide lower-class entertainment, but they cost money and were situated at some distance from many working-class quarters, and once inside the audience was expected to listen quietly rather than respond vocally to the entertainment, as they might at a fairground show.[97] The

91. Some evidence suggests that the dearth of popular public entertainment has been exaggerated. See Catriona Kelly, *Petrushka: The Russian Carnival Puppet Theatre* (Cambridge, 1990), 5–7.

92. Vladimir Nabokov, *Speak Memory* (New York, 1970), 235–36.

93. Zelnik, *A Radical Worker*, 87, 95.

94. Gr, "Sredi molodezhi," *PL*, March 21, 1901.

95. Glickman, *Russian Factory Women*, 208–9.

96. "Narodnaia auditoriia dlia rabochikh," *Niva* 24 (June 18, 1905): 478.

97. My thanks to Richard Stites for pointing out the importance of decorum in entertainment created for the poor by respectable society. See also Lawrence W. Levine, *Highbrow/Lowbrow: The Emergence of Cultural Hierarchy in America* (Cambridge, Mass., 1988), 20–26, 69–81, 112–19, 178–200, on the introduction

Petersburg People's Hall did manage to attract young hooligans, but not to its entertainments. The park in which it was located was one of the prime sites for hooligan assaults. Their targets were the "cultured" workers or People's Hall employees.

Social reformers in philanthropic and voluntary societies were unanimous in calling for more palatable public entertainment and meeting places. A handful of "Children's Houses" (*Detskie doma*—they were not places to live) were established in the years after 1905, at least one of them originating in the soup kitchens set up during 1905 and 1906 for unemployed workers. At first concerned with providing food, clothing, and occasional shelter for the needy children of unemployed or poor workers, the staff at one Children's House on Vasilevskii Island tried to improve the children's inner life as well. This they found extremely difficult because the youths "arrived at this sanctuary straight from the street." The staff was undoubtedly also hampered by their commitment to instill in the children an attraction to work and to "awaken in them a consciousness of the necessity of working." But while the inexperienced staff found their efforts stubbornly resisted at first, they eventually scored some successes with a summer camp and with winter activities, but only because they began to attract what they called more "tranquil" children.[98]

Among judicial professionals these institutions were seen as particularly beneficial preventive measures for juveniles, because they offered both surrogate moral upbringing and the cultural tools for integration into society. They believed that the main obstacle to constructing such institutions was primarily financial: neither the city nor the central government was forthcoming with funds.[99] But the issues involved were invariably more complex. The reform programs and the people staffing them expressed more than a little Victorian intolerance for the lower-class culture they sought to eradicate: if it was not edifying, if it did not raise the cultural level, it surely would corrupt. Left on their own, these reformers

---

of decorum into cultural events and the subsequent loss of mass audiences for "highbrow" culture.

98. "Detskii dom," *Otchet obshch-a pomoshch' detiam rabochikh g. S.-Peterburga za piat' let ego sushchestvovaniia, 1908–1913* (St. Petersburg, 1913), 1–4. See also "Listok: 'Ochagi' dlia bezprizornykh detei," *PL*, March 9, 1914; V. V. Shlezinger, *Opyt otvlecheniia iunoshestva ot rastlevaiushchego vliianiia ulitsy* (St. Petersburg, 1913), 4–19, on activities he organized under sponsorship by the "Society of Children's Towns."

99. Fidler, "O merakh bor'by," 417; M. P. Bekleshov, *Trudy sed'mogo s"ezda*, 197. Many of the debates at the VII Congress concerned funding for various projects, frustrating those who felt it more important to decide what kind of institutions were necessary before deciding how they would be supported.

thought, the *bezprizornye* children of the slums could reflect only the worst aspects of the environment in which they lived. Even those who placed the blame for *bezprizornost* on the economy and social structure rather than on the base morality of urban lower-class culture saw only harmful values in that culture. The usually sensitive Okunev wrote that even the games of urban, working-class children exhibited their propensity for crime. When they became bored with games of "ball" they began to play "bandits," or more often "thieves." Games about thieves soon led to real thievery—at first minor things, like an apple or firewood—until the thieving became a habit.[100] It is hard to believe, however, that middle-class children never played "bandits" in St. Petersburg or, more to the point, that such games produced criminals.

Certainly the taverns and tearooms where children mingled with habitual criminals and others who lived beyond the margins of respectable society were likely to be dangerous places for young children. And it stands to reason that spending time in such establishments would have made crime, prostitution, tramping, and begging seem more like ordinary endeavors than reprehensible, amoral, and frightening occupations.[101] But even taverns and tearooms offered homeless, rootless children something they found nowhere else: companionship, entertainment, and often protection of a sort as well. Alekseii Svirskii inadvertently captured the duality of the slum culture in one of his superb vignettes about the urban underworld. Amid drunken figures, who "run about like madmen before your eyes," the smoky tavern known as The Blindman

> serves as a warm haven in winter for cabdrivers, women of the night, petty thieves, and street youths of both sexes. Late into the night . . . from somewhere . . . appears a child about four years old. . . . Wearing only a shirt, the toddler steps into the room with her tiny, soft little feet. With wide-open eyes of the lightest blue she looks around at the drunken people. . . . When the prostitutes notice her they surround her and begin to coddle her. One wraps the child in her dirty skirt, takes a sticky, shopworn caramel, and puts it in her tiny mouth. Another takes her by the hand and covers her little face with slovenly, wet kisses.[102]

100. Okunev, "Osobyi sud," 730–31.
101. This is assuming that taverns and tearooms were in fact overrun by dangerous and habitual criminals. Thomas Brennan has shown that in Paris popular and police depictions of the tavern as the haven of criminals and the morally degenerate were exaggerated (*Public Drinking and Popular Culture in Eighteenth-Century Paris* [Princeton, 1988]).
102. Svirskii, "Peterburgskie khuligany," 272–73.

The context makes it clear that Svirskii meant to horrify his readers by contrasting the innocence of blue-eyed childhood with debauched womanhood, and to suggest that the child would inevitably follow the path of the women who surrounded her. I am not arguing that, in contrast, we should see the tavern as an ideal environment for raising children, but only that the scene depicted here had some positive features that the author, like the majority of judicial experts, could not see. Where Svirskii perceived in the prostitutes' "slovenly" kisses a sign of depravity, it is possible to read affection, protection, and a kind of mothering that children living in garbage bins or slaving away in brutal workshops might envy. Such blanket condemnation blinded middle-class observers to the appeal street culture had for *bezprizornye* youths, and thus it was difficult for reformers to provide genuinely attractive alternatives.

This censure of lower-class public life was paralleled in the middle-class experts' opinions of the private sphere as well. Affection, loyalty, and respect were absent from portraits of family life, and evidence of their existence was largely ignored. Case histories of the children who passed through the courts or were studied by researchers never acknowledged attractive personality traits or the possibility of positive family relationships, even in instances where evidence of caring can be gleaned from their findings.[103] We know, for example, that some juvenile offenders came from families with "strict" parents, both mothers and fathers, who tried to keep their children out of trouble and punished them for misbehavior.[104] The same criminologists reported numerous cases of parents who tried to have their children arrested, in the hope that punishment might straighten them out.[105] Other parents, single mothers in particular, hoped that in the juvenile shelters or rehabilitation colonies their children would receive better care than their own wages and work schedules allowed them to provide. One of Makovskii's thirteen-year-olds, a boy named E., lived with his mother, although she was too ill to work and could barely keep herself alive on handouts, much less support her son. E.'s mother persuaded a neighbor to accuse E. of stealing a chicken in order to get him

---

103. Case histories can be found in essays by Makovskii, Berman, and others in the collection *Deti-prestupniki*; as well as in the works of Segalov, Semenov, Chichagova, Kimental', Shlezinger, and Tsikin and in Gogel', "Detskaia prestupnost'"; Diomidov, "Rol' alkogolizma"; and Zak, "Kharakteristika."
104. Kimental', "Deiatel'nost' popechitelei," 125–26; Makovskii, "Sotsial'no-ekonomicheskie faktory," 242.
105. "Otchet mirovogo sud'i po delam o maloletnikh za 1911 god," *PMS 1911* (St. Petersburg, 1912), 222; Fidler, "O merakh bor'by," 427.

into a juvenile shelter, simply in order to feed him.[106] In some of these cases parents may have been trying to rid themselves of responsibility for their children, but frequently they appear to have been motivated by care and desperation. Such evidence, partial and ambiguous as it is, of concerned family ties did not find its way into the specialists' analysis of the lower-class family or of the lower-class juvenile criminal.

The specialists' overriding concern with the defects of their subjects' lives is apparent in the kinds of information they requested and recorded. Numerous surveys were carried out among lower-class children in the 1910s, both by the Special Juvenile Court established in St. Petersburg in 1910 and by criminologists interviewing children at urban workhouses. The guardians appointed to supervise convicted juveniles were required to keep a formal notebook that included information about the juveniles' family situation—where and with whom they lived, their parents' financial and employment situation, their parents' physical and psychological state, their drinking habits, and the quality of the relationships between parents and children—and the juveniles' own habits—their physical and psychological state, their tendency to lie, their education and mental development, their "degree of moral degeneracy" (*isporchennost'*), their occupation, the influence of their comrades, their previous record, and their participation in a variety of activities, such as smoking, drinking, reading of crime and adventure novels (Sherlock Holmes was specified by name), time spent in taverns and tearooms, playing billiards or gambling, and if they were girls, whether they worked as prostitutes.

As a result, these observers overlooked positive features of youth culture in the slums—the camaraderie of the streets, the affection and security available even in "haunts and dives," and the less rigid moral code that allowed poor youths to enjoy playing pool and reading Sherlock Holmes. Their emphasis on moral contamination also prevented them from understanding children who were neither depraved nor immoral. The lurid picture their reports presented ignored signs of depression, low self-esteem, loneliness, or other problems that might explain teenage alcohol abuse, self-destructive crime sprees, or hooligan self-assertion. Segalov, for example, recorded the case of an unnamed fifteen-year-old girl, picked up for disturbing the peace only months after her arrival in Moscow from the countryside, who was subject to periodic drinking bouts and suicidal depressions caused, she said, by loneliness and melancholy

106. Makovskii, "Sotsial'no-ekonomicheskie faktory," 249–51; *PMS 1911*, 222.

(*toska*). But these notations appeared in her report almost incidentally and as evidence of her certain future as an "inveterate prostitute." The report emphasized her sexual maturity and "surprisingly dirty underwear," her smoking and drinking, and her unwillingness to scrub floors and carry out slop buckets for an aunt who managed an apartment building.[107]

The specialists' presumption that the juvenile criminals' environment was problem-ridden and that the children were "ruined" might seem appropriate since they were studying children who had committed crimes, but their one-sided critique had a detrimental effect on their efforts to eradicate crime and improve the children's lives. Ignoring positive signs of cultural identification and bonding among lower-class family members and peers precluded remedies rooted in the beneficial aspects of lower-class culture.

Many of these same specialists were the people who had exposed the brutality of the workshop and the other hardships faced by children of the poor. But while their sympathy was with the children's plight, and while several of them blamed "society" for creating the conditions that poor children faced, their understanding of juvenile crime was limited to the narrow world of the slums. None of them thought that juvenile crime might originate in a juvenile's perception of the inequities of the social structure or that it might represent an attack on society itself. A number of important crime and judicial experts did emphasize what they called "social factors" in the genesis of juvenile crime, including some of the more prominent and committed figures, such as Gernet, Makovskii, and Okunev. But these observers also either viewed the children as passive objects susceptible to the moral contamination of their social surroundings or they concentrated exclusively on lower-class society, minimizing its interaction with society at large.

One of the main reasons some observers sought social and economic, or what today we call the "structural," problems underlying crime was to avoid blaming the poor. They saw moral interpretations as an abdication of social responsibility for the conditions that produced juvenile crime, and they sought the social origins of crime in order to design social and practical measures for curtailing it.[108] Many of the socially oriented ana-

---

107. Segalov, *Deti-prestupniki*, 6–7.
108. The debate between proponents of cultural-moral explanations and proponents of structural arguments has been revived repeatedly in the twentieth century, most recently by U.S. social scientists in the 1980s as crime rates and indices of poverty here spiraled upward. See, for example, William Julius Wilson, *The*

lysts were either affiliated with the St. Petersburg Justice of the Peace Court, as was Okunev, or were working with Gernet at Moscow University. Gernet, mentioned earlier in connection with the influence of housing on crime, directed an influential seminar on juvenile crime in 1909. The research produced by the seminar was published in 1912 in the remarkable collection *Deti-prestupniki (Criminal Children)*. Gernet organized the seminar in direct response to the growth of juvenile crime but stated explicitly that its objective was to examine the social conditions that led children to crime, in order to recommend legal action to control juvenile crime.[109] The authors' research was based on local statistics and surveys as well as information about the children's background and experience, often in the children's own words. Consequently, the works in this collection presented the first sustained and realistic portrait of the lives of poor children living in the capital.[110]

The most consistent and outspoken of the social theorists working under Gernet was Iakov Berman, whose contribution to the collection was on juvenile recidivism, a subject particularly important for understanding the genesis of hooliganism. Berman argued that the causes of juvenile recidivism were, first and foremost, poverty, hunger, and need. Children stole not because social conditions prevented their learning to make moral choices but because they were hungry.[111] Berman's conclusion was based on his discovery of the horrendous physical conditions in which the city's poor children were living. Many of the jobs that were available to children under seventeen provided less than enough for survival. It was common for young boys to sell newspapers or take unskilled part-time jobs (often illegally), neither of which provided more than meager and highly irregular income. Okunev confirmed this impression by noting that children often found themselves resorting to such illegal jobs out of need, "often with the consent and encouragement of their parents, because they are too young to work as an apprentice or in a factory." But because it was

Truly Disadvantaged: The Inner City, the Underclass, and Public Policy (Chicago, 1987); Ken Auletta, *The Underclass* (New York, 1982); and for a recent history of twentieth-century cycles redefining poverty and deviancy see Michael B. Katz, *The Undeserving Poor: From the War on Poverty to the War on Welfare* (New York, 1989).

109. M. N. Gernet, "Predislovie," *Deti-prestupniki*, 1–2.

110. Many of these studies have been cited above. Seminar participants had access to the records of the Moscow *mirovoi sud*, the Moscow region's circuit court, the Moscow provincial prison inspector, the Rukavishnikov shelter for juveniles, and the juvenile section of the Moscow city workhouse.

111. Berman, "Retsidiv," 292–332.

illegal for children under eighteen to engage in many trades "the police pick up hundreds of these children each day." "As a result," Okunev continued, "the adolescent population of Petrograd sees each policeman or *dvornik* as his enemy."[112] Signs of poverty and instability were supported by the boys' own explanations for their actions (Berman did not study girls). One sixteen-year-old convicted of theft (his fifth, Berman pointed out) explained that

> only my difficult situation forced me to steal—after serving my sentence for another case, I was thrown out on the street. My parents wouldn't take me in. I was hungry and poorly dressed. I stole some of the things for my mother, to please her, hoping she would take me back.[113]

Another sixteen-year-old, also guilty of theft, explained: "I needed to. I was looking for work with a friend, but I couldn't find anything at all."[114] These were not the "pranks and caprices" of first-time offenders, Berman argued, but a "sad and threatening social anomaly that proceeds from the logic of our society, which needs the depths as a counterweight to the heights."[115] As for the influence of a prison sentence on a young offender, Berman emphasized its social and practical effects. Because they had been pushed off life's path at an early age, it was often difficult for young offenders to find their way back on track. Often after serving a sentence, youths were regarded with suspicion by prospective employers, and thus they were more likely to end up in the ranks of the unemployed. Their families rejected them, leaving them no place to live and no outside support.[116] Berman concluded that juvenile crime was "not solely [the product] of a criminal nature, not simply a habit or an inclination toward evil." It was much simpler: it was "the oldest motive, but it is ever new," and it bore repeating because the usual explanation for juvenile crime portrayed the children as moral degenerates. Berman went on: "If there are some juvenile recidivists with deeply engrained criminal tendencies who are thoroughly ensconced in the life of crime, the majority are not."[117]

Okunev also presented juvenile crime as primarily a "social phenomenon" in his official history of the Special Juvenile Court. An "inescapable"

112. Okunev, "Osobyi sud," 738–39.
113. Berman, "Retsidiv," 311.
114. Ibid., 311–12.
115. Ibid., 312.
116. Ibid., 316–17. The destructive impact of prison terms on juveniles was universally acknowledged.
117. Berman, "Retsidiv," 330.

social problem, juvenile crime was, in Okunev's view, a product of the concentration of people in big cities, the development of factory industry, the poverty of the working-classes, and the high cost of living in the capital, which made theft, for example, almost a necessity.[118] A social phenomenon, Okunev impressed on his readers, demanded social measures to combat it. If *bezprizornost'* were at its root, then it must be fought with day-care centers, kindergartens, shelters, clubs, and an increase in city schools, which would allow children to go to school until they were old enough to work.[119]

Ironically, the evidence these analysts produced to argue for social, and against moral, interpretations of juvenile crime was almost identical with that marshaled by those who focused on *bezprizornost'* and its corrosive moral consequences: homelessness, parental neglect, the lack of regular productive activity or adult supervision, alongside poverty, and hunger. But by transferring the weight of motivation from individual children and their families to the structure of the society in which they lived, the criminologists achieved several ends at once. They could remove the stigma of moral degeneracy from children they viewed as basically innocent, a necessary step toward preventing first-time offenders from committing new crimes. They encouraged people to see that the causes of crime were to be found not within the individual criminal, but within society, which allowed reformers some hope for believing that social action might decrease juvenile crime. If crime were caused by social injustice rather than individual psychology or morality, it could be diminished by improving living and working conditions. If it were poverty and hunger rather than the child's mentality or attitude that led to crime, then food, housing, and assimilation would prevent the alienation and hostility to society that turned juvenile criminals into hooligans.

For all these differences, however, the social structural explanation of juvenile crime shares several features with the moral arguments. First, few experts perceived the milieu and the motives of urban youth in any complexity. For example, few observers subjected the juveniles' words to more than superficial scrutiny. When children caught stealing explained that they were hungry or "had not eaten for days" it does not seem to have occurred to Berman, for example, that the juveniles might know that their answers would win favorable responses. Second, there was little attempt among any of the analysts to sort out the various factors they

---

118. Okunev, "Osobyi sud," 728, 814.
119. Okunev was also the only person to suggest separate schooling for children with special learning or discipline problems ("Osobyi sud," 733–34).

found juvenile criminals to have in common or to understand how they worked to reinforce one another. Both the social-economic and the cultural-moral analysts viewed the entire milieu of the lower-class city in isolation from the rest of society. Even Berman and Makovskii, who exposed the children's wretched conditions, did not see juvenile crime as a response to or an attack on the underlying social and economic structure responsible for those conditions.

Third, both the moral and the social observers of juvenile crime viewed lower-class life from the perspective of respectable society and its values. With only the rarest exceptions, crime specialists, including social theorists, called for cultural measures to curtail and prevent juvenile crime by raising the cultural level of the juveniles and assimilating them into respectable culture.[120] These observers assumed that activities and mores that offended respectable tastes were necessarily corrupting; so they did not try to differentiate the relative importance and influence of various features of lower-class life. They argued that *bezprizornost'* and poverty left children open to the contaminating influences around them, but playing billiards and reading crime fiction are fundamentally different experiences from exposure to open sexuality, ubiquitous alcoholism, and public, ritualized fighting. The point here is not to judge the various experiences on the basis of some corruption quotient, but to determine the varying roles they may have played in influencing a poor youth's life choices. What seemed the abnormal by-products of urban social conditions to respectable society were in fact regular features of lower-class culture (as well as of middle- and upper-class culture, though to different degrees and differently ritualized). While violence may be an obstacle to civilized and equitable social life, it cannot be said to have a uniformly deleterious influence. Inasmuch as ritualized gang violence, holiday brawling, and domestic abuse were commonplace in lower-class culture, their presence alone cannot explain why only some children committed crimes. The same goes for drinking. Alcohol consumption and abuse were so pervasive in Russian culture that they cannot be assumed to have had extraordinary influence on the children who became criminals. Furthermore, some children may have found a safer and more secure existence in the tavern among friends than with abusive parents at home or in a brutal workshop. This particular reading of lower-class culture by proponents of both social-economic and moral-cultural theories of criminal motivation, along with their call for

120. For example, Okunev, "Pervyi s"ezd," 44; Karpinskaia, *Bor'ba s ulitsei*, 11–12; Shlezinger, *Opyt otvlecheniia*, 5–7; N. S-in, "Khuligany i obshchestvo," *PL*, July 18, 1906; Okunev, "Osobyi sud," 733–35.

exclusively cultural measures in the fight against juvenile crime and hooliganism, reflected a deep class and cultural chasm that divided reformers from the youths they wanted to help, and constituted the main obstacle in the legal battle against hooliganism.[121]

③ Punishment, Improvement, and the Prevention of Hooliganism

Negative perceptions of lower-class family life and youth culture were of critical importance because they shaped almost entirely the remedies suggested for preventing juveniles from becoming hooligans. The cultural measures they influenced were intended to extricate the youngsters from the pernicious influences around them and instill moral values, respect for other people, and an appreciation of the need to work. Reformers wanted to keep children away from "vice," especially in prison, to offer them alternatives to taverns and billiards, to find them jobs, and to locate suitable lodgings for them, all in order to help the youths support themselves and, equally important, to integrate them into society. In punishing them, the goal was to offer useful and healing experiences that would demonstrate the superiority of a life of respectable work and activity.[122] In practice these proposals constituted an effort to replace the dysfunctional lower-class family with a surrogate respectable one. "It is not up to this congress to find solutions for poverty and the instability of the majority of working families," Dril' declared in 1908,

> but if the family cannot provide even a rudimentary moral
> education and if as a result the abandoned, uncared-for children
> threaten society, then state and society must provide something in
> place of the family's upbringing, if only in its own protective self-
> interest.[123]

121. Not that a century of social policy has managed to close that breach; today we see the same inability to address the links between culture and social-economic position and the conflicts those links engender between policymakers, social workers, and social welfare recipients. The likelihood of successful reform is further undermined by the political petrification of positions on both sides; see Katz, *The Undeserving Poor*, on the recycling of the categories of poverty that keep governments and social reformers from devising workable policy.
122. Okunev, "Pervyi s"ezd," 43–45; Karpinskaia, *Bor'ba s ulitsei*, 3–5, 9–12; Shlezinger, *Opyt otvlecheniia*, 6–7; "S.-Peterburg, 22-ogo ianvaria," *GK*, January 22, 1911 [lead article]; Okunev, "Osobyi sud," 733–38; "K obuzdaniiu," *PL*, October 17, 1903; N. F. Tsikin, "Patronatnaia pomoshch' maloletnim," *Osobyi sud po delam o maloletnikh: Otchet S.-Peterburgskogo stolichnogo mirovogo sud'i N. A. Okuneva za 1910 god.* (St. Petersburg, 1911), 5–6.
123. Dril', "O merakh bor'by," 22–23.

A handful of new institutions—Children's Houses, reading rooms, clubs—were inspired by such thinking, but the most ambitious and influential project that arose during this period was the Special Juvenile Court of the Petersburg *mirovoi sud*, which opened in St. Petersburg in 1910. The court's stated goal was to provide juvenile criminals with a substitute for the family and cultural life that had driven them to crime. The explicit justification for the new institution was to prevent hooliganism:

> Life is more and more stubbornly creating the necessity to address the most serious attention to the struggle . . . against the noticeably growing problem of juvenile hooliganism, which possesses its own special characteristics and which breeds and cultivates a distinctive cadre of habitual recidivists, who, in turn, infect the weaker youngsters with their influence. Inside the prison and outside they have an extremely harmful effect on first-time offenders.[124]

The structure of the court was based on both the social and the cultural analysis of juvenile crime outlined above: crime was a product of social conditions, and thus it was the responsibility of society to alleviate those conditions, but crimes were committed by *bezprizorniki*—children whose family situation had prevented them from developing an ability to distinguish right from wrong. The plans of the judicial reformers for solving the juvenile crime problem, their implementation and their problems, reveal the attitudes of those in Russian urban society whose response to the 1905–1907 Revolution was to take positive and practical (but not revolutionary) action to ameliorate the social conditions they believed brought about disorder. The structure of the court and its underlying philosophy reveal an optimism about the possibility of assimilating lower-class children into respectable society by means of cultural improvement if the process were begun early enough and the children were sufficiently insulated from the corrupting elements around them.

The Special Juvenile Court was created to take advantage of the provisions of an 1897 law on juveniles that allowed more flexibility in sentencing youths by keeping them out of prison as much as possible, by isolating them from adult inmates when they were sentenced to serve prison terms, and by trying to reduce the stigma of being convicted for a crime at an early age.[125] At the heart of the Special Juvenile Court system was the

---

124. *PMS 1909*, 62–63.
125. On the legislation see *PMS 1909*; A. D. Korotnev, *Maloletnie i nesovershennoletnie prestupniki: Kratkii istoricheskii ocherk* (St. Petersburg, 1903); and A. N. Butovskii, "Zakon o nesovershennoletnikh i ego primenenie v sudebno-mirovoi praktike," *Zhurnal ministerstva iustitsii* 6 (1900).

guardian (*popechitel'*), who was appointed to supervise convicted juveniles put on probation instead of in prison. The law of 1897 allowed the court to appoint as guardian any responsible adult to provide the kind of supervision whose absence had led the child to commit a crime in the first place. Individually the Petersburg Justices of the Peace hoped that guardians would not only supervise and prevent further demoralization but would provide active guidance and assistance to set the children on a positive path.[126] Juveniles had to promise to reform and were warned that more serious punishment would follow if they broke their promise. Juveniles were supposed to avoid their former harmful friends, to leave home only with parental permission, and to quit visiting tearooms and other such places. If the family situation seemed positive, the juvenile was released to the supervision of his or her parent(s), but a guardian was appointed in any case for added supervision.[127] Everything was done to persuade young offenders that they had only made an unfortunate mistake in breaking the law and that society believed they had done so out of ignorance and inexperience rather than malice. Reformers had been struck by young criminals' resignation and fatalism: "Thieving is our business and there's nothing you can do about it," one boy said. "Such is our fate."[128] The founders of the Special Juvenile Court interpreted this to mean that the youths had no confidence that they might escape from a life of crime, so Juvenile Court JPs were supposed to take the time to persuade juveniles that society had not yet irrevocably rejected them. The Justices of the Peace could not imagine that everyday life might have already persuaded lower-class youths that society had long ago turned its back on them.

Reintegration was closely connected with labor and the development of a work ethic. The guardians' official guide stated that "the purpose of guardian supervision is to help the juvenile carry on a life of honest labor,"[129] and as guardian N. F. Tsikin recalled, work was the key to extracting the children from their "former lives and wicked friends."[130] The Special Juvenile Court, it must be noted, was not interested in provid-

126. *PMS 1909*; Gogel', "Detskaia prestupnost'," cols. 1176–77.

127. Okunev, "Osobyi sud," 770–73; see also I. Bocharov, "Pervye osobye sudy po delam o maloletnikh v Rossii," in *Deti-prestupniki*, ed. M. N. Gernet (Moscow, 1912).

128. Okunev, "Osobyi sud," 726–27.

129. "Printsipy raboty popechitelia," in *Osobyi sud po delam o maloletnikh: Otchet S.-Peterburgskogo stolichnogo mirovogo sud'i N. A. Okuneva za 1910 god* (St. Petersburg, 1911), 104; also Okunev, "Osobyi sud," 770–72; Dril', "O merakh bor'by," 22.

130. Tsikin, "Patronatnaia pomoshch'," 1.

ing the lower-class children with social mobility or a step up into the middle class. Their lot in life was to work, and society's goal for them was only that they become respectable workers. The guardians, on the whole, did their best to find youths jobs and instill in them a sense of work ethic and responsibility, but their efforts were at least partly doomed by the conflict between their cultural and their socioeconomic expectations of the results.[131] The contradictions were not lost on contemporary social democrats. When the Moscow Justice of the Peace Court opened its own Special Juvenile Court in 1912, the brand new Bolshevik newspaper *Pravda* responded with an article sarcastically deprecating the court's goal of guiding juveniles toward a "free and productive life." Freedom, *Pravda* noted, meant only that the youths would be "free to work eighteen hours a day, free to go hungry on the patriarchal gruel, free to take the bosses' punches and blows, and free to run out to get vodka for them. From such 'freedom,' children run to the streets."[132]

The point here is not to condemn the guardians for their views or their considerable efforts, but to point out the limits their perceptions placed on their programs. The guardians and Justices of the Peace did not anticipate any of the reasons young poor children may have resisted the "life of honest labor" or were unable to take advantage of its benefits. In addition, while the middle-class reformers expected children to adopt respectable values and behavior once they were removed from a corrupting environment, the guardians offered the children none of the financial or material assistance necessary to make respectability appealing. Why should a fifteen-year-old juvenile delinquent trust a middle-class social worker who had nothing to offer beyond a few days of institutional shelter? The culture of respectability implies a comfortable income earned in rewarding professional occupations. A life of behavioral restraint, responsibility, and discipline can seem appealing only when it holds out a promise of wealth and comfort. It is not that the guardians were insincere in their desire to help the juveniles or that they were interested only in producing conformist drones, but that by offering cultural improvement in the absence of any material benefits they were fighting the battle with one hand tied behind their backs. The ensuing difficulties are evident in the writings of the court's first guardians and other social reformers.

131. Jeffrey Brooks makes a similar point about the educators in the countryside, noting that while teachers wanted to encourage peasants to read, they also wanted them to remain peasants (*When Russia Learned to Read*, 55–56).
132. "Detskie sudy," *Pravda*, April 27, 1912.

During its first two years of operation, the court had five guardians: Semenov, Tsikin, Chichagova, Viktor Kimental, and Andrei Udris. All five of the original guardians had experience as teachers in provincial teacher-training institutes and had done some teaching in *zemstvo* or city schools. Two of the guardians had previously worked with juvenile criminals in colonies and shelters, and two had taught workers in factory classes for adults. Four of the five were men in their early thirties; the one woman was in her mid-fifties in 1910.[133] Each was paid 1,200 rubles for supervising approximately 250 juveniles for varying lengths of time over the course of a year, which was a considerable sum from the point of view of the "poor struggling families" who produced the bulk of the juveniles.[134]

Each of the original guardians quickly discovered that it was hard enough just keeping up with their charges, much less instilling in them new cultural values. The experience was eye-opening and, even for the experienced, deeply troubling. All the guardians reported despair at the conditions in which the juveniles lived and the hardships—psychological and physical—with which the children had to cope each day. Most of the guardians also hinted at their own frustration in helping the youths and even communicating with them. The families were often uncooperative and resentful; the children themselves were hardened by more than their recent brush with the judicial system. Genuine sympathy for the children and their families was expressed in the guardians' reports, along with outrage at the injustice that created the world in which they existed, but little comprehension of the reasons for their own less than warm welcome.[135]

One would hardly expect the creators of such a paternalistic system to have insight into resentment against paternalism, but there were other

---

133. See Okunev, "Osobyi sud," 782, for names, ages, education, and employment records.

134. If we assume, as the evidence suggests, that the juveniles usually came from families of unskilled or poorly paid workers with only one major wage earner, they probably made approximately 200–400 rubles a year; so the guardians' salaries marked a significant economic as well as cultural divide; see Semenov, *Bytovye usloviia*, 7; and on workers' wages see I. I. Kir'ianov, *Zhiznennyi uroven' rabochikh Rossii (konets XIX–nachalo XX v.)* (Moscow, 1979), 89–152. The guardians were paid out of the *mirovoi sud* budget, which was allocated by the City Duma. In 1912 the City Duma approved the appointment of two additional guardians, with a raise to 1,500 rubles per year for each of them. As with the initial legislation for the special court, this request was met with speed rare for the Petersburg City Duma; see *PMS 1914*, 108.

135. For similar experiences in Russian social welfare, see Adele Lindenmeyr, "A Russian Experiment in Voluntarism: The Municipal Guardianships of the Poor, 1894–1914," *Jahrbücher für Geschichte Osteuropas*, vol. 30, no. 3 (1982): 441–44.

factors that complicated the guardians' perceptions of their activities. Government funding for social welfare reform was negligble, and the state's distrust of voluntary associations kept private initiative at a minimum. And despite the activism of the Petersburg JPs and other individuals, apathy toward social problems was prevalent among a large sector of society. Karpinskaia reproached society for ignoring social problems, until "they reach[ed] the homes and palaces of the rich."[136] Thus it was easy for the guardians to focus on the lack of public and private support as impediments to their attempts to transform their juveniles into model citizens. Guardian Kimental, for example, sincerely deplored the youths' desperate material situation, but he clearly felt that economic matters were secondary to his cultural mission. He complained that the guardians "frequently felt incapable of helping these children" mainly because it was "necessary to think first not of moral healing but of satisfying their essential needs."[137] He reported that his work became easier when it became more bureaucratized, as the court and other institutions offered assistance with some of the material problems, such as providing temporary shelter and shoes and clothing—some of the children had been "practically naked" when they were arrested.[138]

The guardians did spend considerable time helping the juveniles find housing and jobs, but it was often frustrating. Their first task after the trial was to find proper lodgings, but as Tsikin recorded, the juveniles under his care frequently had no parents or relatives in St. Petersburg and did not have the means to pay for permanent shelter; so they slept in flophouses or shanties built on the edge of town or in trash heaps. But even the owners of "corners" were disinclined to rent to convicted juveniles.[139] In the first days after the new court opened, some youths slept in the court chambers without mattresses or pillows on benches removed from the public hall and were fed out of donations from court personnel, rather than being imprisoned in cells with adults awaiting trial.[140]

136. Karpinskaia, *Bor'ba s ulitsei*, 5; echoed in Bater, *St. Petersburg*, 212 and passim; apathy among the well-off was a key target of *Peterburgskii listok* articles on city problems and the City Duma; it was a common complaint among social activists: for example, P. N. Litvinov, "O gorodskikh popechitel'stvakh o bednykh v Peterburge," *Gorodskoe delo* 5 (1910); cited in Lindenmeyr, "A Russian Experiment," 444; and among judicial activists: for example, N. A. Okunev, "Bezotsovshchina," *OSDM* 8–9 (1915).
137. Kimental', "Deiatel'nost' popechitelei," 102.
138. Ibid., 102–3; Tsikin, "Patronatnaia pomoshch'," 1–3.
139. Tsikin, "Patronatnaia pomoshch'," 2–3.
140. Ibid., 2–3.

The St. Petersburg Parole Agency (*Obshchestvo patronata*) partially resolved the housing problem by donating funds to open a dormitory for boys awaiting trial or after conviction, to be administered by two of the guardians, Tsikin and Chichagova. In some ways this dormitory embodied the goals of the juvenile court and guardian system. It provided shelter for children who had none, but that was not all. The children "were never left unsupervised." They worked inside the dormitory to keep it clean and orderly and to learn proper work habits. Daily life was strictly routinized, including reading lessons in the evenings and occasionally gymnastics as well.[141] But for all his pride in the success of the dormitory, Tsikin conceded that fewer victories occurred in the areas of working life and moral habits. Work was hard to find because employers always knew the youths had committed crimes. Sometimes when the children found work they were fired after their court-appointed guardian showed up with their passport. *Gazeta-kopeika* offered to hire boys under guardian supervision to sell newspapers, but that gesture of goodwill did not work out. The boys often turned up late and usually managed to "lose" some of their pay, stopping at tearooms on the way home from work or going to tearooms and bypassing work altogether. As for the morality of the boys in the dormitory (and the other juveniles as well), Tsikin believed that the children simply did not possess enough discipline to stay off the streets or resist their temptations.[142] Udris, another guardian, agreed. The typical juvenile, he thought, was accustomed to doing whatever he pleased, and never learned to control his will. A boy needed to be taught how to resist his "wicked and depraved instincts, for the good of others, for the good of society, and for his own good."[143] In contrast Udris noted that they all exhibited a strict sense of justice and fairness, but for him this remained an anomaly.[144]

The one woman guardian, Chichagova, openly expressed frustration with her mission. She found many of the girls she supervised to be incomprehensible, evasive, and incorrigible, though she sympathized with their harrowing and desperate lives. One of her charges was a ten-year-old girl who turned to prostitution after being raped by three boys accompanying her on a boat trip. The girl's story is depressingly familiar. Picked up by the police for illegal soliciting, she was taken to a shelter for girls when she refused to tell the police her name. On release she returned to her

141. Ibid., 3–4; Udris, "Vospitatel'no-ispravitel'nye zavedeniia," 142.
142. Tsikin, "Patronatnaia pomoshch'," 5–6.
143. Udris, "Vospitatel'no-ispravitel'nye zavedeniia," 142–43.
144. Ibid., 143.

parents, but her mother died soon after, and her father was too ill to work; on that account he not only did not discourage her prostitution; he welcomed the income she brought home. She was picked up again by the police and taken to a medical inspection station for prostitutes, where she was found to have a venereal disease. She did not specify her illness in recounting her history for Chichagova except to say that she had been placed in a hospital but found the treatment there useless. She preferred the help and company of the other *shkitsy* (slang for "child-prostitutes") to any of the institutions with which she had had contact. As guardian of such girls Chichagova often felt powerless: "All their stories are so simple and at the same time so awful; but how to help them and what to do, I do not know."[145]

Not all the guardians' experiences were of failure and despair. Kimental, for example, reported cases with ambiguous results as well as those he considered successful. Sometimes, he maintained, the guardian's surveillance (*prismotr*) helped the whole family. A father stopped drinking and found a well-paying job. A boy, whose father had refused to support him any longer, reformed, found a job, and was reunited with his family. Others improved their behavior when removed from their parents and placed in one of the few shelters. Many, however, were returned to their villages, never to be heard of again.[146]

The most interesting success story of this sort comes not from the Juvenile Court itself, but from a doctor, V. V. Shlezinger, who organized similar cultural experiments in assisting convicted juveniles. As a member of the charitable organization that established the St. Petersburg "Children's Village" (*Detskaia derevnia*) Shlezinger organized activities for youths in the belief that hooligans were deeply troubled, but not incorrigible, boys. After working with convicted juveniles for two years, between 1911 and 1913, he was convinced that hooligans continued their rowdy ways only because they never had the opportunity to learn how to behave properly: "The only doors open to them—and they are wide open here in the cultural center of their fatherland—lead to the tavern, debauchery, and disgrace."[147] After two years, Shlezinger found that the boys learned to exhibit proper behavior and attitudes—they had all obtained jobs in factories or workshops, and they tried to act like adults—but he also

---

145. Chichagova, "Otchet popechitel'nitsy," 253–54.
146. Kimental', "Deiatel'nost' popechitelei," 126; also "Vliianie prismotra," *Osobyi sud po delam o maloletnikh: Otchet S.-Peterburgskogo stolichnogo mirovogo sud'i N. A. Okuneva za 1910 god* (St. Petersburg, 1911), 125.
147. Shlezinger, *Opyt otvlecheniia*, 3.

saw that this was fairly superficial. The boys behaved "properly" only to impress the adults at the Children's Village. Nonetheless, Shlezinger found that their main problem was not their shortage of good intentions but their inability to use their free time. They did not want to play children's games on the playground, and they did not want their old pals in the hooligan gangs to laugh at them for participating in activities at the Children's Village. In Shlezinger's assessment the boys' achievements were mixed. On the one hand they showed great interest in social questions, which they debated intensely, but they also enjoyed telling stories about the criminal exploits of their friends, and they all displayed "extremely free views in relation to the property of others," for which many had already served time in prison. To Shlezinger's dismay (but to no one's surprise), a prison sentence only made a boy more awe-inspiring and influential.[148] Against all of this the doctor waged an energetic struggle, and he claimed to have achieved a surprisingly easy victory. He organized a group that the boys themselves named the "Circle for Rational Entertainment" (*kruzhok razumnykh razvlechenii*). The circle received permission to organize a soccer team, which the boys joined enthusiastically; they began to come every day and gradually distanced themselves from the hooligans who had been their friends.

One of Shlezinger's great successes was X., a boy who was especially "lazy" and a well-known troublemaker in the neighborhood and who each year was thrown out of the Children's Village for his rowdiness. In two years he had been to prison five times for petty theft. The other boys admired and liked him for his boldness, his wide experience, and his innately cheerful and rebellious ways. He was also unusually talented: he knew three trades, had a sharp ear and could play several musical instruments, and drew well. But thanks to his "dissipation" and his "lack of discipline," he could never stay in one place or hold a job, preferring drinking, idleness, and theft. One day the circle turned against him for treating his mother cruelly. This was an enormous victory for Shlezinger, but it did not end there. To his great surprise the "slovenly, slothful" X. went out and got himself a job solely in order to remain in the circle.[149]

Shlezinger's successes with individuals and popular activities led him to believe that young hooligans could be reformed because they were not content with their rowdy and disorderly lives; when they could they seized opportunities to construct a more orderly and productive life. Then came

148. Ibid., 6.
149. Ibid., 7–8.

"the drunken day of August 15," when the doctor arrived to find his boys drinking up their holiday pay on the playground. They were thoroughly drunk, "even singing songs," and they instigated a "scandalous" scene when he tried to throw them out. They threatened him, they cried drunken tears, and Shlezinger, by his own account furious and distraught, threatened to resign. All was patched up the next day when the boys returned, "extremely contrite," but Shlezinger's disappointment in them was unequivocal. Moreover, he realized that when the playground closed at the end of the summer, all his hard work would be obliterated "by the streets."[150]

That prediction was largely borne out by the continued rise of juvenile crime and hooliganism. If success is measured by a declining rate of crime, guardian supervision and professional culturalism were a failure. Juvenile crime rates continued to climb. The number of juveniles sentenced to the *mirovoi sud* House of Detention dropped at first when the court began assigning them to guardians instead, as did the number of juveniles tried by Justices of the Peace. But the total number of juveniles tried in the *mirovoi sud* began to rise again within a year after 1910, as did their proportion of total convictions (see table 9 in the Appendix). The number of juveniles assigned to guardians also increased: in 1910, 1,155 juveniles had come under court-appointed supervision; in 1911, 1,321; in 1912, 1,620; and in 1913, 1,860.[151] After the outbreak of World War I, in 1914, crime rates of all kinds, and of juvenile crime in particular, soared. In St. Petersburg so many young people were arrested for theft that the justices and guardians did not know "what to do with them all."[152]

Participants' assessments of the court's success (and that of other cultural measures) are highly ambiguous despite their own predominantly self-confident tone. Certainly court supervision and organized soccer games provided some juvenile offenders with the assistance they needed to escape the desperate poverty and abusive families that may have led them to crime. Supervision helped some children and adolescents find

---

150. Ibid., 15–19.
151. *PMS 1914*, 108.
152. The explosion of crime rates during the war occurred under new social conditions that are beyond the scope of this study. It is worth noting, however, that the sharp upsurge in juvenile crime after 1914 was also seen as the result of family dysfunction. The war increased the number of *bezprizorniki* by drafting their fathers and removing the person responsible for asserting order at home, as Okunev wrote in an article entitled "Bezotsovshchina" (A World without Fathers), 4–5. The journal in which this article appeared became preoccupied, once the war began, with the breakdown of family unity and its relation to crime.

regular work and relatively healthy housing, and they may have managed to enter mainstream working-class life. But for all his successes at the Children's Village, Shlezinger, for example, conceded that he had to wage a constant battle to keep his boys away from those who remained outside the playground gates: the gangs of hooligans who were not tempted by soccer games, dancing parties, and exhibitions on hygiene.[153] The Juvenile Court guardians also felt that they were carrying on an uphill struggle. Their reports suggest that their efforts were useful primarily for those juveniles whose entry into the crime world corresponded with some of the simpler social analysis of criminal motivation discussed above. But such analysis hardly accounts for those who were propelled toward crime and hooliganism by melancholy or rebelliousness or culturally based class conflict. The class and cultural hatred many hooligans expressed by taunting respectable pedestrians on the streets was not mollified by soccer leagues or a steady job. The routine of work itself may have been a source of discontent for the more rebellious hooligans, in which case attempts to instill work discipline would have only fanned the flames.

The middle-class reformers were baffled and dispirited when their efforts to provide cultural development were rebuffed. By late 1914, even the justices connected with the Special Juvenile Court felt the need to resort to more coercive measures.[154] Reports to the 1914 congress on Special Juvenile courts made it clear that the continued growth of juvenile crime, despite the best efforts of the courts, demanded more intrusive steps. A legislative proposal supported by the congress recommended that children be removed from their parents altogether if circumstances proved the parents unfit. Policemen were required to apprehend immediately any child who appeared to be a *bezprizornik* and to take her or him to a shelter. Only as a last resort was a child to be taken to a police station, and then only if there were facilities for isolating children from adults.[155] This was considerably more intrusive than the earlier police policy of interfering in family life only when it was clear that a law had been broken.[156]

---

153. Shlezinger, *Opyt otvlecheniia*, 7–9.
154. For the various coercive measures used to treat *bezprizornost'* after the Bolshevik Revolution see Goldman, "The 'Withering-Away,'" 96–120, 372–74.
155. [Untitled article], *Pravo* 1 (1914): 47–48; "Zakonoproekt o merakh popecheniia nad bezprizornymi maloletnimi i o lishenii roditel'skoi vlasti i ob"iasnitel'naia k nemu zapiska (Priniatyi Pervym Vserossiiskim S"ezdom Deiatelei po voprosam Suda dlia Maloletnikh, sostoiavshimsia v Petrograde v dekabre 1913 goda)," *OSDM* 4 (1915): 3.
156. "Politsiia i sem'ia," *PL*, October 28, 1913.

Unfortunately, the guardians hinted only indirectly at their own feelings about working with juveniles, and they usually attributed their failures with hooligans to the temptations of "the streets." In their reports, however, one can discern a pattern that is common in welfare relationships in other societies. The youths under state supervision or participating in cultural activities like Shlezinger's Children's Village took from the welfare system the kind of assistance they knew they wanted and could use, and they ignored the moral edification that conflicted with their own cultural values and habits.[157] For instance, Shlezinger's boys found jobs and genuinely enjoyed their soccer league, but they refused to give up drinking or admiring the exploits of clever and rebellious criminals. Chichagova's girls accepted shelter when they needed it but resisted the morally uplifting guidance guardians provided in an attempt to extricate them from prostitution, and they rejected institutional medical treatment altogether.

On the whole, then, the study of juvenile crime and hooliganism offered contemporaries some insight into urban youth culture, and the projects based on these studies yielded some partial successes at the time, but they hardly made a dent in the problems of poverty, alienation, and crime that they were trying to alleviate. Similar failures occurred in every Western capital at the time and continue to haunt our cities today, so the following critique is not intended to condemn the Russian experts and reformers, but to explore what this example of social interaction and cultural engineering can show about social dynamics, middle-class professional views of poverty and the poor, and the prospects for social stability in late imperial Petersburg.

▓ Crime, Class, and Culture

The origins of poverty and crime are at once both cultural and social-economic. But, because specialists and policymakers usually understand

---

157. For example, Gareth Stedman Jones, "Working-Class Culture and Working-Class Politics," in *Languages of Class*, 192–205; E. J. Hobsbawm, "Debating the Labour Aristocracy," and other essays in *Workers: Worlds of Labor* (New York, 1984). Linda Gordon argues in *Heroes of Their Own Lives* (New York, 1988), her work on turn-of-the-century domestic abuse in the United States, that clients learned to use social workers as advocates in their own causes, however tangential to the social workers' purposes; David Crew shows how welfare recipients in Weimar Germany used state financial assistance for purposes they defined as priorities, regardless of the state's intent, and that they readily accepted financial assistance while ignoring cultural improvement programs that seemed irrelevant or offensive ("'Eine Elternschaft zu Dritt'—The State as Parent?: Child Welfare and German Families in the Weimar Republic, 1919–1933" [unpublished manuscript]).

crime as either one or the other, the two reinforce each other in ways that have derailed efforts to eradicate crime or improve the lives of the poor and that insure the continuation of hooligan responses to efforts at crime control.

In late imperial Russia, judicial and crime experts first of all rarely looked outside the lower-class milieu for explanations of juvenile criminality. They could imagine youths' motives to have been shaped only by the deplorable conditions of their own world. That slum children might possess a vision of society as a whole and resent their own subordinate place within it or that they might act in response to external stimuli did not enter the middle-class experts' calculations. Nor did they see hooliganism or juvenile crime as a rebellious response to the difficult transition from childhood to adulthood common to members of various classes.[158] In fact, the appeal of the streets lay neither in some mysterious magnetism nor in some inherent moral weakness among *bezprizornye* juveniles. The streets, billiard rooms, tea shops, and beer halls were places where their own culture flourished far from the disapproving gaze of respectable society. However fatal the adolescents' attachment to taverns and flophouses, or for that matter to parents who abused them, it was within this whole environment that their identities were formed. They were not oblivious to the larger society; they were temporarily escaping its weight and its glare. Ultimately, some youths, like Shlezinger's, may have forsaken the most destructive aspects of lower-class culture that prevented them from feeding and housing themselves, but even they refused to abandon wholesale the world they knew. The experience of living between two cultures, and partially adapting to each, is always a painful one. The youths' responses to the efforts made to introduce them to respectable culture show how even assistance or advice that is universally perceived to be "good" can run up against resistance if it comes bound in a package with alien cultural values and expectations. The social workers and judicial reformers underestimated the power of culture to divide people and to divide individuals within themselves. Thus they had little conception of the ways in which people tend to view their own lives positively and to find value in their existence no matter how desperately poor or abused they are. The young juveniles of the Petersburg streets had few models to begin with, but social workers criticized not only the abusive parents and illegal activities; they also attacked the youths' only sources of conviviality and entertainment. Some youths were able to respond by picking and choosing

158. For a partial critique of such theories see Hebdige, *Subculture*, 73–89.

which sorts of advice they might follow, but others must have felt that their whole way of life was under attack.

Second, although the criminologists and justices who studied juveniles did a great deal to publicize the wretched conditions poor children were growing up in, they were not in a position to change the social and economic structure that perpetuated those conditions; therefore they focused their efforts on what they believed they could do. It is important to realize, however, that they chose to focus on cultural measures, as opposed to economic and social ones, to attain their goal of helping "juveniles carry on a life of honest labor." Yet these were youths who had already rejected the world of work. Unless they were teenage—that is, temporary—rebels, in which case they would not become serious hooligan recidivists anyway, these were people who would need tangible enticements to take up a life of respectability. The cultural measures reformers offered were reasonable steps toward a healthier environment for the youths, but they provided few of the economic and social advantages that produced respectable culture in the first place. So by stressing discipline, cleanliness, temperance, and the like, instead of finding them jobs or training or education these programs failed to have lasting impact. It does not even seem to matter that this was a period of social and economic upward mobility for many workers in Russia. Upward mobility was available only to a chosen few, and in the lowest of the lower depths the choices were still bleak.

Finally, when the people bearing cultural improvement were representatives of an economic and political elite—middle-class social workers and Justices of the Peace—their power to intrude must have been readily apparent to the poor and powerless youths. Even good advice and attractive programs can be tarnished as a result. If those same people also bring contempt and disgust for lower-class culture and suggest that the youths' problems stem entirely from their own families and their own streets, there is likely to be conflict, even when areas of agreement can be found.

In some ways, ironically, the juvenile crime specialists came closer to an understanding of hooliganism than anyone else because they realized that crime had a cultural component. They understood the importance of family acculturation, the influence of behavioral models to which children were exposed, and the utility of providing alternative models and activities. But because they did not understand that the poor valued aspects of their lives others considered unsavory and destructive, they cut themselves off from the engrained mental world of their subjects and therefore did not understand why their own way of life did not immediately and fully appeal to slum children. In fact, it was exactly the values that the reformers were trying to instill that hooligans, in their public manifestations, flouted with such bravado on the streets. Therefore, although the justices and social workers were motivated by the need to prevent hooliganism, they may have contributed to its continued growth. Criminologists assumed that *bezprizornost'* blocked juveniles from acquiring knowledge of respectable culture, whereas hooligans not only did not lack such knowledge, they understood respectable culture well enough to mock it vigorously.

Small wonder then that hooliganism remained such an annoying problem. Even sympathetic professional reformers did not know what they were looking at. They thought they saw moral dissipation where a war of values was being waged. They knew that hooliganism was a crime of a different order from childhood pranks, but they believed that hooliganism was the result of increasing exposure to depravity, either through the influence of already demoralized adults or through the juveniles' own experiences in prisons and on the streets. To be sure, these were major influences, but they cannot explain the element of hooliganism that stood outside of such social and moral factors. It does not seem surprising at this remove that a life of petty crime might offer more in the way of pleasure and satisfaction (especially if it brought publicity and notoriety), at least in the short run, than the long, oppressive day in the factory or the capricious tyranny of the workshop. The pervasive fatalism juveniles expressed was ordinarily treated as evidence of the juveniles' weak moral development or lack of imagination, but it is equally possible that the youths were resigned to their life of crime because they did not find any of the other alternatives appealing.

In the late twentieth century we have come to expect the kind of hooligan behavior that alienated poor youths were exhibiting in prerevolutionary Petersburg. But in early twentieth-century cities, urban concentrations of population were still rare enough that many societies were just beginning to examine the special conflicts they created. New interpretations based on a faith in scientific analyses of society and a dimly understood recognition of cultural conflict led Russian reformers and judicial specialists to believe that they were dealing with a new kind of problem. Unlike many liberal jurists of national prominence, they were unwilling to dismiss its importance, but they could not develop an effective policy to deal with it. When cultural measures failed to prevent the growth of hooliganism, they did not question the methods used but proposed more stringent forms of the same methods. Then, as more members of respectable society became disillusioned, they began to question the capacity of the people to respond to enlightenment cultural measures or to develop into what respectable society considered civilized beings. Skepticism about the efficacy of cultural measures and disappointment with the cultural development of the urban lower classes were on the rise just as acute social unrest and hooliganism began to resurface in St. Petersburg and throughout the empire in the 1910s. The specialists' negative views of the lower-class family and their inability to recognize positive features in lower-class culture, both of which were publicized in the respectable and the boulevard press, must have played a role in the subsequent skepticism. The fact that hooliganism, with its implicit iconoclasm and its challenge to respectability, haunted the whole discussion of juvenile crime, the lower-class family, and the culture of the streets had a paradoxical effect. The shadow of hooliganism aroused fears and alerted attention to crime in ways that both reinforced ideas about the need for cultural development and barred understanding of cultural difference. The paradox here is rooted in the conflicting functions served by the discourse on reform.

The criminologists, court officials, and voluntary social workers who studied and worked with urban youths saw themselves as champions of the poor. Their reforms did not constitute, as some Western historians once thought, simple efforts to coerce and control poor youths, and their commitment to cultural improvement was more than a rhetorical facade used purely to exert "social control."[159] The problem with "social control" theories is that they presented the words and deeds of social reformers as little more than disguised weapons of class conflict, without appreciating the complexities of the interaction involved in cultural development projects. In contrast, Foucault's excavation of nineteenth-century reforms stressed the power of culture, and the way we talk about culture, to organize societies. In Foucault's terms, the late imperial Russian reformers redefined deviancy and youth as new categories and new problems: deviant youths were to be corrected and reintegrated rather than ostracized and punished. Correction and rehabilitation provided "modern" and "rational" methods for dealing with deviance (in place of brutal physical

159. See, for example, Humphries, *Hooligans or Rebels?* Stuart Hall et al., *Policing the Crisis: Mugging, the State, and Law and Order* (London, 1978), present a subtler analysis of the mechanisms by which state and cultural institutions, including the press, manipulated the middle class into believing that there was a crime problem, and thereby allowed the police to increase surveillance and control over the poor, but it too emphasizes consciously coercive methods and at the same time ignores the possibility of genuine resistance among the "policed." A representative survey of social control theory historically applied is A. P. Donajgrodzki, ed., *Social Control in Nineteenth-Century Britain* (Totowa, N.J., 1977); more useful are the essays in Stanley Cohen and Andrew Scull, eds., *Social Control and the State* (Oxford, 1983); cogent criticism may be found in Gareth Stedman Jones, "Class Expression versus Social Control? A Critique of Recent Trends in the Social History of 'Leisure,'" in *Languages of Class*, 76–89.

punishment), which allowed reformers to consider themselves progressive, but they were never intended to transform the social hierarchy. In fact, as Foucault makes clear, even when such projects provided the poor with tools for attaining a certain level of security and integration into the industrial economy, they could be as oppressive as sheer political domination, by ensnaring the powerless in a process of "normalization."[160] Russian reformers defined deviancy as an unwillingness or inability to work and to behave peaceably as well as lawfully. Thus work became not only necessary economically; it was society's admission ticket. That some members of the lower classes shared the cultural aspirations of respectable society only served to reinforce the existing structure. By establishing respectable culture as society's norm—making it available to everyone while ignoring the conflicts that it created—reform projects both stabilized society structurally and prevented it from resolving the problems of poverty.

While Foucault describes the larger context in which European societies enforced order and conformity, he does not account for the dynamics of cultural interaction on the individual level; he does not address middle-class motivation underlying reform projects or popular responses to them; and he does not deal with the ways in which subordinate classes interpreted commonly held values, such as the centrality of the family or the need for social harmony, quite independently of efforts to impose cultural conformity.[161] In other words, Foucault does not deal with contemporary perceptions of stability, social problems, resistance, or reform.

To say that the Russian judicial reformers and social workers believed society as a whole would benefit if the lives of poor city youths more closely resembled those of the respectable middle classes is not to accuse them of deliberately or even unconsciously seeking to destroy lower-class autonomy only to serve their own interests. To be sure, assimilation was predicated on the elimination of lower-class culture, but reformers sincerely believed that that would serve the best interests of the poor as well.

160. Foucault, *Discipline and Punish*; Detlev Peukert expands this argument in applying it to youth policy in imperial and Weimar Germany in *Grenzen der Sozialdisziplinierung* (Cologne, 1986); see also David F. Crew, "The Pathologies of Modernity: Detlev Peukert on Germany's Twentieth Century," *Social History*, vol. 17, no. 2 (1992): 319–24.
161. Mark Steinberg discusses common cultures differently interpreted among printers and their bosses in "Culture and Class in a Russian Industry"; see also Tim McDaniels's discussion of conscious workers' efforts to raise their own "moral and intellectual level," their pride in their temperance and self-discipline, as well as their self-righteousness, in *Autocracy, Capitalism, and Revolution*, 183–202 and passim.

And when social mobility has been available, certain aspects of middle-class culture have in fact benefited those who found their way into the middle class. But the judicial professionals had little conception of the dynamics of cultural difference; indeed, they did not view lower-class habits and values as a legitimate culture in the first place. For them, lower-class culture was not something radically different from that of the respectable, civilized classes. It was seen as deficient, an empty vessel to be filled with the proper values and ideas. So while reformers did rescue some boys and girls from abuse and despair, their efforts prompted only partial successes, which reformers usually misread.

Such policies and attitudes provoked particular kinds of reactions: rebellion and resistance were directed toward the contested cultural issues or took the form of idiosyncratic adaptations of the welfare system or of periodic destructive rage, rather than of organized demands for radical structural or revolutionary change. Nonetheless, as social theorists and historians of social welfare systems show us, the powerless subjects of reform and normalization often act *as if* they existed in an autonomous sphere, free from state or other interference. Distortion and adaptation of social welfare, refusal to obey the laws or play along with the conventional rules of behavior, and strategic public displays of defiance and self-assertion could have significant, long-term impact on policy and on everyday life.[162] Such acts never seriously undermined the existing structures of power in Russia, but they forced respectable society to live with heightened fears, ranging from anxiety about personal vulnerability to abstract concern for the future of civilization. In the midst of Russian discourses about hooliganism and judicial reform, society was both more stable and less: the social hierarchy was reinforced by the trivializing of criminal challenges and the ostracizing of lower-class culture, but the respectable classes felt more vulnerable at the same time. During the revival of popular unrest after 1912, similar tactics would be employed by an increasing number of authorities and public voices. The lower classes as a whole were tarred with a brush reserved earlier for hooligans alone, and reports of labor unrest highlighted workers' hooligan characteristics, which cast doubt on the legitimacy of their strikes and demonstrations and heightened their immediately violent and destructive power.

162. Certeau, *The Practice of Everyday Life*, 15–42, and 91–110. For a historical example of acting "as if" that did eventually contribute to concrete change, see Timothy Garton Ash, *The Uses of Adversity* (New York, 1990), 105–19 and passim, on Poles who lived in the 1980s "*as if* they lived in a free country."

5   Violence and Poverty in a City Divided

The intelligentsia should not only stop dreaming of a fusion
with the people—we should fear the people more than all the
executions carried out by the authorities, and hail this
government that alone, with its bayonets and prisons, still
protects us from the fury of the masses.

—Mikhail Gershenzon
Signposts, 1909

After a brief and somewhat illusory hiatus, hooligans returned to the
Petersburg streets in the 1910s. By this time hooliganism had become a
national phenomenon and a symbol with a myriad of uses and meanings.
Between 1912 and 1914, when political discontent and labor unrest were
also simmering, hooliganism not only became a serious crime problem,
but many of its characteristics surfaced in discussions about the working
class and destitute poor. Optimism about social stability and assimilation
subsided, as a result, and the lower classes were further distanced from
the rest of society as all the poor came to be identified with defiant and
criminal elements.

By the 1910s, Petersburg was experiencing conditions not unlike those
that accompanied the first wave of hooliganism before 1905. The 1910s
were years of industrial upsurge and economic change, burgeoning discontent and political unrest, and, perhaps most important of all, renewed
migration from the countryside. Between 1908 and 1914 the capital's
population increased by about 350,000 people, making it a city of about
2.2 million, the fifth largest in Europe.[1] But in other ways St. Petersburg
was a city irrevocably changed by revolution. People experienced the
changes in city life in different ways, depending primarily on which affected them most, but two features of the post-1907 city touched everyone.

---

1. Behind only London, Paris, Vienna, and Berlin. See Kruze and Kutsentov,
"Naselenie Peterburga," 105.

The new wave of migrants confronted a population with vivid memories of a revolution just past. In 1905, for the first time in Russian history, millions of poor and working-class people seized the city's streets, demonstrated their unity, and expressed their demands in public. Even supporters of the mass movement must have been impressed by the people's power to disrupt public life, both for good and for ill. But the popular movement was never entirely peaceful, and the power of the masses also found expression in violence of all kinds, from petty vandalism to military mutinies to the armed uprisings of December 1905.

In subsequent years, the violence of the 1905–1907 Revolution served as a springboard for everything from evaluating the lessons of the revolution and plotting future courses to understanding the national character. Working-class violence has provoked controversy from 1905 to the present day. Lenin and other social democratic leaders began to worry about their ability to control the pace and direction of popular unrest. Revolutionary violence motivated the central government to embark on major police and judicial reform efforts.[2] In belles lettres, popular violence was a catalyst in Blok's exploration of the cultural chasm separating the intelligentsia and the Russian people, and, as we have seen, one of the main characters in Bely's *Petersburg* is a bomb. In *Vekhi* (*Signposts*), the essay collection that created a furor about the role of the intelligentsia and its relationship with the people, revolutionary violence was proof of the moral bankruptcy of the intelligentsia and its failure to lead Russia in the right direction.[3] And as we will see, popular and commercial literature also contributed to placing violence in the spotlight of public discourse.

While Petersburgers were haunted by memories of the revolutionary violence just past, they were also forced to cope with an upsurge in actual

---

2. Neil Weissman, *Reform in Tsarist Russia: The State Bureaucracy and Local Government, 1900–1914* (New Brunswick, N.J., 1981), 202–20; for the critical role of hooliganism in influencing police and court reform, see also *Mezhduvedomstvennaia komissiia po preobrazovaniiu politsii v imperii pod predsedatel'stvom senatora A. A. Makarova* (St. Petersburg, 1910–11); Z. M. Zil'berberg, *Zakon 15 iiunia 1912 goda o preobrazovanii mestnogo suda* (Moscow, 1914).

3. Although revolutionary violence is often mentioned only obliquely in *Vekhi*, responses to revolutionary violence and to the radical intelligentsia's encouragement of violence underlie each essay; see S. Bulgakov, "Heroism and Asceticism," 40–44; M. Gershenzon, "Creative Self-Cognition," 77–81; A. Izgoev, "Educated Youth," 110–11; Struve's article opens with a characterization of 1905 as analogous to the Time of Troubles and the Razin and Pugachev peasant uprisings ("The Intelligentsia and Revolution," 138–41, 146–47, 150–51); Semen Frank, "The Ethic of Nihilism," 170–72; all in *Landmarks: A Collection of Essays on the Russian Intelligentsia, 1909*, trans. Marian Schwartz and ed. Boris Shragin and Albert Todd (New York, 1977).

street violence, which again confronted them as an ever-present fact of daily life. But what kind of violence was this? For Petersburgers (and others) after the revolution, criminal street violence was not entirely divorced from revolution violence, but neither were the two identical. Criminal and revolutionary violence proliferated at approximately the same times and seemed to be rooted in some of the same troubling features of urban social and economic life. All kinds of violent crime were on the rise in the 1910s, but hooliganism accounted for a lion's share of the everyday violence that captured public attention. As a menace that linked a social and cultural challenge with displays of criminal aggression, it blurred the distinctions between political and criminal violence and once again provided useful images for ordering social reality. But hooliganism itself was changing—both hooligan crimes and the images they evoked. As the hooligans became more aggressive, new and more violent crimes fell under the hooligan umbrella. The aspects of hooliganism that prevailed in public discourse in the 1910s were its most hopeless features: hooligans seemed more alienated from society, more incorrigible, more irresponsible. As conditions for the lower classes in St. Petersburg seemed to deteriorate, as the hooligan label was used more freely, and as society's interest in the poor increased, *Peterburgskii listok* and an increasing number of diverse publications discovered in the slums a world permeated with hooligan values and behaviors. This process culminated in the July 1914 general strike, which brought hooligan violence to the fore again, but this time as a factor in an action explicitly associated with the labor movement.

The prevalence of violence—on the streets and in writing—is key to understanding the social polarization and fragmentation of the interrevolutionary years. Violence was often represented as the polar opposite of civilization and culture. It signified a lack of culture (variously defined), a deficient conscience, an immature or bankrupt polity. For some it was the source of Russia's ills, for others a symptom, and for still others the solution that would clear the air of all stale and musty ideas and allow Russia to begin again from scratch. The people who held these diverse views crossed class and other boundaries, so that it is impossible to link ideas with single social groups. Hooligans played a role in shaping this discourse by marking the violent dangers of the street with their taunting defiance, iconoclasm, and threats.

Thus the reasons for the revival of hooliganism and hooligan notoriety when the phenomenon reemerged after 1910 were in part similar to the reasons for the first wave. Hooligans were emboldened by the breakdown of police authority during the renewal of labor activism just as they had been in the early years of the century, especially in 1905–6. And as workers pressed their demands increasingly vocally in 1912 and afterwards, their presence in the city once again became unavoidable, lending threats of hooliganism added potency. By 1912, hooligans were using new tactics, and hooliganism was developing new layers of meaning, which together multiplied the effectiveness of hooliganism as a challenge and a symbol.

⧉ *Hooliganism: "The Beastly Deed"*

Hooligan offenses declined briefly after 1907 only to return, with a vengeance, around 1910. Late in 1906 the police briefly regained control of the streets by expelling hooligans, prostitutes, and other "shady characters" from the city center. Newspaper reports of hooliganism diminished, and according to the chief of the *mirovoi sud* prison, the "energetic police campaign" was responsible for the decrease in the number of hooligans who ended up in the House of Detention in 1906 and 1907.[4]

The decline of hooliganism as news and in crime rates, however, did not indicate the disappearance of hooligans altogether. Court statistics exaggerated the decline of hooliganism because, as discussed previously, most of those apprehended by the police for hooligan offenses between 1907 and 1910 were processed by the *gradonachal'nik* under the authority of binding decrees rather than through the judicial system.[5] If we take such cases into account, hooligan crimes may have reached pre-1905 levels on the streets several years before the Justice of the Peace statistics caught up with them. Already by 1909 the prison administration reported that among increases in those sentenced to *mirovoi* prison terms, the greatest increases were for offenses against public peace and order—typical hooligan crimes.[6]

In addition to the statistical misrepresentations, the exile of hooligans and other "shady characters" from the capital was accompanied by the first widespread appearances of hooliganism in the countryside, suggesting merely a temporary shift of venue. And judging from the immediate

---

4. *PMS 1906*, 205, 210; *PMS 1907*, 202.
5. When the *gradonachal'nik* stopped processing these cases in 1910, the *mirovoi sud* immediately showed an upsurge in trial, conviction, and imprisonment rates for hooligan crimes. Not only did absolute figures for trial and conviction rates rise when the *mirovoi* court regained its full jurisdiction over these crimes, but in 1910 hooligan-like crimes accounted for two-thirds of those sentenced to the *mirovoi* House of Detention, and this percentage rose steadily thereafter. See *PMS 1906*, 199; *PMS 1907*, 202.
6. *PMS 1909*, 170. In 1910 the prison chief stated that in addition to the return of hooliganism to his jurisdiction, the general increase in "police repression of petty crime" was responsible for rising rates, now that those arrested were again appearing before Justices of the Peace; *PMS 1910*, 132.

С-петербургскіе склады алкоголиковъ,

— Укладывай, братцы. плотнѣе! Тамъ еще десятокъ пьяныхъ привезли,—тоже втиснуть надо!

Figure 10. The St. Petersburg Warehouses for Alcoholics (September 5, 1913). (The inscription over the door says "Sobering-up Station.") "Shove 'em in, brothers—tighter! We've got dozens more drunks on the way."

attention hooliganism received in *Gazeta-kopeika* when it began publication in 1908, it is likely that hooligans continued to operate in the neighborhoods of the city's periphery as well. In central St. Petersburg, the sweeps of 1906–7 succeeded in eradicating the sharp increase in hooliganism that coincided with political unrest when hooligans took advantage of the breakdown of authority. But starting in 1908, and especially after 1910, hooligan crime rates reestablished the steady climb that had been interrupted—and transformed—by the revolution. By 1912 *Peterburgskii listok* was portraying St. Petersburg as a city teeming with crime and disorder, against which the police struggled in vain (see figs. 10 and 11).

Renewed coverage of hooliganism in the commercial press briefly preceded the upsurge in working-class unrest sparked by the Lena Gold Fields massacre of 1912, when government troops fired upon striking workers. The differences we see in the representation of hooliganism in this period are a reminder of this crime's elasticity and that newspaper descriptions of hooligan offenses were always at least partly shaped by prevailing social and cultural concerns. Curiosity about the city's poor population was on the rise, but the wariness and hostility toward the lower classes that had been exhibited before 1905 were tinged with fears of mass power and mass violence and a lack of faith in the government's ability to avert lower-class

Чистка столицы отъ „типсвъ"

— Ишь-ты, сколько мусору-то опять накопилось!..

Figure 11. Cleansing the Capital of "Shady Types" (October 28, 1912). "Look at that, will you! See how much trash has piled up again."

disorder. The boulevard press reflected and contributed to the new cultural context of the 1910s.[7] The lifting of most forms of preliminary censorship in 1906 created new possibilities for expression in the press. The relaxation of censorship and the competition among the burgeoning number of newspapers that appeared after the revolution allowed increasing commercialization and an emphasis on news that sells. Crime news had always been popular, but it was given far greater prominence than ever before. More space was allotted to crime stories, and more melodrama evoked by the language used to report crime. In 1910 *Peterburgskii listok* introduced a second crime column. While the old one continued to list criminal offenses, accidents, fires, and so forth, other incidents of the same sort now appeared under the heading "Events of the Petersburg Day" (*Sobytiia*

7. With the appearance of *Gazeta-kopeika* in St. Petersburg and its cousins in many other cities, the term "boulevard press" no longer referred only to the primarily middle-class newspapers such as *Peterburgskii listok*; in this chapter I use the term only when it refers to all the newspapers of the street; otherwise I name the newspapers specifically.

Peterburgskogo dnia), giving crime news in particular added visibility. At least two columns wide and several inches long, "Events" drew attention to crime news with bold headlines and graphic language.

The new visibility and violence of street crime was reflected in (and explained by) the language of crime reporting. Gruesome murders, vicious brawls and attacks, pitiful suicides, and tragic accidents were all treated in more explicit and more dramatic prose than before. Reports in the crime columns emphasized heart-stopping details with vivid, gory language. Blood flowed "in pools"; victims were "beaten to a pulp." Succinct allusions to stab wounds were replaced with grisly specifics. A knifing was now "a multitude of wounds that ripped and bruised the flesh."[8] Victims were no longer simply beaten or stabbed in the side. One man was dragged into a courtyard and then cruelly and horribly beaten until his head was shattered, his nose broken, and his body punctured with stab wounds.[9] The son of an army ensign was attacked by hooligans who "literally riddled [him] with holes."[10] A construction worker, returning home from work late at night on payday, was attacked by hooligans who "knocked him off his feet, stabbed him, tied his mouth, and stripped him. Then they tossed him—bloody, unconscious, and naked—into the canal."[11] Titles of the reports also highlighted violence. "Blood for Blood," "A Nightmarish Crime," and "A Bloody Attack" emphasized the gory consequences of the hooligan threat.[12] The epithet "beast" figured often in various forms in the titles: "A Beastly Murder," "A Beastly Attack," "Hooligan Beastliness," and "A Beastly Hooligan Deed" were all popular, along with the familiar "Rule of the Knife."[13] This is not to say that the boulevard press never used such language before 1905 or that violence did not appear earlier in other popular genres. Isolated examples of blood and gore can be found in *Peterburgskii listok* in the nineteenth century and more often in the serial fiction that appeared in the boulevard press, but, comparing the two periods, one cannot help but be struck by the radical shift in tone

8. "DP: Peterburgskie apashi," *PL*, March 30, 1912.

9. "DP: Zverstvo khuliganov," *PL*, March 21, 1911.

10. K., "Khuligany v Strel'be i ikh rasprava," *PL*, February 1, 1913.

11. "SPd: Zverskoe napadenie khuliganov," *PL*, July 28, 1912.

12. For examples see "SPd," *PL*, February 12, 1912, February 14, 1912, May 4, 1913, May 5, 1913, April 16, 1914.

13. "Zverskoe ubiistvo" was accompanied by a suggestive drawing in *PL*, February 12, 1912; see also examples in "SPd," *PL*, July 28, 1912, March 2, 1913, May 10, 1913, May 12, 1913.

conveyed by the verbal and graphic portrayal of crime that occurred after 1907.[14]

The lurid language of crime reporting was indicative of a change in the tone of the boulevard press as a whole. *Peterburgskii listok* became more explicitly commercial, with larger, more elaborate advertisements.[15] It began to employ bigger, eye-catching headlines with a fashionable art nouveau touch. More drawings accompanied news stories, and cartoons lampooned political and cultural figures more frequently. Indeed much of the reporting in interrevolutionary *Peterburgskii listok* was now genuinely sensationalistic, if that is taken to mean that it was written in such a way as to arouse an emotional and superficial response rather than a thoughtful and reasoned one. The visual presentation of news and information was designed to grab attention, evocative language was used to elicit emotions, and drawings brought points home in an immediate way. In addition, the quantity of light news, human-interest stories, and humor had increased since pre-1905 days.

On the other hand, it is important to remember that *Peterburgskii listok* continued to provide wide coverage of news on national and international issues. It published detailed bulletins on Russia's relations with other nations, daily reports of State Duma meetings when the Duma was in session, news of the Orthodox church and clergy, and elaborate dispatches on important news stories. The Lena Gold Fields massacre was covered and harshly condemned, as was the notorious Beilis case, when the tsarist government knowingly and blatantly supported the false accusation of ritual murder against the Jew Mendel Beilis.[16] The cholera epidemic and other public health hazards, the reform of the local judicial system, na-

14. On violence in popular bandit and detective stories see Brooks, *When Russia Learned to Read*, 186–88; on violence in rural crime, see Frank, "Popular Justice"; and Frierson, "Crime and Punishment"; on early boulevard-press violence see McReynolds, *The News*, 106.

15. In 1906, advertisements typically filled half of the first page of *PL* and the final one or two pages out of approximately six to ten total pages. On September 1, 1913 advertisements covered all of page 1, a corner of page 2, and all of pages 12–18.

16. A *Rech'* writer complained in July 1914 that the boulevard press ignored substantive issues in favor of sensationalistic scandals, such as the attempts to murder Rasputin, but in fact both *Peterburgskii listok* and *Gazeta-kopeika* devoted considerable attention to national and local political issues; *Peterburgskii listok* covered the Beilis trial in minute detail and with scathing criticism of the Ministry of Justice; see "Za nedeliu," *Rech'*, July 7, 1914; on the Beilis case, see, for example, the full-page treatment in *PL*, October 1, 1913; on Lena see articles daily after April 5, 1912.

tional conventions on alcohol abuse and the status of women, to name only a few examples, were reported in detail. And, as before, *Peterburgskii listok* remained an exhaustive source for information about local entertainment and events: society meetings, theatrical productions, art exhibits, sports (bicycle racing was popular in this period), and local government news and scandal. Thus *Peterburgskii listok* was still a valuable source of both news and information for Petersburg readers and a font of scandal, gossip, and sensation. As in the earlier period, the newspaper's sensationalism remains a useful indicator of the rise in concern about crime and poverty, and the heightened, ritualized language of crime reporting allows us to see which details caught the popular imagination and shaped its perception of the urban milieu.

Representations of hooliganism in the 1910s marked different features of the phenomenon than those emphasized during the first wave. In the early years of the century the reporting accentuated the hooligans' ubiquity, moral outrageousness, unabashed insolence, and the threat they posed to public order. After the 1905–1907 Revolution the feature of hooliganism that the new language most consistently stressed was its fearsome physical violence. Serious, even fatal, knife attacks had always been a component of hooliganism in St. Petersburg, but especially after 1912 these brutal attacks came to dominate urban hooliganism. Reports of violent hooligan crimes multiplied, and fewer incidents of hooliganism displayed the outraged propriety of previous years. Only rarely does one find the indignant outcry against hooligan *nakhal'* that so often accompanied hooligan reports before 1905. Irritating people on the streets with rowdy, uncouth behavior, harassing people by bumping into them or whistling at them, and destroying property by throwing rocks through windows were rarely noted in the popular press in the capital after 1910. Nor were there frequent reports of hooligans taking control of whole neighborhoods or ruling over certain streets and squares, not because hooligans were less irritating or less visible than in the past, but because their presence had become so commonplace.

Hooligan *nakhal'* was not altogether missing from popular portraits of hooliganism in this period but tended to surface in publications other than the boulevard press. Svirskii's sketch on hooliganism included several such examples. One young hooligan interviewed in a flophouse tells the author how delighted he would be to find the whole city on strike in the morning, so that he could walk in the middle of the road: "Any fool can walk on the sidewalk. So to walk in the road is like complete freedom! No trams. No carriages. It's great! You walk along, swinging your arms, exactly as you please.''[17] Other sources, as we have seen, including judicial and police reports, and especially reports of hooliganism in the countryside, continued to mix insolent and violent offenses.

The boulevard press, however, concentrated on hooligan violence and by publicizing violent crime contributed to making the city seem a threatening and frightening place. Not only did the crime chronicles report a higher number of more dangerous crimes, described in more graphic language, but many other writers and columnists were at pains to underline the contrast between the danger of hooligan violence after 1910 and that of the years before 1905. In 1912, *Peterburgskii listok* reported that one Petersburg neighborhood "declared war" on hooligans and found it necessary to ask for armed guards to protect residents against hooligan attacks. At a construction site, where hooligan rowdiness and attacks on guards had gotten out of hand, a city official called for "armed battle" against hooligans.[18] *Gazeta-kopeika*, the working-class daily, whose readership was likely to have different social fears but similar concerns for physical safety, also reported an increase in hooligan violence after 1912.[19] The columnist O. I. Blotermants, writing under the pseudonym "Skitalets," wrote in 1913 that "newspapers may be printed on white paper, but in our time their pages seem to be covered with blood."[20] In another article, he noted the unprecedented danger of street violence now that hooligans were armed with revolvers as well as with knives: "They are all armed, as if at war."[21] These are all, to be sure, *representations* of crime as increasingly violent rather than *proof* of an increase in the actual number of violent crimes committed. But these representations demonstrate, at the very least, that a variety of sources, and not only *Peterburgskii listok* with its long-standing fears of hooliganism, portrayed crime as increasingly violent and threatening.

The representations, moreover, are supported by the sharp rise in indictments for all forms of violent crime during this period in St. Petersburg and in the empire as a whole (see table 5 in the Appendix). Murder rates, which more than other crimes tend to be divorced from the kinds of

17. Svirskii, "Peterburgskie khuligany," 252, also 266.
18. "Voina goroda s khuliganami," *PL*, July 24, 1912.
19. Skitalets, "Pod nozhom," *GK*, January 10, 1913.
20. Skitalets, "Ozverenie," *GK*, January 16, 1913.
21. Skitalets, "Pod nozhom," *GK*, January 10, 1913. It is also worth noting that when Moscow and St. Petersburg *mirovoi sud* officials defined hooliganism in 1912 in response to the Ministry of Justice inquiry, the Petersburg justices' description included much more violent crimes among those considered hooliganism. See "Otzyv Moskovskogo," 231–32; *PMS 1913*, 276.

political and cultural considerations discussed here, rose steadily after the turn of the century. Indictments in St. Petersburg were astoundingly high (though prosecution rates were much lower), with 501 indictments for murder in 1908, and 794 in 1913. All kinds of public attacks on women—from aggravating verbal assaults to rape—increased steadily throughout the period. Armed robbery increased by 62 percent between 1901 and 1912, an increase greater than all other forms of theft excluding horse theft.[22]

Violent hooliganism in this period bore some similarity to the back-street muggings of the pre-1905 period, but it also appeared in suggestive new forms and was portrayed in revealing new ways. To begin with, it became common for *Peterburgskii listok* writers to pinpoint a new kind of danger by labeling some violent hooligans "apaches" (*apashi*).[23] By identifying hooligan muggers with Native Americans of fabled savagery, they shifted emphasis away from the overtones of class conflict inherent in pre-1905 depictions of hooligan defiance. The label "apache" distanced the hooligans from the boulevard-press readership—moving them figuratively across the ocean to an alien continent still "wild" by European standards—and it colored hooliganism with the cultural stereotypes of the barbarism and primitivism associated with native peoples who in the eyes of many, represented the polar opposite of civilization. Of course, the word *hooligan* was also foreign, and thus dissonant in Russian, but it was clearly European, and thus closer to home, and it summoned images of buffoonery as well as of danger.

Bloody back-street stabbings, in particular, dominated the crime-column reports of hooliganism in the 1910s. Two *Peterburgskii listok* articles from the spring of 1912 that claimed to describe "the most interesting" and "the most characteristic" cases of the recent rash of hooliganism listed the kind of bloody attack that had become typical, and both articles made it clear that these examples were only a small sample of similar

---

22. Ministerstvo iustitsii, *Svod statisticheskikh svedenii po delum ugolovnym* [1872–1907] (St. Petersburg, 1873–1908); *Svod statisticheskikh svedenii o pod-sudimykh, opravdannykh, i osuzhdennykh* [1908–1914] (St. Petersburg, 1909–15); Mel'nikov, "Kolebaniia prestupnosti," 72.

23. The French used "apache" for knife-wielding muggers who appeared in Paris around 1906; see Nye, *Crime, Madness, and Politics,* 180–226; Zaslavskii, "Bor'ba," 127. Slightly later the German working-class gangs who beat up Hitler Youth groups also called themselves Red Apaches and Navajos; see Rosenhaft, "Organizing the 'Lumpenproletariat,' " 185; and Peukert, *Inside Nazi Germany,* 154–67.

ПЕТЕРБУРГСКІЕ АПАШИ

Figure 12.   Petersburg Apaches (April 25, 1912).

crimes.[24] Reports now usually indicated when attacks ended in fatalities.[25] In late April 1912 the report of a typical hooligan attack was accompanied by a large drawing of the incident: a fairly well-dressed man, hat still on, lying in a pool of blood, with a street policeman kneeling beside him, and a detective looking on sorrowfully but helplessly (fig. 12). Knife-wielding hooligans attacked members of the middle and upper classes somewhat more often in this period, though such attacks were still unusual.[26] The

24. "Peterburgskie apashi," *PL*, March 28, 1912; "SPd," *PL*, April 17, 1912.

25. For examples see *PL*, March 15, 1911, June 17, 1911, March 10, 1912, April 30, 1913, May 26, 1913, August 17, 1913, January 28, 1914. In the past, victims may have died from knife wounds received in hooligan attacks, but reports rarely mentioned it.

26. Among others, a "well-dressed pedestrian": "DP: Zverstvo khuliganov," *PL*, March 21, 1911; a merchant: "DP: Ograblennyi khuliganami," *PL*, May 21, 1911; another merchant: "DP: Kupets—zhertva khuliganov," *PL*, May 22, 1912; a

number of violent attacks on women also rose. *Peterburgskii listok* reported cases in which women were stabbed for refusing to give hooligans money, in which attacks were preceded by a volley of "nasty words," and in which the victims were identified as prostitutes brutalized by men known to them, often their pimps.[27]

Just as in the earlier wave of hooliganism, many of these attacks were committed against strangers "for no reason at all." When causes or motives were given they tended to be presented as extremely petty or incomprehensible, but, unlike in the earlier cases, these conclusions were derived from the hooligans themselves. One hooligan, caught throwing cobblestones at a woman buying oranges from a street peddler, explained himself with a sullen "Just 'cause" (*prosto tak*). In another case four hooligans stabbed a man because he accidentally bumped into one of them on the street.[28] In numerous cases the victims were stabbed or knocked off their feet or beaten "to a pulp" for refusing to hand over whatever money the hooligans demanded, usually just a few kopecks, often for vodka.[29] More often now, weapons of various kinds were mentioned in the reports. The hooligans' weapon of choice was a dagger, but they also used sticks, stones, brass knuckles, *giri*, hammers, and other heavy or pointed objects. Revolvers appeared sometimes and even, in one case, forks and knives stolen from a tea shop.[30]

Mass violence in the form of hooligan brawls also reappeared in the pages of the boulevard press after 1910. One crime specialist writing in this period described fighting as "the hooligans' favorite activity, where they eagerly test their powers."[31] In contrast to 1905–6, when some of

teacher, son of a colonel: "SPd: Khuliganskoe napadenie na realista," *PL*, March 14, 1913.

27. Some examples are "DP: Nozhovshchina," January 3, 1912; "DP: Peterburgskie apashi," January 8, 1912; "SPd," April 17, 1912; "Peterburgskie apashi," March 28, 1912; and "Peterburgskie apashi," May 10, 1912; "SPd: Lovelas-khuligan," January 28, 1913; "SPd: Podvigi khuliganov Aleksandrovskogo parka," April 15, 1914; "DP: Peterburgskie apashi," February 14, 1912; all *PL*.

28. "SPd: Zverskii postupok khuligana," *PL*, May 12, 1913; "DP: Zhertva khuliganov-podrostkov," *PL*, September 25, 1913.

29. For examples see "SPd: Napadenie khuligana na artist," *PL*, January 15, 1911; "DP: Ulichnyi razboi," *PL*, May 19, 1912; "SPd: Khuliganskie napadeniia," *PL*, February 27, 1913; "DP: Khuliganskie napadeniia," *PL*, January 6, 1914.

30. "DP: Peterburgskie apashi," *PL*, April 11, 1912; "SPd: Razboinoe napadenie za Narvskoi zastavoi," *PL*, January 23, 1913; see also reports of brawls in *GK*, January 3 and 10, 1913; [untitled article], *GK*, January 15, 1912; "Proisshestviia: Srazhenie rabochikh," *GK*, July 2, 1912. "Proisshestviia" was *Gazeta-kopeika*'s crime column.

31. A. V. Likhachev, "Ob usilenii nakazanii dlia khuliganov," 93.

the biggest brawls occurred in the city center, most of these took place in outlying, lower-class districts or in the areas of Vasilevskii Island with mixed populations. On numerous occasions the policemen and *dvorniki* arriving on the scene were unable to check the fighting.[32] Many, but not all, of these brawls were identified as episodes of gang warfare.

Gang violence played a larger role in this wave of hooliganism than in the earlier wave. *Peterburgskii listok* informed its readers about warfare among organized youth gangs with established identities, names, leaders, and specified turf. The gang encounters, identified as hooliganism, were nastier and bloodier than either the fighting between the Gaida and the Roshcha gangs immediately after the turn of the century or traditional, recreational brawling, and, as reports often comment, gang fighting usually flared up over petty disputes. But while the immediate pretext for a brawl seemed trivial to *Peterburgskii listok* reporters, they fed long-smoldering animosities and provoked cycles of violent retribution. In 1911 the report of one such reckoning began by noting the "hooligans who love 'loafing' and 'stirring up trouble' (*'nichegonedelanie i vol'nitsa'*) have begun assembling in the taverns on Vasilevskii Island's 7th Line." In one of these taverns a fight broke out "over something trivial" between "Kolka the Tailor" and "Serezha the Coachman," leaders of rival neighborhood gangs. The proprietor called the *dvornik* and the police, who threw the boys out of the tavern and left. A little while later the police returned to find Kolka the Tailor in a pool of blood.[33] Another gang war resulted in the death of a major gang leader, "Black Vaska," and the arrest of ten of the gang members involved in the fatal stabbing.[34] When their case came to court, it acquired considerable public notoriety. A standing-room-only crowd attended the trial, including many of the gang members still at large. The main defendant, Vasily Andreev, maintained that he attacked Black Vaska in self-defense, but neither the prosecutor nor the trial reporter gave him much credence. The prosecutor encouraged the jury to consider the social significance of the case in deciding Andreev's fate, "inasmuch as society is being tormented under the weight of hooliganism." To no one's surprise, the jury found Andreev guilty.[35] The

32. "SPd: Grandioznoe poboishche v Galernoi Gavani," *PL*, August 13, 1912; "Krovavoe poboishche rabochikh," *PL*, September 16, 1912.
33. "SPd: Podvigi khuliganskoi vol'nitsy," *PL*, June 15, 1911.
34. "Gibel' atamana khuliganov," *PL*, August 6, 1912.
35. "Vasil'eostrovskie khuligany: Vchera 13/II v okruzhnom sude," *PL*, February 14, 1913. The *Gazeta-kopeika* report of the same crime and trial echoed the *PL* report; see "Sud: Parad khuliganov," *GK*, February 14, 1913.

violent repercussions from this incident continued to find their way into the crime chronicles throughout the summer and into the fall of 1912, which led one reporter to conclude that "despite all efforts on the part of the police, warring hooligan factions were stirring panic within the local population."[36]

This coverage of gang warfare in the boulevard press suggests a new dimension in public fears of violence between 1912 and 1914 and a sense of revulsion at the squandering of life over trivial or incomprehensible rivalries. The depth of amorality and uncivilized behavior that gang members displayed was underscored by the routine references to the hooligan's weapons—knives, clubs, rocks, and metal shards—and the formulaic "pools of blood." Three-quarters of a century of sociology and efforts at prevention have done nothing to stop gang warfare, but in early twentieth-century Petersburg little effort was made even to probe the causes of youth gang violence. In the interrevolutionary period police and press alike presented gang violence as one more manifestation of the lower-class barbarism hooliganism had come to represent.

The contrast with earlier references to gangs in the boulevard press is striking. In their 1901 letter to *Peterburgskii listok* the "Landlords of the Petersburg Side" mentioned two gangs by name, the Gaida and the Ro-shcha, but their letter conveyed little sense of the hooligans as organized fraternities. They were more concerned with the gang members' petty offenses, their insolence, and their ability to control the streets than with the physical danger they may have posed. Social, more than physical, peril worried the Petersburg Side landowners in 1901. The interrevolutionary portrait of gangs also contrasts sharply with the depiction of the Gaida and Roshcha that appeared in *Peterburgskaia gazeta* in 1905 (which stressed the gangs' honor code). The same contrast, between an earlier, more positive, romanticized tone and the more violent, hostile one in the 1912–14 period, applied to *Peterburgskii listok* depictions of lower-class

---

36. "Gibel' atamana khuliganov," *PL*, August 6, 1912. Police comments on gang activity corroborate information the boulevard press presented, with tantalizing but limited evidence on street gangs. For example, in 1911 the chief of the police department's investigative unit boasted that police efforts in the year past brought gang activity in St. Petersburg under control: there had been five particularly large gangs (Koltovskaia, Roshchinskaia, Peskovskaia, Zheleznovodskaia, and Gai-dovskaia, all mentioned at one time or another in crime reports), but according to the chief of police "[now] only memories of them remain"; a year later he would have cause to eat those words when vicious gang fighting again spilled blood on numerous city streets (cited in Vestnik, "Bor'ba s khuliganami: Beseda s I. O. Nachal'nika sysknoi politsii K. P. Marshalkom," *PG*, August 14, 1911).

life as a whole, as will be discussed below. After 1911, public hooligan fighting (both brawling and gang warfare) seemed less theatrical, less a spectacle than a recognized form of lower-class male behavior. It was no longer a surprise to boulevard-press readers that young, lower-class men beat one another up, whether for recreation, vengeance, or for "no reason at all." In general, there was less emphasis on finding motives for mass fights, other than as incidents of gang warfare, in which case they occurred for "trivial" reasons or for revenge. Brawling had once again become a major disruptive force in the city's social life, but now it was treated more like an ordinary crime, one form of "disturbing the peace."

The elements of social and cultural rebellion had not been entirely eliminated from brawling or other forms of violent hooliganism, but in the boulevard press they had become implicit rather than explicit. The cultural issue that continued to mark these incidents as hooliganism was no longer one of open conflict but rather of yawning cultural difference. The combatants in this cultural conflict had retreated from face-to-face combat to view one another from a greater distance. Hooligans were coming to seem alien in new ways: a breed apart. Hooligan violence became more of an anthropological curiosity that the boulevard press could treat with some detachment. But the absence of direct challenge in this period did not mean that hooliganism lost its social and cultural potency in *Peterburgskii listok*. Hooligan violence was still a sign of the low level of civilization among the lower classes, but now not because it was novel and shocking, rather because it had become common and expected. When, in the past, hooligans chose to offend and assault they seemed to be making conscious choices to defy respectable society. Thus, in theory, they were still susceptible to cultural improvement designed to teach them to refrain from making such choices. But the depiction of hooligans as recklessly and thoughtlessly violent in the 1910s emphasized their disregard for the value of human life, which placed them beyond the cultural influence of respectable society. Hooliganism came to represent an inherent and enduring lack of civilization among certain segments of the poor population. If, as a result, the hooligans did not pose an immediate threat to respectable pedestrians, they posed an even more depressing long-term threat because they now seemed to be impervious to the influence of the uplifting values of cultured society. They seemed altogether beyond redemption. Violent hooligans, brawlers, and muggers were now situated at a greater distance from respectable society, geographically and sociologically, as well as culturally. In this way the boulevard press was able to convey a world in which official authority was weakened, and the social fabric was fraying, but while the future of the country as a whole might be in doubt, the readers of the boulevard press could feel personally secure, at least compared with the period before 1905. Violence was everywhere, but the uncontrolled violence that erupted on the streets of central St. Petersburg in 1905–6 was not being repeated.

The treatment of hooliganism in *Gazeta-kopeika* again provides an illuminating contrast to the portrait painted in *Peterburgskii listok* and *Peterburgskaia gazeta*. While *Gazeta-kopeika* depicted hooliganism as a serious crime problem, it was purely a crime problem. Hooliganism was not seen as a threat to civilized social order but rather as an everyday danger for the inhabitants of the city's lower-class neighborhoods.[37] *Gazeta-kopeika* reported none of the kind of *nakhal'* or rowdiness portrayed in the other boulevard papers. It primarily reported cases of violent physical assault. These it reported with about the same regularity as the other newspapers. Hooliganism was also the subject of a number of articles by *Gazeta-kopeika*'s regular columnist Skitalets. In January 1913 Skitalets received a barrage of letters from workers and other residents of the far western end of Vasilevskii Island in response to a column he had written on the "horrors of hooliganism" in Russian villages. The readers wrote to inform him that the "horrors of hooliganism" were every bit as dangerous in their Petersburg neighborhood as in the countryside. One of the landlords in that neighborhood also wrote, confirming the workers' stories about the hooligans terrorizing his building. They not only "control the streets," he declared, but the hooligans repeatedly entered the building and demanded money from the workers living there. Their boldness was not, it should be emphasized, portrayed as brazen *nakhal'* in the *Gazeta-kopeika* correspondence. When the landlord became enraged and offered to "take up his pen," the workers, fearing retribution, begged him not to publicize their complaints. So he signed his letter "X."[38] The story not only reveals workers' fears of hooliganism but provides a working-class echo of the fears of the "Landlords of the Petersburg Side." Significantly, the working-class version is conspicuously lacking in features of social and cultural conflict.

Cases of abduction and rape were reported relatively infrequently in *Gazeta-kopeika*, but a dozen or so did appear over the course of the years 1912–14. In one case described as hooliganism a group of sixteen- to eighteen-year-olds abducted two teenage girls, the children of well-to-do

37. Occasionally *GK*'s hooligan victims included members of the upper classes. See, for example, "Proisshestviia: Napadenie khuliganov na kuptsa," *GK*, December 29, 1912.
38. Skitalets, "Pod nozhom," *GK*, January 10, 1913.

families, who had lost their way in the dangerous streets at the western end of Vasilevskii Island. The hooligans robbed the girls, undressed them, and then led one off to a shed. She was never seen again. The other girls was beaten and, the article inferred, sexually assaulted. When she awakened the following morning, bruised and alone, she found her way to the local police station.[39] In contrast I was unable to find a single case of rape or abduction reported in *Peterburgskii listok* between 1900 and 1914, and only one case of sexual assault appeared in *Peterburgskaia gazeta* during these years (an unusual one in which a young girl was raped by a policeman), suggesting, perhaps, a respectable ban on some sensitive topics in these newspapers.[40]

Gazeta-kopeika consistently made an unambiguous distinction between respectable workers and the criminal element. That distinction, still clear in *Peterburgskii listok* during the revolutionary disorders in 1905–7, was increasingly blurred later on. In *Peterburgskii listok* and *Peterburgskaia gazeta*, descriptions of the hooligans' social identities reinforced the sense conveyed by reports of their offenses that while hooligan violence was a sign of lower-class degeneracy, it was now located at some clearly defined remove from respectable society. In contrast to the revolutionary period, participants in hooligan offenses were identified more often as workers (or worker-hooligans or workers and hooligans). When their occupations were also listed, however, it is clear that the hooligans' actual occupations had not changed. Even though people engaging in hooligan behavior were now identified either as workers or hooligans, they were still primarily unskilled and casual laborers who worked in factories by day and made trouble after work and on weekends, apprentices and runaway apprentices, and people "with no specified occupation" (*bez opredelennogo zaniatiia*)—a category reserved for those who were considered to be unemployed by choice. People who committed hooligan crimes were referred to as workers and former workers, homeless vagabonds, workers at rival factories, men who went to work in factories but consorted with hooligans and the unemployed after work, unskilled workers, *chernorabochie*, and apprentices. In one case an "unemployed peasant attacked a worker-peasant."[41]

39. "Khuliganstvo v stolitse," *GK*, November 20, 1912.
40. "Sudebnaia khronika: Nasilie gorodovogo nad devushkoi," *PG*, July 6, 1906.
41. "SPd: Podvigi khuliganskoi vol'nitsy," *PL*, June 15, 1911; "SPd: Peterburgskie apashi," *PL*, January 1, 1912; "DP: Nozhevshchina," *PL*, January 16, 1912; "SPd: Peterburgskie apashi," *PL*, March 3, 1912; "SPd: Napadenie na chasovogo," *PL*, August 29, 1912; "SPd: Dikoe khuliganskoe ubiistvo," *PL*, June 5, 1913; "SPd: Khuliganskaia rasprava," *PL*, July 29, 1913; K-v, "Khuliganstvo i shoffery,"

The closer association of hooliganism with the working class might, in another context, be expected to confer a greater legitimacy on hooligans, given the sympathetic treatment the labor movement received in the boulevard press in 1905–7. But times had changed. The violence, irrationality, and pettiness perceived in hooligan behavior and the hooligans' insolent rejection of respectable culture, in other words the features that made hooligans seem impervious to efforts to "raise their intellectual and moral level," to civilize them, now tinted the boulevard-press portrait of workers and other members of the lower classes. This is not to say that the poor population was portrayed as a "dangerous class" in the pathological sense Chevalier intended in his classic study of the connection between the criminal and the non-criminal poor in early nineteenth-century Paris. In contrast to the situation in Russia, in France "it was an unquestioned assumption of middle-class opinion throughout the [nineteenth century] that those most likely to participate in revolution were also those most likely to indulge in crime."[42] In *Peterburgskii listok* and similar publications, the lower-class population was not portrayed as an undifferentiated and actively disruptive or revolutionary force in society. Distinctions were still made between the working poor, the destitute, and the criminal poor. But images of the lower classes (workers included) in a variety of sources increasingly endowed the poor as a whole with the primitivism, lack of culture, and hostility to respectable and civilized values associated with hooliganism. The blurring of distinctions between hooligans and the respectable poor in the 1912–14 period can be found in discussions of two separate issues: living conditions in the city's slum neighborhoods and the upsurge in labor activism. *Peterburgskii listok* and other commercial literature written primarily for middle-class consumption portrayed conditions in the slums and the people who lived there in far more negative terms than they had prior to the great waves of migration in the 1890s and 1910s. Second, in the absence of a general revolutionary movement, the concurrent revival of labor unrest and hooligan activity made them seem closely connected. As we will see, the character of labor unrest in 1914 proved such a perception to be true.

PL, August 17, 1913; "SPd: Napadenie khuliganov na dvornikov," *PL*, September 30, 1913; "DP. Khuliganskaia rasprava," *PL*, January 16, 1914.

42. Robert Tombs, "Crime and the Security of the State: The 'Dangerous Class' and Insurrection in Nineteenth-Century Paris," in *Crime and the Law: The Social History of Crime in Western Europe since 1500*, ed. V. A. C. Gatrell, Bruce Lenman, and Geoffrey Parker (London, 1980), 214; see also Chevalier, *Laboring and Dangerous Classes*.

③ Images of the Poor in Commercial Literature

Shifts in popular opinion are notoriously difficult to pin down and demonstrate. Isolated examples of distrust and hostility toward the poor can be found in the Petersburg press during all the great waves of migration to the city, when new generations of rich and poor, peasant and urbanite, privileged and unprivileged, suddenly confronted each other in high densities. Positive views of the poor were not unknown in the 1910s, and the shifting attitudes were not universal: some forms of poverty continued to be presented sympathetically throughout the period. Nonetheless, *Peterburgskii listok* and other boulevard newspapers, as well as sketches about the poor written for the same audience but published in book form, convey the unmistakable overall impression that attitudes toward the poor population had shifted significantly from a wary sympathy (based as much on ignorance and romanticization as on compassion) to feelings of fear, horror, and contempt.

In most cities concern about the poor ebbs and flows. The 1890s not only witnessed the beginning of the mass peasant influx into the capital, but the decade was marked by an abundant increase in reading material about the city and its poor population. With literacy rising and technology able to speed the gathering and publishing of the news, newspapers attracted a mass audience for the first time, and they provided a wealth of information about the city. A new generation of writers and journalists began addressing the growing middle-class audience. In St. Petersburg, Aleksei Svirskii, A. A. Bakhtiarov, V. I. Binshtok, and many anonymous journalists published articles, exposés, and sketches about the poor and the criminal underworld in commercial newspapers and books.[43]

Sketches, or *ocherki*, complemented the coverage of the social issues dealt with in the news, fiction, and columns of the daily press. The genre differed from the serial fiction about crime and poverty in the mass-circulation press in that it comprised a unique mingling of reportage and fiction. Using firsthand research among the criminal and poor population, sketch writers employed fictional characters, introduced as typical representatives of their milieu, to illustrate social problems. Invented dialogue brought

---

43. Svirskii will be discussed below. Bakhtiarov wrote *Briukho Peterburga* (St. Petersburg, 1888), *Proletariat i ulichnye tipy Peterburga* (St. Petersburg, 1895), *Otpetye liudi* (St. Petersburg, 1903), and *Bosiaki: Ocherki s naturi* (St. Petersburg, 1903); Binshtok wrote *Gde i kak iutitsia Peterburgskaia bednota* (St. Petersburg, 1903). On Moscow writers see Joseph Bradley, "The Writer and the City in Late Imperial Russia," *The Slavonic and East European Review*, vol. 64, no. 3 (July 1986); and McReynolds, *The News*, 145–67.

the characters to life and increased their verisimilitude. The form allowed writers to treat social problems with a depth not possible in short news articles. The use of fictional or composite portraits enabled them to present serious social issues in an accessible and familiar form, without sacrificing the credibility of their "scientific investigation."[44]

By the 1910s the quantity of information about the Petersburg poor reached a high-water mark. Portraits of the people living in inner-city basements and working-class suburbs that were provided daily in the boulevard press, the deluge of commercial (as well as professional) literature about poverty, alcoholism, prostitution, begging, vagabondage, and crime, and the number of city commissions that visited slums and flophouses and were reported in *Peterburgskii listok* reveal a city curious, and worried, about its poor inhabitants—not that this concern enabled the poor to leave their basements behind, or that popular curiosity produced much in the way of practical relief. Curiosity produced neither action nor understanding, and familiarity, in this case, bred contempt.[45]

The declining sympathy found in commercial literature on the poor is striking for its contrast not only with earlier journalistic treatments but with the hopes of the nineteenth-century intelligentsia and with the traditional Russian views of poverty and crime, which had dominated the commercial literature during the first phases of urbanization. As late as the 1890s, Russian attitudes rooted in Orthodox teaching favored the poor and the criminal with sympathy for their plight. Destitution had been understood, in the words of a recent historian, as the "result of a myriad of individual accidents and circumstances, a personal misfortune rather than a social phenomenon."[46] Just as poverty was viewed as something other than a voluntary condition, so was the world of crime a place into

44. The sketch has received scant attention from scholars in comparison with its more famous cousin, the feuilleton. See A. G. Tseitlin, *Stanovlenie realizma v russkoi literature: Russkii fiziologicheskii ocherk* (Moscow, 1965); Maksim Gor'kii, letter to I. F. Zhiga, August 15, 1929, *Sobranie sochinenii v tritsati tomakh*, vol. 30 (Moscow, 1955); E. I. Zhurbina, *Ustoichivye temy* (Moscow, 1974); Gary Saul Morson, *The Boundaries of Genre: Dostoevskii's "Diary of a Writer" and the Traditions of Literary Utopia* (Austin, Tex., 1981); Joseph Frank, *Dostoevsky: The Stir of Liberation, 1860–1865* (Princeton, 1986), 216–25.
45. On popular and official attitudes toward poverty in Moscow that emphasize the work of "reformers" seeking to "civilize" the urban poor, see Bradley, *Muzhik and Muscovite*; in his survey of Moscow literature on the poor Bradley does not note the corrosion of the reformers' faith, but he also does not treat the last decade of tsarist rule as a distinct period.
46. Lindenmeyr, "A Russian Experiment," 434.

which ordinary unfortunates might easily slip in straitened circumstances.[47]

In the period between 1907 and 1914, commercial literature presented an increasingly depressing picture of life for the city's poor. Significantly, the horrifying material conditions in the city's slums described at the end of the tsarist era differed hardly at all from descriptions that had been appearing in waves throughout the nineteenth century: filth, overcrowding, and disease in damp and dark rooms teeming with vermin of all kinds were stock images in the literature on the slums both in Russia and in the West. However, depictions of the inhabitants of the city's slums changed markedly for the worse. The ordinary poor, neither criminal nor hooligan, suffered a fall in these portraits from sympathetic folk to frightening creatures.[48]

Generally speaking, the literature of the 1890s and very early 1900s presented the poor as a colorful lot, worthy of compassion. Their way of life, with its unique songs, language, and curious mores, could be entertaining rather than threatening. The petty criminals among the poor were depicted as people who strayed or fell into a life of crime. Sketches and newspaper columns presented them as victims of society and misfortune, but it was their weakness of character rather than economic injustice that made these people susceptible to misfortune. Only the weak were victimized by society's slings and arrows, but they remained sympathetic, because, despite their moral failings, they were still victims. As victims they presented no serious threat to the health and stability of respectable society, either because they were considered reformable or because they were more dangerous to themselves than to society at large. Indeed, journalists and writers of the 1890s intentionally chose subjects who could be presented sympathetically—prostitutes, alcoholic vagabonds, and petty thieves, rather than hardened, violent criminals—in order to awaken the

47. Such is the perspective in the most famous (and sympathetic) treatment of the Petersburg slums from the 1860s, the mammoth *Peterburgskie trushchoby* by Vsevolod Krestovskii. Published originally in installments in *Otechestvennye zapiski* (1864) and *Peterburgskii listok* (1864–65), it was republished as the first two volumes of V. V. Krestovskii, *Polnoe sobranie sochinenii* (St. Petersburg, 1898). Krestovskii relied heavily on Eugène Sue's *Les mystères de Paris* for his plot, but his exhaustive descriptive details of the life and lingo of the poor and criminal underground were the result of his own research in the prisons, hospitals, courts, and tenements of St. Petersburg. See also a sample of such views in Chalidze, *Criminal Russia*, 3–11; S. V. Maksimov, *Sibir' i katorga* (St. Petersburg, 1891), of which vol. 1 is entitled *Neschastnye* (*The Unfortunates*).
48. Similar shifts in popular literature's images of the poor in England have been discussed by Jones in *Outcast London*, 280–314.

self-satisfied and apathetic middle class to the misfortunes of the poor.[49] Criminals were still treated as people to be saved or reformed. Petty thieves, beggars, and prostitutes were depicted as an exotic and intriguing population, more to be pitied than feared or despised.

Taking such an approach was a humorous 1901 column in *Peterburgskii listok* on popular mores in the capital, entitled "The People's Resort":

> With the arrival of the warm weather everyone is going off to their resorts, and the denizens of the famous Viazemskaia Lavra [an enormous flophouse, well known for sheltering the destitute and criminal] are no exception. Their favorite resort: the shores of the Obvodyni Canal. The rich go to Sicily, people of middle means to the Crimea, those with modest means can get as far as Novaia Derevnia or Ozerki [Petersburg suburbs], but the poor choose the banks of the Obvodnyi. . . . We visited on a Sunday afternoon at about four o'clock. The shores were everywhere covered with people in picturesque poses. Killing time. Playing cards for imaginary stakes.
> —The whole Haymarket, wares included, for the Jack! cried one.
> —The Warsaw station for the Queen. . . ![50]

Others sang and told stories, slept peacefully, drank vodka with pickles, and threw each other into the water. True, they cheated at cards, their tales concerned petty thieving expeditions, both men and women spoke a crude language, and the vodka-drinking troika in this scene was (presumably shockingly) female. But while this article and others like it were patronizing, they were playful, and only mildly censorious; the moral opprobrium was implicit, not laid on with a thick rhetorical brush.

Beggars received a mixed treatment in pre-1905 *Peterburgskii listok*. They were still depicted with considerable sympathy, though they had been viewed as a nuisance and a serious social problem since at least the 1860s. While their claims and needs were often treated with skepticism, and they were increasingly portrayed as swindlers and charlatans, they were for the most part still seen as unfortunates. This was especially true

49. It should be added that the professional criminal underworld was also romanticized at this time: it was often regarded with a mixture of awe and admiration for the code of honor according to which criminals were said to have lived, or as a tantalizing but ultimately costly escape from the restrictions of respectable social life. On the code of honor and the decline of romantic attitudes toward it, see, for example, Aborigen, *Krovavye letopisi Peterburga: Prestupnyi mir i bor'ba s nim* (St. Petersburg, 1914); on criminals' and bandits' escape from society, see Brooks, *When Russia Learned to Read*, 174–213.
50. Dosuzhii (I. N. Gerson), "Narodnyi kurort," *PL*, April 17, 1901.

of the press portrait of children begging: "one of the saddest sights in St. Petersburg."[51] One writer observed in 1902 that it was a shame that the proliferation of beggars in the capital was beginning to dull people's sympathy for them, because they each had "some genuinely tragic past." They were "pitiable," even if "it is probably an act, dreamed up by some professional beggar."[52] Bradley noted that while some writers portrayed the beggars in Moscow as revolting and annoying frauds, they were seen by many others as "picturesque extremes of the ordinary life of the streets," as "possessors of some inner virtue, as quintessential representatives of the Russian people."[53] Suggestions in *Peterburgskii listok* for reducing the extraordinary number of beggars in the capital (some estimated that 30,000 professional beggars roamed Petersburg's streets at the turn of the century) focused on the development of public and private assistance programs.[54]

During the 1905–1907 Revolution the number of beggars in St. Petersburg skyrocketed, and their image in the press began rapidly to deteriorate. By 1912 beggars had lost their folksy charm in the Petersburg boulevard press. Not only had their entreaties become intolerable, but the beggars were almost exclusively portrayed in *Peterburgskii listok* as frauds, who "earn more begging than many regular workers."[55] A letter to the editor expressed pity for the homeless and hungry but wondered whether beggars would ever be capable of developing the work habits and attitudes necessary to settle down and support themselves.[56] One article complained in 1906 that the bureau responsible for keeping an eye on the city's beggars was unable to do its job properly.[57] The bureau responded that the beggars were becoming aggressive and defiant: the revolution ignited ferment among beggars, provoking outbursts, disobedience, and even an open attack on the bureau.[58] Although the situation stabilized after the revolution was suppressed, by 1912 the number of beggars once again reached a staggering height. In 1913 one writer connected beggars directly with the

51. "Deti-brodiazhki," *PL*, March 7, 1901.
52. Avgur, "Komu pomogat'?" *PL*, April 12, 1902.
53. Bradley, *Muzhik and Muscovite*, 253–59.
54. "Nishchenstvo," *PL*, March 4, 1903. In contrast, the police and city officials favored workhouses not only for "discipline" but for punishment of "recidivists"; TsGAOR, fond 102, delo 40, chast' 2, listy 9–26.
55. K. L-dov, "Nishchenstvo v stolitse," *PL*, August 30, 1913; Zriachii (I. N. Gerson), " 'Villa Brodiaga'," *PL*, June 8, 1914; "Interesy dnia: Peterburgskie nishchie," *PG*, August 3, 1906.
56. I. M-v, "Iz kipy zaiavlenii: Deti-nishchenki," *PL*, December 31, 1905.
57. "Gorodskie dela," *PL*, July 20, 1906.
58. "Sredi nishchikh," *PL*, July 20, 1906.

growth of crime.[59] A 1914 article claimed that not only had the number of beggars on the trams grown, but so had their brazenness: "Often just as one is giving them something, they turn into pickpockets, very deftly cleaning out the pockets and wallets of the public. These tram-car beggars can be seen not only on the periphery, but even in the center of the capital."[60] Writing under a new pseudonym, the author of "The People's Resort" observed the degeneration of the neighborhood just east of the Winter Palace: "On Mars Field, the skating rink, observatory, and 'panorama' display are gone. The only remaining structure is a cement shed . . . now known as 'Vagabond Villa,' because it has become a shelter for all sorts of beggars and passportless tramps."[61] In at least one case beggars were identified explicitly as hooligans. A *Peterburgskii listok* reader wrote in to point out that

> anyone wanting proof that hooliganism in Petersburg has
> blossomed in full flower need only take a ride on the Lesnaia horse
> tram. One hardly enters the car (which, by the way, is filthy, with
> rags full of holes for curtains) before being surrounded by beggars:
> men and women, but for the most part children. Impudent and
> familiar, in rags intended to evoke pity, they approach their
> victims and pester them until they can be made to part with three
> or four kopecks.[62]

This view of the poor as aggressor rather than victim and these qualities of degeneracy and doubtful morality dominated other reports about the slums in the 1910s even when they did not include hooligans. This is not to say that the newspaper never distinguished between what it considered the respectable and the degenerate poor, but that now its reporting emphasized the less savory aspects of poverty, including those similar to hooligan characteristics.

Such human-interest stories may have helped sell newspapers, but they also accurately reflected major concerns of the day. During this period national conventions were held in the capital on the problems of prostitution, alcoholism, and crime, to name only the most prominent, which *Peterburgskii listok* duly reported, often in detail. In 1913 and 1914, a number of city conferences and official excursions to the slums were undertaken by St. Petersburg officials to see conditions there for themselves.

59. K. L-dov, "Nishchenstvo v stolitse," *PL*, August 30, 1913.
60. "Listok: Nishchie v tramvaiakh," *PL*, March 8, 1914.
61. Zriachii, " 'Villa Brodiaga'," *PL*, June 18, 1914.
62. M., "Iz kipy zaiavlenii: Khuliganskaia idilliia," *PL*, July 30, 1906.

Their observations were also reported in great detail in *Peterburgskii listok*, introducing the newspaper's readers to the reality behind the crime columns and official pronouncements. These articles offered information about the poor in a context that differed from serial fiction set in the slums and from columnists' feuilletons or commentary on social problems. Fiction presented social background information as incidental and as part of a tale of unique circumstances. Feuilletons and commentary generally came clothed in the opinions of a single individual. However illusory, the articles reporting on official investigations conveyed a higher degree of objectivity and realism, as eyewitness accounts carried out under the mantle of officialdom.

The subject of a number of official investigations in 1913 and 1914 was the "Kholmushki," a huge complex of tenements and shops that housed about 2,500 people in 130 or so apartments.[63] The *Peterburgskii listok* report on the official excursions there featured the casual collusion of poverty and crime in Kholmushki. The police, for example, found it impossible to catch people fencing stolen goods there because shopowners covered themselves by operating under legitimate sales licenses. It seemed that the local inhabitants, even apparently respectable ones, accepted as normal the crime and depravity that surrounded them. The city investigators found drunkards "at every step" lying unconscious in the filth on the road or wobbling along with the help of a drinking pal, but it was not the number of drunks that shocked the investigators; rather, as described in one report,

> they are remarkable for the fact that with very few exceptions and despite the cold and frozen wet snow they appear practically without clothes on. . . . Unfastened trousers, some rags instead of a shirt, and literally not one of the necessities of ordinary human apparel. Here, also, some questionable women with hand baskets even carry on a lively trade in these horrible rags and worse. People undress under the nearest gate and even right on the street, in full view, without attracting any special surprise or curiosity. Obviously this is a common business.[64]

The shift here was primarily one of emphasis, which now stressed the degradations of slum inhabitants rather than their misfortunes. What shocked the official visitors in 1913 was not the number of drunks on the

63. "Peterburgskie trushchoby," *PL*, February 15, 1914.
64. M. B., "Peterburgskie trushchoby," *PL*, October 31, 1913.

streets, but the way the local population accepted their appalling, immodest behavior without blinking.

"Vaskina Village," named for the slumlord who owned the complex of buildings on Vasilevskii Island, was known for its sheltering of "suspicious types" alongside honest workers. A city commission in 1914 found people living in "nasty, dark corners" and in basement apartments whose floors were "literally covered with puddles from sanitation pipes and cesspools." Outside, people were living in cowsheds. The cows and milkmen ate, slept, and lived next to one another. This "seedbed of contagion," where cholera, scarlet fever, diphtheria, and typhus flourished, was all the more dangerous since its 5,000 inhabitants included milkmen, tramdrivers, and cigarette makers who carried the germs all over the capital.[65] Another official expedition visited "Tolkuchka," a market that was "undoubtedly, the source of much disease," where "all the poor of Petersburg come to shop." According to the expedition's report, "secondhand linen and clothing is sold unwashed and undisinfected. And, of course, much of it is stolen goods; so it is sold as quickly as possible."[66]

The dread that crime and disease propagated in these filthy "seedbeds" would spread to the rest of the city permeated the *Peterburgskii listok* reports of official tours of the slums. Fears that moral contagion spread through flophouses and slums like the cholera and typhus also bred there dated at least from the spurt of urbanization that occurred in the 1860s. At that time, the police viewed the housing shortage as a police problem, because the mixture of "honest laborers" with criminals created a potentially dangerous situation.[67] By the 1910s the fears seemed to have become reality. Like the middle-class juvenile crime specialists, boulevard-press writers (though not in *Gazeta-kopeika*) took for granted that the flophouse was a "seedbed of crime" because the criminal and the poor lived side by side there.[68] Epidemics and crime were, of course, genuine threats to the well-being and stability of urban society. But by tying poverty, crime, and disease into one tight knot *Peterburgskii listok* made the poor as a whole responsible for placing the rest of society in jeopardy.

Sympathy for the inhabitants of the city's slums was noticeably absent in these reports. Even when children were discussed, the emphasis was on

65. D., "Uzhasy 'Vas'kinoi derevni'," *PL*, April 27, 1914.
66. D., "Peterburgskie trushchoby: Novaia ekskursiia glasnykh," *PL*, May 4, 1914.
67. Bradley, *Muzhik and Muscovite*, 271–72; see also Zelnik, *Labor and Society*, 279–80.
68. See, for example, B. Ivolgin, "Nochlezhnye doma," *PL*, June 8, 1911.

their lack of parental supervision, their amoral upbringing, their suscepti-
bility to the depraved influence of the street, and the danger that could be
expected from them in the future. The scenes described during this period,
the tone and language used to portray slum dwellers, and the increased
number of articles devoted to slum investigations revived the view of the
poor as an alien species, to whose dwellings it was necessary to travel in
special expeditions. But, unlike earlier portraits, the poor now lacked colorful language and mores, and they had become hopelessly mired in a world
of depravity, destitution, and disease.

The contrast between the images of the 1890s and those of the 1910s
is especially striking in the work of authors whose careers spanned the
whole period. One such writer was Aleksei Svirskii, one of the most prolific
authors of sketches about Petersburg street life, some of which have already been cited. Svirskii was a remarkable writer who grew up in the
slums of St. Petersburg and Zhitomir and later tramped around the empire. In Rostov-on-Don, newspapers began to publish his impressions of
life on the road. Then in the 1890s Svirskii settled in St. Petersburg, where
he became a successful journalist and an unsuccessful publisher.[69] His
sketches about slum dwellers displayed a remarkable shift in both images
and purpose. *The Lost Ones* (*Pogibshie liudi*), a collection of his sketches
published in 1898, was suffused with sympathy for his subjects: vagabonds, homeless beggars, alcoholics, prostitutes, and petty criminals. In
the introduction, Svirskii explained that he felt compelled to write about
the underworld, to describe even its most unpleasant features, in order to
acquaint the well-fed and the comfortable with the poor and the fallen:
"Turn your gaze right over here for a moment, to the gloomy dives. For
one minute, stifle your aversion and look to what depths has fallen your
neighbor, your brother in Christ."[70] The readership Svirskii addressed,

---

69. On Svirskii's own life, see "Avtobiografiia," *Polnoe sobranie sochinenii*, vol.
1 (Moscow and Leningrad, 1930), 21–24; and in the same volume, I. N. Kubikov,
"A. I. Svirskii," 7–18. Svirskii also wrote a long version that is part picaresque
adventure novel, part bildungsroman, *Istoriia moei zhizni* (Moscow, 1947). His
most famous work today is *Ryzhik* (Moscow, 1940), yet another version of his
childhood, written for adolescent readers. In St. Petersburg, Svirskii published a
"boulevard newspaper," *Novaia gazeta*, similar to *Peterburgskii listok* but aimed
at a more literate audience, which ran for a few months in 1906 and 1907; he also
edited and published *Rubikon*, a literary journal that included popular potboilers
alongside works by the leading writers and poets of the Silver Age, which lasted
for eight numbers in 1914.

70. A. I. Svirskii, *Pogibshie liudi*, vol. 1 (St. Petersburg, 1898), 7. See also, for
example, Bakhtiarov, *Proletariat i ulichnye tipy*; id., *Bosiaki*; Binshtok, *Gde i kak
iutitsia Peterburgskaia bednota*; and S. I. Elpat'evskii, "Na perepisi: V Viazemskoi
lavre," *Russkoe bogatstvo* 2 (1897).

the materialistic "new bourgeoisie," had become apathetic to the plight of the poor, though not yet overtly hostile. "But no," he continued, "you haven't the time, you have to try on a new dress, make purchases, prepare for a masquerade."[71]

Svirskii's strategy was to arouse pity and compassion by portraying slum dwellers as people deserving of sympathy—people who shared with the reader basic human characteristics. He chose figures that his genteel readership might easily recognize. Often they had "fallen" from some respectable position in society—an educated civil servant or a highly placed merchant, forced by misfortune to live in poverty among the "dark" and ignorant. He often wrote about the classic "fallen": the innocent girl forced by circumstance into prostitution.[72] None of these characters were evil; they were presented as victims of chance, of some individual injustice, or of just plain bad luck. Most of them were aware of what they had lost and were ashamed of their fall.[73] Explicit social analysis was meager here; long-term causes and solutions were not discussed. Injustice was personal and individual rather than social.

Svirskii successfully humanized these victims of misfortune, whose world was so alien to his readers. Not only was he familiar with the customs and the argot of the world he described, but he had genuine sympathy for its inhabitants and definite, if not especially subtle, ideas about how people ended up there. His naturalistic descriptions make for vivid reading, and his use of reported conversations brings the reader closer to the story, to the unfamiliar characters and settings. Svirskii did not romanticize the life of the underworld—on the contrary, he represented it as a lonely, frightening existence. But the figures that emerged from these early portraits often appeared heroic in their ability to maintain their humanity in such conditions. Even those who appeared to have repressed all moral instinct, Svirskii showed, could be coaxed into confessing their shame and their remorse over the life they were leading. Although they treated each other roughly, often mocked each other, and led lives "resembling moral death," they were still capable of deep kindness toward one another.[74] Even the most desperate characters in these sketches, the regulars in the infamous Makokin flophouse, were relatively tame. Their worse transgression in Svirskii's telling was to arrive early at the overcrowded flop in order to rent a cot and resell it to latecomers at a profit.[75]

71. Svirskii, Pogibshie liudi, vol. 1, p. 7.
72. Ibid., 2, 11–19, 57–71, and passim.
73. Ibid., 19, 26–27, 58.
74. Ibid., 15, 20, 27, 29, and 52–53.
75. Ibid., 54.

Individual misfortune dominated Svirskii's analysis of crime and vice, but he did not ignore the social environment altogether. Svirskii viewed social conditions as alienating, as derailing the development of a moral sensibility, and as preventing proper socialization. This view was similar to that of the prevailing school of criminology in this period, the "sociological" school.[76] But where specialists saw in this a call for social change, Svirskii emphasized the uniqueness of individual circumstances that led to "fall" and criminal transgression. Both viewed transgressors as victims, not entirely responsible for their actions, but Svirskii was relatively sanguine about the threat to society posed by his indigents and criminals.

In discussing prostitutes, for example, Svirskii rejected the notion (which he attributed to Guy de Maupassant) that "laziness and love of finery" led lower-class girls into prostitution.[77] Noting that prostitutes were most often those girls who had been forced to live away from home and work in factories and shops, he explained that they were not only no longer subject to the moral constraints of family life but were vulnerable to the notorious advances of lecherous factory foremen.[78] Similar circumstances explain what drew petty criminals away from legal wage labor. Torn away from the moral upbringing parents offered, some individuals had no strength to resist immoral or illegal propositions or to survive what for others might have been temporary setbacks.

Children, too, entered the ranks of the fallen through a combination of moral weakness and social circumstances. Svirskii estimated that in Rostov-on-Don, where some of his first sketches were set, 200 to 300 children supported themselves solely by begging and stealing. One found children among the fallen, he believed, because the frequency of extramarital sex, especially among workers, produced unwanted children. Not much good could be expected from the offspring of these "fleeting unions," Svirskii wrote, when their mothers worked long days in the factories, and their fathers either wanted nothing to do with them or could not support their families because they lived in a drunken stupor.[79] Still, the one child whose fall from innocence Svirskii described in detail, "Zhenka the Fist," was never depicted as dangerous or evil, only as amoral and misguided: Svirskii began Zhenka's story with a heartfelt declaration of his love for the boy.[80]

---

76. For the basic ideas of the "sociological" school and its debates with the "anthropological" school, see Ostroumov, *Prestupnost' i ee prichiny*, 238–70.

77. Svirskii, *Pogibshie liudi*, vol. 1, pp. 68–69.

78. Ibid., 69–70.

79. Ibid., 219–20.

80. Ibid., 221.

Not all the people who appeared in these early sketches won Svirskii's sympathy, however. A few, briefly glimpsed, foreshadowed what was to come: men and women drinking in the back room of a tearoom, for example, were described as "amoral, crude, and drunk."[81] But even these characters were portrayed as victims. It was society that threatened their survival and their morality; they posed no serious threat to society.

In 1914, Svirskii published another sketch about the Petersburg underworld, "The Hooligans of Petersburg." It was published not in a collection with other sketches or similar literature but in a book designed as an introductory guide to the city, *Petersburg and Its Life.*[82] Svirskii's article is a typical sketch—it describes in evocative language and detail the author's encounters with a motley group of individual hooligans, reproducing their conversations and conveying his moral and social judgments. The other articles, however, are short surveys of the Petersburg economy, history, geography, architecture, museums, scientific institutions, demography, adult education, and working class, written by recognized specialists in a scholarly, if simplified, form. The inclusion of Svirskii's sketch in such a collection testifies both to the importance of the subject and to the reliability of the author. In the midst of the more detached essays the lively style of the sketch reinforced the unrelievedly grim picture Svirskii painted.

In the 1914 sketch, the unfortunate victims and outcasts of 1898 were replaced by desperate and degenerate hooligans, in the words of one of the author's unnamed underworld informants, "an entirely new breed that came into being not long ago."[83] There were no innocent victims now; even the children were already hopelessly depraved. The people in this sketch sank to the lower depths not out of poverty or because they lacked parental guidance, but because they were bad to begin with. The underworld for which Svirskii had once tried to stir sympathy had become an alien otherworld, and the people who lived there, who formerly called forth compassion, now provoked only revulsion and fear.

Svirskii returned to the same flophouses he had described in the 1898 sketches and produced this description of the hooligans and their milieu:

> Three days and two nights I passed among people who had fallen out of life. They are not living, these people, but moldering like charred logs left scattered after a fire. In the gloomy half-light of the dirty dives, in crowded, bug-infested flophouses, in the tearooms and taverns and the dens of cheap debauchery—

81. Ibid., 9, 72–80.
82. Svirskii, "Peterburgskie khuligany." See p. 104, n. 21.
83. Ibid., 258.

everywhere where vodka, women, and children are sold—I encountered people who no longer resembled human beings. There, down below, people believe in nothing, love no one, and are not bothered by anything. Their language is wretched and pallid, consisting of a few dozen vile words and curses. Their songs are the same. I remember how I shuddered when I heard the singing of some ten-year-old child-prostitutes (*shkits*). Flat-chested, scrawny, slovenly girls with weak, unsteady voices glorifying Nevskii, pimps, murder, and wicked diseases. From their childish, but already befouled, lips fell the shameless words of a monstrous song composed of festering evil.[84]

This paragraph streamed from the pen of the same man who in 1898 had informed his readers that the poor, including the criminal, were human beings and deserving of society's compassion and understanding. In 1898 he had written that

all of these outcasts (*otvershennye oborvantsy*) are people. Hearts beat in their chests, just as in the rest of us; they feel and think as we do; and like us they are susceptible to deep suffering and torment.[85]

In the 1914 sketch the physical setting was described in the same stock phrases about dark, damp, and overcrowding that had long characterized writing about the slums; but the people were "of an entirely new breed":

Zhenka is a typical hooligan: he does not recognize any laws, and he has lost all understanding of good and evil. He does not believe in God or the devil, and to everything else, including his own existence, he is totally indifferent.[86]

Svirskii concluded: "I became frightened for him. Fifteen years ago I did not meet such children in the slums."[87]

"Mitka the Lunatic" typified Petersburg's adult hooligans. Mitka was about twenty-five years old; he was tall, lean, and lazy with big, grey eyes "that are twinkling now but were lackluster and apathetic when he was sober."[88] Like the majority of hooligans, Mitka had "a low forehead, a vacant expression, an apathetic face, and, in the local parlance, his brain

84. Ibid., 260.
85. Svirskii, *Pogibshie liudi*, vol. 1, p. 29.
86. Svirskii, "Peterburgskie khuligany," 263.
87. Ibid., 253.
88. Ibid., 268.

is asleep. . . . [His] view of life is simple and categorical: all earthly beings are lice, all people are insects."[89]

The stark dehumanization of these portraits placed the hooligans of 1914 beyond morality, beyond even evil. They were immune to socialization and impervious to rehabilitation. As a result they symbolized the limits of social authority, and they became fearful, rather than pitiable, creatures. Svirskii's sojourn among the hooligans ended "in the grey dawn of a foul morning" as he emerged onto the street after a final night watching degenerate men and women abuse one another in the tavern known as The Blindman. A party of convicts was shuffling down the street toward him, presumably beginning their long journey on foot to prison in Siberia. A coachman, asleep in his carriage, was roused by their steps. The old man crossed himself and, echoing Svirskii's thoughts, mumbled: "Lord save us and have mercy upon us."[90]

It would be difficult to imagine a more striking contrast than that between Svirskii's plea for sympathy in the introduction to his first sketches and the coachman's prayer that ends this one. Svirskii had given up trying to enlighten the public. Now he was sounding a warning. In his earlier pieces he did not call for social change, because he believed that personal weakness and the exigencies of fate would continue to doom individuals to lives outside the bounds of law and conventional morality. Nonetheless, he had felt that society's knowledge and compassion would diminish the power of the circumstances that tempted the weak. By 1914 compassion was barely possible, and knowledge brought disillusionment rather than change, relief, or hope. Throughout his life Svirskii wrote inclusively about the poor: his Petersburg included people on both sides of the law as well as those who slipped back and forth across that line. But in the 1890s Svirskii had chosen to focus on people whose undeveloped moral fiber made them victims of chance and weakness: society's victims. In 1914 his slums were dominated by people whose morals made them little better than beasts: society's foes.

The representations of the poor in *Peterburgskii listok* and in Svirskii's sketches convey not only the hopelessness of poverty in the last years of tsarist rule but also the disillusionment of a particular segment of society with its own efforts. Hopes for "civilizing" the lower classes seemed all the more remote after generations of cultural measures, however halfhearted, had failed to minimize degradation and degeneracy. The

---

89. Ibid., 269.
90. Of all the incantations he might have chosen, Svirskii opted to pray for mercy for *us*, not *them* ("Peterburgskie khuligany," 276).

crime-ridden and disease-infested slums were presented in *Peterburgskii listok* and in sketches as a reminder of the fragility of civilization in St. Petersburg. One excursion to the slums set out to see "what sort of things are possible in the twentieth century, in a city that pretends to call itself 'cultured' and 'advanced.'"[91] The same observers were increasingly skeptical of the influence cultural measures might have in eradicating crime and vice in this population. They were beginning to call into question the value of civilizing efforts still being undertaken to help the poor escape from the destructive effects of poverty. "These holiday hot dogs and glasses of tea," wrote one commentator, and "Sunday soccer games and skiing expeditions" were only a "microscopic drop in the sea," unable to provide even children with the moral education necessary to fight those effects.[92] Significantly, these opinions appeared not in the conservative press, where skepticism concerning cultural measures and a preference for coercion and punishment predominated, but in a politically liberal newspaper, and one that in many ways had been socially more moderate as well.

It is important to remember that these articles about slum social conditions did not appear separately in monographic publications but in newspapers devoted to describing the whole range of city issues and events. The findings of official investigations were published alongside reports of the latest hooligan feats, increasingly bloody crime columns, commentary on local government apathy, news of war and unrest in the Balkans, as well as serial fiction, entertainment news, advertising, and more. These pieces came together, confirming and contradicting one another, to provide a multilayered image of the city and a particular portrait of the lower classes and their place in the city.

The depictions of the poor that appeared between 1912 and 1914 echo those associated with hooliganism that had been appearing since the beginning of the century. Increasingly, the non-criminal poor were identified with hooligan qualities, such as an acceptance of their own degradation and yet an insolent rejection of the leading role and civilizing efforts of the cultured classes. In the boulevard press the association was often only implied, but in Svirskii's sketches the connection was explicit.[93] Thus while the Russian lower classes were not viewed as a single subversive underclass in Chevalier's terms, they were represented in boulevard literature as alien and incorrigible—unable and often unwilling to assimilate to

91. M. B., "Peterburgskie trushchoby," *PL*, October 31, 1913.
92. Izbiratel', "Peterburgskie deti ulitsy," *PL*, February 25, 1914.
93. Svirskii, "Peterburgskie khuligany," 259ff.

civilized society. As such, they hindered the progress and social integration that had been the goal of the educated elite for almost a century.

Historians who have studied society's attitudes toward the poor and criminal in the nineteenth century have shown that some Russian observers were horrified by the "moral decline" of the poor long before the twentieth century.[94] In the 1910s, however, harsh, naturalistic representations of the lower classes were no longer softened by traditional sympathies or by the optimism of the Great Reform era. What then eroded sympathy and optimism? The Revolution of 1905–1907 was an obvious watershed, but the revolution was not the only event to shape public perceptions across class lines. The greatest shifts in perceptions, at least in connection with the issues discussed here, were more closely related to the two great waves of migration to the capital, in the late 1890s and the early 1910s, than to the revolution itself. The sheer number of migrants, their demographic weight and their needs, altered the character of the city and was impossible to ignore. It is not that the new migrants were necessarily rowdier or less submissive. In fact the peasants, women, and children entering the work force in the 1910s may have been more obsequious and less likely to challenge openly the authority of social conventions.[95] But the mass of migrants made their presence felt (in addition to bringing cultural conflict) in the creation of new urban problems, which appeared when their basic material needs were evaded by the municipal and central governments. By the 1910s, solutions to the city's political and social problems seemed particularly elusive. The tsarist government distrusted public initiative and yet offered few programs of its own and little encouragement. In St. Petersburg, the city government was equally bewildered (once it marginally overcame its indifference) in the face of unrelenting poverty, recurring disease, and multiplying crime. The consequences of neglected poverty were—aside from political opposition— alienation, degradation, and hooligan defiance. Yet the actual links between hooliganism and its social sources were difficult to discern and poorly understood.

Old solutions, whether repression or cultural development, seemed increasingly unlikely to alter the situation of the deeply "uncultured." Many people, including those writing for *Peterburgskii listok*, found coercion and repression reprehensible and yet found no new solutions at hand. The despair of the poor was matched by that of many leading voices of

94. For example, Bater, *St. Petersburg*, 201; Zelnik, *Labor and Society*, 240–83; Bradley, *Muzhik and Muscovite*, 249–91.
95. They were also less likely to unionize; see Bonnell, *Roots of Revolution*, 367.

reform. Society leaders on the left and the right expressed a sense of fatigue, exhaustion, and inertia; others spoke of a deep spiritual malaise in the face of the central government's continual pettiness and obstruction.[96] The government's abdication of responsibility for social welfare was deeply felt and sharply criticized in the pages of *Peterburgskii listok*, among other publications. The massacre of workers at the Lena Gold Fields in 1912 not only sparked the resurgence of the labor movement but also elicited sharp condemnation from educated society and the press. In 1913 the central government's disgraceful behavior in the Beilis case became a powerful symbol of its failure to provide moral leadership in troubled times.

The evolution of the mass-circulation press after the 1905–1907 Revolution was also instrumental in shaping readers' attitudes about the poor and about the ability of state and society to resolve social issues. There were more newspapers, each selling more copies and spreading more news about state and society. Whole categories of social issues that had been forbidden earlier entered public discourse when preliminary censorship was abolished in 1906. Much of the news connected with social issues was bad, and hooliganism was mentioned often in connection with other problems. Not only were crime rates in almost every category rising, but the rates were announced repeatedly in the press, and no government official could express confidence about controlling crime. In 1913 when *Peterburgskii listok* writer N. reported that the prison population had been rising steadily since 1897 and that the Ministry of Justice gloomily predicted that it would not soon decrease, he cited a ministry official who blamed hooliganism, "the struggle against which is extraordinarily difficult, it is a broad stream now spilling over its banks."[97] While living standards for the minority of skilled workers were rising in the 1910s, the massive migration of unskilled peasants into a city unprepared to provide for them increased the number of people living at a bare subsistence level.[98] The professional and scientific discussion of these issues in Russia had the ironic effect of making social problems seem all the more difficult, even when the professional specialists were relatively optimistic, as in the case of the local judicial reformers. While in Germany professional attention to crime, poverty, disease, prostitution, and other social prob-

96. I. V. Gessen, Lev Tikhomirov, and S. S. Ol'denburg, quoted in Rogger, "Russia in 1914," 102; S. Galai, "A Liberal's Vision of Russia's Future, 1905–1914: The Case of Ivan Petrunkevich," in *Russian and East European History: Selected Papers from the Second World Congress*, ed. R. C. Elwood (Berkeley, 1984).
97. N, "Rost' prestupnosti," *PL*, September 26, 1913.
98. Kruze and Kutsentov, "Naselenie Peterburga," 115–22.

lems in the imperial and Weimar periods spread confidence that problems could be solved through scientific methods, in Russia the opposite occurred. The sudden publicity for social ills caused by an increase in national meetings and public discussions, combined with the lack of government support for social programs, only intensified despair.[99]

Images of the lower classes were also affected by the kind of issues with which they were juxtaposed in both the boulevard press and leading political journals and official circles. Beginning in the last years of the revolution and continuing after 1907, revolutionary violence and criminal violence each received a great deal of public attention. From the late 1890s the two seemed to ebb and flow side by side. This impression was reinforced in the period between 1912 and 1914 when both labor unrest and hooligan violence were on the rise, but unaccompanied by open revolutionary activity on the part of the educated elite akin to their activities of 1905. As a result, criminal violence and working-class violence were conflated in public images. Some members of the conservative nobility, as well as some urban commentators, believed that the lower-class violence during the 1905–1907 Revolution encouraged and even legitimated peasant, worker, and criminal street violence in subsequent years. Riabchenko, an extreme right-wing observer, wrote that

> after the revolutionary movement . . . that manifested itself in a
> disturbance extremely destructive for the government and whose
> consequences were deeply reflected in popular life, a special type of
> criminal malevolence known as hooliganism, both petty and
> serious, was bolstered and allowed to take root.[100]

Similar views were expressed by respectable scholars. Tarnovskii, the chief statistician for the Ministry of Justice, whose authoritative articles on crime statistics were widely printed in the commercial press, claimed that revolutionary violence pervaded the popular mentality and mingled with justifications for criminal violence:

> The increase in robbery and violence are easily explained by the
> changed psychological mood of the masses . . . at moments when
> society is seized by revolutionary ferment. During periods of
> unrest, the masses idolize the kind of dashing and brave violence
> that comes to the fore, which manifests itself in struggle with the
> government as well as attacks on the person and property of the

99. Detlev J. K. Peukert, *The Weimar Republic: The Crisis of Classical Modernity*, trans. Richard Deveson (New York, 1989), 134–35.
100. Riabchenko, *O bor'be*, 5.

privileged classes. . . . The ordinary criminals . . . acquire their own halo as "warriors" in a struggle against the unjust economic bases of state and society.[101]

Before 1905, Tarnovskii's view of social and cultural progress had been an optimistic one. By 1908 he feared that the commingling of revolutionary and criminal violence presented a serious threat to society in the immediate future.

Similar fears were expressed among moderate leftists and liberals by 1914, though in more muted tones. Gessen wrote in *Rech* that the ominous hostility between classes was not a result of deep-seated disagreements but of an "unhealthy atmosphere" that prevented society from overcoming its differences. That atmosphere was produced not by political infighting but by "the continuing decline of morals, a kind of unquenchable thirst for sensations, the growth of monstrous crimes, and unceasing brazenness."[102] Elsewhere Gessen explained that the thirst for sensations referred not only to the decadent sexuality of the day but to the desire of the "right-wing" reading public for news about violent crime and their eagerness to conclude that the growth of crime was evidence of a "dangerous, undisciplined willfulness." For his part, Gessen believed that there was hopeful evidence of cultural development among the lower classes, and he remained optimistic about lower-class assimilation, but he also understood that more negative views of the people were common, that they were connected to ideas about lower-class criminality, and that they were responsible for polarizing society.[103]

Others among the educated elite, most of whom were liberals, remained firmly optimistic about lower-class cultural development and the potential for social stability. The editors and writers for major daily newspapers from *Russkoe slovo* [The Russian Word] and *Gazeta-kopeika* on the left and center (but not *Peterburgskii listok*) to *Novoe vremia* on the right continued to believe that workers shared their cultural aspirations and in the absence of government authority and respect looked to educated soci-

101. E. N. Tarnovskii, "Dvizhenie prestupnosti v Rossiiskoi imperii, 1899–1908," *Zhurnal ministerstva iustitsii* 9 (1909).
102. I. V. Gessen, "Vnutrennaia zhizn'," *Ezhegodnik gazety Rech' na 1914 god* (St. Petersburg, 1915), 25. His example of "brazenness" was the slashing of Repin's painting, a case that won attention for the futurists, whom Repin blamed for indirectly inciting the attack; see p. 145, n. 114.
103. I. V. Gessen, *Rech'*, January 1, 1914 [lead editorial]. Many leading liberals were less sanguine, as is well known; for Petrunkevich's expectation of the "revenge of the poor" see Galai, "A Liberal's Vision," 112.

ety for leadership.[104] These writers and publicists were proved disastrously wrong in 1917 when the opportunity for common cause finally appeared, yet the educated elite and liberal middle classes found themselves targets of lower-class distrust and scorn. These liberals shared with their contemporaries among social democrats as well as the anti-revolutionary *Vekhi* writers (in other words, the old intelligentsia) a belief in cultural and political tutelage by the intelligentsia. Gessen, Lenin, and Peter Struve (*Vekhi*'s guiding force) all assumed that their own political and cultural codes provided models for the deficient lower classes to adopt. None had a moment's tolerance for characteristic lower-class activities—what Gessen labeled sensationalism, Lenin spontaneity, and Struve mindless violence—which rejected intelligentsia hegemony. Nor did they have the patience to try to understand such behavior. Mikhail Gershenzon's infamous declaration, quoted at the outset of this chapter and seized upon repeatedly in the polemic that followed the publication of *Vekhi*, is an exception here. While Gershenzon made no effort to distinguish criminal from political violence, he understood as well as anyone that radical revolutionary violence not only was a product of socialist agitation but was combined with lower-class self-assertion and hostility toward all the privileged, including the intelligentsia. He recognized how wrong the intelligentsia had been in believing

> that the people differ from us only by the degree of their education, and that if it weren't for the obstacles imposed by authority we would have long since transfused our knowledge into them and become of one flesh with them. That the people's soul is *qualitatively* different from ours never even occurred to us.[105]

On the radical left, of course, social democrats had long been concerned about the potential for eruptions of violence more criminal than revolutionary. The Menshevik response in the 1910s was to celebrate their creation of a worker-intelligentsia, the product of their own political-cultural improvement programs, while the Bolsheviks, and Lenin in particular, were sincerely worried about the workers' capacity for violent action independent of party directive.[106]

104. McReynolds, *The News*, 224–25, 251–52; Thurston, *Liberal City*, 189–90, 212; on *Novoe vremia* see David R. Costello, "*Novoe vremia* and the Conservative Dilemma, 1911–1914," *Russian Review*, vol. 37, no. 1 (1978): 30–50.
105. Gershenzon, "Creative Self-Cognition," 77–81.
106. Haimson, "Social Stability," Part 1, 638–39.

Thus while educated society continued to believe (though from a variety of perspectives) that its own values should provide models for the lower classes, many among the educated began to fear that the poor were sinking below the influence of the cultured elite, and they began to perceive the hostility and bitterness of the poor as directed toward society as a whole. The intelligentsia could not agree on the causes or likely outcome of lower-class discontent, but except among a group of moderate liberals and publicists, expectations for a peaceful outcome were rare. Of course, social tensions alone are not enough to spark major political crises, and other societies have survived similar bouts of social fragmentation. But in St. Petersburg stability was eroded by the widespread perception that Russia's problems could not be resolved. Just as Bely portrayed a city in which fragmentation was spinning out of control, the boulevard literature discussed here presented the degradation of the poor as irreversible and the distance between classes as unbridgeable. [107]

In 1914, conflated perceptions of crime, poverty, and political unrest were reinforced when workers in St. Petersburg began to engage in petty violence in the political and economic struggle. Until 1914 the boulevard press imputed hooligan characteristics to the non-criminal, but still largely marginal, members of the lower classes: beggars, vagabonds, ragpickers, the poorest of the poor, and the inhabitants of the worst slums. However, the disruptive and violent tactics workers employed bore a strong resemblance to the hooligan violence many workers had eschewed in the organized revolutionary struggle of 1905. When they engaged in violence, a variety of newspapers labeled their actions hooliganism. In St. Petersburg this process culminated in the general strike of July 1914. The July general strike exemplifies how hooligan behavior had spread among the lower classes and how images of hooliganism, with all the connotations that had evolved since 1900, provided a symbol that respectable society could use to orient its understanding of the lower classes in action.

The St. Petersburg General Strike of July 1914

At the beginning of July 1914, as the European powers prepared for war, the workers of St. Petersburg organized a massive general strike that involved the active participation of more than half the factory labor force, brought the city's tram and trolley lines to a halt, and closed most of the

107. For accounts of the crisis atmosphere in educated society see Haimson, "Social Stability," Part 2; Rogger, "Russia in 1914"; and W. Bruce Lincoln, *In War's Dark Shadow: The Russians before the Great War* (New York, 1983), 389–99.

manufacturing and commercial establishments in the capital.[108] The strike captured the attention of the highest authorities and was widely reported in the press. From the outset it was remarkable for the violence workers employed to express their hostility to authority and to resist official attempts to terminate the strike. Almost all accounts of the strike, contemporary and historical, have emphasized the workers' violence, but they have differed fundamentally in their interpretations of its significance. Historians in particular have had trouble explaining the violence connected with the strike, in part because they have relied on official police reports and politically liberal and social democratic sources, all of which viewed the labor violence in expressly political terms. But political, and even some social, analyses of labor unrest in 1914 cannot account for the types and extent of violence that occurred during the July strike. After the remarkable discipline and organization in 1905 and two decades of political organizing the inescapable evidence of hooliganism in working-class violence came as a surprise. *Peterburgskii listok* and the other newspapers that labeled the strike violence hooliganism provide a different perspective on the events. In this case, the concept of hooliganism not only provided contemporaries with a symbolic reference point for understanding what happened in July 1914, it also helps us understand an ambiguous instance of working-class unrest.

108. Few historians have analyzed the strike in any detail; see Haimson, "Social Stability"; Haimson and Petrusha, "Two Strike Waves"; Haimson, "Structural Processes of Change and Changing Patterns of Labor Unrest: The Case of the Metal-Processing Industry in Imperial Russia, 1890–1914," in *Strikes, Wars, and Revolutions in an International Perspective*, ed. Leopold Haimson and Charles Tilly (Cambridge, 1989); id., "Labor Unrest in Imperial Russia on the Eve of the First World War: The Roles of Conjunctural Phenomena, Events, and Individual and Collective Actors," in *Strikes, Wars, and Revolutions*; G. A. Arutiunov, *Rabochee dvizhenie v Rossii v periode novogo revoliutsionnogo pod"ema, 1910–1914* (Moscow, 1975); E. E. Kruze, *Peterburgskie rabochie v 1912–1914 godakh* (Moscow and Leningrad, 1961). See also Heather Hogan, "Industrial Rationalization and the Roots of Labor Militance in the St. Petersburg Metalworking Industry, 1901–1914," *Russian Review*, vol. 42, no. 2 (1983); id., "Scientific Management and the Changing Nature of Work in the St. Petersburg Metalworking Industry, 1900–1914," in *Strikes, Wars, and Revolutions*; Robert McKean devotes a chapter to July 1914 in *St. Petersburg between Revolutions: Workers and Revolutionaries, June 1907–February 1917* (New Haven, 1990), 297–317; documents on the strike are in *Rabochee dvizhenie v Petrograde v gody novogo revoliutsionnogo pod"ema, 1912–1917 gg.*, ed. I. I. Korablev (Leningrad, 1958); and *Proletarskaia revoliutsiia* [hereafter *PR*] 8–9 (1924), which also published numerous memoirs: *PR* 30 (1924), 44 (1925); on worker radicalization in 1914, see Bonnell, *Roots of Rebellion*, 390–438.

The Petersburg general strike capped a two-year upsurge in labor unrest sparked by the government's massacre of workers at the Lena Gold Fields in 1912.[109] By July 1914 the situation in the capital was already "extremely tense."[110] In the previous month, there had been 118 strikes, including 59 at metal-processing plants. The upsurge in labor activism coincided with the spread of an acute sense of political crisis among the educated classes, as noted earlier. "We live on a volcano," warned one of the most conservative newspapers in the empire, *Kievlianin (The Kievan)*; this sentiment, however, was echoed in publications from the moderate to the radical left as well.[111]

Word of a general strike among oil-field workers in Baku had reached the capital in June, and support had been growing among workers for a display of solidarity. The Petersburg Committee of the Bolshevik party issued a leaflet calling for workers to leave work one hour early on July 1.[112] When the St. Petersburg *gradonachal'nik* prohibited even the collection of money or provisions for the Baku strikers, rallies and one-hour strikes broke out all over the city. But what was originally called as a sympathy strike in solidarity with the oil workers of Baku was quickly transformed. On July 3, an estimated 12,000 workers attending a rally on the Baku question at the Putilov works refused to obey police demands to disperse. What happened next is unclear. All unofficial sources agree that bullets were fired, leaving 2 men dead and 50 wounded. But the government claimed that the confrontation never occurred and that reports of the melee, spreading quickly around the city, were nothing but rumors.[113]

---

109. The following account is based on the document sources in n. 108 above and the following newspapers: *Peterburgskii listok, Gazeta-kopeika, Rech', Novoe vremia*, and *Trudovaia Pravda*. There is very little disagreement among the sources over the course of events. Among newspapers, the strike was covered most thoroughly in *Peterburgskii listok; PL* included both official communiqués and its own correspondents' reports from around the city. Each newspaper had its own interpretation of the strikers' violence, which will be discussed below.

110. Since the beginning of the year Petersburg workers had been increasingly restive. On the anniversary of Bloody Sunday 100,000 workers had gone on strike, 250,000 workers struck on May Day, and during the course of the month of May, 476,762 workers engaged in political strikes in the capital. Kruze, *Peterburgskie rabochie*, 306, 318–20.

111. Quoted in Rogger, "Russia in 1914," 95.

112. The Bolshevik leaflet explicitly declined to call a general strike ("We still will not now engage in a struggle using Baku's methods. We will now only support the struggle of our Baku comrades"), calling instead for the one-hour strike (*Rabochee dvizhenie*, 209–10).

113. Kruze, *Peterburgskie rabochie*, 307–10; *Rabochee dvizhenie*, 209–14. On government denials, see *Rabochee dvizhenie*, 213; *PL* published the official report in an article by A. Ch., "Den' krovavykh stolknovenii," *PL*, July 5, 1914; and "Za

In any case, the Bolshevik Petersburg Committee responded by calling for a three-day general strike.[114] The next day at least 80,000 workers left the job in outrage over the government violence against the Putilov workers.[115]

During the next few days, Bolshevik organizers repeatedly called on workers to "restrain themselves from excesses,"[116] but in vain. Confrontations between striking workers and government authorities turned to violence from the very start. On the morning of July 4, a Friday, and on July 5, many workers left their jobs to join the growing crowds gathering on the streets for impromptu rallies and demonstrations. Singing revolutionary songs and carrying red flags, strikers marched from factory to factory, encouraging workers to join the strike. Most of the violence in July occurred either in confrontations with the police or troops or in the destruction of city property. In scores of incidents throughout the city, but especially in the Vyborg and Narva districts and along the Obvodnyi Canal, crowds of workers answered government demands to disperse with volleys of rocks and cobblestones. The troops responded with drawn swords and bullets. In Narva on July 4, 9 policemen had to be treated for rock-inflicted injuries, and 4 workers were hospitalized with gunshot wounds.[117] The incidents of July 4 and 5 were evidence of the workers' deep antagonism toward the police and their readiness to engage in direct confrontations with authority, but they were mild compared with the events of the following week.

Because July 6 was a Sunday, plans were made for concerted citywide demonstrations on Monday, July 7. The timing was especially sensitive from the government's point of view, because the strike coincided with the state visit of Raymond Poincaré, the French prime minister, who arrived in the Russian capital to cement relations between Russia and France. In the midst of the international crisis, the government wanted to preserve

---

nedeliu," *Rech'*, July 7, 1914; "K stolknoveniiu na Putilovskom zavode," *GK*, July 5, 1914.

114. *Rabochee dvizhenie*, 214–15.

115. Figures for the number of strikers vary. Arutiunov, *Rabochee dvizhenie v Rossii*, 373, compares Okhranka figures with those published in newspapers (social democratic, moderate liberal) and those culled from official reports. The *Peterburgskii listok* figures fell between the two.

116. Arutiunov, *Rabochee dvizhenie v Rossii*, 365, 371; *Rabochee dvizhenie*, 231–32.

117. *Rabochee dvizhenie*, 216; A. Ch., "Den' krovavykh stolknovenii," *PL*, July 5, 1914.

domestic tranquility in order to display Russia's stability as an ally.[118] Its wish was not granted. Between July 7 and 10 the strike unleashed a storm of violence against the authorities and symbols of authority such as had not been seen since the 1905–1907 Revolution.

Rock and revolver clashes with the police now spread to every factory district of the capital. On Ligovskaia Street (the same "Ligovka" famous for its criminal haunts and hooligan gangs) strikers marching from the Obvodnyi Canal toward Nevskii Prospekt closed factories, shops, and trading stalls and interrupted trolley and horse-tram traffic. At the biscuit and chocolate factory on Ligovskaia, strikers singing revolutionary songs bombarded and broke down the factory gates, which provoked a battle of rocks with the police. The same scene was repeated numerous times in the Vyborg, Narva, and Moscow Gates districts, on Vasilevskii Island and the Petersburg Side, and at railroad stations and along railroad lines. Observers on all sides noticed that women and young children participated in every form of violent confrontation, from throwing rocks to vandalism, which made the clashes all the more disturbing. Some workers, futilely trying to limit the rioting, shut down liquor stores and taverns; others broke into them and looted. Commercial life came to a stop in every district of the city except the very center—along Nevskii Prospekt and in government offices. But while life in the center appeared to be operating more or less normally, Kazan Square had to be closed, and tranquility on the remainder of Nevskii Prospekt was maintained only with extraordinary effort by the police (reinforced with Cossack and military detachments) to divert strikers onto side streets and prevent the workers of Vyborg, Vasilevskii Island, and the Petersburg Side from crossing the Neva.[119]

Liberal *Rech* described the scenes of destruction in some detail; *Novoe vremia*, *Gazeta-kopeika*, and *Peterburgskii listok* reported daily on the accelerating violence, and they all decried the wanton and reckless vandalism. What impressed all contemporary observers as extraordinary and alarming were the workers' attacks on city property, especially the trolley

---

118. Though it seems doubtful, it is hard to know whether the strikers intended their demonstration to coincide with Poincaré's arrival, but some observers believed the workers purposely sought to disrupt the visit. See Rogger, "Russia in 1914," 99–101; "Rabochee dvizhenie," *Rech'*, July 12, 1914; the *Peterburgskii listok* analyst believed that it harmed the peace effort, though workers had not intended it; see V. P-v, "Nedelia zabastovok," *PL*, July 13, 1914.
119. Strikers did reach Nevskii at its intersection with Ligovskaia, near the Nikolaevskii Station, but this was at the far end of Nevskii, barely considered fashionable and central; "Zabastovki i ulichnyi bezporiadki," *Novoe vremia*, July 10, 1914.

and tram lines. In Vyborg, strikers interrupted tram traffic, removed the trams' steering levers, and broke all their windows. Workers evicted passengers, chased away horses, and would have pushed tram cars off their tracks if a police contingent had not arrived to save the trams. On July 7 alone drivers and conductors in seven separate instances were injured by rocks. In the Moscow Gates district, tram traffic was halted altogether along Ligovskaia Street. On July 9, the tramdrivers and conductors themselves refused to work; so tram traffic was almost completely halted. Scores of tram and trolley cars were vandalized—windows broken, seats slashed, and machinery wrecked—causing an estimated 150,000 rubles of damage. Only on Nevskii Prospekt did traffic run without obstacle, but only as a result of special police guards and protection. Furthermore, although many central streets were free from violence or disruption, the absence of trams and trolleys in outlying districts made it difficult for the civil servants and white-collar workers who staffed the central offices and stores to make their way to work in the center.

The vandalism, the interruption of traffic, the building of barricades, the open clashes with the police, and the uprooting of telegraph poles, as well as other isolated forms of violence, such as an attempt to burn down the bridge connecting Vyborg and the Petersburg Side, alarmed the government sufficiently to send the Minister of Internal Affairs on a tour of the ravaged neighborhoods on July 9. But bloody confrontations and violent destruction continued through the day and night of July 10. Trams in many parts of the city ran only under Cossack guard, and a conductor on a Ligovskaia tram who tried to reason peacefully with workers faced a barrage of stones. On the evening of July 10 dozens of violent clashes occurred. In Vyborg 6 young men were reported killed and 20 injured in battles with the police. On Miasnaia Street just north of the Obvodnyi Canal, workers sang revolutionary songs while attacking a tavern with pikes and boards. Arriving policemen were met with flying rocks. Six "ringleaders" were arrested, but not before one policeman was sent unconscious to the hospital. Only on Friday, July 11, were there signs that the strike was losing steam. The trams began running again, though only under heavy guard and despite continued worker attacks. Workers began trickling back to their jobs even on Friday and Saturday, but more than 100,000 workers stayed out, and violent confrontations continued sporadically throughout the weekend. An energetic effort was mounted to repair the broken trolley and tram cars to get them back on the streets. *Peterburg-skii listok* ran a quarter-page drawing of the repairs. On Monday, July 14, at least 70,000 workers were still out, but most factories and plants were open, and no demonstrations occurred. The next day many enterprises returned to regular production schedules. Not until July 17, however, did normal operations resume. Two weeks later Russia was at war.

Leopold Haimson was the first to recognize the significance of the July 1914 general strike and to emphasize the scope and importance of the strikers' violence. Seeking to explain the resurgence of labor unrest between 1912 and 1914, which exploded in the general strike in July 1914, Haimson found that labor activism was concentrated among the more skilled, urbanized, and better-paid workers, rather than among the new migrants or "raw recruits" he had singled out in his earlier essay. He argued that "working-class identity and solidarity" and working-class militance were especially pronounced in the newer, more technologically advanced metal-processing plants, where, as Heather Hogan has shown, the rationalization of production robbed skilled workers of their autonomy, their control over their work, and their pride.[120] Consequently, many 1912–14 strikes took on a new feature. Neither purely political nor economic, they became "demonstrative" in character, as "highly politicized workers" protested the new conditions of their jobs, not on purely economic grounds but in anger over their loss of autonomy and control. Thus, the "politically more militant strata of workers" were involved in a struggle that was not simply "more political" but had become a more "generalized and explosive struggle against all forms of authority."[121] The workers' antagonism toward a broad set of enemies corresponded, according to Haimson, to the Bolsheviks' vision of oppression and brought "politically 'advanced,' 'conscious' workers" into the Bolshevik camp "on the basis of a political identification with and commitment to social democracy."[122]

Haimson's pioneering insight into the way the strike contributed to the process of social polarization and indeed his elaboration of the process of polarization itself have shaped our understanding of the whole period, but his characterization of the strikers and the strike violence as militant, radical, and highly politicized raises some questions. Recently, British historian Robert McKean has argued that the strikers were not in fact acting out of political motives, that the Bolsheviks had little influence on the strike or allegiance from the workers involved, and that the strike was not a sign of imminent revolution: it never included the whole working class of the capital, it did not spark strikes in other cities, and it failed to win the support of educated society. But while outlining the events of

120. Haimson, "Structural Processes," 387–94.
121. Ibid., 397; Haimson and Petrusha, "Two Strike Waves," 132–33, 144.
122. Haimson, "Labor Unrest," 507–9.

the strike, McKean barely acknowledged the strikers themselves, and he dismissed their violence as "impetuous," "ill-advised, one-sided, and fruitless," a sign only of workers' bitterness over factory and economic conditions.[123] The July 1914 strike was indeed a display of generalized anti-authoritarianism, and its violence was significant to contemporaries, but in order to understand that significance we need to examine more closely the strikers involved and their portrayal in contemporary sources. If they were politicized and conscious skilled workers protesting in a general way against their loss of autonomy, why would they resort to the kinds of petty violence associated with unskilled and un-conscious workers? If they were responding to Bolshevik maximalism, why would they engage in behavior the Bolsheviks did everything they could to prevent? Although skilled and highly paid workers in the most technologically advanced plants had new reasons to strike, and although they increasingly switched their allegiance to Bolshevik party representatives and programs, neither shift accounts for the tactics workers used once they got out on the streets. Soviet and Western historians have adduced considerable evidence from police reports, strike statistics, political commentary, and newspapers to show the growing radicalism of Petersburg's workers. They have assumed that worker radicalism was both political and socialist, but they have consistently ignored the actual methods workers used to express their radicalism. Working-class actions in the July 1914 strike confounded both Bolshevik strategy and modern social science theories of working-class evolution. Instead of a mature, organized, disciplined demonstration of political opposition or an outright armed uprising, workers singing revolutionary songs and carrying red flags threw rocks and went on a rampage. They broke windows, assaulted policemen and civil servants, looted liquor stores and taverns, destroyed trams and trolley cars, set fire to a bridge, and uprooted telegraph poles.[124] Violence of this sort had not occurred on anything like this scale since 1906. Yet when similar actions, such as clashes with the police or looting and rioting, had occurred during the 1905–1907 Revolution they were not labeled hooliganism.[125]

123. McKean, St. Petersburg, 306; also see 304–5, 315–17.
124. Hogan even mentions that in two earlier strikes workers smashed time clocks and turnstiles ("Industrial Rationalization" 180). Haimson rightly notes that this kind of violence differed significantly from earlier forms of Luddism because the Russian workers were not trying to return to an earlier work process but rather to regain lost autonomy and control over the modern work process (though even here the distinction is a fine one) ("Structural Processes," 392).
125. Petty violence and vandalism had long been a part of the labor movement in other regions, as Wynn has shown in Workers, Strikes, and Pogroms, his study of the Donbass-Dnepr Bend, but either its role in St. Petersburg was less wide-

The most serious damage the strikers did, and the object of the greatest public censure, was the vandalism of tram lines and cars. *Peterburgskii listok* writers condemned the destruction of the trams as irrational, "stupid, and savage."[126] But the trams were not an irrational choice. The workers must have understood the importance of trams to the smooth functioning of the city economy; thus they were a rational and purposive target (tram lines were specifically mentioned in the Bolshevik leaflet calling for a general strike). Since the tram drivers were reluctant to join the strike, it may have been necessary to destroy the trams to stop them from running. But trams had a personal and symbolic significance for lower-class Petersburgers as well: they were a symbol of economic privilege in a city where most workers could not afford to ride them.[127] While the repair points and terminal stations were located in working-class quarters, the trams themselves served privileged society. Attacking trams may have been self-defeating, but it was neither random nor irrational nor incomprehensible. The strikers used hooligan tactics to take their struggle beyond the workplace and beyond the political arena to assault a symbol of authority and privilege in general.

This was exactly the kind of behavior social democrats sought to eliminate among workers; so its resilience and its magnitude during the last great prewar general strike calls into question the depth of the influence Bolsheviks exerted over workers. The sources' orientation toward political explanations along with historians' expectations of how politicized workers should behave have made it difficult to understand strike violence of this sort.[128] Viewing the violence of July 1914 as a form of hooliganism helps

---

spread or it has been underestimated. Research at this point shows that workers used petty violence only on occasion and in isolated instances; see Surh, *1905*, 196, 313; and Hogan, "Industrial Rationalization," 180.

126. V. P-v, "Nedelia zabastovok," *PL*, July 13, 1914.

127. E. E. Kruze, *Usloviia truda i byta rabochego klassa Rossii v 1900–1914 godakh* (Leningrad, 1981), 95–96. The City Duma discussed lowering the fare, which was higher than even the most expensive tram fares in Western Europe. Semen Kanatchikov recalled that he could afford to ride the horse-drawn trolley when he was employed in Moscow as a skilled pattern maker earning more than a ruble and a half per day, but when he lost his job he was forced to tramp the city on foot looking for work. When he first moved to St. Petersburg and found work in the Vyborg quarter but lived in the Nevskii Gates region he was forced to walk the distance of five or so miles each way until he could find a place to live near his job; see Zelnik, *A Radical Worker*, 76, 86; Bater, *St. Petersburg*, 271–72, 277, 281–84, 320, 332.

128. Both tsarist police reports and social democrats depicted labor unrest as a battle in the war between the state and its political enemies, the revolutionary parties; see, for example, *Rabochee dvizhenie*, 211–12.

resolve questions about who the strikers were and why they resorted to violence.

Peterburgskii listok's correspondents immediately recognized what Haimson called the generalized anti-authoritarianism in the strikers' violence as one of the behaviors the newspaper had long labeled hooliganism. This was the first time, however, that the newspaper labeled as hooligans workers acting as workers, engaging in a labor action. We do not have to accept the pejorative and value-laden or even the cultural connotations associated with hooliganism in *Peterburgskii listok* to see that the tactics strikers used were not some atavistic survival of a primitive stage in the Russian labor movement, but that they resembled hooligan antiauthoritarianism. As one *Peterburgskii listok* writer put it, "This is a strike?!"[129]

Hooligans were people who, for the most part, stood not only outside privileged society, but also outside both the peasant culture that they had left and the working-class culture to which they had not fully assimilated. If their tangential status prevented them from developing a disciplined, political sensibility, it allowed them to develop a keen sense of the balance of power in everyday life. Hooligans used petty violence to intimidate, to attract attention, and to assert their own authority over people with far greater wealth and political power. It should not be surprising that the hooligans' ability to assert their defiance of informal social authority and formal police authority and to intimidate privileged individuals on the streets should appeal to workers whose own autonomy and authority were under attack. By throwing rocks and destroying tram cars, workers on a huge scale were engaging in behavior that resembled the hooligans' assault on privileged society, both literally on the street and more figuratively against the symbols of privilege and authority. Working-class violence in July 1914 needs to be seen at least in part as defiance of the same cultural and social authority that hooligans had been attacking on the streets of the capital since the turn of the century. Strikers may have been acting irresponsibly or even counterproductively, but their actions were directed against specific targets and specific forms of oppression and injustice. As a result, their actions, however undisciplined and however apolitical, did not detract from but contributed to the general revolutionary upheaval. Their rage frightened educated and privileged society, the radical intelligentsia included. Their hooligan turn toward broader, more generally antiauthoritarian action may have been more revolutionary (in the sense that it sprang from a desire to destroy existing power relations and contributed

129. V. P-v, "Nedelia zabastovok," *PL*, July 13, 1914.

to the breakdown of authority), but it was hardly more socialist, much less Bolshevik.[130]

It is probably impossible to determine exactly which workers threw rocks and wrecked tram cars, since arrest records do not usually include such detail.[131] Almost all the primary and historical treatments of July 1914 assume that the violent strikers were from the skilled, urbanized, and militant vanguard; that is, workers who had been attracted to Bolshevik maximalism during the 1912–14 upsurge in labor unrest. During the 1912–14 period it was those from factories with a high percentage of skilled, well-paid, urbanized, and literate workers who were most likely to engage in political and demonstrative (that is, generally antiauthoritarian) strikes.[132] Newspapers and police reports all associated the violent actions of July 1914 with workers singing revolutionary songs and carrying red flags. If it is true that the violent strikers of 1914 were among the highly skilled and highly politicized, then their adoption of hooligan tactics shows a remarkable rejection of social democratic tutelage and worker-intelligentsia cultural aspirations, as well as a significant shift in their disciplined mentality to encompass symbolic attacks on privileged society at large.

But while the evidence for the involvement of such workers is suggestive, it is not conclusive. The factories where strikes most often occurred (one of the measures of labor radicalism) were the new, technologically advanced factories where the most militant workers were employed. But these factories also engaged increasing numbers of unskilled, "new" workers: peasants, women, and children. Furthermore, there is no hard evi-

130. As Haimson noted, Lenin himself feared that the Bolsheviks' maximalist appeal would unleash popular violence; see Haimson, "Social Stability," Part 1, 639; and Bonnell, *Roots of Revolution*, 406.
131. *Sosloviia*, age, place of origin, length of residence in St. Petersburg, or place of employment are not definitive evidence of skill or radicalism. Even occupation, which rarely appears in documents connected with strikes or demonstrations, is ambiguous, since many occupational categories included skilled and unskilled jobs. Haimson has shown that workers in cities with a high concentration of industry, a high concentration of large plants, and higher average levels of pay had a higher propensity to strike. He also shows that metalworkers in the capital accounted for a vastly disproportionate number of strikers, and metal plants for a disproportionate number of strikes during the 1912–14 period, but none of this is conclusive evidence that the people who threw rocks and wrecked trams were highly skilled, highly paid, or highly politicized, nor does it prove that the workers who sang revolutionary songs were the same workers who flung rocks at policemen, or that the rock throwers were also tram wreckers; see Haimson and Petrusha, "Two Strike Waves," 113–22.
132. Haimson and Petrusha, "Two Strike Waves," 113–22.

dence to prove that the rock throwers and tram wreckers were not the same kinds of people who engaged in hooligan rowdiness in 1905–7 or after: that is, the less skilled, marginal, temporary or casual workers. The crowds that sang revolutionary songs and carried red flags were undoubtedly composed of a wide variety of workers. Although women and teenagers were not unknown among skilled and radical workers, they were rare. Yet women and young children were seen throwing rocks, wrecking trams, and uprooting telegraph poles, and at least one woman stood out in the crowd that tried to stop the railroad traffic. There is no telling whether militant workers led incidents of violence or whether violence occurred when the politically oriented leaders were superseded by those in the crowd with more violent proclivities and no idea how to sing the "Marseillaise" or "Internationale."[133]

If hooligan tactics were carried out primarily by unskilled workers or standard hooligan types, rather than the skilled and politicized, we have to rethink our understanding of the strike as a revolutionary moment and reconsider the appearance of labor violence as evidence of a turn toward labor militance. It is difficult, in this case, to see 1914 as a step toward a working-class *socialist* revolution rooted in a more-or-less developed proletarian consciousness. On the other hand, the appearance of widespread hooliganism in the midst of the general strike in July 1914 makes it clear that workers, broadly defined, had evolved a very clear sense of their place in society, of links among all workers, even if only in opposition to privileged society and its police protectors, and they found a willingness to demonstrate together against society. Unlike 1905–6, when hooliganism usually followed in the wake of labor demonstrations, here the two coincided. This concurrence certainly created a more dangerous and unstable situation (not only, I might add, for the tsarist government but for any postrevolutionary state as well), though not necessarily a more radical or socialist one.

This was exactly the scenario social democrats had always feared. Workers' petty violence would endanger the movement as a whole by opening the door to spontaneous and self-destructive actions, thereby allowing the movement to slip from social democratic control. Social democrats also feared that popular violence would undermine society's sympathy for the workers' cause, considered necessary until autocracy was

---

133. *Rabochee dvizhenie*, 216–38; A. P-ii, "Zabastovki v stolitse," *PL*, July 10, 1914; id., "Zabastovki v stolitse," *PL*, July 11, 1914; V. P-v, "Nedelia zabastovok," *PL*, July 13, 1914; "Zabastovki i ulichnye bezporiadki," *NV*, July 10, 1914.

overthrown.[134] Judging from press coverage of July 1914, this came about only in part and based not exclusively on political criteria. The liberals who wrote for *Rech* were more concerned with attacking the government than commenting directly on the workers' violence. Their coverage of the strike described the violent confrontations not in daily reports from around the city as *Peterburgskii listok* did, but in a few highly evocative descriptions of chaotic rioting and destruction. Commentators wrote that the events represented an understandable response to the government's willingness to quell the strike with force, but an unstated horror comes through in the juxtaposition of the workers' rioting and the liberals' dispassionate critique.[135] One *Rech* correspondent wrote that despite the existence of a constitution, the labor movement had been forced underground, where workers were prone to adopt extremist slogans, and had come to the point where workers were "prepared to do anything and stop at nothing."[136] In general, *Rech* writers stuck to their position that social ills could not be solved in a country where basic civil and political rights were not guaranteed. They underscored the workers' deep bitterness, and they warned readers that any semblance of calm during and after the strike was deceptive, but they avoided criticizing the workers, and, in fact, while *Rech* writers described the violence, they refrained from analyzing the many issues that violence raised.

Novoe vremia also reported extensively on the July 1914 strike and, as a conservative newspaper, naturally deplored the strikers' hooligan tactics. But *Novoe vremia* writers, perhaps surprisingly, did not dismiss the strikers' violence as the work of an irrational mob.[137] Instead they recognized from the beginning the social and cultural roots of lower-class hostility toward the government and privileged society. *Novoe vremia*'s lengthy analysis of the strike's violence was highly critical of the government for prohibiting the development of popular, even socialist, political activity, which would have channeled worker discontent into legal, peaceful forms. Unlike *Rech*, *Novoe vremia* went on to blame society as well. "It is possible," one article began,

> that never before has the capital of the empire felt so painfully the disintegration of life, the fragmentation of the group interests of

134. It is not entirely clear that liberal sympathy for the workers' cause was all that advantageous to workers, but Marxists considered it necessary at this historical stage.

135. *Rech'*, July 12, 1914 [lead editorial].

136. "Rabochee dvizhenie," *Rech'*, July 12, 1914.

137. *Novoe vremia* viewed hooliganism as the result of government incompetence and neglect even before the 1914 violence; see Costello, "*Novoe vremia*," 46–47.

the various strata of the population, which are growing and deepening every day. Our leadership and central government should understand that an entire human anthill is forming, which has become independent of the center and absolutely alien to it spiritually. It is animated by aspirations and inclinations that mystify us, and to an obvious degree is already hostile to us.[138]

The author saw no logic or idea behind the strikers' violence and agreed that it was self-defeating: "Turning over tram cars is not the same as turning over the government or the social structure." But at the same time the writer recognized that the violence was a "grave blow at all society, . . . savage violence against the peaceful population."[139] *Novoe vremia* blamed the government for ignoring workers' needs and hindering the free development of "cultural and class consciousness among workers," which led workers only into the arms of agitators. "But let's be fair and impartial," it went on,

the moral responsibility for the very possibility of such criminal and destructive use of the dark working-class crowd undeniably lies with the authorities and *with society*, which did not devote enough attention to resolving expeditiously the most vital issues raised by the Worker Question.[140]

Strike violence did alienate the sympathies of society, but it also focused attention on the broader responsibility of elite society and on the cultural and social hostility the unprivileged harbored against society in a way that economic and political strikes aimed directly against employers and the government could not. To the extent that labor violence awakened society to its responsibility for social problems and to the extent that it displayed working-class power and its bitterness against society at large it should not be considered an exclusively self-defeating weapon.

Peterburgskii listok's commentary on the strike was even less sympathetic than that of the conservative *Novoe vremia*. Although *Peterburgskii listok* remained moderately liberal on political issues and critical of both the central and local government's activities on behalf of the capital's poor population, the coverage of July 1914 is evidence of the newspaper's increasingly critical perspective on the working classes. From the first days of the strike, when workers and police exchanged rocks and bullets, but even before widespread hooligan vandalism and rioting occurred, *Peter-*

138. "V tine revoliutsionnogo khuliganstva," *NV*, July 11, 1914.
139. Ibid.
140. Ibid.; my emphasis.

burgskii listok presented the events from the perspective of the police and the central authorities. Its correspondents depicted the clashes as battles in which the legitimate forces of order were besieged by unruly and aggressive workers.[141] *Peterburgskii listok* deplored the workers' violence, withheld support for the workers, and showed no sympathy for their cause. The labor issues involved and the workers' political grievances were mentioned only briefy in each article and usually only after the summation of the day's violence.[142] Like other newspapers, *Peterburgskii listok* labeled as hooligans the workers engaged in violence and emphasized the "hooligan" nature of the strikers' tactics, by which was meant their defiant, reckless, incomprehensible, and irresponsible behavior. Even where the newspaper distinguished between "hooligan" strikers and "well-known" or "long-time" hooligans, they were shown acting in concert. The strike was characterized in *Peterburgskii listok* by the close connection between hooligans and workers as well as between hooliganism and labor militance.[143]

This was in sharp contrast to the newspaper's stance in 1905–7, when *Peterburgskii listok* clearly differentiated hooliganism (mugging, rioting, and rock throwing at policemen) from labor strikes and demonstrations and strongly supported the latter. It also differs from the newspaper's coverage of working-class demonstrations as recently as the months immediately preceding July. On the anniversary of the 1905 Bloody Sunday massacre, a one-day strike involving 140,000 workers produced political demonstrations all along Nevskii Prospekt. Detailed coverage appeared the next day in *Peterburgskii listok* in an exceptionally prominent article with a big, bold headline. The report depicted an "unrecognizable" Nevskii Prospekt as marching workers (and "almost no students"), surrounded by a tight cordon of police brigades, made their way along the street, stopping to sing revolutionary songs at strategic spots along the avenue, in front of the Kazan Cathedral, the City Duma, the Armenian Church, the Arcade department store, and the Imperial Library. The tension between the workers and the police who surrounded them was palpable, and the potential for an eruption very high. Nonetheless, *Peterburgskii listok* made clear that it viewed the police effort as excessive and did not view the workers

141. A. Ch., "Den' krovavykh stolknovenii," *PL*, July 5, 1914; id., "Zabastovka rabochikh," *PL*, July 6, 1914.
142. A. P-ii, "Zabastovki v stolitse," *PL*, July 10, 1914.
143. "Zabastovki v stolitse," *PL*, July 8, 1914; A. P-ii, "Zabastovki v stolitse," *PL*, July 10, 1914, July 11, 1914, and July 13, 1914.

as "dangerous."[144] Even later on in the spring, when striking workers began fighting the police with rocks and cobblestones, *Peterburgskii listok* presented the events as seriously disruptive but avoided censuring the workers involved.[145]

In other words, it was not workers' violence per se that was appalling in July 1914 but the furious and irresponsible destruction of public property that in the eyes of *Peterburgskii listok* (and *Novoe vremia* and *Gazeta-kopeika* as well) had no connection with workers' legitimate economic needs or political desires. *Peterburgskii listok*'s editorial comment on the July strike emphasized the workers' irrationality and self-destructiveness.[146] Instead of blaming the government for ignoring working-class needs, the correspondent P-v condemned the workers for launching a strike that interfered with arms production and national security when Europe was on the precipice of war, a type of strike prohibited even in the "most enlightened and advanced" states. P-v claimed to have no quarrel with economic strikes that truly benefited workers, but found neither rhyme nor reason in the events of the week past. For P-v (and the other strike correspondents) the July violence ought to have made the general strike an anomaly, as distinct as hooliganism had been in 1905–7 from what he called "the real, serious labor movement," which, as P-v put it, was "tarnished by the street outbursts." But by 1914 the increasing willingness of workers to proclaim their revolutionary spirit openly and, more important, to employ violence against authority made workers and hooligans less easy to distinguish.

Because *Peterburgskii listok* had focused on hooliganism for more than a decade, it provided a historical perspective for understanding the violence of July 1914 by making explicit what was implicit in other accounts. The workers' adoption of behavior that the newspaper had been the first to identify and publicize, their "wild and savage" attack against state and society, could be seen in *Peterburgskii listok* only as a deterioration of the labor movement, not as a sign of increasing militance or radicalism. This interpretation corresponds to the newspaper's increasingly negative view of the lower classes as a whole.

The *Peterburgskii listok* perspective on the July general strike suggests solutions to some of the unanswered questions about violence in earlier accounts. We still do not know who or what kind of workers participated in the strike violence, but since activist workers and their intelligentsia

144. "Deviatoe ianvaria v Peterburge," *PL*, January 10, 1914.
145. For example, "Vcherashnye zabastovki rabochikh," *PL*, March 14, 1914.
146. V. P-v, "Nedelia zabastovok," *PL*, July 13, 1914.

mentors almost always eschewed reckless violence, it seems logical to look elsewhere. For the first time hooligan violence occurred on a large scale in direct connection with strike activities; thus it differed from earlier hooliganism, which had always either followed labor unrest, as in 1905–6, or occurred independently of labor activism in ordinary street rowdiness and assaults. We need first of all to remember that the lines separating workers, casual workers, and sometime hooligans remained fluid and accommodated a great deal of flow back and forth. It seems likely that the violent strikers were grouped somewhere in between habitual hooligans and "militant" or "conscious" workers. In that case we must conclude that some ordinary workers—men, women, and children—adopted hooligan tactics and shared something of the hooligan mentality that encouraged the use of extreme public methods of defiance and self-assertion to lash out at symbols of authority and at authority itself. In other words, workers acting as workers had some hooligan attributes: their violence resembled hooliganism in its fury, its defiance, and its attack on local symbols and powers rather than on central political ones. If the July violence left few permanent traces in the way of significant concessions or improvements, it made a deep impression on privileged observers of all kinds, and we can reasonably imagine that it marked the experience of the participants as well. Furthermore, there was method in the strikers' madness. Though the July violence may have been self-defeating, the targets of violence were anything but meaningless or incomprehensible. Trams, policemen, Cossacks, power lines, and bridges were all either symbols or instruments of power and authority in the city. So while *Peterburgskii listok* decried the violence as irresponsible, its identification of the violence as hooliganism alerts us to a layer of cultural and social defiance in the labor movement that was inherent in hooliganism. The general anti-authoritarianism Haimson discerned among skilled workers was, in fact, a more widespread attribute of lower-class protest as a whole during these last years of imperial rule.

o   o   o   o

By using violence to attack authority in general and by provoking society's revulsion at the sight, the strike of July 1914 made a major contribution to the polarization of society along lines associated with hooliganism, between the "cultured" and the "uncultured." The illustrated weekly magazine *Niva* made this explicit by criticizing workers' participation in vandalism and political demonstrations, calling for them to limit themselves to "normal and cultured" behavior: peaceful strikes over immediate economic issues.[147] But polarization was not occurring exclusively between the critical actors of 1905—the workers and the intelligentsia. Historians have focused on that split, in part because contemporaries did, but in part because they have seen that alliance as crucial to any attempt to overthrow the autocracy. This study of hooliganism, poverty, and violence makes it clear that polarization occurred in relative degrees and among a multiplicity of social groups. While workers adopted hooligan tactics in 1914, there is no corresponding evidence of a decline in the animosity between skilled, urbanized workers and the unskilled or casual, "new" workers. And, as the disparate treatments of labor violence in *Rech, Novoe vremia,* and *Peterburgskii listok* show, there was by 1914 considerable variation among attitudes in educated, privileged, and respectable society toward the poor population as a whole, the legitimacy of working-class grievances and actions, and the potential for social stability. This study should also make it clear that relations between the workers and the intelligentsia occurred in an urban environment amid a great diversity of people in new and shifting social groups who may have had little direct impact on the outcome of major political events, but who formed the parameters within which the politically active behaved and were understood.

The July 1914 strike exposed the disintegration of the hopeful ties that united the privileged and the poor in 1905. While many people saw fragmentation and polarization in 1914, only a prescient few explicitly understood the basic social and cultural aspects of popular antagonism toward society. Those who did linked polarization with anti-social behavior like hooliganism. *Novoe vremia* understood that link only partially; *Peterburgskii listok* only implicitly. Gessen only reluctantly saw popular criminality as a cause of polarization, but coverage of the general strike in *Rech* showed that, even among liberals, labor violence and lower-class animosity were eroding belief in the potential for a common front. The most famous apocalyptic seer in this period was, of course, Alexander Blok, whose speeches and essays on the chasm separating educated society from the people caused a furor in 1908, when he began voicing his ideas. He was denounced by the radical intelligentsia and dismissed by the artistic intelligentsia, but his ideas were increasingly echoed toward 1914, and they were vindicated by the popular fury against society that was un-

147. "Kul'turnaia bor'ba s zabastovkami (voprosy vnutrennei zhizni)," *Niva,* May 3, 1914.

leashed first in July 1914 and then in the 1917 revolutions.[148] Blok pointed
out over and over again that educated society had never understood what
the people wanted and that the intelligentsia had itself become ossified and
obsolete as a leading force in society. He believed that the greatest creative
force in Russia resided in the people but that centuries of oppression and
misunderstanding had turned the people not only against the government
but against all of privileged society and had transformed their creative
potential into a violent, destructive rage. In one of the essays he wrote
on this theme, "Stikhiia i kul'tura" (The Elemental and Culture), Blok
portrayed the people as a volcano ready to erupt. But Blok's view was
never specifically political. It was rooted in an acute, if immobilizing,
understanding of cultural difference and its consequences. Therefore it is
no accident that Blok's illustration of the people's spirit in "Stikhiia i
kul'tura" was a hooligan song:

У нас ножики литые,	Our little knives are made of steel
Гири кованые,	Our rocks on ropes are iron-cast
Мы ребята холостые,	We've been around
Практикованные . . .	We've seen it all . . .
Пусть нас жарят и калят,	Let 'em broil us and roast us
Размазуриков-ребят—	We're the boys who steal from everyone
Мы начальству не уважим,	Even the cops don't really scare us
Лучше сядем в каземат . . .	A spell in jail will be just fine . . .
Ах ты, книжка-складенец,	Oh you, switch-blade of mine,
В каторгу дорожка,	This road leads to hard labor
Пострадает молодец	Where a bold lad
За тебя немножко . . .	Will suffer for you a little . . .[149]

148. On Blok, the development of his social ideas, and some of the responses to
these ideas, see Avril Pyman, *The Life of Aleksandr Blok*, 2 vols. (Oxford, 1979).
149. "Stikhiia i kul'tura," *Sobranie sochinenii v shesti tomakh*, vol. 4 (Leningrad,
1982), 123. Blok's source for the song was Nikolai Kliuev, the "peasant-poet,"
with whom he carried on an extended and at times rancorous correspondence. The
song clearly mixes two genres: the first eight lines are typical of hooligan *chastushki*, recorded in European Russia in the early twentieth century, while the last
four lines more closely resemble much older songs associated with Siberian exile,
prison, and hard labor, whose roots are in rural folk tale and song; see N. M.
Iadrintsev, *Russkaia obshchina v tiur'me i ssylke* (St. Petersburg, 1872), 86–123;
Maksimov, *Sibir' i katorga*, 331–75; K. M. Azadovskii, "Olonetskaia derevnia
posle pervoi russkoi revoliutsii (stat'ia N. A. Kliueva 'S rodnogo berega')," *Russkii
fol'klor* 15 (1975): 199–209.

Blok's view of popular rebellion encompassed the brazen defiance of cultural norms and social authority that could be equally self-destructive and life-affirming. Although Blok has been dismissed as a politically naive mystic, his lack of political acumen was matched by an extraordinary instinct for the cultural and social dislocations of his time. In fact, it was precisely his neglect of the political that allowed him to see the power inherent in the hooligan's elemental contempt for culture and to see that contempt spreading among the people.

Epilogue

Hooliganism was no ordinary crime. Without an audience, hooligans would not have existed. They would have been common criminals engaging in common crimes, remarkable only for their proliferating numbers. Their acts took on special meaning and power because they performed them in a way that provoked a potent response, and at a time when the issues they dramatized were of particular concern. If hooliganism had remained a phenomenon of the boulevard press, it would still have represented a curious and revealing instance of the role cultural conflict played in the formation of urban cultures and classes (as it did to varying extents elsewhere in Europe). But in Russia, from 1905 on, hooligan behavior became a useful means of protesting an increasing number of amorphous social and cultural authorities, and hooliganism became a widely used image, category, and symbol in the depiction and understanding of social reality in a changing, disintegrating world.

A number of conditions contributed to making hooliganism into a wider phenomenon, a useful symbol, and a social obsession. Hooligans, understandably, frightened people, both people who encountered obnoxious hooligans on the streets and those who read about their behavior in the newspaper. In a period when the city's public spaces were "swarming" with a million new inhabitants and when all kinds of authorities—government, police, intelligentsia, family—were under attack, hooligans' public insolence, defiance, and violence dramatized the challenge to tradition and authority. Hooligans also came to represent the dangers inherent in loosening constraints on society. Even when hooligans victimized people far from the centers of power, the increase in their numbers, the apparent pettiness of their motives, and the savagery of their attacks suggested that certain members of the lower classes were either very beastly or very angry and that the mechanisms of social control were no longer functioning.

Hooliganism flourished in the last years of tsarist rule because the conflicts that hooliganism exposed brought to the surface issues that were at the center of public concern. As civil society expanded and redefined itself to include increasingly diverse sectors of respectable society and as the traditional centers of high culture, such as St. Petersburg, were inundated with masses of the uncultured, consensus among the educated about the character and purpose of Russian culture was breaking down. A cultured society remained the goal of the educated, yet it was no longer clear what constituted a cultured society, who might belong to it, and by what criteria, or whether true civilization was still within Russia's grasp. Hooligans provided evidence of the country's inability to civilize itself by their uninhibited displays of all sorts of "uncultured" behavior in public, mocking and frightening those most sensitive to the fragile line dividing civilization from barbarism. Through such behavior they made manifestly clear the existence of another culture, the fragmentation of Russian society along cultural lines, and the erosion of popular deference toward traditional or conventional cultural authorities. In fact, Russian culture was fragmenting under numerous economic and political pressures, many of which were unconnected with hooligan offenses, but hooliganism, with its defiance, violence, unpredictability, and use of cultural weapons, symbolized the erosion of the unity, authority, tradition, and optimism that had characterized the last decade and a half of the imperial era.

Ironically, the hooligan challenge to culturalism and fears for the future of Russian civilization arose just when cultural development was making real headway. Literacy and education were spreading, and cultural events of all kinds were popular among the people, when they had access to them. Perhaps most ironically, newspapers offered the greatest evidence of popular cultural development in Russian society. Despite the old intelligentsia's disparagement of the boulevard press and despite fears expressed in *Peterburgskii listok* that the poor would never imbibe enough culture to be assimilated into respectable society, the immense readership of newspapers like *Peterburgskii listok* and *Gazeta-kopeika* was proof of the existence of a popular literate culture, which was a necessary step in cultural development.

The spread of culture was transforming social conventions and values as well. As the public sphere widened, hooligans and avant-garde artists were not the only ones confronting old standards with new kinds of public behavior. All sorts of people entered the public sphere for the first time or on a new scale: women, elected politicians, workers, professionals, and social reformers of many kinds. Disparate conventions of behavior collided with one another on the streets of the capital but also on village roads, inside the St. Petersburg Duma, on the pages of the diverse newspapers from which readers might choose, and in proliferating forms of commercial culture: literature, theater, films, and music among them. Hooligan challenges to respectable, civilized society came at a time when the cultural ideology of educated society, indeed educated society itself, was splintering. And cultural pluralism did not sit well with the Russian intelligentsia, old or new, both of whom wanted their own standards accepted as the norm. By 1900, when actual urban social and cultural diversity were already well established, they were not readily acknowledged. Consequently, many people believed that the power of traditional norms was on the wane, and they feared the breakdown of the traditional cultural institutions that had preserved order in their communities, such as the family, church, class structure, and state. These were processes set in motion by a variety of forces, but hooliganism dramatized them, advertised them, and eventually came to symbolize them.

The roles hooliganism played in the political upheavals of the period also contributed to cultural conflict and social polarization. The proliferation of hooliganism—from the confounding of police power to the confrontation with all authorities during the revolutionary years to the more diverse challenges of the 1910s—testified to the breakdown of informal and formal authority. Hooligans were most active and most frightening when social and political authority was already weak—in 1905–7 and 1912–14. During these times of political crisis hooligans were emboldened to act on a much larger scale. They contributed to the disintegration of police and state power, giving hooliganism additional political significance for demonstrating the government's loss of control. By 1914, the adoption of hooligan tactics in organized labor demonstrations was viewed by respectable society as evidence not only of the deterioration of the labor movement but of the failure on the part of state and society to exert their proper authority over the masses and assert sufficient leadership. The July 1914 general strike suggests that hooligan rage was spreading among ordinarily more disciplined workers. While the boulevard press and other newspapers interpreted this as evidence of moral or cultural deterioration among the lower classes, it might just as easily be seen as a sign of rising lower-class consciousness; not necessarily radical consciousness, but a genuine bitterness about continuing injustice, a sense that the problems they faced stemmed from a diffuse coalition of government and privileged society, and a willingness to use violence and to attack symbolic targets in order to be heard.

The political, social, and cultural implications of hooligan behavior made manifest the chasm between privileged and poor in Russia and the growing hostility on both sides. If widespread contempt for the poor among Russian elites does not seem remarkable or surprising, remember that sympathy, pity, and optimism about cultural development dominated views of crime and poverty before 1905. In addition, during the years leading up to the 1905–1907 Revolution, the obvious indifference, if not opposition, of the tsar to the goals of almost every segment of society allowed highly divergent social groups to unite with the intelligentsia against the autocracy and to forget for a time the gaping differences that divided them. But in the years after 1905, hooliganism was associated with two issues that were very likely to trouble society: violence and open displays of the "uncultured" behavior associated with the raw, unassimilated masses. Even people who remained optimistic about cultural development, such as the judicial specialists and social workers who studied youth culture, discovered the cultural chasm dividing them from their poor subjects to be much wider than they expected. On the eve of the war, pessimism regarding the possibility of creating a harmonious society was often expressed not in political terms or in the context of social and economic change, but in terms of cultural difference and conflict. Even those who believed that unjust social conditions lay at the root of the low moral level of the people could not explain the apparent impenetrability of lower-class culture. Their discussions focused on lower-class behavior, habits, and customs, and hooliganism represented an extreme form of lower-class lack of culture.

Other societies in the Western world witnessed similar processes of massive urban in-migration and cultural diversification, but Russian society seemed especially ill equipped to deal with the social fragmentation that followed. In the United States, to take just one example, Lawrence Levine has shown how American social elites, who also found lower-class, migrant culture disturbing, were able to create a new cultural discourse to incorporate the new social reality. Levine argues that they invented concepts of "high" and "low" culture, which conceded diversity but ranked various cultural products in a way that maintained, and indeed reinforced, the old social hierarchy.[1] Nothing like this happened in Russia until after 1917, when cultural fragmentation was resolved by imposing a single culture in a far more drastic and coercive manner. Before 1917, however, Russian cultural elites, who had long nurtured the dream of a single, unified culture (diametrically opposed to the American pluralistic discourse), were unable to reconstruct a workable cultural discourse to accommodate modern diversity. The lack of any real leadership within the autocracy and the immaturity of the Russian public sphere provided articulate Russians with little experience in dealing with difference and conflict on a mass scale. And revolutionary politics intensified existing divisions in realms outside politics. As William Wagner suggested recently, instability in late imperial Russia was not due to the absence of a middle class, as

1. Levine, *Highbrow/Lowbrow.*

historians have claimed, but to the presence of multiple middle classes, divided over basic political and ideological issues.[2] In this regard Germany may come closest among modern Western societies to the Russian experience, with its own middle classes fairly rigidly divided between commercial and intellectual circles. But bourgeois society was more deeply rooted in Germany, and a comparable period of severe fragmentation and loss of direction appeared there only *after* World War I. And then, of course, tensions over social and cultural diversity were "resolved" when Germany, too, succumbed to a unitary culture, drastically coerced.[3] Comparative studies of middle-class culture in Europe and the United States during this period would clarify some of these issues, but one thing seems clear: in Russia, with the exception of a small optimistic liberal wing, educated society *perceived* social and cultural divisions as intense, problematic, and destabilizing. These perceptions derived from a variety of experiences, but they produced similar expressions of pessimism regarding the future of Russian culture.

Such fragmentation had political consequences both before and after 1917. First, the challenge to the autocracy came from a society divided along social and cultural, as well as political, lines. Second, resistance to informal and amorphous forms of authority and privilege had already established its own conventions and ritual behaviors. And, third, it was clear that hostility toward culturalism and culturalist projects had a foundation among the lower classes. Not that every member of the urban poor rejected the literacy and refined manners of respectable society; far from it. But a significant segment of the lower classes resisted culturalism "from above." Blok may not have been representative of the educated elite, but his sentiments were echoed in *Peterburgskii listok* continually after 1912, when he criticized culturalism as mere reforms, which could not withstand the "mighty floods of popular resentment that were barely restrained by the feeble dikes of civilization and a decaying state."[4]

The hooligans' animosity toward privilege and toward the cultural trappings of privilege did not disappear after 1917, and the Soviet state periodically used campaigns against hooliganism to rid itself of troublesome elements. From 1914 through the early 1920s the disorders of war, revolution, and civil war bred criminal acts in record numbers, but the

2. William Wagner, "Ideology, Identity," in *Between Tsar and People*, 162–63. For a similar argument in the specifically political realm, see Emmons, *Political Parties*, 375–79.
3. David Blackbourn and Geoff Eley, *The Peculiarities of German History: Bourgeois Society and Politics in Nineteenth-Century Germany* (New York, 1984).
4. Quoted in Rogger, "Russia in 1914," 95.

preoccupation with larger disorders kept hooliganism out of the news. Hooligan crimes occurred, of course, and one can read about them in the press (especially in 1917, when the prisons spilled open),[5] but the discourse on hooliganism and the power struggle it enacted were postponed. In the mid-1920s, as the economy recovered and cities revived, a new process of self-identification began under the socialist state, with its own hierarchies and cultural programs. In 1924–25 a campaign against hooliganism was initiated, and it was clearly used, this time by political authorities and economic managers as well as by criminologists, to define the "respectable" proletarian worker and to stigmatize disruptive and nonproductive behaviors, as well as to control crime.[6] Hooliganism (like prostitution) was expected to disappear along with capitalism; so it also became a case study for criminologists in explaining why crime persisted under socialism.[7] For their part, hooligans understood perhaps better than anyone that the cultural projects of the new regime involved a set of values and didactic methods much like the culturalism of the prerevolutionary intelligentsia and respectable middle classes. Hooligan targets expanded accordingly during this period to include Bolshevik culture clubs, reading rooms, theatrical circles, and statues of Lenin.

In the 1930s, as state control over both life and language increased, crimes that blurred the lines between annoying practical jokes and anti-state actions were often labeled hooliganism. In one case, a pair of pranksters who played a practical joke on a model "Stakhanovite" worker were considered too petty to be labeled serious class enemies but were tried for hooligan sabotage. And in 1935 another campaign against hooliganism was launched.[8] In the 1940s and 1950s hooliganism continued to appear in the newspapers, with new social campaigns producing new kinds of hooliganism. The kind of street hooliganism associated with the 1900s–1920s was curtailed by mass arrests of homeless and abandoned youths and a ban on popular forms of crime reporting.[9] But in 1940, when

5. Tsuyoshi Hasegawa, "Crime and Revolution in Petrograd, 1917" (unpublished manuscript).
6. *Khuliganstvo i ponozhevshchina* (Moscow, 1927); *Khuliganstvo i khuligany: Sbornik* (Moscow, 1929); Neil Weissman, "The Soviet Campaign against Hooliganism in the 1920s" (unpublished paper).
7. *Khuliganstvo i prestuplenie: Sbornik* (Moscow and Leningrad, 1927).
8. *Sovetskaia iustitsiia* 14 (1936): 3; quoted in Chalidze, *Criminal Russia*, 84; Peter Solomon, *Soviet Criminal Justice under Stalin* (Cambridge, forthcoming).
9. Mikhail Dyomin, *The Day Is Born of Darkness: A Personal Account of the Soviet Criminal Underworld*, trans. Tony Kahn (New York, 1976); Goldman, "The 'Withering-Away,'" 360–72.

the Stalinist campaign to reassert traditional family structures was under way, *Pravda* identified as hooligans, for example, men who ran out on their family obligations or refused to pay alimony.[10]

A new boom in hooligan crimes occurred with the loosening of social and cultural constraints in the 1960s and 1970s, and the hooligan wave accelerated with the explosion of public expression in the Gorbachev era. Hooligan street crime reappeared, but again, as throughout the Soviet period, political uses were added to more purely social and cultural ones. During the 1970s, accusations of hooliganism were used against political dissidents, and in 1987 when a young German flyer successfully and astonishingly evaded Soviet military detection to fly deep into Russian territory and land his light aircraft beside the Kremlin walls in the center of Moscow, he was indicted for "malicious hooliganism." What all these offenses had in common was that they were perceived by the authorities as trivial, but brazen, insolent acts that launched deadly serious and humiliating attacks on established authority.

Does the persistence of hooliganism mean that it is in some way endemic to Russian culture? Blok certainly thought so, and it is not difficult to find an acknowledgment, and even a celebration, of mischievous and insolent iconoclasm in writers before and since.[11] But it takes two to tango. Hooliganism acquires power as a discourse only when there is a sufficiently imposing tradition and authority to outrage or attack; so it can be endemic only to the portion of the population that stands outside convention and power. Historically in Russia that has been a sizable lot. The tsar's monopoly on political power and public expression, combined with the extraordinary disparity of wealth and the tiny size of the privileged elite, increased the reasons for mass alienation and popular fury as well as elite fears of the masses. Furthermore, hooliganism is the tactic of people without more powerful weapons at their disposal; so hooligans can act only when traditional authorities are already weakened. They tend to be outsiders: people living on the margins of their society whose public voices have been muted by poverty, exclusion, distance, or change itself: workers without work, peasants between field and factory, artists without a market, or writers abroad. Russian history, of course, has been marked by long periods in

10. *Pravda*, June 1, 1940.
11. Recently Tatiana Tolstaia has adopted a hooligan persona in her journalistic performances and public appearances. Her essays in *Moscow News*, for example, are self-consciously provocative: a recent column opens with an epigraph by Rozanov: "Slobbering, bug-eyed—that's me. You don't like me? Too bad! That's how I am," no. 20, May 17–24, 1992, 15.

which the powerful have been able to accumulate an overbearing weight of authority, interrupted from time to time by radical reform projects and the unleashing of public expression.[12] Yet each period of reform has been marked by disappointment and the continuation of at least some traditions of authority. During three centuries of intermittent spurts of modernization the periods of reform have each been marked by outbursts of hooliganism: ordinary petty crimes that provoke new levels of fear because they symbolize the perils of change, and genuine attacks or expressions of bitterness and rage at the failed promises of change. Sideswipes at burdensome powers and expressions of popular rage are obviously not unique to Russia, but they do appear to be woven tightly into the historical fabric there.

12. The weight of authority accumulates in both politics and culture in Russia: what other country can match the double whammy cult of Pushkin and cult of Stalin? On Andrei Siniavskii's recent hooligan critique of Pushkin see *Progulki s Pushkinym* (Paris, 1975); and Stephanie Sandler, "Sex, Death, and Nation in the *Strolls with Pushkin* Controversy," *Slavic Review*, vol. 51, no. 2 (1992).

Appendix

Tables

Table 1. Action Taken on All Crimes

St. Petersburg *Mirovoi Sud* and House of Detention

Year	Indictments	Convictions	Incarcerations
1897	64,712	43,878	15,625
1898	75,931	51,750	18,705
1899	88,819	60,718	21,281
1900	113,213	78,715	25,968
1901	116,598	82,228	26,596
1902	109,586	76,719	24,284
1903	122,829	81,748	22,827
1904	121,921	72,625	18,484
1905	105,347	68,787	14,957
1906	100,516	62,554	14,157
1907	105,372	64,912	11,787
1908	112,061	68,864	13,913
1909	111,195	80,274	16,277
1910	125,458	88,103	17,905
1911	131,633	93,943	17,318
1912	135,683	95,095	16,688
1913	149,447	95,915	10,242
1914	117,842	86,265	17,090

Source: *S.-Peterburgskie stolichnye sudebnye mirovye ustanovleniia i arestnyi dom, Otchety.*

Table 2. Indictments for All Crimes in Relation to St. Petersburg
Population

St. Petersburg *Mirovoi Sud*

Year	Indictments	Population
1902	179,374	1,299,000
1903	208,955	1,344,000
1904	211,011	1,369,900
1905	200,522	1,406,800
1906	209,150	1,453,000
1907	214,258	1,492,500
1908	245,938	1,533,000
1909	254,133	1,574,700
1910	269,129	1,617,600
1911	275,300	1,661,500
1912	288,724	1,706,000
Increase, 1902–1912	109,350 (61%)	407,000 (31.3%)

Source: *S.-Peterburgskie stolichnye sudebnye mirovye ustanovleniia i arestnyi dom za 1913 g., Otchety*, 102.

Note: Population includes districts and suburbs only within *mirovoi sud* jurisdiction.

Table 3. Action Taken on Offenses against Public Peace and Order, Articles 35–52

St. Petersburg *Mirovoi Sud* and House of Detention

Year	Indictments	Convictions	Incarcerations
1897	26,455	20,652	9,057
1898	30,986	23,887	10,865
1899	40,423	31,039	13,620
1900	59,181	46,306	18,864
1901	62,521	49,040	19,470
1902	57,244	44,651	17,136
1903	62,710	45,543	15,425
1904	61,650	40,406	11,994
1905	53,240	37,795	9,576
1906	46,539	31,950	8,518
1907	40,232	27,182	6,442
1908	44,258	29,866	6,768
1909	39,838	—	8,752
1910	46,690	—	10,631
1911	39,396	—	11,304
1912	—	40,787	10,761
1913	—	39,855	6,258
1914	—	45,431	—

Source: *S.-Peterburgskie stolichnye sudebnye mirovye ustanovleniia i arestnyi dom, Otchety.*

Table 4. Incarcerations for Offenses against Public Peace and Order,
Not Including Public Drunkenness, Articles 35–52 (minus 42)

St. Petersburg House of Detention

Year	Incarcerations	% of Total Incarcerations
1897	8,811	56.4
1898	—	—
1899	11,827	55.6
1900	10,534	50.6
1901	11,235	42.2
1902	10,892	44.9
1903	11,873	51.9
1904	9,390	50.8
1905	8,517	56.9
1906	7,846	55.5
1907	5,915	50.2
1908	6,028	43.3
1909	7,900	48.6
1910	9,806	54.8
1911	10,414	60.2
1912	10,011	60.0
1913	5,847	57.1
1914	—	—

Source: *S.-Peterburgskie stolichnye sudebnye mirovye ustanovleniia i arestnyi dom, Ot-chety.*

Table 5. Indictments for Major Crimes

St. Petersburg Region Circuit Court

Year	Murder	Armed Robbery	Assault	Rape Abduction	Assault	Theft[a]
1900	227	427	1,171	182	216	2,197
1901	253	446	1,471	207	271	2,572
1902	252	476	1,504	180	233	2,836
1903	285	656	—	—	—	—
1904	337	611	1,748	168	302	3,094
1905	422	1,211	2,292	194	351	3,630
1906	584	1,747	1,650	229	437	4,697
1907	580	1,521	818[b]	249	384	4,210
1908	501	1,181	800	229	461	4,108
1909	575	1,143	834	284	460	4,356
1910	510	989	841	313	475	4,245
1911	642	973	891	285	447	4,983
1912	668	1,111	911	328	568	5,164
1913	794	1,328	929	338	598	5,777
1914	616[c]	841	616	262	488	6,073

Source: *Svod statisticheskikh svedenii po delam ugolovnym.*

[a] Includes all theft except armed robbery and horse or cow theft.

[b] Less serious cases were transferred to the Justice of the Peace Court beginning March 18, 1906.

[c] January through July 1914.

Table 6. Action Taken on Threats, Assaults, and Violations of Honor, Articles 130–43

St. Petersburg *Mirovoi Sud* and House of Detention

Year	Indictments	Convictions	Incarcerations
1897	8,056	2,512	1,142
1898	9,044	3,099	1,201
1899	9,911	3,136	1,232
1900	10,588	3,767	1,195
1901	10,460	4,140	1,275
1902	10,633	4,293	1,298
1903	11,810	4,748	1,361
1904	12,503	5,116	1,306
1905	11,904	5,321	1,174
1906	11,925	5,701	1,266
1907	13,271	6,377	1,104
1908	13,421	6,734	1,157
1909	13,673	—	1,070
1910	14,671	—	1,180
1911	—	8,102	1,149
1912	—	8,210	1,349
1913	—	9,512	1,152
1914	—	9,624	—

Source: *S.-Peterburgskie stolichnye sudebnye mirovye ustanovleniia i arestnyi dom, Otchety.*

Table 7. Juvenile Convictions

St. Petersburg Region Circuit Court (All Crimes) and *Mirovoi Sud* (Crimes Carrying Punishment of Imprisonment)

Year	Total Convictions	Index 1901 = 1	Juvenile Convictions	Index 1901 = 1	% of Total
1901	119,764	100	3,543	100	3.0
1902	119,902	100	3,173	90	2.6
1903	120,195	100	3,135	89	2.6
1904	110,828	93	3,640	103	3.3
1905	100,215	86	3,218	91	3.2
1906	112,497	94	3,221	91	2.8
1907	137,963	115	3,899	110	2.8
1908	154,175	129	4,628	131	3.0
1909	164,718	138	6,137	173	3.7
1910	161,904	135	7,483	211	4.6

Source: *Zhurnal ministerstva iustitsii* 10 (1913): 45.

Table 8. Juvenile Convictions as Percentage of Total Convictions for All Crimes

Russia and Germany

Year	Russia			Germany		
	Total Con-victions	Juvenile Con-victions	% of Total	Total Con-victions	Juvenile Con-victions	% of Total
1901	119,674	3,543	3.0	484,262	49,667	10.3
1902	119,902	3,173	2.6	499,000	51,044	10.2
1903	120,195	3,135	2.6	492,468	50,217	10.2
1904	110,828	3,640	3.3	505,158	50,027	9.9
1905	100,215	3,218	3.2	508,102	51,498	10.1
1906	112,497	3,221	2.8	524,113	55,270	10.5
1907	137,963	3,899	2.8	520,787	54,110	10.4
1908	154,175	4,628	3.0	540,083	54,692	10.1
1909	164,718	6,137	3.7	536,603	49,689	9.3
1910	161,904	7,483	4.6	538,225	51,315	9.5

Source: *Zhurnal ministerstva iustitsii* 10 (1913): 45, 49.

Table 9. Juvenile Convictions as Percentage of Total Convictions
St. Petersburg *Mirovoi Sud*

Year	Total Convictions	Juvenile Convictions	% of Total
1900	78,715	1,113	1.4
1901	82,228	1,283	1.6
1902	76,719	1,302	1.7
1903	81,748	1,328	1.6
1904	72,625	1,466	2.0
1905	68,787	1,492	2.2
1906	62,554	1,378	2.2
1907	64,912	1,427	2.2
1908	68,864	1,627	2.4
1909	80,274	2,434	3.0
1910	88,103	2,848	3.2
1911	93,943	1,917	2.0[a]
1912	95,095	2,032	2.1
1913	95,915	2,156	2.3
1914	86,265	2,120	2.5
1915	39,073	3,239	8.3[b]

Source: *S.-Peterburgskie stolichnye sudebnye mirovye ustanovleniia i arestnyi dom, Otchety.*

[a] First full year of Special Juvenile Court.

[b] Following outbreak of World War I.

Table 10. Occupations of Parents of Girls under Court Supervision
Special Juvenile Court, *Mirovoi Sud*

	Fathers		Mothers	
	Total	*%*	*Total*	*%*
Farming	66	25.7	81	23.5
Factory Work	58	22.3	45	13
Artisanal Work	29	11.2	16	4.6
Domestic Service	24	9.3	20	6
Casual Labor	43	16	35	10.1
Trade	14	5.5	20	6
Other	12	5	—	—
Laundry	—	—	30	8.7
Taking Boarders	—	—	28	8.1
Living with Husband	—	—	62	18
Unemployed	12	5	7	2

Source: E. I. Chichagova, "O prestupnosti devushek za piatiletie ot 1910 g. po 1915 g. po dannym osobogo suda po delam o maloletnikh v Petrograde," *Osobyi sud po delam o maloletnikh* 6 (1915): 13.

Bibliography

I. DOCUMENTS

A. ARCHIVAL

Tsentral'nyi Gosudarstvennyi Arkhiv Oktiabr'skoi Revoliutsii
[TsGAOR]. Fond 102. Departament politsii.

B. PUBLISHED DOCUMENTS

Alfavitnyi sbornik rasporiazhenii po S.-Peterburgskomu Gradona-chal'stvu i politsii, izvlechennykh iz prikazov za 1891–1901 gg. Edited by I. P. Vysotskii. St. Petersburg, 1902.

Alfavitnyi sbornik rasporiazhenii po S.-Peterburgskomu Gradona-chal'stvu i politsii, izvlechennykh iz prikazov za vremia s 1902 po 10 iiulia 1904. Edited by I. P. Vysotskii. St. Petersburg, 1904.

Gosudarstvennaia duma. *Stenograficheskie otchety.* St. Petersburg, 1906–16.

Otchet X obshchego sobraniia russkoi gruppy mezhdunarodnogo soiuza kriminalistov, 13–16 fevralia 1914 g. Petrograd, 1916.

Otchet o deiatel'nosti S-Peterburgskoi sysknoi politsii za 1903 god. St. Petersburg, 1904.

Prilozhenie k vsepoddaneishemu otchetu po S.-Peterburgskomu gradona-chal'stvu za 1901 god. St. Petersburg, 1902.

Rabochee dvizhenie v Petrograde v gody novogo revoliutsionnogo pod''ema, 1912–1917 gg.: Dokumenty i materialy. Edited by I. I. Korablev. Leningrad, 1958.

Revoliutsionnoe dvizhenie v Rossii vesnoi i letom 1905 g. 2 vols. Edited by N. S. Trusova. Moscow, 1957–61.

S.-Peterburg po perepisi 15 dekabria 1900 goda, Naselenie. St. Petersburg, 1903.

S.-Peterburg po perepisi 15 dekabria 1910 goda, Naselenie. St. Petersburg, 1912.

S.-Peterburgskie (later Petrogradskii) stolichnye sudebnye mirovye usta-noveniia i arestnyi dom, Otchet. St. Petersburg, 1867–1918.

Statisticheskii ezhegodnik S.-Peterburga. St. Petersburg, 1898–1907.

Svod statisticheskikh svedenii o podsudimykh, opravdannikh, i osu-zhdennykh. St. Petersburg, 1909–15.

Svod statisticheskikh svedenii po delam ugolovnym. St. Petersburg, 1873–1908.

Trudy sed'mogo s''ezda predstavitelei russkikh ispravitel'nykh zavedenii dlia maloletnikh, Okt. 1908 goda. Moscow, 1909.

Trudy shestogo s''ezda predstavitelei russkikh ispravitel'nykh zavedenii dlia maloletnikh, Mai 1904 goda. Moscow, 1904.

Trudy vos'mogo s''ezda predstavitelei russkikh vospitatel'no-ispravitel'nykh zavedenii dlia nesovershennoletnikh, Okt. 1911 goda. St. Petersburg, 1913.

Ulozhenie o nakazaniiakh ugolovnykh i ispravitel'nikh 1885 goda. 16th ed., revised and updated. St. Petersburg, 1912.

Ustav o nakazaniiakh, nalagaemykh mirovymi sud'iami, 1885 g. St. Petersburg, 1906.

Vserossiiskaia politicheskaia stachka v oktiabre 1905 goda. Edited by L. M. Ivanov. Moscow and Leningrad, 1955.

Vtoroi period revoliutsii, 1906–1907 gody. 4 vols. Moscow, 1957–65.

Vysshii pod''em revoliutsii 1905–1907 gg.: Vooruzhennye vostaniia, Noiabr'–Dekabr' 1905 goda. Edited by A. L. Sidorov. Moscow, 1955.

II. NEWSPAPERS AND JOURNALS

Individual newspaper articles are cited in the notes only.

Birzhevye vedomosti

Gazeta-kopeika

Golos

Gorodskoe delo

Iuridicheskaia gazeta

Iuridicheskii vestnik

Iurist

Izvestiia St. Peterburgskoi gorodskoi dumy

Moskovskii listok

Niva

Novoe vremia

Peterburgskaia gazeta

Peterburgskii listok

Pravda

Pravo

Rech'

Russkoe bogatstvo

Russkoe slovo

S.-Peterburgskie vedomosti

Sudebnaia gazeta

Sudebnoe obozrenie

Sud i zhizn'

Tiuremnyi vestnik

Vedomosti S-Peterburgskogo gradonachal'stva

Vestnik evropy
Vestnik politsii
Vestnik prava
Vestnik S.-Peterburgskogo Gradonachal'nika i stolichnoi politsii
Zhurnal ministerstva iustitsii
Zhurnal ugolovnogo prava i protsessa

III. BOOKS, ARTICLES, AND UNPUBLISHED WORKS

Abbott, Robert J. "Crime, Police, and Society in St. Petersburg, Russia, 1866–1878." *The Historian* 40 (1977).

Aborigen. *Krovavye letopisi Peterburga: Prestupnyi mir i bor'ba s nim.* St. Petersburg, 1914.

Adams, Bruce Friend. "Criminology, Penology, and Prison Administration in Russia, 1863–1917." Ph.D. diss., University of Maryland, 1981.

Arutiunov, G. A. *Rabochee dvizhenie v Rossii v periode novogo revoliutsionnogo pod"ema, 1910–1914.* Moscow, 1975.

Ascher, Abraham. *The Revolution of 1905: Russia in Disarray.* Stanford, 1990.

Avrich, Paul. *The Russian Anarchists.* Princeton, 1967.

Babushkin, Ivan. *Recollections (1893–1900).* Moscow, 1957.

Baker, Keith Michael. "Politics and Public Opinion under the Old Regime: Some Reflections." In *Press and Politics in Prerevolutionary France,* edited by Jack R. Censer and Jeremy D. Popkin. Berkeley, 1987.

Bakhrushin, S. V. *Maloletnie nishchie i brodiagi v Moskve (Istoricheskii ocherk).* Moscow, 1913.

Bakhtiarov, A. A. *Bosiaki: Ocherki s natury.* St. Petersburg, 1903.

———. *Briukho Peterburga.* St. Petersburg, 1888.

———. *Otpetye liudi.* St. Petersburg, 1903.

———. *Proletariat i ulichnye tipy Peterburga: Bytovye ocherki.* St. Petersburg, 1895.

Bakhtin, Mikhail. *Rabelais and His World.* Translated by Helene Iswolsky. Bloomington, Ind., 1984.

Barrows, Susanna. *Distorting Mirrors: Visions of the Crowd in Late Nineteenth-Century France.* New Haven, 1981.

Bashilov, P. P. "O khuliganstve kak prestupnom iavlenii ne predusmotrennym zakonom." *Zhurnal ministerstva iustitsii* 2 (1913).

Bater, James H. "Between Old and New: St. Petersburg in the Late Imperial Era." In *The City in Late Imperial Russia,* edited by Michael F. Hamm. Bloomington, Ind., 1986.

———. *St. Petersburg: Industrialization and Change.* Montreal, 1976.

Bely, Andrei. *Petersburg.* Translated by Robert A. Maguire and John E. Malmstad. Bloomington, Ind., 1978.

Bentovin, B. "Spasanie 'padshikh' i khuliganstvo." *Obrazovanie* 11–12 (1905).

Berlanstein, Lenard R. "Vagrants, Beggars, and Thieves: Delinquent Boys in Mid-Nineteenth-Century Paris." *Journal of Social History*, vol. 12, no. 4 (1979).

Berman, Iakov. *P'ianstvo i prestupnost'*. Petrograd, 1914.

———. "Retsidiv v detskoi prestupnosti." In *Deti-prestupniki*, edited by M. N. Gernet. Moscow, 1912.

Bernstein, Laurie. "Sonia's Daughters: Prostitution and Society in Russia." Ph.D. diss., University of California, Berkeley, 1987.

Bethea, David M. *The Shape of Apocalypse in Modern Russian Fiction*. Princeton, 1989.

Binshtok, V. I. *Gde i kak iutitsia Peterburgskaia bednota*. St. Petersburg, 1903.

Blagoveshchenskii, P. A. *O bor'be s khuliganstvom: Iz eparkhial'noi zhizni*. Petrograd, 1914.

Blok, Aleksander. *Rossiia i intelligentsiia*. Petersburg, 1919.

Bocharov, I. "Pervye osobye sudy po delam o maloletnikh v Rossii." In *Deti-prestupniki*, edited by M. N. Gernet. Moscow, 1912.

Bonnell, Victoria E. *Roots of Rebellion: Workers' Politics and Organizations in St. Petersburg and Moscow, 1900–1914*. Berkeley, 1983.

———, ed. and trans. *The Russian Worker: Life and Labor under the Tsarist Regime*. Berkeley, 1983.

Bowlt, John E. "David Burliuk, The Father of Russian Futurism." *Canadian-American Slavic Studies*, vol. 20, nos. 1–2 (1986).

Bradley, Joseph. "The Moscow Workhouse and Urban Welfare Reform in Russia." *Russian Review*, vol. 41, no. 3 (1982).

———. *Muzhik and Muscovite: Urbanization in Late Imperial Russia*. Berkeley, 1985.

Breitman, G. N. *Prestupnyi mir: Ocherki iz byta professional'nykh prestupnikakh*. Kiev, 1901.

Brennan, Thomas. *Public Drinking and Popular Culture in Eighteenth-Century Paris*. Princeton, 1988.

Brewer, John, and John Styles, eds. *An Ungovernable People: The English and Their Law in the Seventeenth and Eighteenth Centuries*. New Brunswick, N.J., 1980.

Brooks, Jeffrey. "Popular Philistinism and the Course of Russian Modernism." In *History and Literature: Theoretical Problems and Russian Case Studies*, edited by Gary Saul Morton. Stanford, 1986.

———. "Readers and Reading at the End of the Tsarist Era." In *Literature and Society in Imperial Russia, 1800–1914*, edited by William Mills Todd III. Stanford, 1978.

———. *When Russia Learned to Read: Literacy and Popular Literature, 1861–1917*. Princeton, 1985.

Brower, Daniel. "Labor Violence in Russia in the Late Nineteenth Century." *Slavic Review*, vol. 41, no. 3 (1982).

————. *The Russian City between Tradition and Modernity, 1850–1900.* Berkeley, 1990.

————. "Urban Russia on the Eve of World War I: A Social Profile." *Journal of Social History*, vol. 13, no. 3 (1980).

Brown, Edward J. *Mayakovsky: A Poet in the Revolution.* Princeton, 1973.

Brusianin, V. "O khuliganakh i khuliganstve." *Novyi zhurnal dlia vsekh* 4 (1913).

Bushnell, John. *Mutiny amid Repression: Russian Soldiers in the Revolution of 1905–1907.* Bloomington, Ind., 1985.

Butovskii, A. N. "Zakon o nesovershennoletnikh i ego primenenie v sudebno-mirovoi praktike." *Zhurnal ministerstva iustitsii* 6 (1900).

Buzinov, Aleksei. *Za nevskoi zastavoi.* Moscow and Leningrad, 1930.

Carden, Patricia. "The Aesthetic of Performance in the Russian Avant-Garde." *Canadian-American Slavic Studies*, vol. 19, no. 4 (1985).

Censer, Jack R., and Jeremy D. Popkin. "Historians and the Press." In *Press and Politics in Prerevolutionary France*, edited by Jack R. Censer and Jeremy D. Popkin. Berkeley, 1987.

Certeau, Michel de. *The Practice of Everyday Life.* Translated by Steven Rendall. Berkeley, 1988.

Chalidze, Valery. *Criminal Russia: Essays on Crime in the Soviet Union.* Translated by P. S. Falla. New York, 1977.

Chartier, Roger. *The Cultural Uses of Print.* Translated by Lydia G. Cochrane. Princeton, 1987.

————. "Culture as Appropriation: Popular Cultural Uses in Early Modern France." In *Understanding Popular Culture*, edited by Stephen Kaplan. Berlin, 1984.

————. "Texts, Printings, Readings." In *The New Cultural History*, edited by Lynn Hunt. Berkeley, 1989.

————. "Text, Symbols, and Frenchness." *Journal of Modern History*, vol. 57, no. 4 (1985).

Charykov, Kh. M. *Sotsiologicheskaia shkola v nauke ugolovnogo prava.* Moscow, 1910.

————. *Uchenie o faktorakh prestupnosti: Sotsiologicheskaia shkola v nauke ugolovnogo prava.* Moscow, 1910.

Chevalier, Louis. *Laboring Classes and Dangerous Classes in Paris during the First Half of the Nineteenth Century.* Translated by Frank Jellinek. Princeton, 1973.

Chibnall, Steve. *Law-and-Order News: An Analysis of Crime Reporting in the British Press.* London, 1977.

Chichagova, E. I. "O prestupnosti devushek za piatiletie ot 1910 g. po 1915 g. po dannym osobogo suda po delam o maloletnikh v Petrograde." *Osobyi sud po delam o maloletnikh* 6 (1915).

———. "Otchet popechitel'nitsy." *Osobyi sud po delam o maloletnikh: Otchet S.-Peterburgskogo stolichnogo mirovogo sud'i N. A. Okuneva za 1910 god.* St. Petersburg, 1911.

Chubinskii, M. P. "O khuliganstve." *Izvestiia S.-Peterburgskogo politekhnicheskogo instituta* 21 (1914).

Chukovsky, Kornei. *Alexander Blok as Man and Poet.* Translated and edited by Diana Burgin and Katherine O'Connor. Ann Arbor, Mich., 1982.

Clowes, Edith W., Samuel D. Kassow, and James L. West. *Between Tsar and People: Educated Society and the Quest for Public Identity in Late Imperial Russia.* Princeton, 1991.

Cobb, R. C. *The Police and the People: French Popular Protest, 1789–1820.* London, 1970.

Cohen, Stanley. *Folk Devils and Moral Panics: The Creation of the Mods and Rockers.* London, 1972.

Cohen, Stanley, and Andrew Scull, eds. *Social Control and the State: Historical and Comparative Essays.* Oxford, 1983.

Costello, David. "*Novoe vremia* and the Conservative Dilemma, 1911–1914." *Russian Review,* vol. 37, no. 1 (1978).

Darnton, Robert. *The Great Cat Massacre and Other Episodes in French Cultural History.* New York, 1985.

———. "The Symbolic Element in History." *Journal of Modern History,* vol. 58, no. 1 (1986).

Davydov, N. V., and N. N. Polianskii, eds. *Sudebnaia reforma.* 2 vols. Moscow, 1915.

"X s"ezd russkoi gruppy mezhdunarodnogo soiuza kriminalistov." *Pravo* 10 (1914).

"Detskii dom." *Otchet obshch-a pomoshch' detiam rabochikh g. S.-Peterburga za piat' let ego sushchestvovaniia, 1908–1913.* St. Petersburg, 1913.

Diomidov, I. [M.] "Alkogolizm, kak faktor prestupnosti nesovershennoletnikh." In *Deti-prestupniki,* edited by M. N. Gernet. Moscow, 1912.

———. "Rol' alkogolizma v etiologii prestupleniia nesovershennoletnikh." *Trudy sed'mogo s"ezda predstavitelei russkikh ispravitel'nykh zavedenii dlia maloletnikh, Okt. 1908 goda.* Moscow, 1909.

Dioneo [I. V. Shklovskii]. "Iz Anglii." *Russkoe bogatstvo* 9 (1898).

Doroshevich, V. M. *Sobranie sochinenii.* 12 vols. Moscow, 1907.

Dril', D. A. "O merakh bor'by s prestupnost'iu nesovershennoletnikh." *Trudy sed'mogo s"ezda predstavitelei russkikh ispravitel'nykh zavedenii dlia maloletnikh, Okt. 1908 goda.* Moscow, 1909.

Elpat'evskii, S. I. "Bezchinstvo." *Russkoe bogatstvo* 5 (1912).

———. "Na perepisi: V Viazemskoi lavre." *Russkoe bogatstvo* 2 (1897).

Emel'ianchenko, I. "Bezdomnye." *Sovremennyi mir* 1 (1913).

Emmons, Terence. *The Formation of Political Parties and the First National Elections in Russia.* Cambridge, Mass., 1983.

Engel, Barbara Alpern. *Between the Fields and the City: Women, Work, and Family in Russia, 1861–1914.* Cambridge, forthcoming.

———. "St. Petersburg Prostitutes in the Late Nineteenth Century: A Personal and Social Profile." *Russian Review*, vol. 48, no. 1 (1989).

Engelstein, Laura. "Gender and the Juridical Subject: Prostitution and Rape in Nineteenth-Century Russian Criminal Codes." *Journal of Modern History*, vol. 60, no. 3 (1988).

———. *Moscow, 1905: Working-Class Organization and Political Conflict.* Stanford, 1982.

Esin, B. I. *Russkaia dorevoliutsionnaia gazeta, 1702–1917: Kratkii ocherk.* Moscow, 1971.

———. *Russkaia gazeta i gazetnoe delo v Rossii.* Moscow, 1981.

Faleev, N. I. "Arestantskie deti." *Zhurnal ministerstva iustitsii* 7 (1905).

Fidler, A. A. "Ob organizatsii shirokoi pomoshchi bezprizornym, zabroshennym i t. p. detiam." *Trudy vos'mogo s''ezda predstavitelei russkikh vospitatel'no-ispravitel'nykh zavedenii dlia nesovershennoletnikh, Okt. 1911 goda.* St. Petersburg, 1913.

———. "O merakh bor'by s detskoiu prestupnost'iu." *Trudy shestogo s''ezda predstavitelei russkikh ispravitel'nykh zavedenii dlia maloletnikh, Mai 1904 goda.* Moscow, 1904.

Fomenko, K. I. *Khuliganstvo.* Kiev, 1913.

Foucault, Michel. *The Archeology of Knowledge.* Translated by A. M. Sheridan Smith. New York, 1972.

———. *Discipline and Punish: The Birth of the Prison.* Translated by Alan Sheridan. New York, 1977.

Frank, Stephen. "Cultural Conflict and Criminality in Rural Russia, 1861–1900." Ph.D. diss., Brown University, 1987.

———. "Popular Justice, Community, and Culture among the Russian Peasantry, 1870–1900." *Russian Review*, vol. 46, no. 3 (1987).

Freeze, Gregory. "The Estate (*Soslovie*) Paradigm and Russian Social History." *American Historical Review*, vol. 91, no. 1 (1986).

Fridman, M. I. "Rabochie i partiia narodnoi svobody." *Rech'*, April 1, 1906.

Frierson, Cathy. "Crime and Punishment in the Russian Village: Concepts of Criminality at the End of the Nineteenth Century." *Slavic Review*, vol. 46, no. 1 (1987).

Galai, S. "A Liberal's Vision of Russia's Future, 1905–1914: The Case of Ivan Petrunkevich." In *Russian and East European History*, edited by R. C. Elwood. Berkeley, 1984.

Gatrell, V. A. C. "The Decline of Theft and Violence in Victorian and Edwardian England." In *Crime and the Law: The Social History of Crime in Western Europe since 1500*, edited by V. A. C. Gatrell, Bruce Lenman, and Geoffrey Parker. London, 1980.

Gatrell, V. A. C., and T. B. Hadden. "Criminal Statistics and Their Interpretation." In *Nineteenth-Century Society: Essays in the Use of*

Quantitative Methods for the Study of Social Data, edited by E. A. Wrigley. Cambridge, 1972.

Gatrell, V. A. C., Bruce Lenman, and Geoffrey Parker, eds. *Crime and the Law: The Social History of Crime in Western Europe since 1500.* London, 1980.

Gernet, M. N. "Prestupnost' i zhilishcha bedniakov." *Pravo* 42 (1903).

———, ed. *Deti-prestupniki.* Moscow, 1912.

———, ed. *Prestupnyi mir Moskvy.* Moscow, 1924.

Gessen, I. [V.] "Vnutrennaia zhizn'." *Ezhegodnik gazety Rech' na 1913 god.* St. Petersburg, 1914.

———. "Vnutrennaia zhizn'." *Ezhegodnik gazety Rech' na 1914.* St. Petersburg, 1915.

Giliarovskii, V. A. *Moskva i Moskvichi.* Moscow, 1979.

Gillis, J. R. *Youth and History: Tradition and Change in European Age Relations, 1770–Present.* New York, 1981.

Gilroy, Paul. *"There Ain't No Black in the Union Jack": The Cultural Politics of Race and Nation.* Chicago, 1991.

Glickman, Rose. *Russian Factory Women: Workplace and Society, 1880–1914.* Berkeley, 1984.

Gogel', S. K. "Detskaia prestupnost' v S. Peterburge v 1910 godu, po dannym popechitelei detskogo suda." *Pravo* 20 (1911).

———. *Rol' obshchestva v dele bor'by s prestupnost'iu.* St. Petersburg, 1906.

Goldman, Wendy Z. "The 'Withering Away' and the Resurrection of the Soviet Family, 1917–1936." Ph.D. diss., University of Pennsylvania, 1987.

Goranovskii, M. A. *Khuliganstvo i mery bor'by s nim.* Grodno, 1913.

———. "Sluchainoe vpadenie v prestuplenii krazhi liudei s bezukoriz-nennym proshlym, kak smiagchaiushchee vinu obstoiatel'stvo po ustavu o nakazaniiakh." *Zhurnal ministerstva iustitsii* 7 (1901).

Gor'kii, Maksim. *Sobranie sochinenii v tritsati tomakh.* Vol. 30. Moscow, 1955.

Graham, Stephen. "One of the Higher Intelligentsia." *The Russian Review*, vol. 1, no. 4 ([London] 1912).

Gramsci, Antonio. *Selections from the Prison Notebooks.* Edited and translated by Quentin Hoare and Geoffrey Nowell Smith. New York, 1971.

Gray, Camilla. *The Russian Experiment in Art: 1863–1922.* New York, 1962.

Grigor'ev, N. I. *Alkogolizm i prestupnost' v Sankt-Peterburge.* St. Petersburg, 1900.

———. "Ustroistvo priiutov dlia vytrezvleniia p'ianykh." *Gorodskoe delo* 18 (1910).

Grimm, E. "Povorot." *Rech'*, April 4, 1906.

Gromov, V. I. "Bezmotivnoe prestuplenie." *Zhurnal ministerstva iustitsii* 5 (1913).

Haimson, Leopold. "Labor Unrest in Imperial Russia on the Eve of the First World War: The Roles of Conjunctural Phenomena, Events, and Individual and Collective Actors." In *Strikes, Wars, and Revolutions in an International Perspective*, edited by Charles Tilly and Leopold Haimson. Cambridge, 1989.

―――. "The Problem of Social Stability in Urban Russia, 1905–1917." *Slavic Review*, vol. 23, no. 4 (1964) [Part 1]; vol. 24, no. 1 (1965) [Part 2].

―――. "Structural Processes of Change and Changing Patterns of Labor Unrest: The Case of the Metal-Processing Industry in Imperial Russia, 1890–1914." In *Strikes, Wars, and Revolutions in an International Perspective*, edited by Charles Tilly and Leopold Haimson. Cambridge, 1989.

―――, ed. *The Politics of Rural Russia, 1905–1907*. Bloomington, Ind., 1979.

Haimson, Leopold, and Ronald Petrusha. "Two Strike Waves in Imperial Russia, 1905–1907, 1912–1914." In *Strikes, Wars, and Revolutions in an International Perspective*, edited by Charles Tilly and Leopold Haimson. Cambridge, 1989.

Hamm, Michael F., ed. *The City in Late Imperial Russia*. Bloomington, Ind., 1986.

―――, ed. *The City in Russian History*. Lexington, Ky., 1976.

Harper, Samuel N. "Exceptional Measures in Russia." *The Russian Review*, vol. 1, no. 4 ([London] 1912).

Hay, Douglas, Peter Linebaugh, and E. P. Thompson, eds. *Albion's Fatal Tree: Crime and Society in Eighteenth-Century England*. London, 1975.

Hebdige, Dick. *Subculture: The Meaning of Style*. London, 1979.

Henshel, Richard L., and Robert A. Silverman, eds. *Perception in Criminology*. New York, 1975.

Hobsbawm, E. J. *Primitive Rebels: Studies in Archaic Forms of Social Movement in the Nineteenth and Twentieth Centuries*. Manchester, 1959.

―――. *Workers: Worlds of Labor*. New York, 1984.

――― et al. "Conference Report: Distinctions Between Socio-Political and Other Forms of Crime." *Society for the Study of Labor History Bulletin* 25 (1972).

Hogan, Heather. "Industrial Rationalization and the Roots of Labor Militance in the St. Petersburg Metalworking Industry, 1901–1914." *Russian Review*, vol. 42, no. 2 (1983).

―――. "Scientific Management and the Changing Nature of Work in the St. Petersburg Metalworking Industry, 1900–1914." In *Strikes*,

Wars, and Revolutions in an International Perspective, edited by Charles Tilly and Leopold Haimson. Cambridge, 1989.

Hoggart, Richard. The Uses of Literacy. London, 1957.

Hosking, Geoffrey A. The Russian Constitutional Experiment: Government and Duma, 1907–1914. Cambridge, 1973.

Humphries, Stephen. Hooligans or Rebels? An Oral History of Working-Class Childhood and Youth, 1889–1939. Oxford, 1981.

Hunt, Lynn, ed. The New Cultural History. Berkeley, 1989.

Ignatieff, Michael. A Just Measure of Pain: The Penitentiary in the Industrial Revolution, 1750–1850. London, 1978.

Isaev, M. "Khuliganstvo: Iuridicheskii ocherk." In Khuliganstvo i khuligany: Sbornik. Moscow, 1929.

Ivanov, V. Chto takoe khuliganstvo? Orenburg, 1915.

Johnson, Eric, and Vincent E. McHale. "Socioeconomic Aspects of the Delinquency Rate in Imperial Germany, 1882–1914." Journal of Social History, vol. 13, no. 3 (1980).

Jones, David. Crime, Protest, Community, and Police in Nineteenth-Century Britain. London, 1982.

Jones, Gareth Stedman. Languages of Class: Studies in English Working-Class History, 1832–1982. Cambridge, 1983.

———. Outcast London: A Study in the Relationship between Classes in Victorian Society. 2d ed. New York, 1984.

Juviler, Peter H. "Contradictions of Revolution: Juvenile Crime and Rehabilitation." In Bolshevik Culture, edited by Abbott Gleason, Peter Kenez, and Richard Stites. Bloomington, Ind., 1985.

———. Revolutionary Law and Order: Politics and Social Change in the U.S.S.R. New York, 1976.

Karaffa-Korbut, K. B. "Nochlezhnye doma v bol'shikh russkikh gorodakh." Gorodskoe delo 10 (1912).

Karpinskaia, I. Bor'ba s ulitsei. Moscow, 1906.

Kelly, Catriona. Petrushka: The Russian Carnival Puppet Theatre. Cambridge, 1990.

Khuliganstvo i khuligany: Sbornik. Moscow, 1929.

Khuliganstvo i ponozhevshchina. Moscow, 1927.

Khuliganstvo i prestuplenie: Sbornik. Moscow and Leningrad, 1927.

"Khuliganstvo v gorodakh," Gorodskoe delo 4 (1913).

Kimental', V. V. "Deiatel'nost' popechitelei (Ocherk godovoi raboty popechitelei)." Osobyi sud po delam o maloletnikh: Otchet S.-Peterburgskogo stolichnogo mirovogo sud'i N. A. Okuneva za 1910 god. St. Petersburg, 1911.

Kir'ianov, I. I. Zhiznennyi uroven' rabochikh Rossii (konets XIX–nachalo XX v.). Moscow, 1979.

Kleinbort, L. M. Istoriia bezrabotnitsy v Rossii, 1857–1919. Moscow, 1925.

Kniazev, V. "Sovremennaia derevnia o sebe samoi: Chastushki Peterburg-skoi gubernii." *Sovremennik* 4 (1912).

de Kochko, General A. *Souvenirs d'un détective russe.* Paris, 1930.

Koenker, Diane. "Urban Families, Working-Class Youth Groups, and the 1917 Revolution in Moscow." In *The Family in Imperial Russia: New Lines of Historical Research,* edited by David L. Ransel. Urbana, Ill., 1978.

Korotnev, A. D. *Maloletnie i nesovershennoletnie prestupniki: Kratkii istoricheskii ocherk.* St. Petersburg, 1903.

Krasovskii, D. D. *O maloletnikh i nesovershennoletnikh prestupnikakh.* Warsaw, 1898.

Krestovskii, V. V. *Peterburgskie trushchoby.* Vols. 1 and 2 of *Polnoe sobranie sochinenii.* St. Petersburg, 1898.

Kroeber, A. L., and Clyde Kluckhohn. *Culture: A Critical Review of Concepts and Definitions.* New York, n.d.

Krukones, James H. "To the People: The Russian Government and the Newspaper *Sel'skii Vestnik* (Village Herald), 1881–1917." Ph.D. diss., University of Wisconsin, 1983.

Krumbmiller, V. V. *Zlobodnevnyi vopros: Khuliganstvo i bor'ba s nim, Po povodu proekta Ministra iustitsii.* Khar'kov, 1913.

Kruze, E. E. *Peterburgskie rabochie v 1912–1914 godakh.* Moscow and Leningrad, 1961.

———. *Usloviia truda i byta rabochego klassa Rossii v 1900–1914 go-dakh.* Leningrad, 1981.

Kruze, E. E., and D. G. Kutsentov. "Naselenie Peterburga." In *Ocherki istorii Leningrada,* vol. 3, edited by B. M. Kochakov. Moscow and Leningrad, 1956.

Kucherov, Samuel. *Courts, Lawyers, and Trials under the Last Three Tsars.* New York, 1953.

Kurnin, A. "Bezrabotnye na Khitrovom rynke v Moskve." *Russkoe bogatstvo* 2 (1898).

"K voprosu o merakh bor'by s khuliganstvom." *Zhurnal ugolovnogo prava i protsessa* 4 (1913).

Lebedev, V. "K istorii kulachnykh boev na Rusi." *Russkaia starina* 7–8 (1913).

Lemke, M. K. "V mire usmotreniia." *Vestnik prava,* vol. 35, no. 7 (1905).

Lewin, Moshe. *The Making of the Soviet System: Essays in the Social History of Interwar Russia.* New York, 1985.

Likhachev, A. V. "Ob usilenii nakazanii dlia khuliganov." *Zhurnal ministerstva iustitsii* 5 (1913).

Lindenmeyr, Adele. "Public Poor Relief and Private Charity." Ph.D. diss., Princeton University, 1980.

———. "A Russian Experiment in Voluntarism: The Municipal Guardianships of the Poor." *Jahrbücher für Geschichte Osteuropas,* vol. 30, no. 3 (1982).

Linton, Derek S. *"Who Has the Youth, Has the Future"*: The Campaign to Save Young Workers in Imperial Germany. Cambridge, 1991.

Liublinskii, P. "Khuliganstvo i ego sotsial'no-bytovye korni." *Khuliganstvo i khuligany: Sbornik.* Moscow, 1929.

Livshits, Benedikt. *The One and a Half-Eyed Archer.* Translated by John E. Bowlt. Newtonville, Mass., 1977.

Lodhi, Abdul Quiyum, and Charles Tilly. "Urbanization, Crime, and Collective Violence in Nineteenth-Century France." *American Journal of Sociology* 79 (1973).

Lotman, Iurii M. "The Decembrist in Daily Life (Everyday Behavior as a Historical-Psychological Category)." In *The Semiotics of Russian Cultural History,* edited by Alexander D. Nakhimovsky and Alice Stone Nakhimovsky. Ithaca, N.Y., 1985.

Lotman, Iurii M., and Boris A. Uspenskii. "Binary Models in the Dynamics of Russian Culture (to the End of the Eighteenth Century)." In *The Semiotics of Russian Cultural History,* edited by Alexander D. Nakhimovsky and Alice Stone Nakhimovsky. Ithaca, N.Y., 1985.

Luchinskii, N. F. "Mery bor'by s prazdnoshataistvom i khuliganstvom." *Tiuremnyi vestnik* 3 (1915).

McDaniels, Tim. *Autocracy, Capitalism, and Revolution in Russia.* Berkeley, 1988.

MacDonald, Michael. "Suicide and the Rise of the Popular Press in England." *Representations* 22 (1988).

McKean, Robert B. *St. Petersburg between the Revolutions: Workers and Revolutionaries, June 1907–February 1917.* New Haven, 1990.

McReynolds, Louise. *The News under Russia's Old Regime: The Development of a Mass-Circulation Press.* Princeton, 1991.

Maguire, Robert A., and John E. Malmstad. "The Line, the Circle, the Spiral—of Symbolism." In *Andrey Bely: Spirit of Symbolism,* edited by John E. Malmstad. Ithaca, N.Y., 1987.

Makarevich, N. A. *S.-Peterburgskoi arestnyi dom v 1881–1910 gg.* St. Petersburg, 1912.

Makletsov, A. "K voprosu o iuridicheskoi otsenke khuliganstva." *Iuridicheskii vestnik* 2 (1913).

Makovskii, N. N. "Sotsial'no-ekonomicheskie faktory detskoi prestupnosti v Moskve." In *Deti-prestupniki,* edited by M. N. Gernet. Moscow, 1912.

Maksimov, S. V. *Sibir' i katorga.* St. Petersburg, 1891.

Maliantovich, P. N., and N. K. Murav'ev. *Zakony politicheskikh i obshchestvennykh prestupleniiakh: Prakticheskii kommentarii.* St. Petersburg, 1910.

Malyshev, Sergei. *Unemployed Councils in St. Petersburg in 1906.* London, 1931.

Manning, Roberta T. *The Crisis of the Old Order in Russia: Gentry and Government.* Princeton, 1982.

Markov, Vladimir. *Russian Futurism: A History*. Berkeley, 1968.

Marx, Karl. "The Class Struggles in France: 1848–1850." In *Political Writings*. Vol. 2, *Surveys from Exile,* edited by David Fernbach. New York, 1974.

———. "Manifesto of the Communist Party." In *Political Writings*. Vol. 1, *The Revolutions of 1848,* edited by David Fernbach. New York, 1974.

May, M. "Innocence and Experience: The Evolution of the Concept of Juvenile Delinquency in the Mid-Nineteenth Century." *Victorian Studies* 17 (1973).

Mel'nikov, A. P. "Kolebaniia prestupnosti v tekushchem stoletii." *Zhurnal ministerstva iustitsii* 5–6 (1917).

Mertvyi, A. "Khuliganstvo." *Utro Rossii*, November 11, 1912.

Mikhnevich, V. *Iazvy Peterburga: Opyt istoriko-statisticheskogo issledovaniia nravstvennosti stolichnogo naselenii*. St. Petersburg, 1886.

Mironov, K. *Iz vospominaniia rabochego*. Moscow, 1906.

Morson, Gary Saul. *The Boundaries of Genre: Dostoevskii's "Diary of a Writer" and the Traditions of Literary Utopia*. Austin, Tex., 1981.

[Mosolov, A. I.] *Doklad chlena Postoiannogo soveta A. I. Mosolova po voprosu o razvitii khuliganstva*. St. Petersburg, 1913.

Mulukaev, R. S. *Obshcheugolovnaia politsiia dorevoliutsionnoi Rossii*. Moscow, 1979.

Nabokov, V. D. "Desiatyi s"ezd kriminalistov." *Pravo* 9 (1914).

———. *Sbornik statei po ugolovnomu pravu*. St. Petersburg, 1904.

Naimark, Norman M. "Terrorism and the Fall of Imperial Russia." University Lecture, Boston University, 1986.

Neuberger, Joan. "Stories of the Street: Hooliganism in the St. Petersburg Popular Press." *Slavic Review*, vol. 48, no. 2 (1989).

Nye, Robert A. *Crime, Madness, and Politics in Modern France: The Medical Concept of National Decline*. Princeton, 1984.

Okunev, N. A. "Bezotsovshchina," *Osobyi sud po delam o maloletnikh* 8–9 (1915).

———. "Bezprizornost' maloletnikh, kak posledstvie voiny." *Osobyi sud po delam o maloletnikh* 1 (1914).

———. "Osobyi sud po delam o maloletnikh." *Petrogradskii mirovoi sud za piat'desiat' let, 1866–1916*. Petrograd, 1916.

———. "Pervyi s"ezd deiatelei po voprosam suda dlia maloletnikh." *Uchitel' i shkola* 3 (1914).

———. *Trudy pervogo s"ezda deiatelei po voprosam suda dlia maloletnikh, SPb. Dekabr 1913*. Petrograd, 1915.

Orlovsky, Daniel. "The Lower Middle Strata in Revolutionary Russia." In *Between Tsar and People: Educated Society and the Quest for Public Identity in Late Imperial Russia,* edited by E. W. Clowes, S. D. Kassow, and J. L. West. Princeton, 1991.

Ostroumov, S. S. *Ocherki po istorii ugolovnoi statistiki dorevoliutsionnoi Rossii*. Moscow, 1961.

————. *Prestupnost' i ee prichiny v dorevoliutsionnoi Rossii.* 2d ed. Moscow, 1980.

"Otzyv Moskovskogo stolichnogo mirovogo s"ezda o ministerskom zakonoproekte o merakh bor'by s khuliganstvom." *Iuridicheskii vestnik* 3 (1913).

Owen, Thomas C. *Capitalism and Politics in Russia: A Social History of the Moscow Merchants, 1855–1905.* Cambridge, 1981.

Pearson, Geoffrey. *Hooligan: A History of Respectable Fears.* London, 1983.

Perrot, Michelle. "Delinquency and the Penitentiary System in Nineteenth-Century France." In *Deviants and the Abandoned in French Society: Selections from the Annales: Economies, Sociétés, Civilisations,* vol. 4, edited by Robert Forster and Orest Ranum and translated by Elborg Forster and Patricia M. Ranum. Baltimore, 1978.

Pervoe desiatiletie S.-Peterburgskogo arestnogo doma, 1881–1891. St. Petersburg, 1891.

Petrishev, A. "Khronika vnutrennei zhizni: O khuliganakh." *Russkoe bogatstvo* 1 (1913).

Petrogradskii mirovoi sud za piat'desiat' let, 1866–1916. 2 vols. St. Petersburg, 1916.

Peukert, Detlev J. K. *Grenzen der Sozialdisziplinierung.* Cologne, 1986.
————. *Inside Nazi Germany: Conformity, Opposition, and Racism in Everyday Life.* Translated by Richard Deveson. New Haven, 1987.
————. *The Weimar Republic: The Crisis of Classical Modernity.* Translated by Richard Deveson. New York, 1989.

Philips, David. *Crime and Authority in Victorian England: The Black Country, 1835–1860.* London, 1977.

Pokrovskaia, M. I. *Po podvalam, cherdakam i ugolovym kvartiram Peterburga.* St. Petersburg, 1903.

Porter, David, and Cathy King, eds. *Blood and Laughter: Caricatures from the 1905 Revolution.* London, 1983.

Prikliuchenie odnogo khuligana. Kiev, 1908.

Proffer, Carl, and Ellendea Proffer, eds. *The Ardis Anthology of Russian Futurism.* Ann Arbor, Mich., 1980.

Pushnov, I. A. "Vvedenie mirovykh sudebnykh ustanovlenii." *Petrogradskii mirovoi sud za piat'desiat' let.* Petrograd, 1916.

Pyman, Avril. *The Life of Aleksandr Blok.* 2 vols. Oxford, 1979.

Radzinowicz, Sir Leon, and Marvin E. Wolfgang, eds. *Crime and Justice.* 3 vols. 2d ed. New York, 1977.

Ransel, David L. "Infant-Care Cultures in the Russian Empire." In *Russia's Women: Accommodation, Resistance, Transformation,* edited by Barbara E. Clements, Barbara A. Engel, and Christine D. Worobec. Berkeley, 1991.
————, ed. *The Family in Imperial Russia: New Lines of Historical Research.* Urbana, Ill., 1978.

Riabchenko, A. E. *O bor'be s khuliganstvom, vorovstvom, i brodiazh-nichestvom.* St. Petersburg, 1914.

Rieber, Alfred J. *Merchants and Entrepreneurs in Imperial Russia.* Chapel Hill, N.C., 1982.

Rigberg, Benjamin. "The Efficacy of Tsarist Censorship Operations, 1894–1917." *Jahrbücher für Geschichte Osteuropas* 14 (1966).

———. "The Tsarist Press Law, 1894–1905." *Jahrbücher für Geschichte Osteuropas* 13 (1965).

Rodionov, I. A. *Nashe prestuplenie (Ne vred, a byl').* 1st ed. St. Petersburg, 1909.

Rogger, Hans. "The Beilis Case: Anti-Semitism and Politics in the Reign of Nicholas II." *Slavic Review,* vol. 25, no. 4 (1966).

———. "Russia in 1914." *Journal of Contemporary History,* vol. 1, no. 4 (1966).

Rosenberg, William G. "Kadets and the Politics of Ambivalence." In *Essays on Russian Liberalism,* edited by Charles E. Timberlake. Columbia, Mo., 1972.

Rosenberg, William G., and Diane P. Koenker. "The Limits of Formal Protest: Worker Activism and Social Polarization in Petrograd and Moscow, March to October, 1917." *American Historical Review,* vol. 92, no. 2 (1987).

Rosenhaft, Eve. "Organizing the 'Lumpenproletariat': Cliques and Communists in Berlin during the Weimar Republic." In *The German Working Class, 1888–1933,* edited by Richard J. Evans. London, 1982.

Rozentsveig, G. "Khuligan." *Iurist* 2 (1904).

———. "Sudebnye etiudy: Brodiachaia armiia." *Iurist* 28 (1904).

Ruble, Blair A. "From Palace Square to Moscow Square: St. Petersburg's Century-Long Retreat from Public Space." In *Reshaping Russian Architecture: Western Technology, Utopian Dreams,* edited by William Brumfield. Cambridge, 1990.

Ruckman, Jo Ann. *The Moscow Business Elite: A Social and Cultural Portrait of Two Generations, 1840–1905.* DeKalb, Ill., 1984.

Rudé, George. *Criminal and Victim: Crime and Society in Early Nineteenth-Century England.* Oxford, 1985.

———. *The Crowd in the French Revolution.* Oxford, 1959.

———. *The Crowd in History: A Study of Popular Disturbances in France and England, 1730–1848.* New York, 1964.

Schiller, Dan. *Objectivity and the News: The Public and the Rise of Commercial Journalism.* Philadelphia, 1981.

Scott, A. Maccallum. *Through Finland to St. Petersburg.* London, 1913.

Scott, James C. *Weapons of the Weak: Everyday Forms of Peasant Resistance.* New Haven, 1985.

Segalov, T. E. *Deti-prestupniki: Iz vpechatlenii vracha pri detskom sude.* Moscow, 1914.

Semenov, V. P. *Bytovye usloviia zhizni mal'chikov*. St. Petersburg, n.d.

Shklovsky, Viktor. *Vladimir Mayakovsky and His Circle*. Translated by Lily Feiler. New York, 1972.

Shlezinger, V. V. *Opyt otvlecheniia iunoshestva ot rastlevaiushchego vliianiia ulitsy*. St. Petersburg, 1913.

Shragin, Boris, and Albert Todd, eds., and Marian Schwartz, trans. *Landmarks: A Collection of Essays on the Russian Intelligentsia, 1909*. New York, 1977.

Shuster, U. A. *Peterburgskie rabochie v 1905–1907 gg*. Leningrad, 1976.

Shustikov, A. A. "Khuliganstvo v derevne i ego poeziia." *Vologodskii listok*, June 23, 1913.

Simakov, V. I. *Sbornik derevenskikh chastushek*. Iaroslavl', 1913.

Skidan, V. V. *O bor'be s khuliganstvom: Doklad Ekaterinodarskoi gorodskoi dumy*. Ekaterinodar, 1913.

Skrobotov, N. A. *Peterburgskii listok za tridtsat'-piat' let, 1864–1899*. St. Petersburg, 1914.

Slobin, Greta Nachtailer. "The Ethos of Performance in Remizov." *Canadian-American Slavic Studies*, vol. 19, no. 4 (1985).

Stachura, Peter D. *The Weimar Republic and the Younger Proletariat*. New York, 1989.

Steinberg, Mark. "Consciousness and Conflict in Russian Industry: The Printers of St. Petersburg and Moscow, 1885–1905." Ph.D. diss., University of California, Berkeley, 1987.

———. "Culture and Class in a Russian Industry: The Printers of St. Petersburg, 1860–1905." *Journal of Social History*, vol. 23, no. 3 (1990).

Stevens, Jennie. "Children of the Revolution: Soviet Russia's Homeless Children (Besprizorniki) in the 1920s." *Russian History* 9 (1982).

Stites, Richard. *Revolutionary Dreams: Utopian Vision and Experimental Life in the Russian Revolution*. Oxford, 1989.

Stone, Christopher. "Vandalism: Property, Gentility, and the Rhetoric of Crime in New York City, 1890–1920." *Radical History Review* 26 (1982).

Suleiman, Susan R., and Inge Crosman, eds. *The Reader in the Text: Essays on Audience and Interpretation*. Princeton, 1980.

Surh, Gerald. *1905 in St. Petersburg: Labor, Society, and Revolution*. Stanford, 1989.

Sutton, Richard. "Crime and Social Change in Russia after the Great Reforms: Laws, Courts, and Criminals, 1874–1894." Ph.D. diss., Indiana University, 1984.

Sveshnikov, N. *Peterburgskie Viazemskie trushchoby*. St. Petersburg, 1900.

Svirskii, A. I. *Istoriia moei zhizni*. Moscow, 1947.

———. "Peterburgskie khuligany: Ocherki." In *Peterburg i ego zhizn'*. St. Petersburg, 1914.

————. *Pogibshie liudi.* 3 vols. St. Petersburg, 1898.

————. *Polnoe sobranie sochinenii.* 3 vols. Moscow and Leningrad, 1930.

Szeftel, Marc. "The Form of Government of the Russian Empire prior to the Constitutional Reforms of 1905–1906." In *Essays in Russian and Soviet History in Honor of Geroid Tanquary Robinson,* edited by J. S. Curtiss. New York, 1963.

Tagantsev, N. S. *Russkoe ugolovnoe pravo: Chast' obshchaia.* St. Petersburg, 1902.

Tarnovskii, E. N. "Dvizhenie chisla nesovershennoletnikh (10–17 let) osuzhdennykh v sviazi s obshchim rostom prestupnosti v Rossii za 1901–1910 gg." *Zhurnal ministerstva iustitsii* 10 (1913).

————. "Dvizhenie prestupnosti v Rossiiskoi imperii za 1899–1908 gg." *Zhurnal ministerstva iustitsii* 9 (1909).

Taylor, Ian, Paul Walton, and Jock Young. *The New Criminology: For a Social Theory of Deviance.* London, 1975.

Thompson, E. P. "Folklore, Anthropology, and Social History." *Indian Historical Review* 3 (1977).

————. "The Moral Economy of the English Crowd in the Eighteenth Century." *Past and Present* 50 (1971).

————. *Whigs and Hunters: The Origins of the Black Act.* London, 1975.

Thurston, Robert W. *Liberal City, Conservative State: Moscow and Russia's Urban Crisis, 1906–1914.* New York, 1987.

————. "Police and People in Moscow, 1906–1914." *Russian Review,* vol. 39, no. 3 (1980).

Tilly, Charles. *From Mobilization to Revolution.* Reading, Mass., 1978.

Tilly, Louise. "The Food Riot as a Form of Political Conflict in France." *Journal of Interdisciplinary History* 2 (1972).

Tobias, J. J. *Crime and Industrial Society in the Nineteenth Century.* London, 1967.

Tomachevsky, K. "Vladimir Mayakovsky." In *Victory over the Sun,* translated by Ewa Bartos and Victoria Nes Kirby. In *Drama Review,* vol. 15, no. 4 (1971).

Tombs, Robert. "Crime and the Security of the State: The 'Dangerous Class' and Insurrection in Nineteenth-Century Paris." In *Crime and the Law: The Social History of Crime in Western Europe since 1500,* edited by V. A. C. Gatrell, Bruce Lenman, and Geoffrey Parker. London, 1980.

Trainin, A. "Khuliganstvo." *Pravo* 10–11 (1914).

————. "Prestupnost' goroda i derevni v Rossii." *Russkaia mysl'* 7 (1909).

Tseitlin, A. G. *Stanovlenie realizma v russkoi literature: Russkii fiziologicheskii ocherk.* Moscow, 1965.

Tsikin, N. F. "Patronatnaia pomoshch' maloletnim." *Osobyi sud po delam o maloletnikh: Otchet S.-Peterburgskogo stolichnogo mirovogo sud'i N. A. Okuneva za 1910 god.* St. Petersburg, 1911.

Udris, A. P. "Vospitatel'no-ispravitel'nye zavedeniia." *Osobyi sud po delam o maloletnikh: Otchet S.-Peterburgskogo stolichnogo mirovogo sud'i N. A. Okuneva za 1910 god.* St. Petersburg, 1911.

Utevskii, B. "Khuliganstvo v epokhu 1905–1914 gg." *Khuliganstvo i khuligany: Sbornik.* Moscow, 1929.

Valkenier, Elizabeth Kridl. "Il'ia Repin and David Burliuk." *Canadian-American Slavic Studies,* vol. 20, nos. 1–2 (1986).

Verner, Andrew. *The Crisis of Russian Autocracy: Nicholas II and the 1905 Revolution.* Princeton, 1990.

Victory over the Sun. Translated by Ewa Bartos and Victoria Nes Kirby. In *Drama Review,* vol. 15, no. 4 (1971).

Vilenskii, B. V. *Sudebnaia reforma i kontrreforma.* Saratov, 1969.

Vsesviatskii, P. V. "Prestupnost' i zhilishchnyi vopros." *Pravo* 20 (1909).

Vystavkina, E. "Bezprizornye." *Zhenskoe delo,* December 1, 1914.

Wagner, W. G. "Tsarist Legal Policies at the End of the Nineteenth Century: A Study in Inconsistencies." *Slavonic and East European Review* 54 (1976).

Weinberg, Robert. *The Revolution of 1905 in Odessa: Blood on the Steps.* Bloomington, Ind., forthcoming.

———. "Workers, Pogroms, and the 1905 Revolution in Odessa." *Russian Review,* vol. 46, no. 1 (1987).

Weissman, Neil. *Reform in Tsarist Russia: The State Bureaucracy and Local Government, 1900–1914.* New Brunswick, N.J., 1981.

———. "Regular Police in Tsarist Russia, 1900–1914." *Russian Review,* vol. 44, no. 1 (1985).

———. "Rural Crime in Tsarist Russia: The Question of Hooliganism, 1905–1914." *Slavic Review,* vol. 37, no. 2 (1978).

Wildman, Allan K. *The Making of a Workers' Revolution: Russian Social Democracy, 1891–1903.* Chicago, 1967.

Williams, Raymond. *Keywords: A Vocabulary of Culture and Society.* New York, 1983.

Wortman, Richard. *The Development of a Russian Legal Consciousness.* Chicago, 1976.

Wright, Gordon. *Between the Guillotine and Liberty: Two Centuries of the Crime Problem in France.* New York, 1983.

Wynn, Charters. *Workers, Strikes, and Pogroms: The Donbass-Dnepr Bend in Late Imperial Russia, 1870–1905.* Princeton, 1992.

Yablonskaya, M. N. *Women Artists of Russia's New Age, 1900–1935.* Edited and translated by Anthony Parton. London, 1990.

Zak, A. I. "Kharakteristika detskoi prestupnosti." In *Deti-prestupniki,* edited by M. N. Gernet. Moscow, 1912.

———. "Kinomotograf i detskaia prestupnost'." *Zhurnal ugolovnogo prava i protsessa* 4 (1913).

Zaslavskii, D. "Bor'ba s khuliganstvom." *Sovremennyi mir* 1 (1913).

Zdanevich, Ilya, and Mikhail Larionov. "Why We Paint Ourselves: A Futurist Manifesto." In *Russian Art of the Avant-Garde: Theory and Criticism, 1902–1934*, edited and translated by John E. Bowlt. New York, 1976.

Zelnik, Reginald E. *Labor and Society in Tsarist Russia: The Factory Workers of St. Petersburg, 1855–1870*. Stanford, 1971.

————. "Russian Bebels: An Introduction to the Memoirs of Semen Kanatchikov and Matvei Fisher." *Russian Review*, vol. 35, no. 3 (1976) [Part 1]; vol. 35, no. 4 (1976) [Part 2].

————, ed. and trans. *A Radical Worker in Tsarist Russia: The Autobiography of Semen Ivanovich Kanatchikov*. Stanford, 1986.

Zhilkin, I. "Provintsial'noe obozrenie." *Vestnik evropy* 2 and 4 (1913).

Zhurbina, E. I. *Ustoichivye temy*. Moscow, 1974.

Zviagintseva, A. P. "Organizatsiia i deiatel'nost' militsii vremennogo pravitel'stva Rossiia v 1917 goda." Candidate's diss., Moscow, 1972.

Index

Compositor: Maryland Composition
Text: 10/13 Aldus
Display: Aldus
Printer and Binder: Braun-Brumfield

DATE DUE

DEC 0 7 2006			